GEOMETRY WITH AN INTRODUCTION TO COSMIC TOPOLOGY

GEOMETRY WITH AN INTRODUCTION TO COSMIC TOPOLOGY

– *Author* –
Paraman Boyinepalli,
Jegathiswaran Damaraju

BIO - GREEN
BOOKS

BIO-GREEN BOOKS
New Delhi - 110 002

ISBN: 9789389183962 (Hardback)

Published by : **BIO-GREEN BOOKS**
4736/23, Ansari Road, Darya Ganj,
New Delhi – 110 002
Phone: 011-23245578, 35004336
E-mail: biogreenbooks@gmail.com

Printed at : **Replika Press Pvt. Ltd.**

Preface

Geometry and Cosmic Topology are two branches of mathematics that deal with the study of shapes and spaces. While geometry focuses on the properties of shapes and their relationships, cosmic topology investigates the possible shapes and topologies of the universe. Geometry is one of the oldest branches of mathematics and has been studied for thousands of years. It deals with the properties of points, lines, planes, and solid objects, and their relationships. Euclidean geometry is the most well-known branch of geometry, which deals with the properties of flat space. However, there are other types of geometries, such as spherical geometry, which studies the properties of objects on the surface of a sphere, and hyperbolic geometry, which studies the properties of objects on surfaces with a negative curvature. Cosmic topology is a relatively new field of study that emerged in the 1980s. It explores the possible shapes and topologies of the universe, taking into account the laws of physics and cosmology. It is based on the theory of general relativity, which describes the properties of gravity and the structure of the universe. According to this theory, the universe is expanding, and its shape and topology are determined by the distribution of matter and energy in it.

One of the key concepts in cosmic topology is the idea that the universe may have a non-trivial topology. This means that the universe may have a shape that is not simply connected, like a torus or a Möbius strip. This has important implications for the large-scale structure of the universe, such as the distribution of galaxies and the cosmic microwave background radiation. Geometry and cosmic topology are closely related, as the study of the shape and topology of the universe requires an understanding of the properties of space and the relationships between objects. Moreover, the study of cosmic topology has led to new developments in geometry, such as the study of hyperbolic and elliptic geometries on surfaces. Geometry and Cosmic Topology are two fascinating branches of mathematics that deal with the properties of shapes and spaces, and the possible shapes and topologies of the universe. Both fields have important applications in physics, cosmology, and other areas of science, and their study has led to new developments and insights in mathematics.

The present book covers a range of topics related to geometry, including complex numbers, transformations, hyperbolic geometry, elliptic geometry, and cosmic topology. The book is written in clear and accessible language and includes many examples, illustrations, and exercises that encourage readers to engage actively with the material and develop their problem-solving skills. The book combines ideas from geometry, algebra, and topology to provide a comprehensive view of the subject. The book includes historical context and background information about the development of geometry, making it a rich resource for anyone interested in the history of mathematics. The book is suitable for students, researchers, and educators in the fields of mathematics, physics, astronomy, and cosmology.

We are grateful to all those persons as well as various books, manuals, periodicals, magazines, journals etc. that helped in the preparation of this book. In spite of the best efforts, it is possible that some errors may have occurred into the compilation and editing of the book. Further queries, constructive suggestions and criticisms for the improvement of the book are always welcomed and shall be thankfully acknowledged.

Paraman Boyinepalli
Jegathiswaran Damaraju

Contents

Preface v

1. **An Invitation to Geometry** 1
   - Introduction
   - A Brief History of Geometry
   - Geometry on Surfaces: A First Look
2. **The Complex Plane** 15
   - Basic Notions
   - Polar Form of a Complex Number
   - Division and Angle Measure
   - Complex Expressions
3. **Transformations** 29
   - Basic Transformations of C
   - Inversion
   - The Extended Plane
   - Möbius Transformations
   - Möbius Transformations: A Closer Look
4. **Geometry** 71
   - The Basics
   - Möbius Geometry
5. **Hyperbolic Geometry** 81
   - The Poincaré Disk Model
   - Figures of Hyperbolic Geometry
   - Measurement in Hyperbolic Geometry
   - Area and Triangle Trigonometry
   - The Upper Half-Plane Model
6. **Elliptic Geometry** 121
   - Antipodal Points
   - Elliptic Geometry
   - Measurement in Elliptic Geometry

- Revisiting Euclid's Postulates

7. **Geometry on Surfaces** **145**
   - Curvature
   - Elliptic Geometry with Curvature $k > 0$
   - Hyperbolic Geometry with Curvature $k < 0$
   - The Family of Geometries (X_k, G_k)
   - Surfaces
   - Polygonal Surfaces
   - Geometry of Surfaces
   - Quotient Spaces

8. **Cosmic Topology** **195**
   - Three-Dimensional Geometry and 3-Manifolds
   - Cosmic Crystallography
   - Circles in the Sky
   - Our Universe

Index **225**

1

An Invitation to Geometry

How can it be that mathematics, being after all a product of human thought which is independent of experience, is so admirably appropriate to the objects of reality?

—Albert Einstein

Out of nothing I have created a strange new universe.

—János Bolyai

1.1 Introduction

Imagine you are a two-dimensional being living in a two-dimensional universe. Mathematicians in this universe often represent its shape as an infinite plane, exactly like the xy-plane you've used as the canvas in your calculus courses.

Your two-dimensional self has been taught in geometry that the angles of any triangle sum to 180°. You may have even constructed some triangles to check. Builders use the Pythagorean theorem to check whether two walls meet at right angles, and houses are sturdy.

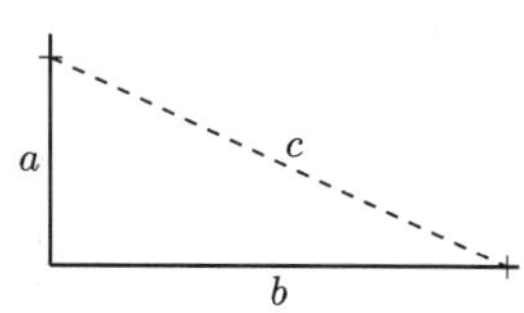

Figure 1.1.1 Measure a, b, and c and check whether $a^2 + b^2 = c^2$. If equality holds, the corner is square!

The infinite plane model of the two-dimensional universe works well enough for most purposes, but cosmologists and mathematicians, who notice that everything within the universe is finite, consider the possibility that the universe itself is finite. Would a finite universe have a boundary? Can it have an edge, a point beyond which one cannot travel? This possibility is unappealing because a boundary point would be physically different from the rest of space. But how can a finite universe have no boundary?

In a stroke as bold as it is simple, a two-dimensional mathematician suggests that the universe looks like a rectangular region with opposite edges identified.

Consider a flat, two-dimensional rectangle. In fact, visualize a tablet screen. Now imagine that you are playing a video game called Asteroids. As you shoot the asteroids and move your ship around the screen, you find that if you go off the top of the screen your ship reappears on the bottom; and if you go off the screen to the left you reappear on the right. In Figure 1.1.2, p. 2 there are just five asteroids. One has partially moved off the top of the screen and reappeared below, while a second is half way off the right hand "edge" and is reappearing to the left.

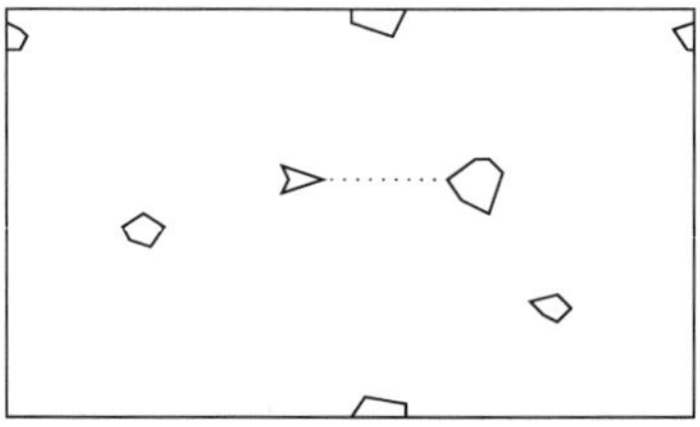

Figure 1.1.2 A finite two-dimensional world with no boundary.

Thus, the top edge of the rectangle has been identified, point by point, with the bottom edge. In three dimensions one can physically achieve this identification, or gluing, of the edges. In particular, one can bend the rectangle to produce a cylinder, being careful to join only the top and bottom edges together, and not any other points. The left and right edges of the rectangle have now become the left and right circles of the cylinder, which themselves get identified, point by point. Bend the cylinder to achieve this second gluing, and one obtains a donut, also called a torus.

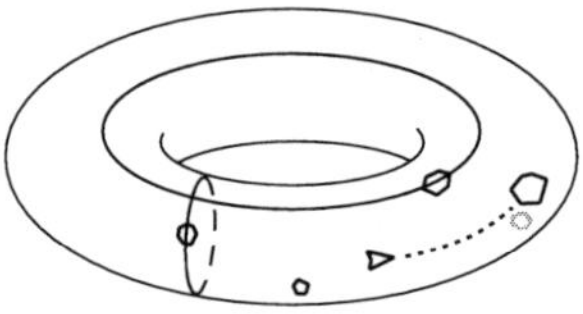

Figure 1.1.3 The video screen in Figure 1.1.2, p. 2 is equivalent to a torus.

Of course your two-dimensional self would not be able to see this torus surface in 3-space, but you could understand the space perfectly well in its rectangle-with-edges-identified form. It is clearly a finite area universe without any edge.

A sphere, like the surface of a beach ball, is another finite area two-dimensional surface without any edge. A bug cruising around on the surface of a sphere will observe that locally the world looks like a flat plane, and that the surface has no edges.

Consideration of a finite-area universe leads to questions about the type of geometry that applies to the universe. Let's look at a sphere. On small scales Euclidean geometry works well enough: small triangles have angle sum essentially equal to 180°, which is a defining feature of Euclidean geometry. But on a larger scale, things go awry. A very large triangle drawn on the surface of the sphere has an angle sum far exceeding 180°. (By triangle, we mean three points on the surface, together with three paths of shortest distance between the points. We'll discuss this more carefully later.)

Consider the triangle formed by the north pole and two points on the equator in Figure 1.1.4, p. 3. The angle at each point on the equator is 90°, so the total angle sum of the triangle exceeds 180° by the amount of the angle at the north pole. We conclude that a non-Euclidean geometry applies to the sphere on a global scale.

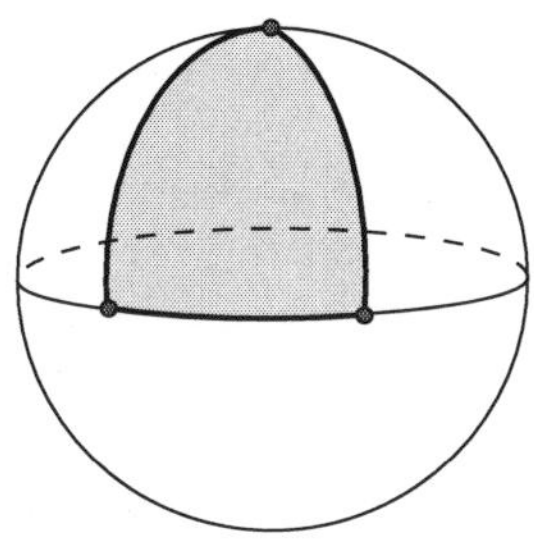

Figure 1.1.4 A triangle on a sphere.

In fact, there is a wonderful relationship between the topology (shape) of a surface, and the type of geometry that it inherits, and a primary goal of this book is to arrive at this relationship, given by the pristine Gauss-Bonnet equation

$$kA = 2\pi\chi.$$

We won't explain this equation here, but we will point out that geometry is on the left side of the equation, and topology is on the right. So, if a two-dimensional being can deduce what sort of global geometry holds in her world, she can greatly reduce the possible shapes for her universe. Our immediate task in the text is to study the other, non-Euclidean types of geometry that may apply on surfaces.

1.2 A Brief History of Geometry

Geometry is one of the oldest branches of mathematics, and most important among texts is Euclid's *Elements.* His text begins with 23 definitions, 5 postulates, and 5 common notions. From there Euclid starts proving results about geometry using a rigorous logical method, and many of us have been asked to do the same in high school.

Euclid's *Elements* served as *the* text on geometry for over 2000 years, and it has been admired as a brilliant work in logical reasoning. But one of Euclid's five postulates was also the center of a hot debate. It was this debate that ultimately led to the non-Euclidean geometries that can be applied to different surfaces.

Here are Euclid's five postulates:

1. One can draw a straight line from any point to any point.

2. One can produce a finite straight line continuously in a straight line.

3. One can describe a circle with any center and radius.

4. All right angles equal one another.
5. If a straight line falling on two straight lines makes the interior angles on the same side less than two right angles, the two straight lines, if produced indefinitely, meet on that side on which the angles are less than two right angles.

Does one postulate not look like the others? The first four postulates are short, simple, and intuitive. Well, the second might seem a bit odd, but all Euclid is saying here is that you can produce a line segment to any length you want. However, the 5th one, called the **parallel postulate**, is not short or simple; it sounds more like something you would try to prove than something you would take as given.

Indeed, the parallel postulate immediately gave philosophers and other thinkers fits, and many tried to prove that the fifth postulate followed from the first four, to no avail. Euclid himself may have been bothered at some level by the parallel postulate since he avoids using it until the proof of the 29th proposition in his text.

In trying to make sense of the parallel postulate, many equivalent statements emerged. The two equivalent statements most relevant to our study are these:

> $5'$. Given a line and a point not on the line, there is exactly one line through the point that does not intersect the given line.
>
> $5''$. The sum of the angles of any triangle is $180°$.

Reformulation $5'$ of the parallel postulate is called *Playfair's Axiom* after the Scottish mathematician John Playfair (1748-1819). This version of the fifth postulate will be the one we alter in order to produce non-Euclidean geometry.

The parallel postulate debate came to a head in the early 19th century. Farkas Bolyai (1775-1856) of Hungary spent much of his life on the problem of trying to prove the parallel postulate from the other four. He failed, and he fretted when his son János (1802-1860) started following down the same tormented path. In an oft-quoted letter, the father begged the son to end the obsession:

> For God's sake, I beseech you, give it up. Fear it no less than the sensual passions because it too may take all your time and deprive you of your health, peace of mind and happiness in life.[1]

But János continued to work on the problem, as did the Russian mathematician Nikolai Lobachevsky (1792-1856). They independently discovered that a well-defined geometry is possible in which the first four postulates hold, but the fifth doesn't. In particular, they demonstrated that the fifth postulate *is not a necessary consequence* of the first four.

In this text we will study two types of non-Euclidean geometry. The first type is called hyperbolic geometry, and is the geometry that Bolyai and Lobachevsky discovered. (The great Carl Friedrich Gauss (1777-1855) had also discovered this geometry; however, he did not publish his work because he feared it would be too controversial for the establishment.) In hyperbolic geometry, Euclid's fifth postulate is replaced by this:

[1]See for instance, Martin Gardner's book *The Colossal Book of Mathematics*, W.W. Norton & Company (2001), page 176.

> 5H. Given a line and a point not on the line, there are *at least two* lines through the point that do not intersect the given line.

In hyperbolic geometry, the sum of the angles of any triangle is less than 180°, a fact we prove in Chapter 5.

The second type of non-Euclidean geometry in this text is called elliptic geometry, which models geometry on the sphere. In this geometry, Euclid's fifth postulate is replaced by this:

> 5E. Given a line and a point not on the line, there are *zero* lines through the point that do not intersect the given line.

In elliptic geometry, the sum of the angles of any triangle is greater than 180°, a fact we prove in Chapter 6.

The Pythagorean Theorem. The celebrated Pythagorean theorem depends upon the parallel postulate, so it is a theorem of Euclidean geometry. However, we will encounter non-Euclidean variations of this theorem in Chapters 5 and 6, and present a unified Pythagorean theorem in Chapter 7, a result that appeared recently in [20].

The Pythagorean theorem appears as Proposition 47 at the end of Book I of Euclid's *Elements*, and we present Euclid's proof below. The Pythagorean theorem is fundamental to the systems of measurement we utilize in this text, in both Euclidean and non-Eucidean geometries. We also remark that the final proposition of Book I, Proposition 48, gives the converse that builders use: If we measure the legs of a triangle and find that $c^2 = a^2 + b^2$ then the angle opposite c is right. The interested reader can find an online version of Euclid's *Elements* here [29].

Theorem 1.2.1 The Pythagorean Theorem. *In right-angled triangles the square on the side opposite the right angle equals the sum of the squares on the sides containing the right angle.*

PROOF. Suppose we have right triangle ABC as in Figure 1.2.2, p. 6 with right angle at C, and side lengths a, b, and c, opposite corners A, B and C, respectively. In the figure we have extended squares from each leg of the triangle, and labeled various corners. We have also constructed the line through C parallel to AD, and let L and M denote the points of intersection of this line with AB and DE, respectively. One can check that ΔKAB is congruent to ΔCAD. Moreover, the area of ΔKAB is one half the area of the square AH. This is the case because they have equal base (segment KA) and equal altitude (segment AC). By a similar argument, the area of ΔDAC is one half the area of the parallelogram AM. This means that square AH and parallelogram AM have equal areas, the value of which is b^2.

One may proceed as above to argue that the areas of square BG and parallelogram BM are also equal, with value a^2. Since the area of square BD, which equals c^2, is the sum of the two parallelogram areas, it follows that $a^2 + b^2 = c^2$. □

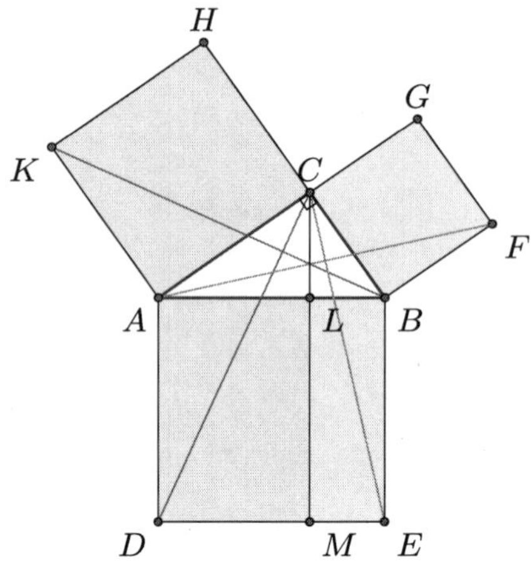

Figure 1.2.2 Proving the Pythagorean theorem

The arrival of non-Euclidean geometry soon caused a stir in circles outside the mathematics community. Fyodor Dostoevsky thought non-Euclidean geometry was interesting enough to include in *The Brothers Karamazov*, first published in 1880. Early in the novel two of the brothers, Ivan and Alyosha, get reacquainted at a tavern. Ivan discourages his younger brother from thinking about whether God exists, arguing that if one cannot fathom non-Euclidean geometry, then one has no hope of understanding questions about God.[2]

One of the first challenges of non-Euclidean geometry was to determine its logical consistency. By changing Euclid's parallel postulate, was a system created that led to contradictory theorems? In 1868, the Italian mathematician Enrico Beltrami (1835-1900) showed that the new non-Euclidean geometry could be constructed within the Euclidean plane so that, as long as Euclidean geometry was consistent, non-Euclidean geometry would be consistent as well. Non-Euclidean geometry was thus placed on solid ground.

This text does not develop geometry as Euclid, Lobachevsky, and Bolyai did. Instead, we will approach the subject as the German mathematician Felix Klein (1849-1925) did.

Whereas Euclid's approach to geometry was additive (he started with basic definitions and axioms and proceeded to build a sequence of results depending on previous ones), Klein's approach was subtractive. He started with a space and a group of allowable transformations of that space. He then threw out all concepts that did not remain unchanged under these transformations. Geometry, to Klein, is the study of objects and functions that remain unchanged under allowable transformations.

Klein's approach to geometry, called the **Erlangen Program** after the university at which he worked at the time, has the benefit that all three geometries (Euclidean, hyperbolic and elliptic) emerge as special cases from a general space and a general set of transformations.

The next three chapters will be devoted to making sense of and working through the preceding two paragraphs.

[2]See, for instance, *The Brothers Karamazov*, Fyodor Dostoevsky (a new translation by Richard Pevear and Larissa Volokhonsky), North Point Press (1990), page 235.

Like so much of mathematics, the development of non-Euclidean geometry anticipated applications. Albert Einstein's theory of special relativity illustrates the power of Klein's approach to geometry. Special relativity, says Einstein, is derived from the notion that the laws of nature are invariant with respect to Lorentz transformations.[3]

Even with non-Euclidean geometry in hand, Euclidean geometry remains central to modern mathematics because it *is* an excellent model for our local geometry. The angles of a triangle drawn on this paper *do* add up to 180°. Even "galactic" triangles determined by the positions of three nearby stars have angle sum indistinguishable from 180°.

However, on a larger scale, things might be different.

Maybe we live in a universe that looks flat (i.e., Euclidean) on smallish scales but is curved globally. This is not so hard to believe. A bug living in a field on the surface of the Earth might reasonably conclude he is living on an infinite plane. The bug cannot sense the fact that his flat, visible world is just a small patch of a curved surface (Earth) living in three-dimensional space. Likewise, our apparently Euclidean three-dimensional universe might be curving in some unseen fourth dimension so that the global geometry of the universe might be non-Euclidean.

Under reasonable assumptions about space, hyperbolic, elliptic, and Euclidean geometry are the only three possibilities for the global geometry of our universe. Researchers have spent significant time poring over cosmological data in hopes of deciding which geometry is ours. Deducing the geometry of the universe can tell us much about the shape of the universe and perhaps whether it is finite. If the universe is elliptic, then it must be finite in volume. If it is Euclidean or hyperbolic, then it can be either finite or infinite. Moreover, each geometry type corresponds to a class of possible shapes. And, if that isn't exciting enough, the overall geometry of the universe may be fundamentally connected to the fate of the universe. Clearly there is no more grand application of geometry than to the fate of the universe!

Exercises

1. Use Euclid's parallel postulate to prove the alternate interior angles theorem. That is, in Figure 1.2.3, p. 7(a), assume the line BD is parallel to the line AC. Prove that $\angle BAC = \angle ABD$.

2. Use Euclid's parallel postulate and the previous problem to prove that the sum of the angles of any triangle is 180°. You may find Figure 1.2.3, p. 7(b) helpful, where segment CD is parallel to segment AB.

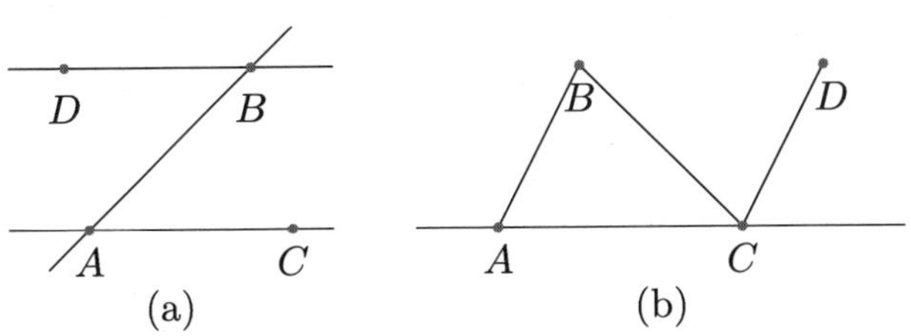

Figure 1.2.3 Two consequences of the parallel postulate.

[3] *Relativity: The Special and General Theory*, Crown Publications Inc (1961), p. 148.

1.3 Geometry on Surfaces: A First Look

Think for a minute about the space we live in. Think about objects that live in our space. Do the features of objects change when they move around in our space? If I pick up this paper and move it across the room, will it shrink? Will it become a broom?

If you draw a triangle on this page, the angles of the triangle will add to 180°. In fact, *any* triangle drawn *anywhere* on the page has this property. Euclidean geometry on this flat page (a portion of the plane) is **homogeneous**: the local geometry of the plane is the same at all points. Our three-dimensional space appears to be homogeneous as well. This is nice, for it means that if we buy a 5 ft^3 freezer at the appliance store, it doesn't shrink to 0.5 ft^3 when we get it home. A sphere is another example of a homogenous surface. A two-dimensional bug living on the surface of a sphere could not tell the difference (geometrically) between any two points on the sphere.

The surface of a donut in three-dimensional space (see Figure 1.3.1, p. 8) is not homogeneous, and a two-dimensional bug living on this surface *could* tell the difference between various points. One approach to discovering differences in geometry involves triangles.

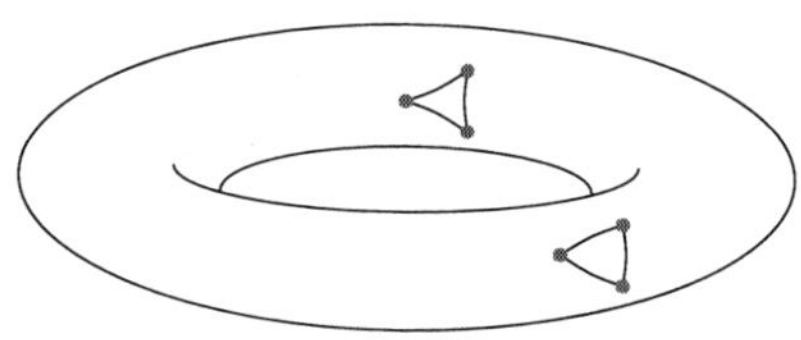

Figure 1.3.1 This torus surface is not homogeneous.

It is an important matter to decide what we mean, exactly, by a triangle on a surface. A triangle consists of three points and three edges connecting these points. An edge connecting point A to point B is drawn to represent the *path of shortest distance* between A and B. Such a path is called a **geodesic**. For the two-dimensional bug, a "straight line" from A to B is simply the shortest path from A to B.

On a sphere, geodesics follow great circles. A **great circle** is a circle drawn on the surface of the sphere whose center (in three-dimensional space) corresponds to the center of the sphere. Put another way, a great circle is a circle of maximum diameter drawn on the sphere. The circles a and b in Figure 1.3.2, p. 8 are great circles, but circle c is not.

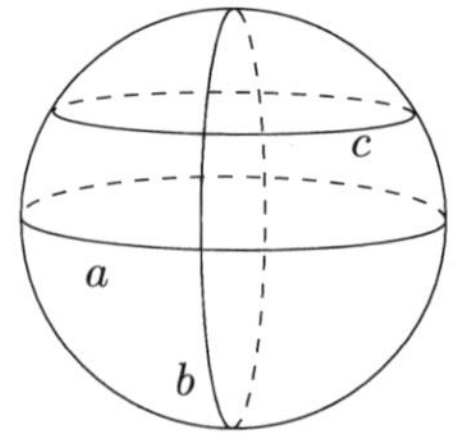

Figure 1.3.2 Geodesics on the sphere are great circles.

In the Euclidean plane, geodesics are Euclidean lines. One way to determine a geodesic on a surface physically is to pin some string at A and draw the string tight on the surface to a point B. The taut string will follow the geodesic from A to B. In Figure 1.3.3, p. 9 we have drawn geodesic triangles on three different surfaces.

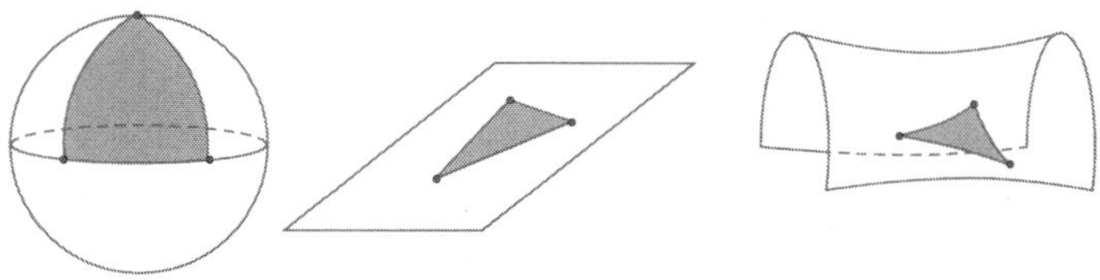

Figure 1.3.3 Depending on the shape of the surface, geodesic triangles can have angle sum greater than, less than, or equal to 180°.

Getting back to the donut, a two-dimensional bug could use triangles to tell the difference between a "convex" point on an outer wall, and a "saddle-shaped" point on an inner wall (see Figure 1.3.1, p. 8). A bug could draw a triangle about the convex point, determine the angle sum, and then move around the surface to a saddle-shaped point, and determine the angle sum of a new triangle (whose legs are the same length as before). The bug would scratch her head at the different angle sums before realizing she'd stumbled upon something big. She'd go home, write up the result, emphasizing the fact that a triangle in the first "convex" region will have angle sum greater than 180°, while a triangle in the "saddle-shaped" region will have angle sum less than 180°. This happy bug will conclude her donut surface is not homogeneous. She will then sit back and watch the accolades pour in. Perhaps even a Nobel prize. Thus, small triangles and their angles can help a two-dimensional bug distinguish points on a surface.

The donut surface is not homogeneous, so let's build one that is.

Example 1.3.4 The Flat Torus.

Consider again the world of Figure 1.1.2, p. 2. This world is called a *flat torus*. At every spot in this world, the pilot of the ship would report flat surroundings (triangle angles add to 180°). Unlike the donut surface living in three dimensions, the flat torus *is* homogeneous. Locally, geometry is the same at every point, and thanks to a triangle check, this geometry is Euclidean. But the world as a whole is much different than the Euclidean plane. For instance, if the pilot of the ship has a powerful enough telescope, he'd be able to see the back of his ship. Of course, if the ship had windows just so, he'd be able to see the back of his head. The flat torus is a finite, Euclidean two-dimensional world without any boundary.

Example 1.3.5 Coneland.

Here we build cones from flat wedges, and measure angles of some triangles.

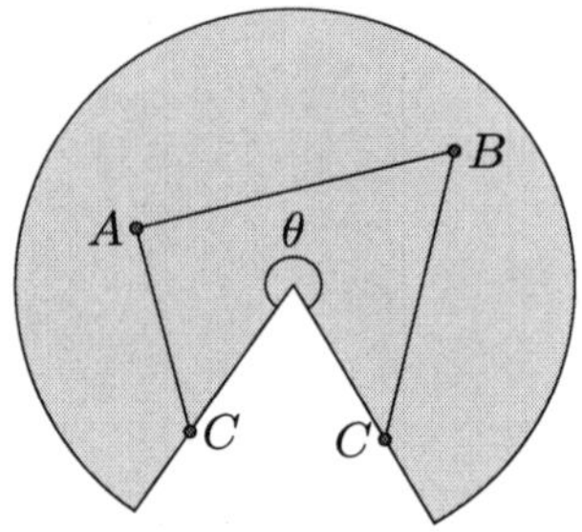

Figure 1.3.6 A triangle on a cone.

a. Begin with a circular disk with a wedge removed, like a pizza missing a slice or two. Joining the two radial edges produces a cone. Try it with a cone of your own to make sure it works. Now, with the cone flat again, pick three points, labeled A, B, and C, such that C is on the radial edge. This means that in this flattened version of the cone, point C actually appears twice: once on each radial edge, as in Figure 1.3.6, p. 10. These two representatives for C should get identified when you join the radial edges.

b. Draw the segments connecting the three points. You should get a triangle with the tip of the cone in its interior. (This triangle should actually look like a triangle if you re-form the cone.) If you don't get the tip of the cone on the inside of the triangle, adjust the points accordingly.

c. With your protractor, carefully measure the angle θ subtended by the circular sector. To emphasize θ's role in the shape of the cone, we let $S(\theta)$ denote the cone surface determined by θ.

d. With your protractor, carefully measure the three angles of your triangle. The angle at point C is the sum of the angles formed by the triangle legs and the radial segments. Let Δ denote the sum of these three angles.

e. State a conjecture about the relationship between the angle θ and Δ, the sum of the angles of the triangle. Your conjecture can be in the form of an equation. Then prove your conjecture. Hint: if you draw a segment connecting the 2 copies of point C, what is the angle sum of the quadrilateral $ABCC$?

Example 1.3.7 Saddleland.

Repeat the previous exercise but with circle wedges having $\theta > 2\pi$. Identifying the radial edges in this case produces a saddle-shaped surface. [To create such a circle wedge we can tape together two wedges of equal radius. One idea: Start with a disk with one radial cut, and a wedge of equal radius.

Tape one radial edge of the wedge to one of the slit radial edges of the disk. Then, identifying the other radial edges should produce Saddleland.]

Remember, a *homogeneous surface* is a space that has the same local geometry at every point. Our flat torus is homogeneous, having Euclidean geometry at every point. However, our cones $S(\theta)$ in the previous exercises are not homogeneous (unless θ happens to be 2π). If a triangle in $S(\theta)$ does not contain the tip of the cone in its interior, then the angles of the triangle will add to π radians, but if the triangle does contain the tip of the cone in its interior, then the angle sum will not be π radians. A two-dimensional bug, then, could conclude that $S(\theta)$ is not homogeneous.

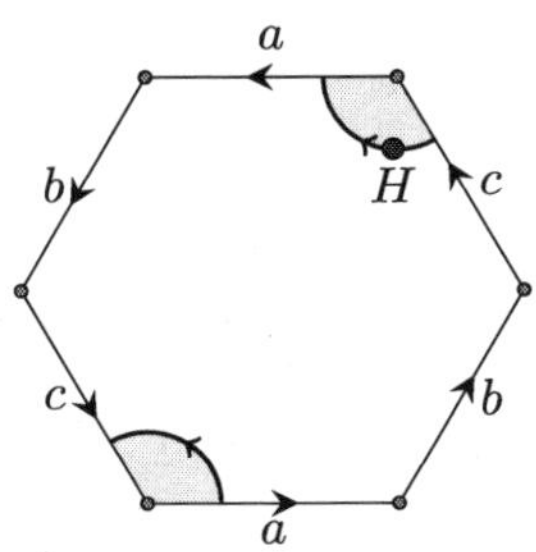

Figure 1.3.8 A hexagonal video screen

Example 1.3.9 A non-Euclidean surface.

Consider the surface obtained by identifying the edges of the hexagon as indicated in Figure 1.3.8, p. 11. In particular, the edges are matched according to their labels and arrow orientation. So, if a ship flies off the hexagonal screen at a spot on the edge marked a, say, then it reappears at the matching spot on the other edge marked a.

Suppose the pilot of a ship wants to fly around one of the corners of the hexagon. If she begins at point H, say, and flies counterclockwise around the upper right corner as indicated in the diagram, she would fly off the screen at the top near the start of an a edge. So, as she made her journey, she would reappear in the lower left corner near the start of the other a edge. Continuing around she would complete her journey after circling this second corner.

However, the angle of each corner is 120°, and gluing them together will create a cone point, as pictured below. Similarly, she would find that the other corners of the hexagon meet in groups of two, creating two additional cone points. As with the Coneland Example 1.3.5, p. 9, the pilot can distinguish a corner point from an interior point here. She can look at triangles: a triangle containing one of the cone points will have angle sum greater than 180°; any other triangle will have angle sum equal to 180°.

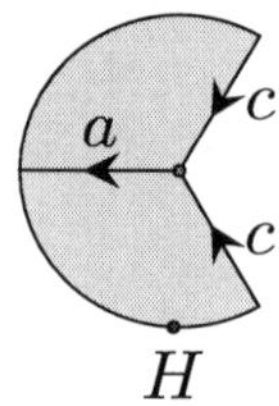

So the surface is not homogeneous, *if it is drawn in the plane.* However, the surface does *admit* a homogeneous geometry. We can get rid of the cone points if we can increase each corner angle of the hexagon to 180°. Then, two corners would come together to form a perfect 360° patch about the point.

But how can we increase the corner angles? Put the hexagon on the sphere! Imagine stretching the hexagon onto the northern hemisphere of a sphere (see Figure 1.3.10, p. 12). In this case we can think of the 6 points of our hexagon as lying on the equator. Then each corner angle *is* 180°, each edge is still a line (geodesic), and when we glue the edges, each pair of corner angles adds up to exactly 360°, so the surface is homogeneous. The homogeneous geometry of this surface is the geometry of the sphere (elliptic geometry), not the geometry of the plane (Euclidean geometry).

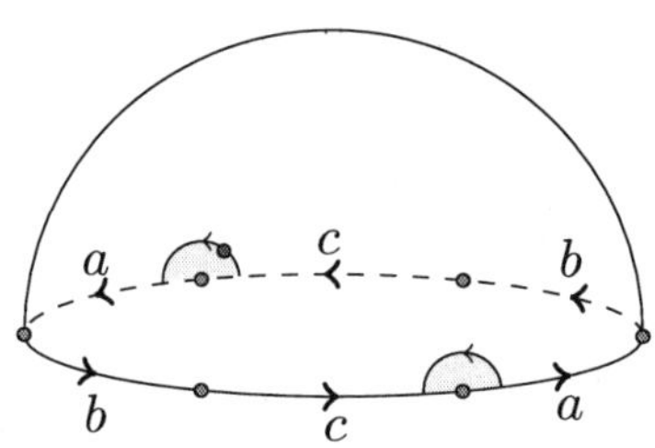

Figure 1.3.10 A surface with homogeneous elliptic geometry.

It turns out *every* surface can be given one of three types of homogeneous geometry: Euclidean, hyperbolic, or elliptic. We will return to the geometry of surfaces (and of our universe) after we develop hyperbolic and elliptic geometry. If it doesn't make a whole lot of sense right now, don't sweat it, but please use these facts as motivation for learning about these non-Euclidean geometries.

Exercises

1. Work through the Coneland Example 1.3.5, p. 9.

2. Work through the Saddleland Example 1.3.7, p. 10.

3. *Circumference vs Radius in Coneland and Saddleland.* In addition to triangles, a two-dimensional bug can use circles to screen for different geometries. In particular, a bug can study the relationship between the radius and the circumference of a circle. To make sure we think like the bug, here's how we define a circle on a surface: Given a point P on the surface, and a real number $r > 0$, the circle centered at P with radius r is the set of all points r

units away from P, where the distance between two points is the length of the shortest path connecting them (the geodesic).

a. Pick your favorite circle in the plane. What is the relationship between the circle's radius and circumference? Is your answer true for *any* circle in the plane?

b. Consider the Coneland surface of Example 1.3.5, p. 9. Construct a circle centered at the tip of the cone and derive a relationship between its circumference and its radius. Is $C = 2\pi r$ here? If not, which is true: $C > 2\pi r$ or $C < 2\pi r$?

c. Consider the Saddleland surface of Example 1.3.7, p. 10. Construct a circle centered at the tip of the saddle and derive a relationship between its circumference and its radius. Is $C = 2\pi r$ here? If not, which is true: $C > 2\pi r$ or $C < 2\pi r$?

2

The Complex Plane

To study geometry using Klein's Erlangen Program, we need to define a space and a group of transformations of the space. Our space will be the complex plane.

2.1 Basic Notions

The set of complex numbers is obtained algebraically by adjoining the number i to the set $\mathbb{R}$ of real numbers, where i is defined by the property that $i^2 = -1$. We will take a geometric approach and define a **complex number** to be an ordered pair (x, y) of real numbers. We let $\mathbb{C}$ denote the set of all complex numbers,

$$\mathbb{C} = \{(x, y) \mid x, y \in \mathbb{R}\}.$$

Given the complex number $z = (x, y)$, x is called the **real part** of z, denoted $\text{Re}(z)$; and y is called the **imaginary part** of z, denoted $\text{Im}(z)$. The set of real numbers is a subset of $\mathbb{C}$ under the identification $x \leftrightarrow (x, 0)$, for any real number x.

Addition in $\mathbb{C}$ is componentwise,

$$(x, y) + (s, t) = (x + s, y + t),$$

and if k is a real number, we define **scalar multiplication** by

$$k \cdot (x, y) = (kx, ky).$$

Within this framework, $i = (0, 1)$, meaning that any complex number (x, y) can be expressed as $x + yi$ as suggested here:

$$\begin{aligned}(x, y) &= (x, 0) + (0, y)\\ &= x(1, 0) + y(0, 1)\\ &= x + yi.\end{aligned}$$

The expression $x + yi$ is called the **Cartesian form** of the complex number. This form can be helpful when doing arithmetic of complex numbers, but it can also be a bit gangly. We often let a single letter such as z or w represent a complex number. So, $z = x + yi$ means that the complex number we're calling z corresponds to the point (x, y) in the plane.

It is sometimes helpful to view a complex number as a vector, and complex addition corresponds to vector addition in the plane. The same holds for scalar multiplication. For instance, in Figure 2.1.1, p. 16 we have represented $z = 2 + i$, $w = -1 + 1.5i$, as well as $z + w = 1 + 2.5i$, as vectors from the origin to these points in $\mathbb{C}$. The complex number $z - w$ can be represented by the vector from w to z in the plane.

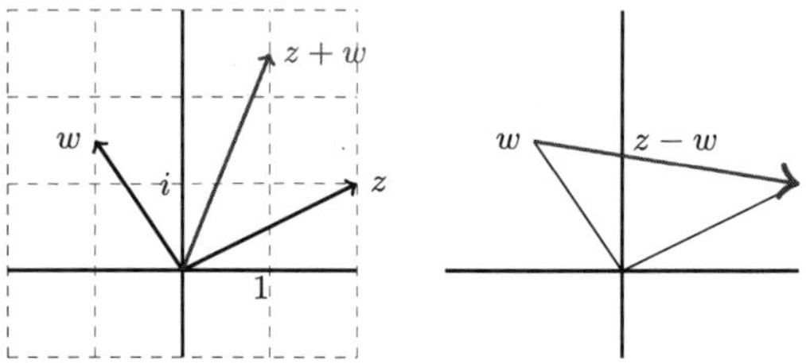

Figure 2.1.1 Complex numbers as vectors in the plane.

We define **complex multiplication** using the fact that $i^2 = -1$.

$$\begin{aligned}(x + yi) \cdot (s + ti) &= xs + ysi + xti + yti^2 \\ &= (xs - yt) + (ys + xt)i.\end{aligned}$$

The **modulus** of $z = x + yi$, denoted $|z|$, is given by

$$|z| = \sqrt{x^2 + y^2}.$$

Note that $|z|$ gives the Euclidean distance of z to the point (0,0).

The **conjugate** of $z = x + yi$, denoted $\overline{z}$, is

$$\overline{z} = x - yi.$$

In the exercises the reader is asked to prove various useful properties of the modulus and conjugate.

Example 2.1.2 Arithmetic of complex numbers.

Suppose $z = 3 - 4i$ and $w = 2 + 7i$.

Then $z + w = 5 + 3i$, and

$$\begin{aligned}z \cdot w &= (3 - 4i)(2 + 7i) \\ &= 6 + 28 - 8i + 21i \\ &= 34 + 13i.\end{aligned}$$

A few other computations:

$$\begin{aligned}4z &= 12 - 16i \\ |z| &= \sqrt{3^2 + (-4)^2} = 5 \\ \overline{zw} &= 34 - 13i.\end{aligned}$$

Exercises

1. In each case, determine $z + w$, sz, $|z|$, and $z \cdot w$.

a. $z = 5 + 2i$, $s = -4$, $w = -1 + 2i$

b. $z = 3i$, $s = 1/2$, $w = -3 + 2i$

c. $z = 1 + i$, $s = 0.6$, $w = 1 - i$

2. Show that $z \cdot \overline{z} = |z|^2$, where $\overline{z}$ is the conjugate of z.

3. Suppose $z = x + yi$ and $w = s + ti$ are two complex numbers. Prove the following properties of the conjugate and the modulus.

a. $|w \cdot z| = |w| \cdot |z|$.

b. $\overline{zw} = \overline{z} \cdot \overline{w}$.

c. $\overline{z + w} = \overline{z} + \overline{w}$.

d. $z + \overline{z} = 2\text{Re}(z)$. (Hence, $z + \overline{z}$ is a real number.)

e. $z - \overline{z} = 2\text{Im}(z)i$.

f. $|z| = |\overline{z}|$.

4. A **Pythagorean triple** consists of three integers (a, b, c) such that $a^2+b^2 = c^2$. We can use complex numbers to generate Pythagorean triples. Suppose $z = x + yi$ where x and y are positive integers. Let

$$a = Re(z^2) \qquad b = Im(z^2) \qquad c = z\overline{z}.$$

a. Prove that $a^2 + b^2 = c^2$.

b. Find the complex number $z = x + yi$ that generates the famous triple (3,4,5).

c. Find the complex number that generates the triple (5,12,13).

d. Find five other Pythagorean triples, generated using complex numbers of the form $z = x + yi$, where x and y are positive integers with no common divisors.

2.2 Polar Form of a Complex Number

A point (x, y) in the plane can be represented in polar form (r, θ) according to the relationships in Figure 2.2.1, p. 17.

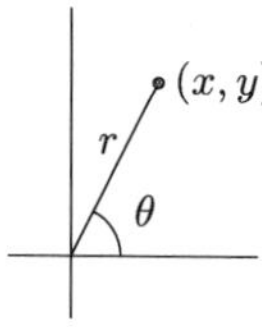

$$x = r\cos(\theta)$$
$$y = r\sin(\theta)$$

Figure 2.2.1 Polar coordinates of a point in the plane

Using these relationships, we can rewrite

$$\begin{aligned} x + yi &= r\cos(\theta) + r\sin(\theta)i \\ &= r(\cos(\theta) + i\sin(\theta)). \end{aligned}$$

This leads us to make the following definition. For any real number θ, we define

$$e^{i\theta} = \cos(\theta) + i\sin(\theta).$$

For instance, $e^{i\pi/2} = \cos(\pi/2) + i\sin(\pi/2) = 0 + i \cdot 1 = i$.

Similarly, $e^{i0} = \cos(0) + i\sin(0) = 1$, and it's a quick check to see that $e^{i\pi} = -1$, which leads to a simple equation involving the most famous numbers in mathematics (except 8), truly an all-star equation:

$$e^{i\pi} + 1 = 0.$$

If $z = x + yi$ and (x, y) has polar form (r, θ) then $z = re^{i\theta}$ is called the **polar form** of z. The non-negative scalar $|r|$ is the modulus of z, and the angle θ is called the **argument** of z, denoted $\arg(z)$.

Example 2.2.2 Exploring the polar form.

On the left side of the following diagram, we plot the points $z = 2e^{i\pi/4}, w = 3e^{i\pi/2}, v = -2e^{i\pi/6}, u = 3e^{-i\pi/3}$.

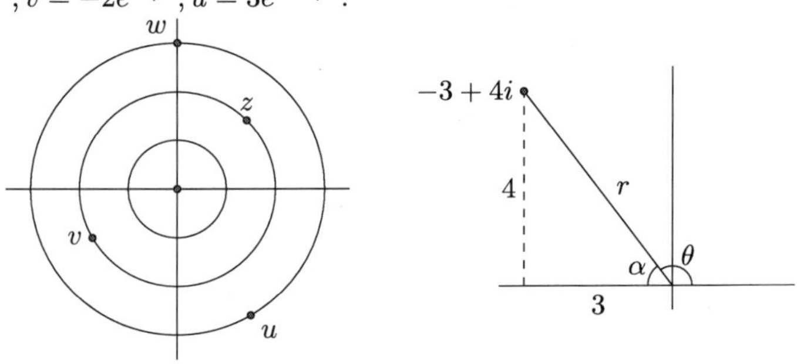

To convert $z = -3 + 4i$ to polar form, refer to the right side of the diagram. We note that $r = \sqrt{9 + 16} = 5$, and $\tan(\alpha) = 4/3$, so $\theta = \pi - \tan^{-1}(4/3) \approx 2.21$ radians. Thus,

$$-3 + 4i = 5e^{i(\pi - \tan^{-1}(4/3))} \approx 5e^{2.21i}.$$

Theorem 2.2.3 *The product of two complex numbers in polar form is given by*

$$re^{i\theta} \cdot se^{i\beta} = (rs)e^{i(\theta+\beta)}.$$

PROOF. We use the definition of the complex exponential and some trigonometric identities.

$$\begin{aligned} re^{i\theta} \cdot se^{i\beta} &= r(\cos\theta + i\sin\theta) \cdot s(\cos\beta + i\sin\beta) \\ &= (rs)(\cos\theta + i\sin\theta) \cdot (\cos\beta + i\sin\beta) \\ &= rs[\cos\theta\cos\beta - \sin\theta\sin\beta + (\cos\theta\sin\beta + \sin\theta\cos\beta)i] \\ &= rs[\cos(\theta+\beta) + \sin(\theta+\beta)i] \end{aligned}$$

$$= rs[e^{i(\theta+\beta)}].$$

□

Thus, the product of two complex numbers is obtained by multiplying their magnitudes and adding their arguments, and

$$\arg(zw) = \arg(z) + \arg(w),$$

where the equation is taken modulo 2π. That is, depending on our choices for the arguments, we have $\arg(vw) = \arg(v) + \arg(w) + 2\pi k$ for some integer k.

Example 2.2.4 Polar form with $r \geq 0$.

When representing a complex number z in polar form as $z = re^{i\theta}$, we may assume that r is non-negative. If $r < 0$, then

$$\begin{aligned} re^{i\theta} &= -|r|e^{i\theta} \\ &= (e^{i\pi}) \cdot |r|e^{i\theta} \quad \text{since } -1 = e^{i\pi} \\ &= |r|e^{i(\theta+\pi)}, \quad \text{by Theorem 2.2.3, p. 18.} \end{aligned}$$

Thus, by adding π to the angle if necessary, we may always assume that $z = re^{i\theta}$ where r is non-negative.

Exercises

1. Convert the following points to polar form and plot them: $3 + i$, $-1 - 2i$, $3 - 4i$, $7{,}002{,}001$, and $-4i$.

2. Express the following points in Cartesian form and plot them: $z = 2e^{i\pi/3}$, $w = -2e^{i\pi/4}$, $u = 4e^{i5\pi/3}$, and $z \cdot u$.

3. Modify the all-star equation to involve 8. In particular, write an expression involving $e, i, \pi, 1$, and 8, that equals 0. You may use no other numbers, and certainly not 3.

4. If $z = re^{i\theta}$, prove that $\overline{z} = re^{-i\theta}$.

2.3 Division and Angle Measure

The **division** of the complex number z by $w \neq 0$, denoted $\frac{z}{w}$, is the complex number u that satisfies the equation $z = w \cdot u$.

For instance, $\frac{1}{i} = -i$ because $1 = i \cdot (-i)$.

In practice, division of complex numbers is not a guessing game, but can be done by multiplying the top and bottom of the quotient by the conjugate of the bottom expression.

Example 2.3.1 Division in Cartesian form.

We convert the following quotient to Cartesian form:

$$\begin{aligned}\frac{2+i}{3+2i} &= \frac{2+i}{3+2i}\cdot\frac{3-2i}{3-2i}\\ &= \frac{(6+2)+(-4+3)i}{9+4}\\ &= \frac{8-i}{13}\\ &= \frac{8}{13}-\frac{1}{13}i.\end{aligned}$$

Example 2.3.2 Division in polar form.

Suppose we wish to find z/w where $z = re^{i\theta}$ and $w = se^{i\beta} \neq 0$. The reader can check that

$$\frac{1}{w} = \frac{1}{s}e^{-i\beta}.$$

Then we may apply Theorem 2.2.3, p. 18 to obtain the following result:

$$\begin{aligned}\frac{z}{w} &= z\cdot\frac{1}{w}\\ &= re^{i\theta}\cdot\frac{1}{s}e^{-i\beta}\\ &= \frac{r}{s}e^{i(\theta-\beta)}.\end{aligned}$$

So,

$$\arg\left(\frac{z}{w}\right) = \arg(z) - \arg(w)$$

where equality is taken modulo 2π.

Thus, when dividing by complex numbers, we can first convert to polar form if it is convenient. For instance,

$$\frac{1+i}{-3+3i} = \frac{\sqrt{2}e^{i\pi/4}}{\sqrt{18}e^{i3\pi/4}} = \frac{1}{3}e^{-i\pi/2} = -\frac{1}{3}i.$$

Angle Measure. Given two rays L_1 and L_2 having common initial point, we let $\angle(L_1, L_2)$ denote the **angle between rays** L_1 and L_2, measured from L_1 to L_2. We may rotate ray L_1 onto ray L_2 in either a counterclockwise direction or a clockwise direction. We adopt the convention that angles measured counterclockwise are positive, and angles measured clockwise are negative, and admit that angles are only well-defined up to multiples of 2π. Notice that

$$\angle(L_1, L_2) = -\angle(L_2, L_1).$$

To compute $\angle(L_1, L_2)$ where z_0 is the common initial point of the rays, let z_1 be any point on L_1, and z_2 any point on L_2. Then

$$\begin{aligned}\angle(L_1, L_2) &= \arg\left(\frac{z_2 - z_0}{z_1 - z_0}\right)\\ &= \arg(z_2 - z_0) - \arg(z_1 - z_0).\end{aligned}$$

Example 2.3.3 The angle between two rays.

Suppose L_1 and L_2 are rays emanating from $2+2i$. Ray L_1 proceeds along the line $y = x$ and L_2 proceeds along $y = 3 - x/2$ as pictured.

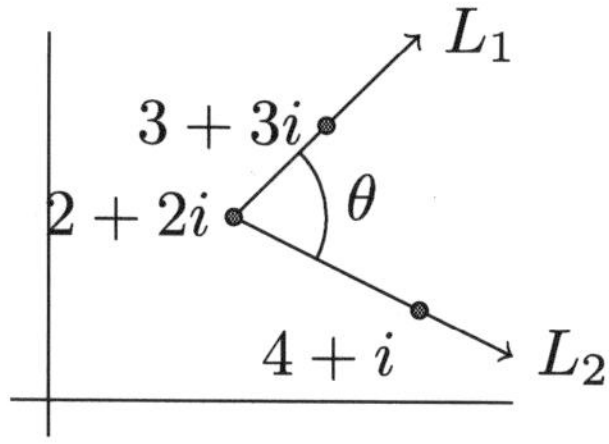

To compute the angle θ in the diagram, we choose $z_1 = 3 + 3i$ and $z_2 = 4 + i$. Then

$$\angle(L_1, L_2) = \arg(2 - i) - \arg(1 + i) = -\tan^{-1}(1/2) - \pi/4 \approx -71.6°.$$

That is, the angle from L_1 to L_2 is 71.6° in the clockwise direction.

The angle determined by three points.

If u, v, and w are three complex numbers, let $\angle uvw$ denote the angle θ from ray $\overrightarrow{vu}$ to $\overrightarrow{vw}$. In particular,

$$\angle uvw = \theta = \arg\left(\frac{w - v}{u - v}\right).$$

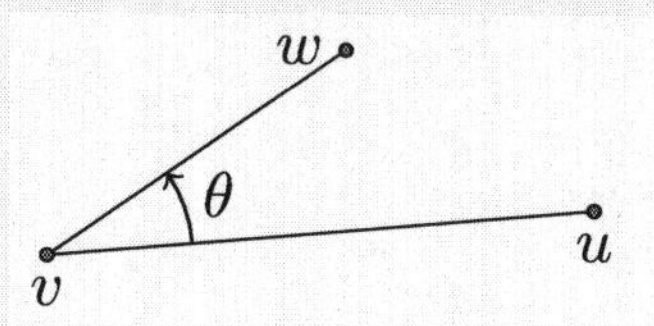

For instance, if $u = 1$ on the positive real axis, $v = 0$ is the origin in $\mathbb{C}$, and z is any point in $\mathbb{C}$, then $\angle uvz = \arg(z)$.

Exercises

1. Express $\frac{1}{x+yi}$ in the form $a + bi$.

2. Express these fractions in Cartesian form or polar form, whichever seems more convenient.

$$\frac{1}{2i}, \quad \frac{1}{1+i}, \quad \frac{4+i}{1-2i}, \quad \frac{2}{3+i}.$$

3. Prove that $|z/w| = |z|/|w|$, and that $\overline{z/w} = \overline{z}/\overline{w}$.

4. Suppose $z = re^{i\theta}$ and $w = se^{i\alpha}$ are as shown below. Let $u = z \cdot w$. Prove that $\Delta 01z$ and $\Delta 0wu$ are similar triangles.

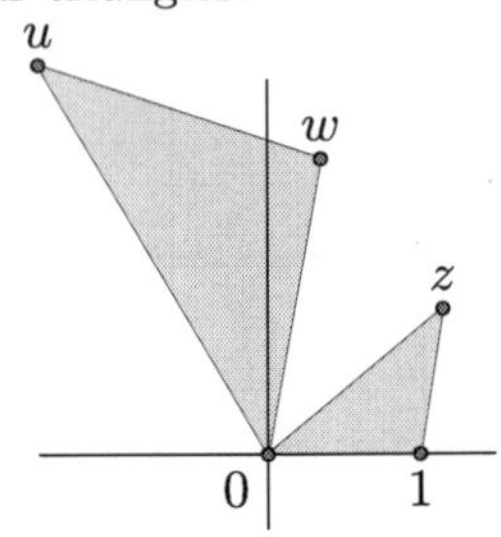

5. Determine the angle $\angle uvw$ where $u = 2+i$, $v = 1+2i$, and $w = -1+i$.

6. Suppose z is a point with positive imaginary component on the unit circle shown below, $a = 1$ and $b = -1$. Use the angle formula to prove that angle $\angle bza = \pi/2$.

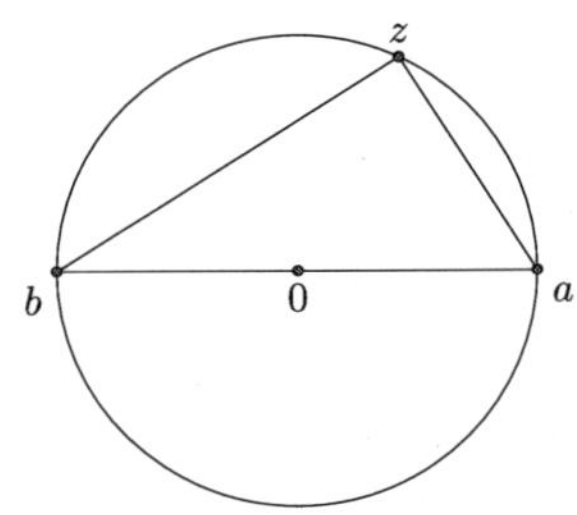

2.4 Complex Expressions

In this section we look at some equations and inequalities that will come up throughout the text.

Example 2.4.1 Line equations.

The standard form for the equation of a line in the xy-plane is $ax+by+d=0$. This line may be expressed via the complex variable $z = x+yi$. For an arbitrary complex number $\beta = s+ti$, note that

$$\begin{aligned}\beta z + \overline{\beta z} &= \big[(sx-ty)+(sy+tx)i\big] + \big[(sx-ty)-(sy+tx)i\big] \\ &= 2sx - 2ty.\end{aligned}$$

It follows that the line $ax+by+d=0$ can be represented by the equation

$$\alpha z + \overline{\alpha z} + d = 0 \qquad \text{(equation of a line)}$$

where $\alpha = \frac{1}{2}(a-bi)$ is a complex constant and d is a real number.

Conversely, for any complex number α and real number d, the equation

$$\alpha z + \overline{\alpha z} + d = 0$$

determines a line in $\mathbb{C}$.

We may also view any line in $\mathbb{C}$ as the collection of points equidistant from two given points.

Theorem 2.4.2 *Any line in $\mathbb{C}$ can be expressed by the equation $|z-\gamma| = |z-\beta|$ for suitably chosen points γ and β in $\mathbb{C}$, and the set of all points (Euclidean) equidistant from distinct points γ and β forms a line.*

PROOF. Given two points γ and β in $\mathbb{C}$, z is equidistant from both if and only if $|z-\gamma|^2 = |z-\beta|^2$. Expanding this equation, we obtain

$$\begin{aligned}(z-\gamma)(\overline{z-\gamma}) &= (z-\beta)(\overline{z-\beta})\\ |z|^2 - \overline{\gamma}z - \gamma\overline{z} + |\gamma|^2 &= |z|^2 - \overline{\beta}z - \beta\overline{z} + |\beta|^2\\ \overline{(\beta-\gamma)}z + (\beta-\gamma)\overline{z} + (|\gamma|^2 - |\beta|^2) &= 0.\end{aligned}$$

This last equation has the form of a line, letting $\alpha = \overline{(\beta-\gamma)}$ and $d = |\gamma|^2 - |\beta|^2$.

Conversely, starting with a line we can find complex numbers γ and β that do the trick. In particular, if the given line is the perpendicular bisector of the segment $\gamma\beta$, then $|z-\gamma| = |z-\beta|$ describes the line. We leave the details to the reader. □

Example 2.4.3 Quadratic equations.

Suppose z_0 is a complex constant and consider the equation $z^2 = z_0$. A complex number z that satisfies this equation will be called a square root of z_0, and will be written as $\sqrt{z_0}$.

If we view $z_0 = r_0 e^{i\theta_0}$ in polar form with $r_0 \geq 0$, then a complex number $z = re^{i\theta}$ satisfies the equation $z^2 = z_0$ if and only if

$$re^{i\theta} \cdot re^{i\theta} = r_0 e^{i\theta_0}.$$

In other words, z satisfies the equation if and only if $r^2 = r_0$ and $2\theta = \theta_0$ (modulo 2π).

As long as r_0 is greater than zero, we have two solutions to the equation, so that z_0 has two square roots:

$$\pm\sqrt{r_0}e^{i\theta_0/2}.$$

For instance, $z^2 = i$ has two solutions. Since $i = 1e^{i\pi/2}$, $\sqrt{i} = \pm e^{i\pi/4}$. In Cartesian form, $\sqrt{i} = \pm(\frac{\sqrt{2}}{2} + \frac{\sqrt{2}}{2}i)$.

More generally, the complex quadratic equation $\alpha z^2 + \beta z + \gamma = 0$ where α, β, and γ are complex constants, will have one or two solutions. This marks an important difference from the real case, where a quadratic equation might not have any real solutions. In both cases we may use the quadratic formula to hunt for roots, and in the complex case we have solutions

$$z = \frac{-\beta \pm \sqrt{\beta^2 - 4\alpha\gamma}}{2\alpha}.$$

For instance, $z^2 + 2z + 4 = 0$ has two solutions:

$$z = \frac{-2 \pm \sqrt{-12}}{2} = -1 \pm \sqrt{3}i$$

since $\sqrt{-1} = i$.

Example 2.4.4 Solving a quadratic equation.

Consider the equation $z^2 - (3+3i)z = 2 - 3i$. To solve this equation for z we first rewrite it as

$$z^2 - (3+3i)z - (2-3i) = 0.$$

We use the quadratic formula with $\alpha = 1$, $\beta = -(3+3i)$, and $\gamma = -(2-3i)$, to obtain the solution(s)

$$z = \frac{3 + 3i \pm \sqrt{(3+3i)^2 + 4(2-3i)}}{2}$$
$$z = \frac{3 + 3i \pm \sqrt{8+6i}}{2}.$$

To determine the solutions in Cartesian form, we need to evaluate $\sqrt{8+6i}$. We offer two approaches. The first approach considers the following task: Set $x + yi = \sqrt{8+6i}$ and solve for x and y directly by squaring both sides to obtain a system of equations.

$$\begin{aligned} x + yi &= \sqrt{8+6i} \\ (x+yi)^2 &= 8+6i \\ x^2 - y^2 + 2xyi &= 8+6i. \end{aligned}$$

Thus, we have two equations and two unknowns:

$$x^2 - y^2 = 8 \quad (1)$$
$$2xy = 6. \quad (2)$$

In fact, we also know that $x^2+y^2 = |x+yi|^2 = |(x+yi)^2| = |8+6i| = 10$, giving us a third equation

$$x^2 + y^2 = 10. \quad (3)$$

Adding equations (1) and (3) yields $x^2 = 9$ so $x = \pm 3$. Substituting $x = 3$ into equation (2) yields $y = 1$; substituting $x = -3$ into (2) yields $y = -1$. Thus we have two solutions:

$$\sqrt{8+6i} = \pm(3+i).$$

We may also use the polar form to determine $\sqrt{8+6i}$. Consider the right triangle determined by the point $8 + 6i = 10e^{i\theta}$ pictured in the following diagram.

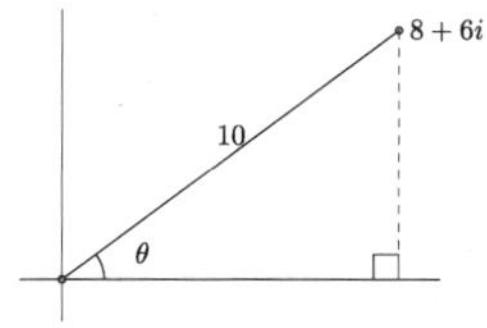

We know $\sqrt{8+6i} = \pm\sqrt{10}e^{i\theta/2}$, so we want to find $\theta/2$. Well, we can determine $\tan(\theta/2)$ easily enough using the half-angle formula

$$\tan(\theta/2) = \frac{\sin(\theta)}{1+\cos(\theta)}.$$

The right triangle in the diagram shows us that $\sin(\theta) = 3/5$ and $\cos(\theta) = 4/5$, so $\tan(\theta/2) = 1/3$. This means that any point $re^{i\theta/2}$ lives on the line through the origin having slope 1/3, and can be described by $k(3+i)$ for some scalar k. Since $\sqrt{8+6i}$ has this form, it follows that $\sqrt{8+6i} = k(3+i)$ for some k. Since $|\sqrt{8+6i}| = \sqrt{10}$, it follows that $|k(3+i)| = \sqrt{10}$, so $k = \pm 1$. In other words, $\sqrt{8+6i} = \pm(3+i)$.

Now let's return to the solution of the original quadratic equation in this example:

$$z = \frac{3+3i \pm \sqrt{8+6i}}{2}$$
$$z = \frac{3+3i \pm (3+i)}{2}.$$

Thus, $z = 3+2i$ or $z = i$.

Example 2.4.5 Circle equations.

If we let $z = x+yi$ and $z_0 = h+ki$, then the complex equation

$$|z - z_0| = r \qquad \text{(equation of a circle)}$$

describes the circle in the plane centered at z_0 with radius $r > 0$.

To see this, note that

$$\begin{aligned} |z - z_0| &= |(x-h) + (y-k)i| \\ &= \sqrt{(x-h)^2 + (y-k)^2}. \end{aligned}$$

So $|z - z_0| = r$ is equivalent to the equation $(x-h)^2 + (y-k)^2 = r^2$ of the circle centered at z_0 with radius r.

For instance, $|z - 3 - 2i| = 3$ describes the set of all points that are 3 units away from $3+2i$. All such z form a circle of radius 3 in the plane, centered at the point $(3, 2)$.

Example 2.4.6 Complex expressions as regions.

Describe each complex expression below as a region in the plane.

a. $|1/z| > 2$.

Taking the reciprocal of both sides, we have $|z| < 1/2$, which is the interior of the circle centered at 0 with radius 1/2.

b. $\text{Im}(z) < \text{Re}(z)$.

Set $z = x + yi$ in which case the inequality becomes $y < x$. This inequality describes all points in the plane under the line $y = x$, as pictured below.

c. $\text{Im}(z) = |z|$.

Setting $z = x + yi$, this equation is equivalent to $y = \sqrt{y^2 + x^2}$. Squaring both sides we obtain $0 = x^2$, so that $x = 0$. It follows that $y = \sqrt{y^2} = |y|$ so the equation describes the points $(0, y)$ with $y \geq 0$. These points determine a ray on the positive imaginary axis.

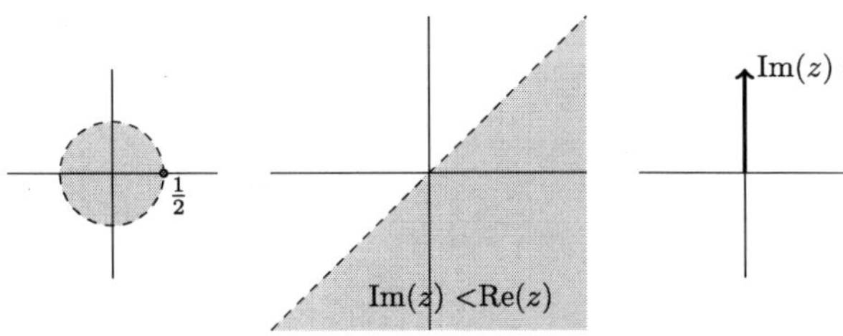

Moving forward, lines and circles will be especially important objects for us, so we end the section with a summary of their descriptions in the complex plane.

Lines and circles in $\mathbb{C}$.

Lines and circles in the plane can be expressed with a complex variable $z = x + yi$.

- The line $ax + by + d = 0$ in the plane can be represented by the equation

$$\alpha z + \overline{\alpha z} + d = 0$$

where $\alpha = \frac{1}{2}(a - bi)$ is a complex constant and d is a real number.

- The circle in the plane centered at z_0 with radius $r > 0$ can be represented by the equation

$$|z - z_0| = r.$$

Exercises

1. Use a complex variable to describe the equation of the line $y = mx + b$. Assume $m \neq 0$. In particular, show that this line is described by the equation

$$(m + i)z + (m - i)\overline{z} + 2b = 0.$$

2. In each case, sketch the set of complex numbers z satisfying the given condition.

a. $|z + i| = 3$.

b. $|z + i| = |z - i|$.

c. $\mathrm{Re}(z) = 1$.

d. $|z/10 + 1 - i| < 5$.

e. $\mathrm{Im}(z) > \mathrm{Re}(z)$.

f. $\mathrm{Re}(z) = |z - 2|$.

3. Suppose u, v, w are three complex numbers not all on the same line. Prove that any point z in $\mathbb{C}$ is uniquely determined by its distances from these three points.

4. Find all solutions to the quadratic equation $z^2 + iz - (2 + 6i) = 0$.

3

Transformations

Transformations will be the focus of this chapter. They are functions first and foremost, often used to push objects from one place in a space to a more convenient place, but transformations do much more. They will be used to *define* different geometries, and we will think of a transformation in terms of the sorts of objects (and functions) that are unaffected by it.

3.1 Basic Transformations of $\mathbb{C}$

We begin with a definition.

Definition 3.1.1 Given two sets A and B, a function $f : A \to B$ is called **one-to-one** (or 1-1) if whenever $a_1 \neq a_2$ in A, then $f(a_1) \neq f(a_2)$ in B. The function f is called **onto** if for any b in B there exists an element a in A such that $f(a) = b$. A **transformation** on a set A is a function $T : A \to A$ that is one-to-one and onto. ◊

Following are two schematics of functions. In the first case, $f : A \to B$ is onto, but not one-to-one. In the second case, $g : A \to B$ is one-to-one, but not onto.

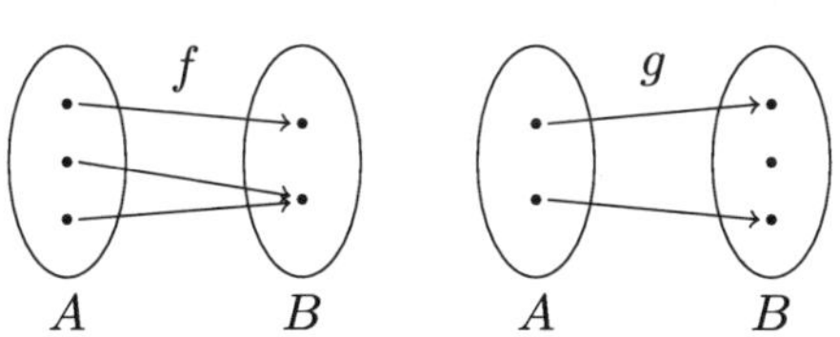

A transformation T of A has an inverse function, T^{-1}, characterized by the property that the compositions $T^{-1} \circ T(a) = a$ and $T \circ T^{-1}(a) = a$ for all a in A. The inverse function T^{-1} is itself a transformation of A and it "undoes" T in this sense: For elements z and w in A, $T^{-1}(w) = z$ if and only if $T(z) = w$.

In this section we develop the following basic transformations of the plane, as well as some of their important features.

Basic Transformations of $\mathbb{C}$.

- General linear transformation: $T(z) = az + b$, where a, b are in $\mathbb{C}$ with $a \neq 0$.
- Special cases of general linear transformations:
  - Translation by b: $T_b(z) = z + b$.
  - Rotation by θ about 0: $R_\theta(z) = e^{i\theta}z$.
  - Rotation by θ about z_0: $R(z) = e^{i\theta}(z - z_0) + z_0$.
  - Dilation by factor $k > 0$: $T(z) = kz$.
- Reflection across a line L: $r_L(z) = e^{i\theta}\overline{z} + b$, where b is in $\mathbb{C}$, and θ is in $\mathbb{R}$.

Example 3.1.2 Translation.

Consider the fixed complex number b, and define the function $T_b : \mathbb{C} \to \mathbb{C}$ by

$$T_b(z) = z + b.$$

The notation helps us remember that z is the variable, and b is a complex constant. We will prove that T_b is a transformation, but this fact can also be understood by *visualizing* the function. Each point in the plane gets moved by the vector b, as suggested in the following diagram.

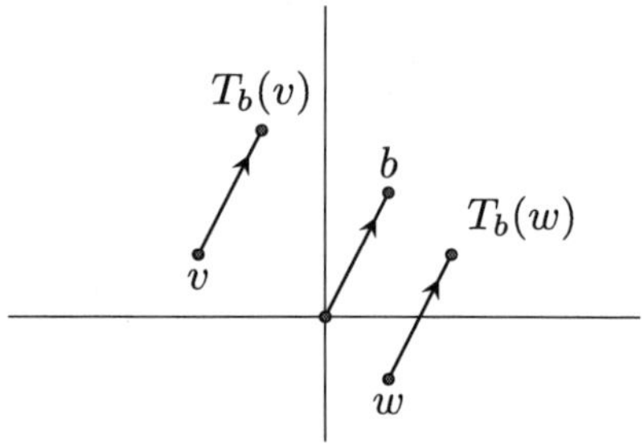

For instance, the origin gets moved to the point b, (i.e., $T_b(0) = b$), and every other point in the plane gets moved the same amount and in the same direction. It follows that two different points, such as v and w in the diagram, cannot get moved to the same image point (thus, the function is one-to-one). Also, any point in the plane is the image of some other point (just follow the vector $-b$ to find this "pre-image" point), so the function is onto as well.

We now offer a formal argument that the translation T_b is a transformation. Recall, b is a fixed complex number.

That T_b is onto:

To show that T_b is onto, let w denote an arbitrary element of $\mathbb{C}$. We must find a complex number z such that $T_b(z) = w$. Let $z = w - b$. Then $T_b(z) = z + b = (w - b) + b = w$. Thus, T is onto.

That T_b is one-to-one:

To show that T_b is 1-1 we must show that if $z_1 \neq z_2$ then $T_b(z_1) \neq T_b(z_2)$. We do so by proving the *contrapositive*. Recall, the contrapositive of a statement of the form "If P is true then Q is true" is "If Q is false then P is false." These statements are logically equivalent, which means we may prove one by proving the other. So, in the present case, the contrapositive of "If $z_1 \neq z_2$ then $T_b(z_1) \neq T_b(z_2)$" is "If $T_b(z_1) = T_b(z_2)$, then $z_1 = z_2$." We now prove this statement.

Suppose z_1 and z_2 are two complex numbers such that $T_b(z_1) = T_b(z_2)$. Then $z_1 + b = z_2 + b$. Subtracting b from both sides we see that $z_1 = z_2$, and this completes the proof.

Example 3.1.3 Rotation about the origin.

Let θ be an angle, and define $R_\theta : \mathbb{C} \to \mathbb{C}$ by $R_\theta(z) = e^{i\theta} z$.

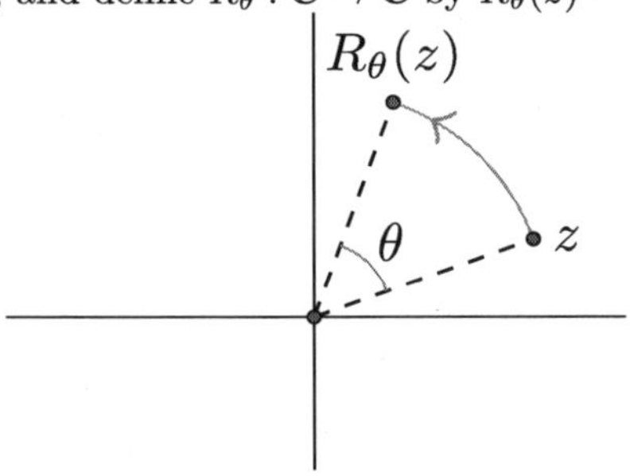

This transformation causes points in the plane to rotate about the origin by the angle θ. (If $\theta > 0$ the rotation is counterclockwise, and if $\theta < 0$ the rotation is clockwise.) To see this is the case, suppose $z = re^{i\beta}$, and notice that

$$R_\theta(z) = e^{i\theta} re^{i\beta} = re^{i(\theta+\beta)}.$$

Example 3.1.4 Rotation about any point.

To achieve a rotation by angle θ about a general point z_0, send points in the plane on a three-leg journey: First, translate the plane so that the center of rotation, z_0, goes to the origin. The translation that does the trick is T_{-z_0}. Then rotate each point by θ about the origin (R_θ). Then translate every point back (T_{z_0}). This sequence of transformations has the desired effect and can be tracked as follows:

$$z \xmapsto{T_{-z_0}} z - z_0 \xmapsto{R_\theta} e^{i\theta}(z - z_0) \xmapsto{T_{z_0}} e^{i\theta}(z - z_0) + z_0.$$

In other words, the desired rotation R is the composition $T_{z_0} \circ R_\theta \circ T_{-z_0}$ and

$$R(z) = e^{i\theta}(z - z_0) + z_0.$$

That the composition of these three transformations is itself a transformation follows from the next theorem.

Theorem 3.1.5 *If T and S are two transformations of the set A, then the composition $S \circ T$ is also a transformation of the set A.*

PROOF. We must prove that $S \circ T : A \to A$ is 1-1 and onto.

That $S \circ T$ is onto:

Suppose c is in A. We must find an element a in A such that $S \circ T(a) = c$.
Since S is onto, there exists some element b in A such that $S(b) = c$.
Since T is onto, there exists some element a in A such that $T(a) = b$.
Then $S \circ T(a) = S(b) = c$, and we have demonstrated that $S \circ T$ is onto.

That $S \circ T$ is 1-1:

Again, we prove the contrapositive. In particular, we show that if $S \circ T(a_1) = S \circ T(a_2)$ then $a_1 = a_2$.
If $S(T(a_1)) = S(T(a_2))$ then $T(a_1) = T(a_2)$ since S is 1-1.
And $T(a_1) = T(a_2)$ implies that $a_1 = a_2$ since T is 1-1.
Therefore, $S \circ T$ is 1-1. □

Example 3.1.6 Dilation.

Suppose $k > 0$ is a real number. The transformation $T(z) = kz$ is called a **dilation**; such a map either stretches or shrinks points in the plane along rays emanating from the origin, depending on the value of k.

Indeed, if $z = x + yi$, then $T(z) = kx + kyi$, and z and $T(z)$ are on the same line through the origin. If $k > 1$ then T stretches points away from the origin. If $0 < k < 1$, then T shrinks points toward the origin. In either case, such a map is called a dilation.

Given complex constants a, b with $a \neq 0$ the map $T(z) = az + b$ is called a **general linear tranformation**. We show in the following example that such a map is indeed a transformation of $\mathbb{C}$.

Example 3.1.7 General Linear Transformations.

Consider the general linear transformation $T(z) = az + b$, where a, b are in $\mathbb{C}$ and $a \neq 0$. We show T is a transformation of $\mathbb{C}$.

That T is onto:

Let w denote an arbitrary element of $\mathbb{C}$. We must find a complex number z such that $T(z) = w$. To find this z, we solve $w = az + b$ for z. So, $z = \frac{1}{a}(w - b)$ should work (since $a \neq 0$, z is a complex number). Indeed, $T(\frac{1}{a}(w - b)) = a \cdot \left[\frac{1}{a}(w - b)\right] + b = w$. Thus, T is onto.

That T is one-to-one:

To show that T is 1-1 we show that if $T(z_1) = T(z_2)$, then $z_1 = z_2$.

If z_1 and z_2 are two complex numbers such that $T(z_1) = T(z_2)$, then $az_1 + b = az_2 + b$. By subtracting b from both sides we see that $az_1 = az_2$, and then dividing both sides by a (which we can do since $a \neq 0$), we see that $z_1 = z_2$. Thus, T is 1-1 as well as onto, and we have proved T is a transformation.

Note that dilations, rotations, and translations are all special types of general linear transformations.

We will often need to figure out how a transformation moves a collection of points such as a triangle or a disk. As such, it is useful to introduce the following notation, which uses the standard convention in set theory that $a \in A$ means the element a is a member of the set A.

Definition 3.1.8 Suppose $T : A \to A$ is a transformation and D is a subset of A. The **image** of D, denoted $T(D)$, consists of all points $T(x)$ such that $x \in D$. In other words,

$$T(D) = \{a \in A \mid a = T(x) \text{ for some } x \in D\}.$$

◊

For instance, if L is a line and T_b is translation by b, then it is reasonable to expect that $T(L)$ is also a line. If one translates a line in the plane, it ought to keep its linear shape. In fact, lines are preserved under any general linear transformation, as are circles.

Theorem 3.1.9 *Suppose T is a general linear transformation.*
a. T maps lines to lines.
b. T maps circles to circles.

PROOF. a. We prove that if L is a line in $\mathbb{C}$ then so is $T(L)$. A line L is described by the line equation

$$\alpha z + \overline{\alpha z} + d = 0$$

for some complex constant α and real number d. Suppose $T(z) = az+b$ is a general linear transformation (so $a \neq 0$). All the points in $T(L)$ have the form $w = az + b$ where z satisfies the preceeding line equation. It follows that $z = \frac{1}{a}(w - b)$ and when we plug this into the line equation we see that

$$\alpha\frac{w-b}{a} + \overline{\alpha}\overline{\frac{w-b}{a}} + d = 0$$

which can be rewritten

$$\frac{\alpha}{a}w + \frac{\overline{\alpha}}{\overline{a}}\overline{w} + d - \frac{\alpha b}{a} - \frac{\overline{\alpha b}}{\overline{a}} = 0.$$

Now, for any complex number β the sum $\beta + \overline{\beta}$ is a real number, so in the above expression, $d - (\frac{\alpha b}{a} + \frac{\overline{\alpha b}}{\overline{a}})$ is a real number. Therefore, all w in $T(L)$ satisfy a line equation. That is, $T(L)$ is a line.

b. The proof of this part is left as an exercise. □

Example 3.1.10 The image of a disk.

The image of the disk $D = \{z \in \mathbb{C} \mid |z - 2i| \leq 1\}$ under the transformation $T : \mathbb{C} \to \mathbb{C}$ given by $T(z) = 2z + (4 - i)$ is the disk $T(D)$ centered at $4 + 3i$ with radius 2 as pictured below.

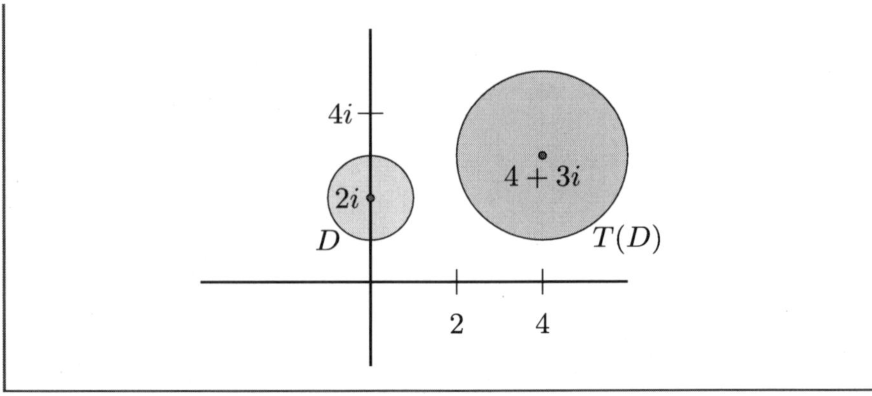

We will be interested in working with transformations that preserve angles between smooth curves. A **planar curve** is a function $\boldsymbol{r} : [a, b] \to \mathbb{C}$ mapping an interval of real numbers into the plane. A curve is **smooth** if its derivative exists and is nonzero at every point. Suppose $\boldsymbol{r}_1$ and $\boldsymbol{r}_2$ are two smooth curves in $\mathbb{C}$ that intersect at a point. The **angle** between the curves measured from $\boldsymbol{r}_1$ to $\boldsymbol{r}_2$, which we denote by $\angle(\boldsymbol{r}_1, \boldsymbol{r}_2)$, is defined to be the angle between the tangent lines at the point of intersection.

Definition 3.1.11 A transformation T of $\mathbb{C}$ **preserves angles at point** z_0 if $\angle(\boldsymbol{r}_1, \boldsymbol{r}_2) = \angle(T(\boldsymbol{r}_1), T(\boldsymbol{r}_2))$ for all smooth curves $\boldsymbol{r}_1$ and $\boldsymbol{r}_2$ that intersect at z_0. A transformation T of $\mathbb{C}$ **preserves angles** if it preserves angles at all points in $\mathbb{C}$. A transformation T of $\mathbb{C}$ **preserves angle magnitudes** if, at any point in $\mathbb{C}$, $|\angle(\boldsymbol{r}_1, \boldsymbol{r}_2)| = |\angle(T(\boldsymbol{r}_1), T(\boldsymbol{r}_2))|$ for all smooth curves $\boldsymbol{r}_1$ and $\boldsymbol{r}_2$ intersecting at the point. ◊

Theorem 3.1.12 *General linear transformations preserve angles.*

PROOF. Suppose $T(z) = az + b$ where $a \neq 0$. Since the angle between curves is defined to be the angle between their tangent lines, it is sufficient to check that the angle between two lines is preserved. Suppose L_1 and L_2 intersect at z_0, and z_i is on L_i for $i = 1, 2$, as in the following diagram.

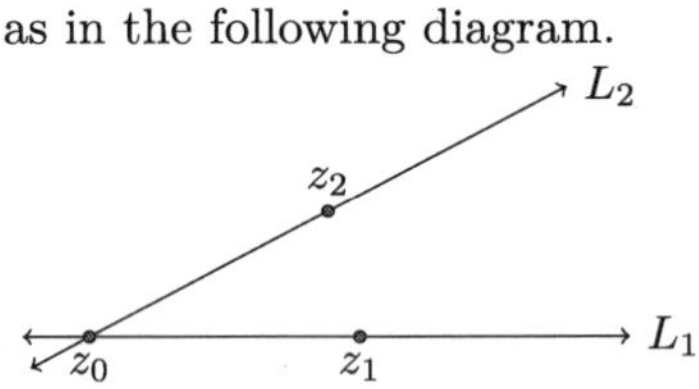

Then,

$$\angle(L_1, L_2) = \arg\left(\frac{z_2 - z_0}{z_1 - z_0}\right).$$

Since general linear transformations preserve lines, $T(L_i)$ is the line through $T(z_0)$ and $T(z_i)$ for $i = 1, 2$ and it follows that

$$\begin{aligned}\angle(T(L_1), T(L_2)) &= \arg\left(\frac{T(z_2) - T(z_0)}{T(z_1) - T(z_0)}\right)\\ &= \arg\left(\frac{az_2 + b - az_0 - b}{az_1 + b - az_0 - b}\right)\end{aligned}$$

$$= \arg\left(\frac{z_2 - z_0}{z_1 - z_0}\right)$$
$$= \angle(L_1, L_2).$$

Thus T preserves angles. □

Definition 3.1.13 A **fixed point** of a transformation $T : A \to A$ is an element a in the set A such that $T(a) = a$. ◊

If $b \neq 0$, the translation T_b of $\mathbb{C}$ has no fixed points. Rotations of $\mathbb{C}$ and dilations of $\mathbb{C}$ have a single fixed point, and the general linear transformation $T(z) = az + b$ has one fixed point as long as $a \neq 1$. To find this fixed point, solve

$$z = az + b$$

for z. For instance, the fixed point of the transformation $T(z) = 2z + (4 - i)$ of Example 3.1.10, p. 33 is found by solving $z = 2z + 4 - i$, for z, which yields $z = -4 + i$. So, while the map $T(z) = 2z + (4 - i)$ moves the disk D in the example to the disk $T(D)$, the point $-4 + i$ happily stays where it is.

Definition 3.1.14 A **Euclidean isometry** is a transformation T of $\mathbb{C}$ with the feature that $|T(z) - T(w)| = |z - w|$ for any points z and w in $\mathbb{C}$. That is, a Euclidean isometry preserves the Euclidean distance between any two points. ◊

Example 3.1.15 Some Euclidean isometries of ℂ.

It is perhaps clear that translations, which move each point in the plane by the same amount in the same direction, ought to be isometries. Rotations are also isometries. In fact, the general linear transformation $T(z) = az+b$ will be a Euclidean isometry so long as $|a| = 1$:

$$\begin{aligned}|T(z) - T(w)| &= |az + b - (aw + b)| \\ &= |a(z - w)| \\ &= |a||z - w|.\end{aligned}$$

So, $|T(z) - T(w)| = |z - w| \iff |a| = 1$. Translations and rotations about a point in $\mathbb{C}$ are general linear transformations of this type, so they are also Euclidean isometries.

Example 3.1.16 Reflection about a line.

Reflection about a line L is the transformation of $\mathbb{C}$ defined as follows: Each point on L gets sent to itself, and if z is not on L, it gets sent to the point z^* such that line L is the perpendicular bisector of segment zz^*.

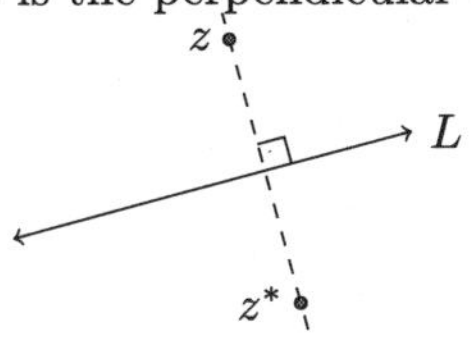

Reflection about L is defined algebraically as follows. If L happens to be the real axis then

$$r_L(z) = \overline{z}.$$

For any other line L we may arrive at a formula for reflection by rotating and/or translating the line to the real axis, then taking the conjugate, and then reversing the rotation and/or translation.

For instance, to describe reflection about the line $y = x + 5$, we may translate vertically by $-5i$, rotate by $-\frac{\pi}{4}$, reflect about the real axis, rotate by $\frac{\pi}{4}$, and finally translate by $5i$ to get the composition

$$\begin{aligned} z &\mapsto z - 5i \\ &\mapsto e^{-\frac{\pi}{4}i}(z - 5i) \\ &\mapsto \overline{e^{-\frac{\pi}{4}i}(z - 5i)} = e^{\frac{\pi}{4}i}(\overline{z} + 5i) \\ &\mapsto e^{\frac{\pi}{4}i} \cdot e^{\frac{\pi}{4}i}(\overline{z} + 5i) = e^{\frac{\pi}{2}i}(\overline{z} + 5i) \\ &\mapsto e^{\frac{\pi}{2}i}(\overline{z} + 5i) + 5i. \end{aligned}$$

Simplifying (and noting that $e^{\frac{\pi}{2}i} = i$), the reflection about the line $L : y = x + 5$ has formula

$$r_L(z) = i\overline{z} - 5 + 5i.$$

In general, reflection across any line L in $\mathbb{C}$ will have the form

$$r_L(z) = e^{i\theta}\overline{z} + b$$

for some angle θ and some complex constant b.

Reflections are more basic transformations than rotations and translations in that the latter are simply careful compositions of reflections.

Theorem 3.1.17 *A translation of $\mathbb{C}$ is the composition of reflections about two parallel lines. A rotation of $\mathbb{C}$ about a point z_0 is the composition of reflections about two lines that intersect at z_0.*

Proof. Given the translation $T_b(z) = z + b$ let L_1 be the line through the origin that is perpendicular to segment $0b$ as pictured in Figure 3.1.18, p. 37(a). Let L_2 be the line parallel to L_1 through the midpoint of segment $0b$. Also let r_i denote reflection about line L_i for $i = 1, 2$.

Now, given any z in $\mathbb{C}$, let L be the line through z that is parallel to vector b (and hence perpendicular to L_1 and L_2). The image of z under the composition $r_2 \circ r_1$ will be on this line. To find the exact location, let z_1 be the intersection of L_1 and L, and z_2 the intersection of L_2 and L, (see the figure). To reflect z about L_1 we need to translate it along L twice by the vector $z_1 - z$. Thus $r_1(z) = z + 2(z_1 - z) = 2z_1 - z$.

Next, to reflect $r_1(z)$ about L_2, we need to translate it along L twice by the vector $z_2 - r_1(z)$. Thus,

$$r_2(r_1(z)) = r_1(z) + 2(z_2 - r_1(z)) = 2z_2 - r_1(z) = 2z_2 - 2z_1 + z.$$

Notice from Figure 3.1.18, p. 37(a) that $z_2 - z_1$ is equal to $b/2$. Thus $r_2(r_1(z)) = z + b$ is translation by b.

Rotation about the point z_0 by angle θ can be achieved by two reflections. The first reflection is about the line L_1 through z_0 parallel to the real axis, and the second reflection is about the line L_2 that intersects L_1 at z_0 at an angle of $\theta/2$, as in Figure 3.1.18, p. 37(b). In the exercises you will prove that this composition of reflections does indeed give the desired rotation. □

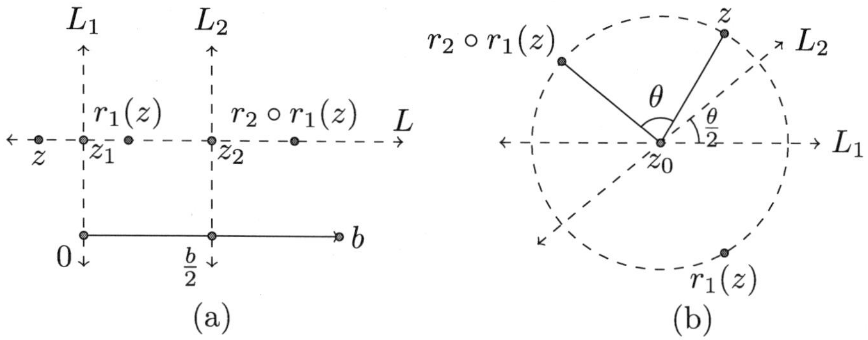

Figure 3.1.18 (a) Translations and (b) rotations are compositions of reflections.

We list some elementary features of reflections in the following theorem. We do not prove them here but encourage you to work through the details. We will focus our efforts in the following section on proving analogous features for inversion transformations, which are reflections about circles.

Theorem 3.1.19 *Reflection across a line is a Euclidean isometry. Moreover, any reflection sends lines to lines, sends circles to circles, and preserves angle magnitudes.*

In fact, one can show that *any* Euclidean isometry can be expressed as the composition of at most three reflections. See, for instance, Stillwell [10] for a proof of this fact.

Theorem 3.1.20 *Any Euclidean isometry is the composition of, at most, three reflections.*

Exercises

1. Is $T(z) = -z$ a translation, dilation, rotation, or none of the above?

2. Show that the general linear transformation $T(z) = az + b$, where a and b are complex constants, is the composition of a rotation, followed by a dilation, followed by a translation.

3. Prove that a general linear transformation maps circles to circles.

4. Suppose T is a rotation by 30° about the point 2, and S is a rotation by 45° about the point 4. What is $T \circ S$? Can you describe this transformation geometrically?

5. Suppose $T(z) = iz + 3$ and $S(z) = -iz + 2$. Find $T \circ S$. What type of transformation is this?

6. Find a formula for a transformation of $\mathbb{C}$ that maps the open disk $D = \{z \mid |z| < 2\}$ to the open disk $D' = \{z \mid |z - i| < 5\}$. Is this transformation unique, or can you think of two different ones that work?

7. Find a formula for reflection about the vertical line $x = k$.

8. Find a formula for reflection about the horizontal line $y = k$.

9. Find a formula for reflection in the plane about the line $y = mx + b$, where $m \neq 0$.

10. Prove that the construction in Figure 3.1.18, p. 37(b) determines the desired rotation.

11. $S(z) = kz$ is a dilation about the origin. Find an equation for a dilation of $\mathbb{C}$ by factor k about an arbitrary point z_0 in $\mathbb{C}$.

3.2 Inversion

Inversion offers a way to reflect points across a circle. This transformation plays a central role in visualizing the transformations of non-Euclidean geometry, and this section is the foundation of much of what follows.

Suppose C is a circle with radius r and center z_0. **Inversion in the circle** C sends a point $z \neq z_0$ to the point z^* defined as follows: First, construct the ray from z_0 through z. Then, let z^* be the unique point on this ray that satisfies the equation

$$|z - z_0| \cdot |z^* - z_0| = r^2.$$

The point z^* is called the **symmetric point** to z with respect to C.

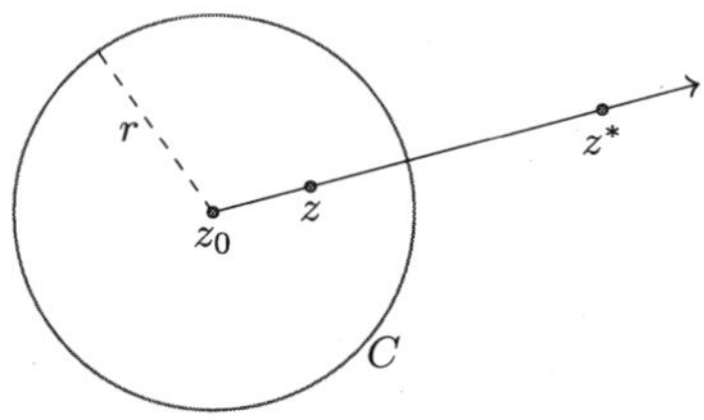

Inversion in a circle centered at z_0 is a transformation on the set $\mathbb{C} - \{z_0\}$ consisting of all complex numbers except z_0. We usually denote inversion in the circle C by by $i_C(z) = z^*$. In the next section we will discuss how to extend this transformation in a way to include the center z_0.

You will work through several features of circle inversions in the exercises, including how to construct symmetry points with compass and ruler (see Figure 3.2.18, p. 48). We note here that i_C fixes all the points on the circle C, and points inside the circle get mapped to points outside the circle and vice versa. The closer z gets to the center of the circle, the further $i_C(z)$ gets from the circle.

Example 3.2.1 Inversion in the unit circle.

The **unit circle** in $\mathbb{C}$, denoted $\mathbb{S}^1$, is the circle with center $z_0 = 0$ and radius $r = 1$. The equation for the point z^* symmetric to a point $z \neq 0$

with repsect to $\mathbb{S}^1$ thus reduces from $|z - z_0| \cdot |z^* - z_0| = r^2$ to

$$|z| \cdot |z^*| = 1.$$

Moreover, z^* is just a scaled version of z since they are on the same ray through the origin. That is, $z^* = kz$ for some positive real number k. Plug this description of z^* into the symmetry point equation to see $|z| \cdot |kz| = 1$, which implies $k = 1/|z|^2$. Thus, $z^* = (1/|z|^2)z$. Moreover, $|z|^2 = z \cdot \overline{z}$, so inversion in the unit circle $\mathbb{S}^1$ may be written as

$$i_{\mathbb{S}^1}(z) = 1/\overline{z}.$$

The following formula for inversion about an arbitrary circle can be obtained by composition of inversion in the unit circle with some general linear transformations. The details are left to Exercise 3.2.1, p. ??.

Inversion in the circle C centered at z_0 with radius r.

Inversion in the circle C centered at z_0 with radius r is given by

$$i_C(z) = \frac{r^2}{\overline{(z - z_0)}} + z_0.$$

Example 3.2.2 Inverting some figures in a circle.

Below we have inverted a circle, the letter 'M,' and a small grid across the circle C centered at z_0. It looks as if the image of the circle is another circle, which we will soon prove is the case. We will also prove that lines not intersecting the center of C get inverted into circles. It follows that the line segments in the 'M' get mapped to arcs of circles.

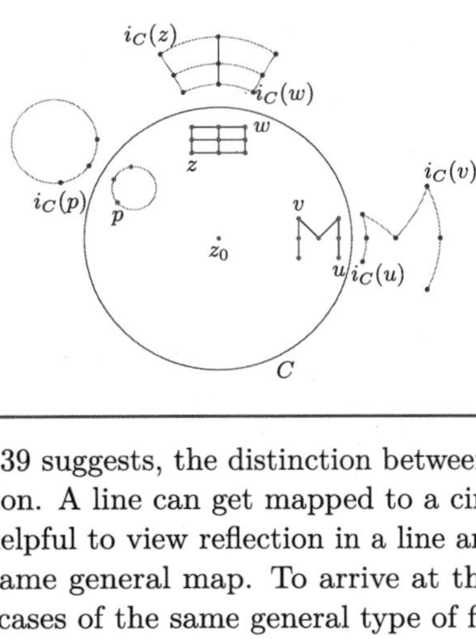

As Example 3.2.2, p. 39 suggests, the distinction between lines and circles gets muddied a bit by inversion. A line can get mapped to a circle and vice versa. In what follows, it will be helpful to view reflection in a line and inversion in a circle as special cases of the same general map. To arrive at this view we first make lines and circles special cases of the same general type of figure.

Definition 3.2.3 A **cline** is a Euclidean circle or line. Any cline can be described algebraically by an equation of the form

$$cz\overline{z} + \alpha z + \overline{\alpha z} + d = 0$$

where $z = x + yi$ is a complex variable, α is a complex constant, and c, d are real numbers. If $c = 0$ the equation describes a line, and if $c \neq 0$ and $|\alpha|^2 > cd$ the equation describes a circle. ◊

The word "cline" (pronounced 'Klein') might seem a bit forced, but it represents the shift in thinking we aim to achieve. We need to start thinking of lines and circles as different manifestations of the same general class of objects. What class? The class of clines.

Letting $\alpha = a + bi$ and $z = x + yi$, the cline equation $cz\overline{z} + \alpha z + \overline{\alpha z} + d = 0$ can be written as

$$c(x^2 + y^2) + [ax - by + (ay + bx)i] + [ax - by - (ay + bx)i] + d = 0$$

which simplifies to

$$c(x^2 + y^2) + 2(ax - by) + d = 0.$$

If $c = 0$ then we have the equation of a line, and if $c \neq 0$ we have the equation of a circle, so long as $a^2 + b^2 > cd$. In this case, the equation can be put into standard form by completing the square. Let's run through this.

If $c \neq 0$,

$$\begin{aligned} c(x^2 + y^2) + 2ax - 2by + d &= 0 \\ x^2 + \frac{2a}{c}x + y^2 - \frac{2b}{c}y &= -\frac{d}{c} \\ x^2 + \frac{2a}{c}x + \left(\frac{a}{c}\right)^2 + y^2 - \frac{2b}{c}y + \left(\frac{b}{c}\right)^2 &= -\frac{d}{c} + \left(\frac{a}{c}\right)^2 + \left(\frac{b}{c}\right)^2 \\ \left(x + \frac{a}{c}\right)^2 + \left(y - \frac{b}{c}\right)^2 &= \frac{a^2 + b^2 - cd}{c^2} \end{aligned}$$

and we have the equation of a circle so long as the right-hand side (the radius term) is positive. In other words, we have the equation of a circle so long as $a^2 + b^2 > cd$. We summarize this information below.

The cline equation.

Given $c, d \in \mathbb{R}$, $\alpha \in \mathbb{C}$, if $c \neq 0$, the cline equation

$$cz\overline{z} + \alpha z + \overline{\alpha z} + d = 0$$

gives a circle with center z_0 and radius r, where

$$z_0 = \left(-\frac{\text{Re}(\alpha)}{c}, \frac{\text{Im}(\alpha)}{c}\right) \quad \text{and} \quad r = \sqrt{\frac{|\alpha|^2 - cd}{c^2}},$$

so long as $|\alpha|^2 > cd$. If $c = 0$, the cline equation gives a line.

From now on, if you read the phrase "inversion in a cline," know that this means inversion in a circle or reflection about a line, and if someone hands you a cline C, you might say, "Thanks! By the way, is this a line or a circle?"

We note here the construction of a cline through three points in $\mathbb{C}$. This construction is used often in later chapters to generate figures in non-Euclidean geometry.

Theorem 3.2.4 *There exists a unique cline through any three distinct points in* $\mathbb{C}$.

PROOF. Suppose u, v, and w are distinct complex numbers. If v is on the line through u and w then this line is the unique cline through the three points. Otherwise, the three points do not lie on a single line, and we may build a circle through these three points as demonstrated in Figure 3.2.5, p. 41. Construct the perpendicular bisector to segment uv, and the perpendicular bisector to segment vw. These bisectors will intersect because the three points are not collinear. If we call the point of intersection z_0, then the circle centered at z_0 through w is the unique cline through the three points. □

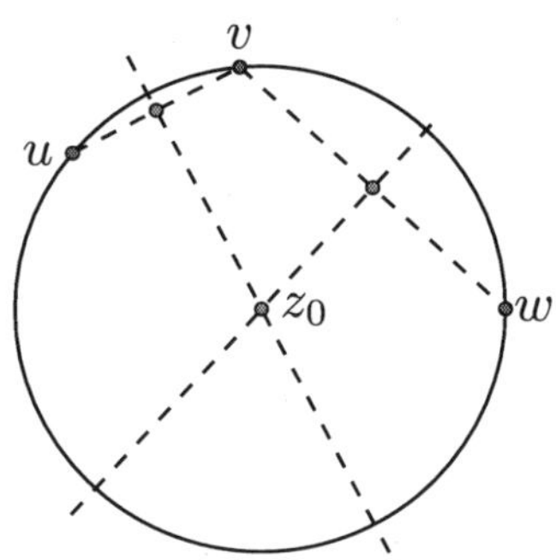

Figure 3.2.5 Constructing the unique circle through three points not on a single line.

Theorem 3.2.6 *Inversion in a circle maps clines to clines. In particular, if a cline goes through the center of the circle of inversion, its image will be a line; otherwise the image of a cline will be a circle.*

PROOF. We prove the result in the case of inversion in the unit circle. The general proof will then follow, since any inversion is the composition of this particular inversion together with translations and dilations, which also preserve clines by Theorem 3.1.9, p. 33.

Suppose the cline C is described by the cline equation

$$cz\overline{z} + \alpha z + \overline{\alpha z} + d = 0,$$

where $c, d \in \mathbb{R}$, $\alpha \in \mathbb{C}$.

We want to show that the image of this cline under inversion in the unit circle, $i_{\mathbb{S}^1}(C)$, is also a cline. Well, $i_{\mathbb{S}^1}(C)$ consists of all points $w = 1/\overline{z}$, where z satisfies the cline equation for C. We show that all such w live on a cline.

If $z \neq 0$ then we may multiply each side of the cline equation by $1/(z \cdot \overline{z})$ to obtain

$$c + \alpha\frac{1}{\overline{z}} + \overline{\alpha}\frac{1}{z} + d\frac{1}{z}\frac{1}{\overline{z}} = 0.$$

But since $w = 1/\overline{z}$ and $\overline{w} = 1/z$, this equation reduces to

$$c + \alpha \cdot w + \overline{\alpha} \cdot \overline{w} + dw\overline{w} = 0,$$

or

$$dw\overline{w} + \alpha \cdot w + \overline{\alpha} \cdot \overline{w} + c = 0.$$

Thus, the image points w form a cline equation. If $d = 0$ then the original cline C passed through the origin, and the image cline is a line. If $d \neq 0$ then C did not pass through the origin, and the image cline is a circle. (In fact, we must also check that $|\alpha|^2 > dc$. This is the case because the original cline equation ensures $|\alpha|^2 > cd$.) □

We will call two clines **orthogonal** if they intersect at right angles. For instance, a line is orthogonal to a circle if and only if it goes through the center of the circle. One very important feature of inversion in C is that clines orthogonal to C get inverted to themselves. To prove this fact, we first prove the following result, which can be found in Euclid's *Elements* (Book III, Proposition 36).

Lemma 3.2.7 *Suppose C is the circle with radius r centered at o, and p is a point outside C. Let $s = |p - o|$. If a line through p intersects C at points m and n, then*

$$|p - m| \cdot |p - n| = s^2 - r^2.$$

PROOF. Suppose the line through p does not pass through the center of C, as in the diagram below. Let q be the midpoint of segment mn, and let $d = |q - o|$ as in the diagram. Note also that the line through q and o is the perpendicular bisector of segment mn. In particular, $|m - q| = |q - n|$.

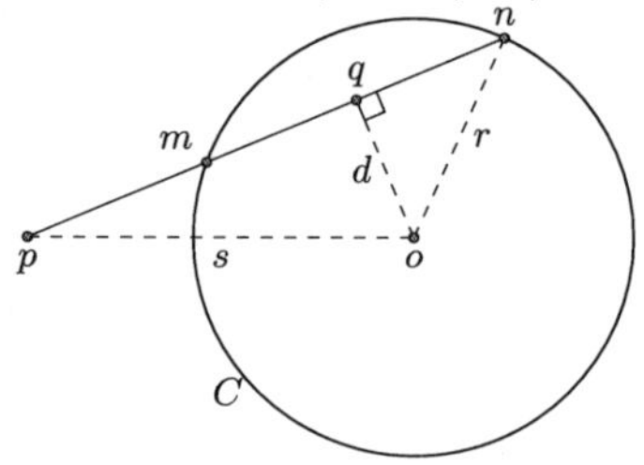

The Pythagorean theorem applied to Δpqo gives

$$|p - q|^2 + d^2 = s^2, \tag{1}$$

and the Pythagorean theorem applied to Δnqo gives

$$|q - n|^2 + d^2 = r^2. \tag{2}$$

By subtracting equation (2) from (1), we have

$$|p - q|^2 - |q - n|^2 = s^2 - r^2,$$

which factors as

$$(|p - q| - |q - n|)(|p - q| + |q - n|) = s^2 - r^2.$$

Since $|p - q| - |q - n| = |p - m|$ and $|p - q| + |q - n| = |p - n|$, the result follows.

The case that the line through p goes through the center of C is left as an exercise. □

We note that the quantity $s^2 - r^2$ in the previous lemma is often called the power of the point p with respect to the circle C. That is, if circle C has radius r

and a point p is a distance s from the center of C then the quantity $s^2 - r^2$ is called the **power of the point** p.

Theorem 3.2.8 *Suppose C is a circle in $\mathbb{C}$ centered at z_0, and $z \neq z_0$ is not on C. A cline through z is orthogonal to C if and only if it goes through z^*, the point symmetric to z with respect to C.*

PROOF. Assume C is the circle of radius r centered at z_0, and D is a cline through a point $z \neq z_0$ not on C. Let z^* denote the point symmetric to z with respect to C.

First, suppose D is a line through z. A line through z passes through z^* if and only if it passes through the center of C, which is true if and only if the line is orthogonal to C. Thus, the line D through z contains z^* if and only if it is orthogonal to C, and the theorem is proved in this case.

Now assume D is a circle through z. Let o and k denote the center and radius of D, respectively. Set $s = |z_o - o|$, and let t denote a point of intersection of C and D as pictured below.

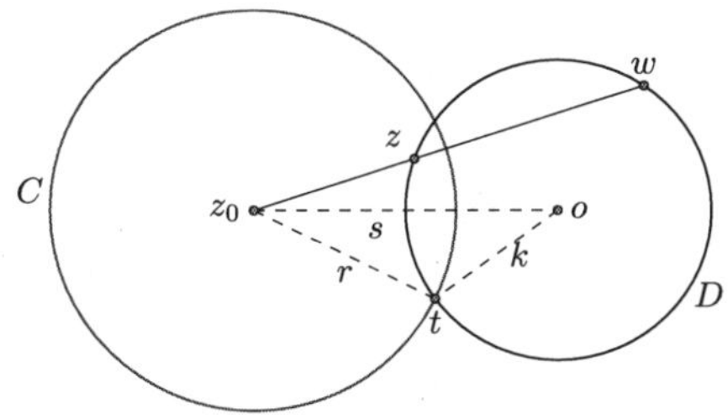

We must argue that C and D are orthogonal if and only if z^* is on D. Now, C and D are orthogonal if and only if $\angle otz_0$ is right, which is the case if and only if $r^2 = s^2 - k^2$ by the Pythagorean theorem. Applying Lemma 3.2.7, p. 42 to the point z_0 (which is outside D) and the line through z_0 and z, we see that

$$|z_0 - z| \cdot |z_0 - w| = s^2 - k^2, \tag{1}$$

where w is the second point of intersection of the line with circle D.

Note also that as symmetric points, z and z^* satisfy the equation

$$|z_0 - z| \cdot |z_0 - z^*| = r^2. \tag{2}$$

Thus, if we assume z^* is on D, then it must be equal to the point w, in which case equations (1) and (2) above tell us $s^2 - k^2 = r^2$. It follows that D is orthogonal to C. Conversely, if D is orthogonal to C, then $s^2 - k^2 = r^2$, so $|z_0 - w| = |z_0 - z^*|$. Since z^* and w are both on the ray $\overrightarrow{z_0 z}$ it must be that $z^* = w$. In other words, z^* is on D. □

Corollary 3.2.9 *Inversion in C takes clines orthogonal to C to themselves.*

Theorem 3.2.10 *Inversion in a cline preserves angle magnitudes.*

PROOF. The result was stated for lines in Theorem 3.1.19, p. 37. Here we assume C is a circle of inversion. Consider two curves $\boldsymbol{r_1}$ and $\boldsymbol{r_2}$ that intersect at a point z that is not on C or at the center of C. Recall, $\angle(\boldsymbol{r_1}, \boldsymbol{r_2}) = \angle(L_1, L_2)$ where L_i is the line tangent to curve $\boldsymbol{r_i}$ at z, for $i = 1, 2$. We may describe this angle with two circles C_1 and C_2 tangent to the tangent lines L_1 and L_2, respectively, with the additional feature that the circles meet the circle of inversion C at right angles, as in Figure 3.2.11, p. 44. Indeed, C_1 is the circle through z and z^* whose center is at the intersection of lines m_1 and k, where m_1 is the line through z that is perpendicular to L_1, and k is the perpendicular bisector of segment zz^*. Circle C_2 also goes through z and z^*, and its center is on the intersection of k and the line m_2 through z that is perpendicular to L_2.

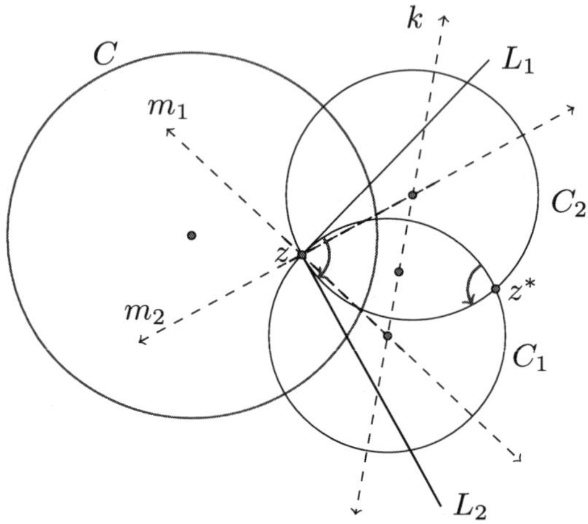

Figure 3.2.11 Inversion in a circle preserves angle magnitudes.

The advantage to describing $\angle(L_1, L_2)$ with these circles is that the image of the angle, $\angle(i_C(L_1), i_C(L_2))$, is also described by these two circles, at their other intersection point z^*. Notice that these angles will have opposite signs. For instance, in Figure 3.2.11, p. 44, our initial angle is negative, described by sweeping arc C_1 clockwise onto C_2, but in the image, we sweep $i_C(C_1)$ counterclockwise onto $i_C(C_2)$. We leave it as an exercise for the reader to check that the angle of intersection of C_1 and C_2 at z^* is the same magnitude as the angle between C_1 and C_2 at z.

Now we show that inversion preserves angle magnitudes for angles that occur on the circle C (i.e., z is on C). Let C' be a concentric circle to C. Then $i_C(z) = S \circ i_{C'}$ where S is a dilation of $\mathbb{C}$ whose fixed point is the common center of circles C and C' (see Exercise 3.2.12, p. ??). Since our angle is not on circle C', $i_{C'}$ preserves the magnitude of the angle by reason of the preceding argument. The dilation S preserves angles according to Theorem 3.1.12, p. 34. Thus i_C preserves angle magnitudes as well. We leave the case of the angle occurring at the origin to the next section. Bearing that exception in mind, this completes the proof. □

Another important feature of inversion in a cline is that it preserves symmetry points.

Theorem 3.2.12 Inversion preserves symmetry points. *Let i_C denote inversion in a cline C. If p and q are symmetric with respect to a cline D, then $i_C(p)$ and $i_C(q)$ are symmetric with respect to the cline $i_C(D)$.*

PROOF. Assume C is the cline of inversion, and assume p and q are symmetric with respect to a cline D as in Figure 3.2.13, p. 45 (where C and D are represented as circles).

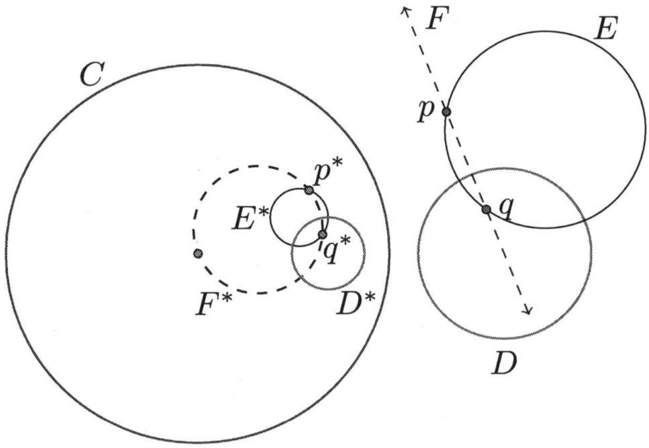

Figure 3.2.13 Inversion preserves symmetry points: If p and q are symmetric with respect to D and we invert about cline C then the image points are symmetric with respect to the image of D.

We may construct two clines E and F that go through p and q. In the figure, cline E is a circle and cline F is a line. These clines intersect D at right angles (Theorem 3.2.8, p. 43). Since inversion preserves clines and angle magnitudes, we know that $E^* = i_C(E)$ and $F^* = i_C(F)$ are clines intersecting the cline $D^* = i_C(D)$ at right angles. Both E^* and F^* contain $p^* = i_C(p)$, so they both contain the point symmetric to p^* with respect to D^* (Theorem 3.2.8, p. 43), but the only other point common to both E^* and F^* is $q^* = i_C(q)$. Thus, p^* and q^* are symmetric with respect to D^*. □

We close the section with two applications of inversion.

Theorem 3.2.14 Apollonian Circles Theorem. *Let p, q be distinct points in $\mathbb{C}$, and $k > 0$ a positive real number. Let D consist of all points z in $\mathbb{C}$ such that $|z - p| = k|z - q|$. Then D is a cline.*

PROOF. If $k = 1$, the set D is a Euclidean line, according to Theorem 2.4.2, p. 23, so we assume $k \neq 1$. Let C be the circle centered at p with radius 1. Suppose z is an arbitrary point in the set D. Inverting about C, let $z^* = i_C(z)$ and $q^* = i_C(q)$ as in the following diagram.

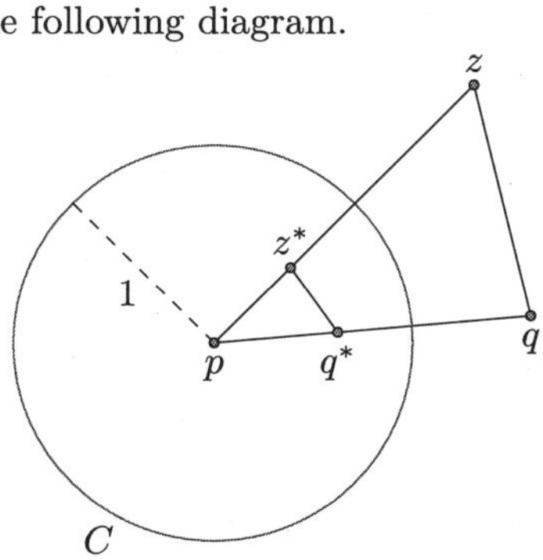

Observe first that Δpz^*q^* and Δpqz are similar.

Indeed, $|p-z|\cdot|p-z^*| = 1 = |p-q|\cdot|p-q^*|$ by the definition of the inversion transformation, so we have equal side-length ratios

$$\frac{|p-z^*|}{|p-q|} = \frac{|p-q^*|}{|p-z|},$$

and the included angles are equal, $\angle q^*pz^* = \angle qpz$.

It follows that

$$\frac{|z-q|}{|p-q|} = \frac{|z^*-q^*|}{|z^*-p|},$$

from which we derive

$$\begin{aligned}|z^*-q^*| &= |z^*-p|\cdot\frac{|z-q|}{|p-q|}\\ &= [|z^*-p|\cdot|z-p|]\cdot\frac{|z-q|}{|z-p|}\cdot\frac{1}{|p-q|}\\ &= 1\cdot\frac{1}{k}\cdot\frac{1}{|p-q|}.\end{aligned}$$

Thus, the set D of all points z satisfying $|z-p| = k|z-q|$ has image $i_C(D)$ under this inversion consisting of all points z^* on a circle centered at q^* with radius $(k|p-q|)^{-1}$. Since inversion preserves clines and p is not on $i_C(D)$, it follows that D itself is a circle. □

As we let k run through all positive real numbers, we obtain a family of clines, called the **circles of Apollonius of the points p and q**. We note that p and q are symmetric with respect to each cline in this family (see Exercise 3.3.2, p. ??).

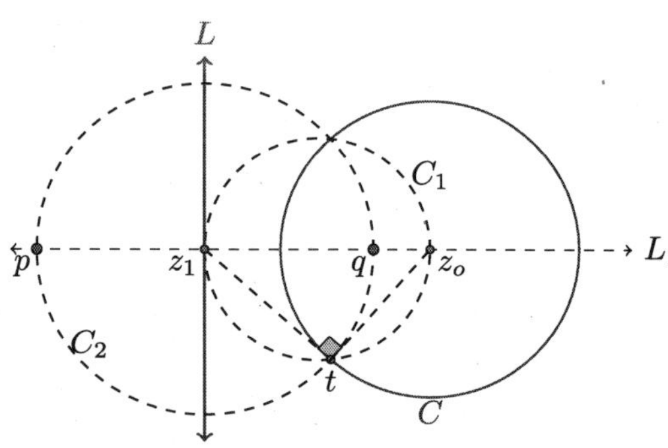

Figure 3.2.15 Finding two points symmetric with respect to a line and circle.

Theorem 3.2.16 *Suppose we have two clines that do not intersect, and at least one of them is a circle. Then there exist two points, p and q, that are symmetric with respect to both clines.*

PROOF. First, assume one cline is a line L, and the other is a circle C centered at the point z_0 as pictured in Figure 3.2.15, p. 46. Let L_1 be the line through z_0 that is perpendicular to L, and let z_1 be the point of intersection of L and L_1. Next, construct the circle C_1 having the diameter z_0z_1. Circle C_1 intersects circle C at some point, which we call t. Notice that $\angle z_0tz_1$ is right, and so the circle C_2 centered at z_1 through t is orthogonal to C. Furthermore, the center of C_2, z_1, lies on line L, so C_2 is orthogonal to L. Let p and q be the two points at which C_2 intersects L_1. By construction, and by using Theorem 3.2.8, p. 43, p and q are symmetric to both C and L.

Now, suppose C_1 and C_2 are circles that do not intersect. We may first perform an inversion in a circle C that maps C_1 to a line C_1^*, and C_2 to another circle, C_2^*, as suggested in Figure 3.2.17, p. 47 (any circle C centered on a point of C_1 works). Then by reason of the preceeding argument, there exist two points p and q that are symmetric with respect to C_1^* and C_2^*. Since inversion preserves symmetry points, $i_C(p)$ and $i_C(q)$ are symmetric with respect to both $i_C(C_1^*)$ and $i_C(C_2^*)$. But $i_C(C_1^*) = C_1$ and $i_C(C_2^*) = C_2$ so we're found two points symmetric to both C_1 and C_2. (In fact, we have one exception. If C_1 and C_2 are concentric circles, this strategy will produce points $i_C(p)$ and $i_C(q)$, one of which is the center of C, and we have not yet extended the notion of inversion to include the center. We do so in the next section in such a way that the theorem applies to this exceptional case as well.)

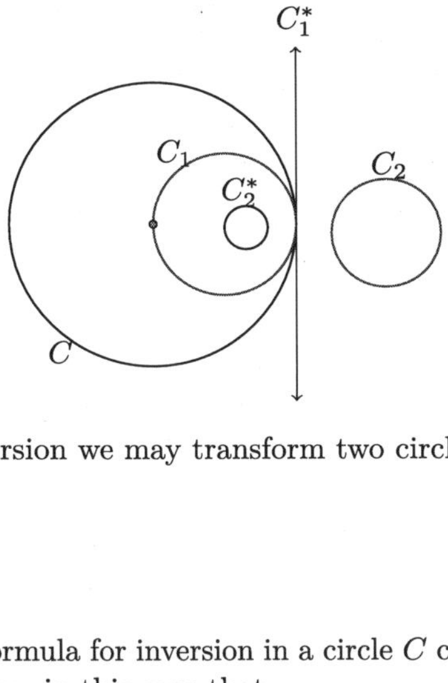

Figure 3.2.17 By inversion we may transform two circles to a circle and a line.

□

Exercises

1. Prove the general formula for inversion in a circle C centered at z_0 with radius r. In particular, show in this case that

$$i_C(z) = \frac{r^2}{\overline{(z - z_0)}} + z_0.$$

2. *Constructing the symmetric point to z when z is inside the circle of inversion.* Prove that for a point z inside the circle C with center z_0 (Figure 3.2.18, p. 48(a)), the following construction finds the symmetry point of z. (1) Draw the ray from z_0 through z. (2) Construct the perpendicular to this ray at z. Let t be a point of intersection of this perpendicular and C. (3) Construct the radius z_0t. (4) Construct the perpendicular to this radius at t. The symmetric point z^* is the point of intersection of this perpendicular and ray $\overrightarrow{z_o z}$.

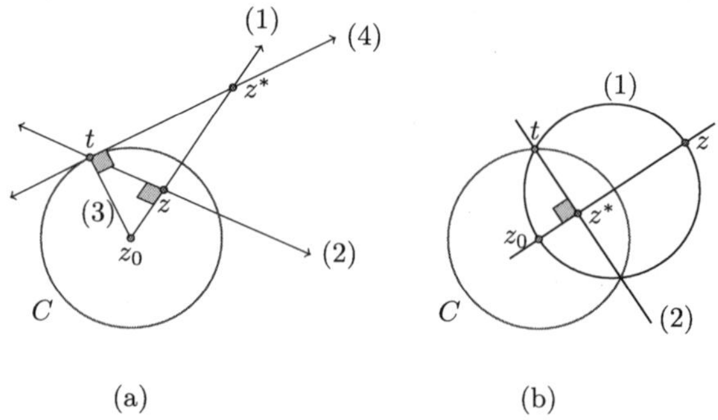

Figure 3.2.18 Constructing the symmetric point (a) if z is inside the circle of inversion; (b) if z is outside the circle of inversion.

3. *Constructing the symmetric point to z when z is outside the circle of inversion.* Prove that for a point z outside the circle C with center z_0 (Figure 3.2.18, p. 48(b)), the following construction finds the symmetry point of z. (1) Construct the circle having diameter z_0z. Let t be a point of intersection of the two circles. (2) Construct the perpendicular to z_0z through t. Let z^* be the intersection of this perpendicular with segment z_0z.

4. Suppose T_1 is inversion in the circle $|z| = r_1$, and T_2 is inversion in the circle $|z| = r_2$, where $r_1, r_2 > 0$. Prove that $T_2 \circ T_1$ is a dilation. Conversely, show any dilation is the composition of two inversions.

5. Determine the image of the line $y = mx + b$ (when $b \neq 0$) under inversion in the unit circle. In particular, show that the image is a circle with center $(-m/2b, 1/2b)$ and radius $\sqrt{(m^2+1)/4b^2}$.

6. Determine the image of the line L given by $y = 3x + 4$ under inversion in the unit circle. Give a careful plot of the unit circle, the line L, and the image of L under the inversion.

7. Prove that inversion in the unit circle maps the circle $(x-a)^2 + (y-b)^2 = r^2$ to the circle

$$\left(x - \frac{a}{d}\right)^2 + \left(y - \frac{b}{d}\right)^2 = \left(\frac{r}{d}\right)^2$$

where $d = a^2 + b^2 - r^2$, provided that $d \neq 0$.

8. Determine in standard form the image of the circle C given by $(x-1)^2 + y^2 = 4$ under inversion in the unit circle. Give a careful plot of the unit circle, the circle C, and the image of C under the inversion.

9. True or False? If a circle C gets mapped to another circle under inversion in the unit circle, then the center of C gets mapped to the center of the image circle, $i_{\mathbb{S}^1}(C)$. If the statement is true, prove it; if it is false, provide a counterexample.

10. Suppose C and D are orthogonal circles. Corollary 3.2.9, p. 43 tells us that inversion in C maps D to itself. Prove that this inversion also takes the interior of D to itself.

11. Finish the proof of Theorem 3.2.10, p. 43 by showing that the angle of intersection at z^* equals the angle of intersection at z in Figure 3.2.11, p. 44.

12. Suppose C is the circle $|z - z_0| = r$ and C' is the circle $|z - z_0| = r'$. Find the stretch factor k in the dilation $S(z) = k(z - z_0) + z_0$ so that $i_C = S \circ i_{C'}$.

13. Complete the proof of Lemma 3.2.7, p. 42 by proving the case in which the line through p passes through the center of C.

3.3 The Extended Plane

Consider again inversion about the circle C given by $|z - z_0| = r$, and observe that points close to z_0 get mapped to points in the plane far away from from z_0. In fact, a sequence of points in $\mathbb{C}$ whose limit is z_0 will be inverted to a sequence of points whose magnitudes go to ∞. Conversely, any sequence of points in $\mathbb{C}$ having magnitudes marching off to ∞ will be inverted to a sequence of points whose limit is z_0.

With this in mind, we define a new point called **the point at infinity**, denoted ∞. Adjoin this new point to the plane to get the **extended plane**, denoted as $\mathbb{C}^+$. Then, one may extend inversion in the circle C to include the points z_0 and ∞. In particular, inversion of $\mathbb{C}^+$ in the circle C centered at z_0 with radius r, $i_C : \mathbb{C}^+ \to \mathbb{C}^+$, is given by

$$i_C(z) = \begin{cases} \frac{r^2}{\overline{(z-z_0)}} + z_0 & \text{if } z \neq z_0, \infty; \\ \infty & \text{if } z = z_0; \\ z_0 & \text{if } z = \infty \end{cases}.$$

Viewing inversion as a transformation of the extended plane, we define z_0 and ∞ to be symmetric points with respect to the circle of inversion.

The space $\mathbb{C}^+$ will be the canvas on which we do all of our geometry, and it is important to begin to think of ∞ as "one of the gang," just another point to consider. All of our translations, dilations, and rotations can be redefined to include the point ∞.

So where is ∞ in $\mathbb{C}^+$? You approach ∞ as you proceed in either direction along any line in the complex plane. More generally, if $\{z_n\}$ is a sequence of complex numbers such that $|z_n| \to \infty$ as $n \to \infty$, then we say $\lim_{n\to\infty} z_n = \infty$. By convention, we assume ∞ is on every line in the extended plane, and reflection across any line fixes ∞.

Theorem 3.3.1 *Any general linear transformation extended to the domain $\mathbb{C}^+$ fixes ∞.*

PROOF. If $T(z) = az + b$ where a and b are complex constants with $a \neq 0$, then by limit methods from calculus, as $|z_n| \to \infty$, $|az_n + b| \to \infty$ as well. Thus, $T(\infty) = \infty$. □

So, with new domain $\mathbb{C}^+$, we modify our fixed point count for the basic transformations:

- The translation T_b of $\mathbb{C}^+$ fixes one point (∞).

- The rotation about the origin R_θ of $\mathbb{C}^+$ fixes 2 points (0 and ∞).
- The dilation $T(z) = kz$ of $\mathbb{C}^+$ fixes 2 points, (0 and ∞).
- The reflection $r_L(z)$ of $\mathbb{C}^+$ about line L fixes all points on L (which now includes ∞).

Example 3.3.2 Some transformations not fixing ∞.

The following function is a transformation of $\mathbb{C}^+$

$$T(z) = \frac{i+1}{z+2i},$$

a fact we prove in the next section. For now, we ask where T sends ∞, and which point gets sent to ∞.

We tackle the second question first. The input that gets sent to ∞ is the complex number that makes the denominator 0. Thus, $T(-2i) = \infty$.

To answer the first question, take your favorite sequence that marches off to ∞, for example, $1, 2, 3, \ldots$. The image of this sequence, $T(1), T(2), T(3), \ldots$ consists of complex fractions in which the numerator is constant, but the denominator grows unbounded in magnitude along the horizontal line $\text{Im}(z) = 2$. Thus, the quotient tends to 0, and $T(\infty) = 0$.

As a second example, you can check that if

$$T(z) = \frac{iz + (3i+1)}{2iz+1},$$

then $T(i/2) = \infty$ and $T(\infty) = 1/2$.

We emphasize that the following key results of the previous section extend to $\mathbb{C}^+$ as well:

- There exists a unique cline through any three distinct points in $\mathbb{C}^+$. (If one of the given points in Theorem 3.2.4, p. 41 is ∞, the unique cline is the line through the other two points.)
- Theorem 3.2.8, p. 43 applies to all points z not on C, including $z = z_0$ or ∞.
- Inversion about a cline preserves angle magnitudes at all points in $\mathbb{C}^+$ (we discuss this below).
- Inversion preserves symmetry points for all points in $\mathbb{C}^+$ (Theorem 3.2.12, p. 44 holds if p or q is ∞).
- Theorem 3.2.16, p. 46 now holds for all clines that do not intersect, including concentric circles. If the circles are concentric, the points symmetric to both of them are ∞ and the common center.

Stereographic Projection. We close this section with a look at stereographic projection. By identifying the extended plane with a sphere, this map offers a very useful way for us to think about the point ∞.

Definition 3.3.3 The **unit 2-sphere,** denoted $\mathbb{S}^2$, consists of all the points in 3-space that are one unit from the origin. That is,

$$\mathbb{S}^2 = \{(a, b, c) \in \mathbb{R}^3 \mid a^2 + b^2 + c^2 = 1\}.$$

◊

We will usually refer to the unit 2-sphere as simply "the sphere." Stereographic projection of the sphere onto the extended plane is defined as follows. Let $N = (0, 0, 1)$ denote the north pole on the sphere. For any point $P \neq N$ on the sphere, $\phi(P)$ is the point on the ray $\overrightarrow{NP}$ that lives in the xy-plane. See Figure 3.3.4, p. 51 for the image of a typical point P of the sphere.

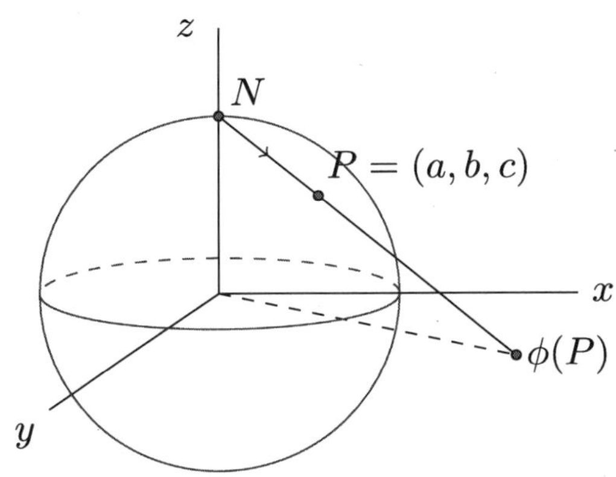

Figure 3.3.4 Stereographic projection.

The stereographic projection map ϕ can be described algebraically. The line through $N = (0, 0, 1)$ and $P = (a, b, c)$ has directional vector $\overrightarrow{NP} = \langle a, b, c - 1\rangle$, so the line equation can be expressed as

$$\vec{r}(t) = \langle 0, 0, 1\rangle + t\langle a, b, c - 1\rangle.$$

This line intersects the xy-plane when its z coordinate is zero. This occurs when $t = \frac{1}{1-c}$, which corresponds to the point $(\frac{a}{1-c}, \frac{b}{1-c}, 0)$.

Thus, for a point (a, b, c) on the sphere with $c \neq 1$, stereographic projection $\phi : \mathbb{S}^2 \to \mathbb{C}^+$ is given by

$$\phi((a, b, c)) = \frac{a}{1 - c} + \frac{b}{1 - c}i.$$

Where does ϕ send the north pole? To ∞, of course. A sequence of points on $\mathbb{S}^2$ that approaches N will have image points in $\mathbb{C}$ with magnitudes that approach ∞.

Angles at ∞. If we think of ∞ as just another point in $\mathbb{C}^+$, it makes sense to ask about angles at this point. For instance, any two lines intersect at ∞, and it makes sense to ask about the angle of intersection at ∞. We can be guided in answering this question by stereographic projection, thanks to the following theorem.

Theorem 3.3.5 *Stereographic projection preserves angles. That is, if two curves on the surface of the sphere intersect at angle θ, then their image curves in $\mathbb{C}^+$ also intersect at angle θ.*

Thus, if two curves in $\mathbb{C}^+$ intersect at ∞ we may define the angle at which they intersect to equal the angle at which their pre-image curves under stereographic projection intersect. The angle at which two parallel lines intersect at ∞ is 0. Furthermore, if two lines intersect at a finite point p as well as at ∞, the angle at which they intersect at ∞ equals the negative of the angle at which they intersect at p. As a consequence, we may say that inversion about a circle preserves angle magnitudes at all points in $\mathbb{C}^+$.

Exercises

1. In each case find $T(\infty)$ and the input z_0 such that $T(z_0) = \infty$.

a. $T(z) = (3 - z)/(2z + i)$.

b. $T(z) = (z + 1)/e^{i\pi/4}$.

c. $T(z) = (az + b)/(cz + d)$.

2. Suppose D is a circle of Apollonius of p and q. Prove that p and q are symmetric with respect to D.

3. Determine the inverse stereographic projection function $\phi^{-1} : \mathbb{C}^+ \to \mathbb{S}^2$. In particular, show that for $z = x + yi \neq \infty$,

$$\phi^{-1}(x, y) = \left(\frac{2x}{x^2 + y^2 + 1}, \frac{2y}{x^2 + y^2 + 1}, \frac{x^2 + y^2 - 1}{x^2 + y^2 + 1}\right).$$

3.4 Möbius Transformations

Consider the function defined on $\mathbb{C}^+$ by $T(z) = (az + b)/(cz + d)$ where a, b, c and d are complex constants. Such a function is called a **Möbius transformation** if $ad - bc \neq 0$. Transformations of this form are also called fractional linear transformations. The complex number $ad - bc$ is called the **determinant** of $T(z) = (az + b)/(cz + d)$, and is denoted as $\text{Det}(T)$.

Theorem 3.4.1 *The function*

$$T(z) = \frac{az + b}{cz + d}$$

is a transformation of $\mathbb{C}^+$ if and only if $ad - bc \neq 0$.

PROOF. First, suppose $T(z) = (az + b)/(cz + d)$ and $ad - bc \neq 0$. We must show that T is a transformation. To show T is one-to-one, assume $T(z_1) = T(z_2)$. Then

$$\frac{az_1 + b}{cz_1 + d} = \frac{az_2 + b}{cz_2 + d}.$$

Cross multiply this expression and simplify to obtain

$$(ad - bc)z_1 = (ad - bc)z_2.$$

Since $ad - bc \neq 0$ we may divide this term out of the expression to see $z_1 = z_2$, so T is 1-1 and it remains to show that T is onto.

Suppose w in $\mathbb{C}^+$ is given. We must find $z \in \mathbb{C}^+$ such that $T(z) = w$. If $w = \infty$, then $z = -d/c$ (which is ∞ if $c = 0$) does the trick, so assume $w \neq \infty$. To find z such that $T(z) = w$ we solve the equation

$$\frac{az + b}{cz + d} = w$$

for z, which is possible so long as a and c are not both 0 (causing the z terms to vanish). Since $ad - bc \neq 0$, we can be assured that this is the case, and solving for z we obtain

$$z = \frac{-dw + b}{cw - a}.$$

Thus T is onto, and T is a transformation.

To prove the converse we show the contrapositive. We suppose $ad - bc = 0$ and show $T(z) = (az + b)/(cz + d)$ is not a transformation by tackling two cases.

Case 1: $ad = 0$. In this case, $bc = 0$ as well, so a or d is zero, and b or c is zero. In all four scenarios, one can check immediately that T is not a transformation of $\mathbb{C}^+$. For instance, if $a = c = 0$ then $T(z) = b/d$ is neither 1-1 nor onto $\mathbb{C}^+$.

Case 2: $ad \neq 0$. In this case, all four constants are non-zero, and $a/c = b/d$. Since $T(0) = b/d$ and $T(\infty) = a/c$, T is not 1-1, and hence not a transformation of $\mathbb{C}^+$. □

Note that in the preceeding proof we found the inverse transformation of a Möbius transformation. This inverse transformation is itself a Möbius transformation since its determinant is not 0. In fact, its determinant equals the determinant of the original Möbius transformation. We summarize this fact as follows.

Theorem 3.4.2 *The Möbius transformation*

$$T(z) = \frac{az + b}{cz + d}$$

has the inverse transformation

$$T^{-1}(z) = \frac{-dz + b}{cz - a}.$$

In particular, the inverse of a Möbius transformation is itself a Möbius transformation.

If we compose two Möbius transformations, the result is another Möbius transformation. Proof of this fact is left as an exercise.

Theorem 3.4.3 *The composition of two Möbius transformations is again a Möbius transformation.*

Just as translations and rotations of the plane can be constructed from reflections across lines, the general Möbius transformation can be constructed from inversions about clines.

Theorem 3.4.4 *A transformation of $\mathbb{C}^+$ is a Möbius transformation if and only if it is the composition of an even number of inversions.*

PROOF. We first observe that any general linear transformation $T(z) = az + b$ is the composition of an even number of inversions. Indeed, such a map is a dilation and rotation followed by a translation. Rotations and translations are each compositions of two reflections (Theorem 3.1.17, p. 36), and a dilation is the composition of two inversions about concentric circles (Exericise 3.2.4, p. ??). So, in total, we have that $T(z) = az + b$ is the composition of an even number of inversions.

Now suppose T is the Möbius transformation $T(z) = (az + b)/(cz + d)$. If $c = 0$ then T is a general linear transformation of the form $T(z) = \frac{a}{d}z + \frac{b}{d}$, and we have nothing to show.

So we assume $c \neq 0$. By doing some long division, the Möbius transformation can be rewritten as

$$T(z) = \frac{az + b}{cz + d} = \frac{a}{c} + \frac{(bc - ad)/c}{cz + d},$$

which can be viewed as the composition $T_3 \circ T_2 \circ T_1(z)$, where $T_1(z) = cz + d$, $T_2(z) = 1/z$ and $T_3(z) = \frac{bc-ad}{c}z + \frac{a}{c}$. Note that T_1 and T_3 are general linear transformations, and

$$T_2(z) = \frac{1}{z} = \overline{\left[\frac{1}{\overline{z}}\right]}$$

is inversion in the unit circle followed by reflection about the real axis. Thus, each T_i is the composition of an even number of inversions, and the general Möbius transformation T is as well.

To prove the other direction, we show that if T is the composition of two inversions then it is a Möbius transformation. Then, if T is the composition of any even number of inversions, it is the composition of half as many Möbius transformations and is itself a Möbius transformation by Theorem 3.4.3, p. 53.

Case 1: T is the composition of two circle inversions. Suppose $T = i_{C_1} \circ i_{C_2}$ where C_1 is the circle $|z - z_1| = r_1$ and C_2 is the circle $|z - z_2| = r_2$. For $i = 1, 2$ the inversion may be described by

$$i_{C_i} = \frac{r_i^2}{\overline{z - z_i}} + z_i,$$

and if we compose these two inversions we do in fact obtain a Möbius transformation. We leave the details of this computation to the reader but note that the determinant of the resulting Möbius transformation is $r_1^2 r_2^2$.

Case 2: T is the composition of one circle inversion and one line reflection. Reflection in the line can be given by $r_L(z) = e^{i\theta}\overline{z} + b$ and inversion in the circle C is given by $i_C = \frac{r^2}{\overline{z - z_o}} + z_o$ where z_0 and r are the center and radius of the circle, as usual. Work out the composition and you'll see that we have a Möbius transformation with determinant $e^{i\theta}r^2$ (which is non-zero). Its inverse, the composition $i_C \circ r_L$, is also a Möbius transformation.

Case 3: T is the composition of two reflections. Either the two lines of reflection are parallel, in which case the composition gives a translation, or they intersect, in which case we have a rotation about the point of intersection (Theorem 3.1.17, p. 36). In either case we have a Möbius transformation.

It follows that the composition of any even number of inversions yields a Möbius transformation. □

Since Möbius transformations are composed of inversions, they will embrace the finer qualities of inversions. For instance, since inversion preserves clines, so do Möbius transformations, and since inversion preserves angle magnitudes, Möbius transformations preserve angles (as an *even* number of inversions).

Theorem 3.4.5 *Möbius transformations take clines to clines and preserves angles.*

The following fixed point theorem is useful for understanding Möbius transformations.

Theorem 3.4.6 *Any Möbius transformation* $T : \mathbb{C}^+ \to \mathbb{C}^+$ *fixes 1, 2, or all points of* $\mathbb{C}^+$.

PROOF. To find fixed points of $T(z) = (az + b)/(cz + d)$ we want to solve

$$\frac{az+b}{cz+d} = z$$

for z, which gives the quadratic equation

$$cz^2 + (d - a)z - b = 0. \tag{1}$$

If $c \neq 0$ then, as discussed in Example 2.4.3, p. 23, equation (1) *must* have 1 or 2 solutions, and there are 1 or 2 fixed points in this case.

If $c = 0$ and $a \neq d$, then the transformation has the form $T(z) = (az + b)/d$, which fixes ∞. From equation (1), $z = b/(d - a) \neq \infty$ is a fixed point as well. So we have 2 fixed points in this case.

If $c = 0$ and $a = d$, then equation (1) reduces to $0 = -b$, so $b = 0$ too, and the transformation is the identity transformation $T(z) = (az + 0)/(0z + a) = z$. This transformation fixes every point. □

With this fixed point theorem in hand, we can now prove the Fundamental Theorem of Möbius Transformations, which says that if we want to induce a one-to-one and onto motion of the entire extended plane that sends my favorite three points (z_1, z_2, z_3) to your favorite three points (w_1, w_2, w_3), as dramatized below, then there is a Möbius transformation that will do the trick, and there's *only* one.

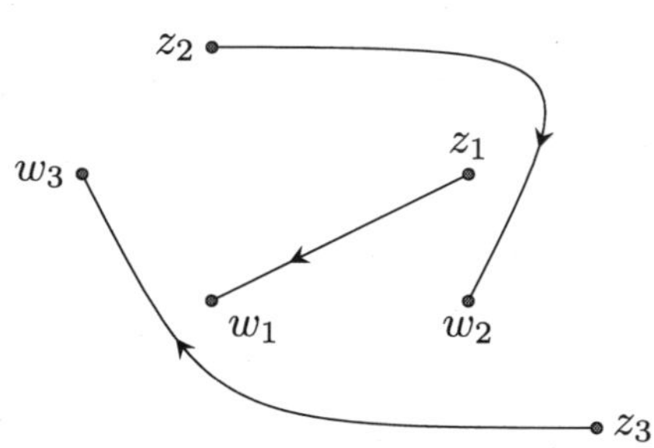

Figure 3.4.7 We can build a Möbius transformation that sends $z_1 \mapsto w_1$, $z_2 \mapsto w_2$, and $z_3 \mapsto w_3$.

Theorem 3.4.8 Fundamental Theorem of Möbius Transformations. *There is a unique Möbius transformation taking any three distinct points of* $\mathbb{C}^+$ *to any three distinct points of* $\mathbb{C}^+$.

PROOF. Suppose z_1, z_2, and z_3 are distinct points in $\mathbb{C}^+$, and w_1, w_2, and w_3 are distinct points in $\mathbb{C}^+$. We show there exists a unique Möbius transformation that maps $z_i \mapsto w_i$ for $i = 1, 2, 3$. To start, we show there exists a map, built from inversions, that maps $z_1 \mapsto 1$, $z_2 \mapsto 0$ and $z_3 \mapsto \infty$. We do so in the case that $z_3 \neq \infty$. This special case is left to the exercises.

First, invert about any circle centered at z_3. This takes z_3 to ∞ as desired. Points z_1 and z_2 no doubt get moved, say to z_1' and z_2', respectively, neither of which is ∞. Second, do a translation that takes z_2' to 0. Such a translation will keep ∞ fixed, and take z_1' to some new spot z_1'' in $\mathbb{C}$. Third, rotate and dilate about the origin, (which keeps 0 and ∞ fixed) so that z_1'' moves to 1. This process yields a composition of inversions that maps $z_1 \mapsto 1$, $z_2 \mapsto 0$, and $z_3 \mapsto \infty$. However, this composition actually involves an *odd* number of inversions, so it's not a Möbius transformation. To make a Möbius transformation out of this composition, we do one last inversion: reflect across the real axis. This keeps 1, 0, and ∞ fixed. Thus, there *is* a Möbius transformation taking any three distinct points to the points $1, 0$, and ∞. For now, we let T denote the Möbius transformation that maps $z_1 \mapsto 1$, $z_2 \mapsto 0$ and $z_3 \mapsto \infty$.

One can similarly construct a Möbius transformation, call it S, that takes $w_1 \mapsto 1$, $w_2 \mapsto 0$, and $w_3 \mapsto \infty$.

If we let S^{-1} denote the inverse transformation of S, then the composition $S^{-1} \circ T$ is a Möbius transformation, and this transformation does what we set out to accomplish as suggested by Figure 3.4.9, p. 56. In particular,

$$S^{-1} \circ T(z_1) = S^{-1}(1) = w_1$$
$$S^{-1} \circ T(z_2) = S^{-1}(0) = w_2$$
$$S^{-1} \circ T(z_3) = S^{-1}(\infty) = w_3.$$

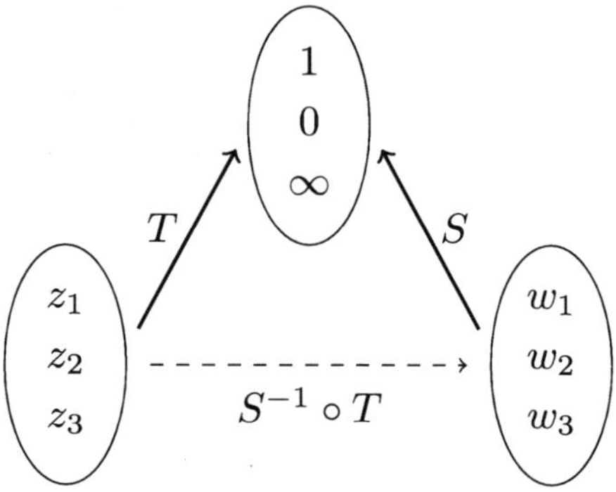

Figure 3.4.9 A schematic for building a Möbius transformation that sends $z_i \mapsto w_i$ for $i = 1, 2, 3$. Go through the points $1, 0, \infty$.

Finally, to prove that this Möbius transformation is unique, assume that there are two Möbius transformations U and V that map $z_1 \mapsto w_1$, $z_2 \mapsto w_2$ and $z_3 \mapsto w_3$. Then $V^{-1} \circ U$ is a Möbius transformation that fixes z_1, z_2, and z_3. According to Theorem 3.4.6, p. 55 there is only one Möbius transformation that fixes more than two points, and this is the identity transformation. Thus $V^{-1} \circ U(z) = z$ for all $z \in \mathbb{C}^+$. Similarly, $U \circ V^{-1}(z) = z$, and it follows that $U(z) = V(z)$ for all $z \in \mathbb{C}^+$. That is, U and V are the same map. □

There is an algebraic description of the very useful Möbius transformation mapping $z_1 \mapsto 1$, $z_2 \mapsto 0$ and $z_3 \mapsto \infty$ that arose in the proof of Theorem 3.4.8,

p. 55:

$$T(z) = \frac{(z - z_2)}{(z - z_3)} \cdot \frac{(z_1 - z_3)}{(z_1 - z_2)}.$$

The reader can check that the map works as advertised and that it is indeed a Möbius transformation. (While it is clear that the transformation has the form $(az+b)/(cz+d)$, it might not be clear that the determinant is nonzero. It is, since the z_i are distinct.) We also note that if one of the z_i is ∞, the form of the map reduces by cancellation of the terms with ∞ in them. For instance, if $z_2 = \infty$, the map that sends $z_1 \mapsto 1$, $\infty \mapsto 0$ and $z_3 \mapsto \infty$ is $T(z) = (z_1 - z_3)/(z - z_3)$.

The Möbius transformation that sends any three distinct points to 1, 0, and ∞ is so useful that it gets its own name and special notation.

Definition 3.4.10 The **cross ratio** of 4 complex numbers z, w, u, and v, where w, u, and v are distinct, is denoted $(z, w; u, v)$, and

$$(z, w; u, v) = \frac{z - u}{z - v} \cdot \frac{w - v}{w - u}.$$

◊

If z is a variable, and w, u, and v are distinct complex constants, then $T(z) = (z, w; u, v)$ is the (unique!) Möbius transformation that sends $w \mapsto 1$, $u \mapsto 0$, and $v \mapsto \infty$.

Example 3.4.11 Building a Möbius transformation.

Find the unique Möbius transformation that sends $1 \mapsto 3$, $i \mapsto 0$, and $2 \mapsto -1$.

One approach: Find $T(z) = (z, 1; i, 2)$ and $S(w) = (w, 3; 0, -1)$. In this case, the transformation we want is $S^{-1} \circ T$.

To find this transformation, we set the cross ratios equal:

$$\begin{aligned}
(z, 1; i, 2) &= (w, 3; 0, -1) \\
\frac{z - i}{z - 2} \cdot \frac{1 - 2}{1 - i} &= \frac{w - 0}{w + 1} \cdot \frac{3 + 1}{3 - 0} \\
\frac{-z + i}{(1 - i)z - 2 + 2i} &= \frac{4w}{3w + 3}.
\end{aligned}$$

Then solve for w:

$$\begin{aligned}
-3zw + 3iw + 3i - 3z &= 4[(1 - i)z - 2 + 2i]w \\
-3z + 3i &= [3z - 3i + 4[(1 - i)z - 2 + 2i]]w \\
w &= \frac{-3z + 3i}{(7 - 4i)z + (-8 + 5i)}.
\end{aligned}$$

Thus, our Möbius transformation is

$$V(z) = \frac{-3z + 3i}{(7 - 4i)z + (-8 + 5i)}.$$

It's quite easy to check our answer here. Since there is exactly one Möbius transformation that does the trick, all we need to do is check whether $V(1) = 3, V(i) = 0$ and $V(2) = -1$. Ok... yes... yes... yep! We've got our map!

Theorem 3.4.12 Invariance of Cross Ratio. *Suppose z_0, z_1, z_2, and z_3 are four distinct points in $\mathbb{C}^+$, and T is any Möbius transformation. Then*

$$(z_0, z_1; z_2, z_3) = (T(z_0), T(z_1); T(z_2), T(z_3)).$$

PROOF. Let T be an arbitrary Möbius transformation, and define $S(z) = (z, z_1; z_2, z_3)$, which sends $z_1 \mapsto 1$, $z_2 \mapsto 0$, and $z_3 \mapsto \infty$. Notice, the composition $S \circ T^{-1}$ is a Möbius transformation that sends $T(z_1) \mapsto 1$, $T(z_2) \mapsto 0$, and $T(z_3) \mapsto \infty$. So this map can be expressed as a cross ratio:

$$S \circ T^{-1}(z) = (z, T(z_1); T(z_2), T(z_3)).$$

Plugging $T(z_0)$ into this transformation, we see

$$S \circ T^{-1}(T(z_0)) = (T(z_0), T(z_1); T(z_2), T(z_3)).$$

On the other hand, $S \circ T^{-1}(T(z_0)) = S(z_0)$, which equals $(z_0, z_1; z_2, z_3)$. So we have proved that

$$(z_0, z_1; z_2, z_3) = (T(z_0), T(z_1); T(z_2), T(z_3)).$$

□

Example 3.4.13 Do four points lie on a single cline?

In addition to defining maps that send points to 1, 0, and ∞, the cross ratio can proclaim whether four points lie on the same cline: If $(z, w; u, v)$ is a real number then the points are all on the same cline; if $(z, w; u, v)$ is complex, then they aren't. The proof of this fact is left as an exercise.

Take the points $1, i, -1, -i$. We know these four points lie on the circle $|z| = 1$, so according to the statement above, $(1, i; -1, -i)$ is a real number. Let's check:

$$\begin{aligned}(1, i; -1, -i) &= \frac{1+1}{1+i} \cdot \frac{i+i}{i+1} \\ &= \frac{2}{1+i}\frac{2i}{1+i} \\ &= \frac{4i}{(1-1)+2i} \\ &= \frac{4i}{2i} \\ &= 2. \qquad \text{(Yep!)}\end{aligned}$$

Another important feature of inversion that gets passed on to Möbius transformations is the preservation of symmetry points. The following result is a corollary to Theorem 3.2.12, p. 44.

Corollary 3.4.14 *If z and z^* are symmetric with respect to the cline C, and T is any Möbius transformation, then $T(z)$ and $T(z^*)$ are symmetric with respect to the cline $T(C)$.*

We close the section with one more theorem about Möbius transformations.

Theorem 3.4.15 *Given any two clines C_1 and C_2, there exists a Möbius transformation T that maps C_1 onto C_2. That is, $T(C_1) = C_2$.*

PROOF. Let p_1 be a point on C_1 and q_1 and q_1^* symmetric with respect to C_1. Similarly, let p_2 be a point on C_2 and q_2 and q_2^* be symmetric with respect to C_2. Build the Möbius transformation that sends $p_1 \mapsto p_2$, $q_1 \mapsto q_2$ and $q_1^* \mapsto q_2^*$. Then $T(C_1) = C_2$. □

Exercises

1. Find a transformation of $\mathbb{C}^+$ that rotates points about $2i$ by an angle $\pi/4$. Show that this transformation has the form of a Möbius transformation.

2. Find the inverse transformation of $T(z) = \frac{3z+i}{2z+1}$.

3. Prove Theorem 3.4.3, p. 53. That is, suppose T and S are two Möbius transformations and prove that the composition $T \circ S$ is again a Möbius transformation.

4. Prove that any Möbius transformation can be written in a form with determinant 1, and that this form is unique up to sign.

5. Find the unique Möbius transformation that sends $1 \mapsto i$, $i \mapsto -1$, and $-1 \mapsto -i$. What are the fixed points of this transformation? What is $T(0)$? What is $T(\infty)$?

6. Repeat the previous exercise, but send $2 \to 0$, $1 \to 3$ and $4 \to 4$.

7. Prove this feature of the cross ratio: $\overline{(z, z_1; z_2, z_3)} = (\overline{z}, \overline{z_1}; \overline{z_2}, \overline{z_3})$.

8. Prove that the cross ratio of four distinct real numbers is a real number.

9. Prove that the cross ratio of four distinct complex numbers is a real number if and only if the four points lie on the same cline.

10. Do the points $2 + i, 3, 5$, and $6 + i$ lie on a single cline?

11. More on Möbius transformations.

a. Give an example of a Möbius transformation T such that $\overline{T(z)} \neq T(\overline{z})$ for some z in $\mathbb{C}^+$.

b. Suppose T is a Möbius transformation that sends the real axis onto itself. Prove that in this case, $\overline{T(z)} = T(\overline{z})$ for all z in $\mathbb{C}$.

12. Is there a Möbius transformation that sends 1 to 3, i to 4, -1 to $2 + i$ and $-i$ to $4 + i$?

13. Find the fixed points of these transformations on $\mathbb{C}^+$. Remember that ∞ can be a fixed point of such a transformation.

a. $T(z) = \dfrac{2z}{3z - 1}$

b. $T(z) = iz$

c. $T(z) = \dfrac{-iz}{(1 - i)z - 1}$

14. Find a Möbius transformation that takes the circle $|z| = 4$ to the straight line $3x + y = 4$.

15. Find a non-trivial Möbius transformation that fixes the points -1 and 1, and call this transformation T. Then, let C be the imaginary axis. What is the image of C under this map. That is, what cline is $T(C)$?

16. Suppose z_1, z_2, z_3 are distinct points in $\mathbb{C}^+$. Show that by an even number of inversions we can map $z_1 \mapsto 1$, $z_2 \mapsto 0$, and $z_3 \mapsto \infty$ in the case that $z_3 = \infty$.

3.5 Möbius Transformations: A Closer Look

To visualize Möbius transformations it is helpful to focus on fixed points and, in the case of two fixed points, on two families of clines with respect to these points.

Given two points p and q in $\mathbb{C}^+$, a **type I cline of p and q** is a cline that goes through p and q, and a **type II cline of p and q** is a cline with respect to which p and q are symmetric. Type II clines are also called circles of Apollonius (see Exercise 3.3.2, p. **??**). Figure 3.5.1, p. 60 shows some type I and type II clines of p and q. The type II clines of p and q are dashed.

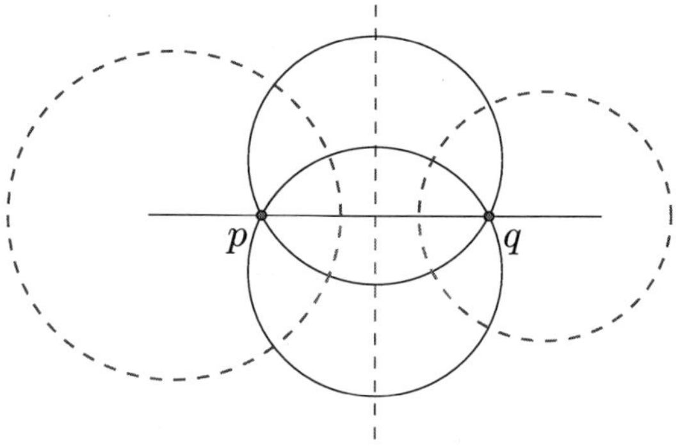

Figure 3.5.1 Type I clines (solid) and Type II clines (dashed) of p and q.

By Theorem 3.2.8, p. 43, any type II cline of p and q intersects any type I cline of p and q at right angles. Furthermore, because Möbius transformations preserve clines and symmetry points, we can be assured that Möbius transformations preserve type I clines as well as type II clines. In particular, if C is a type I cline of p and q, then $T(C)$ is a type I cline of $T(p)$ and $T(q)$. Similarly, if C is a type II cline of p and q, then $T(C)$ is a type II cline of $T(p)$ and $T(q)$. We can use this to our advantage.

For instance, the type I clines of the points 0 and ∞ are, precisely, lines through the origin, while the type II clines of 0 and ∞ are circles centered at the origin. (Remember, inversion in a circle takes the center of the circle to ∞.) The type I clines in this case are clearly perpendicular to the type II clines, and they combine to create a coordinate system of the plane (polar coordinates), as pictured in Figure 3.5.2, p. 61(a).

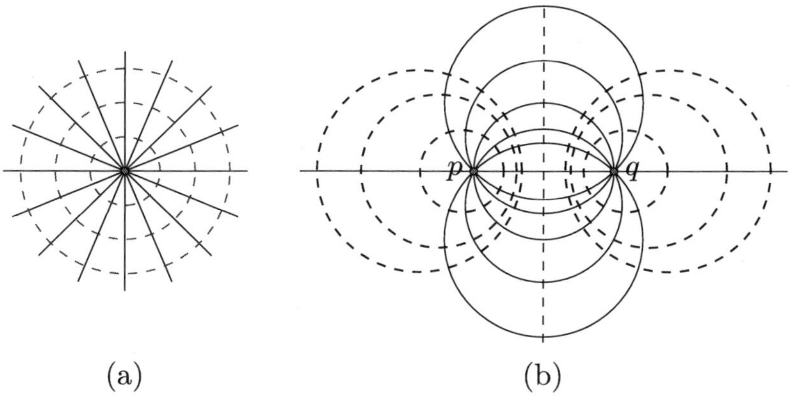

Figure 3.5.2 (a) Type I clines (solid) and type II clines (dashed) of points 0 and ∞ (solid); (b) A Möbius transformation sending $0 \mapsto p$ and $\infty \mapsto q$ sends type I and II clines of 0 and ∞ to type I and II clines of p and q, respectively.

We can move this system of clines by considering a Möbius transformation that maps 0 to p and ∞ to q (where $p, q \neq \infty$). Lines through the origin get mapped to type I clines of p and q, and circles centered at the origin get mapped to type II clines of p and q. The result is a system of clines that serves as a general coordinate system for the plane. Each point z in the plane is at the intersection of a single type I cline of p and q and a single type II cline of p and q, and these two clines intersect at right angles.

Let's get back to fixed points and how they can help us describe Möbius transformations. We consider the case that 0 and ∞ are fixed before proceeding to the general case.

Example 3.5.3 Fixing 0 and ∞.

Suppose $T(z) = (az + b)/(cz + d)$ is a Möbius transformation that fixes 0 and ∞. In this case, the form of the Möbius transformation can be simplified. In particular, since $T(0) = 0$, it follows that $b = 0$. And since $T(\infty) = \infty$, it follows that $c = 0$. Thus, $T(z) = \frac{a}{d}z$ which may be written as

$$T(z) = re^{i\theta}z.$$

With T in this form, it is clear that if T fixes 0 and ∞, then T is a combination of a dilation (by factor r) and a rotation about the origin (by a factor θ). We may assume that $r > 0$ in the above equation, because if it is negative, we can turn it into a positive constant by adding π to the angle of rotation.

A dilation by r will push points along lines through the origin. These lines are precisely the type I clines of 0 and ∞. All points in the plane either head toward ∞ (if $r > 1$) or they all head toward 0 (if $0 < r < 1$). Of course, if $r = 1$ there is no dilation.

Meanwhile, rotation about 0 by θ pushes points along circles centered at the origin. These circles are precisely the type II clines of 0 and ∞.

Now suppose T is a Möbius transformation that fixes two finite points p and q (neither is ∞). Let

$$S(z) = \frac{z-p}{z-q}$$

be a Möbius transformation that takes p to 0 and q to ∞. Let U be the Möbius transformation determined by the composition equation

$$U = S \circ T \circ S^{-1}. \tag{1}$$

Notice

$$U(0) = S \circ T \circ S^{-1}(0) = S \circ T(p) = S(p) = 0,$$

and

$$U(\infty) = S \circ T \circ S^{-1}(\infty) = S \circ T(q) = S(q) = \infty.$$

That is, U is a Möbius transformation that fixes 0 and ∞. So, by Example 3.5.3, p. 61, U is a rotation, a dilation, or some combination of those, and U looks like $U(z) = re^{i\theta}z$.

In any event, focusing on T again and using equation (1), which can be rewritten as $S \circ T = U \circ S$, we arrive at the following equation, called the normal form of the Möbius transformation in this case.

Normal form, two fixed points.

The normal form of a Möbius transformation T fixing distinct points p and q (neither of which is ∞):

$$\frac{T(z)-p}{T(z)-q} = re^{i\theta} \cdot \frac{z-p}{z-q}$$

This normal form is much more illuminating than the standard a, b, c, d form because, although the map is still described in terms of four constants (p, q, r, θ), each constant now has a simple geometric interpretation: p and q are fixed points, r is a dilation factor along type I clines of p and q, and θ is a rotation factor around type II clines of p and q.

In particular, thanks to composition equation (1) we can view T as the composition $T = S^{-1} \circ U \circ S$. With this view, T moves points according to a three-leg journey. Think of a general point z clinging to the intersection of a single type II cline of p and q and a single type I cline of p and q (see Figure 3.5.4, p. 63).

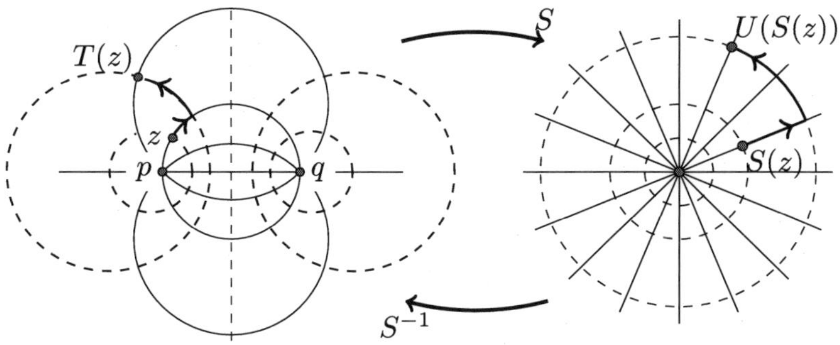

Figure 3.5.4 Tracking the image of z if T fixes p and q.

First, z gets sent via S to $S(z)$, which is at the intersection of a line through the origin and a circle centered at the origin. Second, U (which has the form $U(z) = re^{i\theta}z$), sends $S(z)$ along this line through the origin (by dilation factor r), and then around a new circle centered at the origin (by rotation factor θ) to the point $U(S(z))$. Third, S^{-1} sends $U(S(z))$ back to the intersection of a type I cline of p and q and a type II cline of p and q. This point of intersection is $S^{-1}(U(S(z)))$ and is equivalent to $T(z)$.

Though fatigued, our well-traveled point realizes there's a shortcut. Why go through this complicated wash? We can understand T as follows: T will push points along type I clines of p and q (according to the dilation factor r) and along type II clines of p and q (according to the rotation factor θ).

We emphasize two special cases of this normal form. If $|re^{i\theta}| = 1$ there is no dilation, and points simply get rotated about type II clines of p and q as in Figure 3.5.5, p. 63. Such a Möbius transformation is called an **elliptic Möbius transformation**.

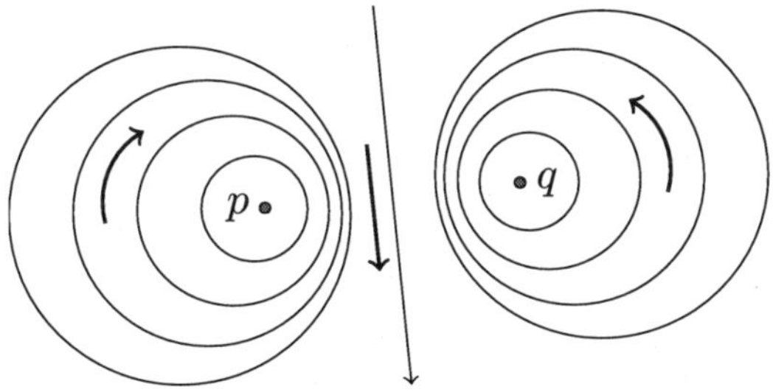

Figure 3.5.5 An elliptic Möbius transformation fixing p and q swirls points around type II clines of p and q.

The second special case occurs when $\theta = 0$. Here we have a dilation factor r, but no rotation. All points move along type I clines of p and q, as in Figure 3.5.6, p. 64. A Möbius transformation of this variety is called a **hyperbolic Möbius transformation**. A hyperbolic Möbius transformation fixing p and q either sends all points away from p and toward q or vice versa, depending on the value of r.

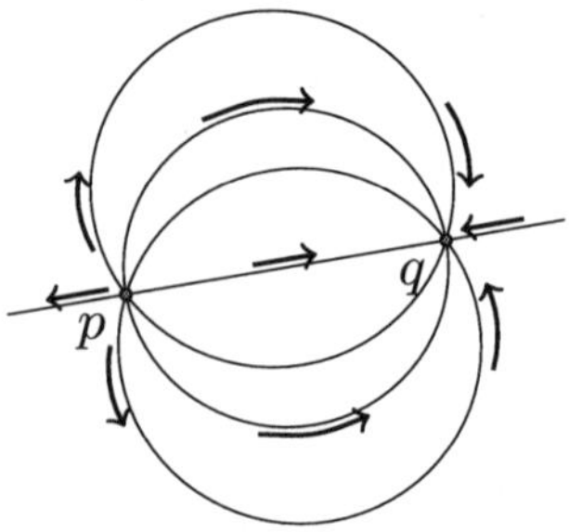

Figure 3.5.6 A hyperbolic Möbius transformation fixing p and q pushes points away from one fixed point and toward the other along type I clines of p and q.

If we are not in one of these special cases, then T is simply a combination of these two, and a Möbius transformation of this type is often called **loxodromic**.

If a Möbius transformation fixes two finite points, say p and q, and it is not the identity transformation, then some finite point gets sent to ∞. Moreover, ∞ gets sent to some finite point. The point sent to infinity is called the **pole** of the transformation and is often denoted z_∞. That is, $T(z_\infty) = \infty$. The **inverse pole of T** is the image of ∞ under the map, which is often denoted as w_∞. That is, $T(\infty) = w_\infty$. There is a simple relationship between the four points p, q, z_∞, and w_∞.

Lemma 3.5.7 *Suppose T is a Möbius transformation that fixes distinct finite points p and q, sends z_∞ to ∞, and sends ∞ to w_∞. Then $p + q = z_\infty + w_\infty$.*

PROOF. Suppose T satisfies the conditions of the lemma. Then T has normal form

$$\frac{z-p}{z-q} = \lambda \frac{T(z)-p}{T(z)-q},$$

where $\lambda = re^{i\theta}$. Plug $z = z_\infty$ into the normal form to see

$$\frac{z_\infty - p}{z_\infty - q} = \lambda \cdot 1.$$

Plug $z = \infty$ into the normal form to see

$$1 = \lambda \frac{w_\infty - p}{w_\infty - q}.$$

Next solve each equation for λ, set them equal, cross multiply, and simplify as follows to get the result:

$$\begin{aligned} \frac{z_\infty - p}{z_\infty - q} &= \frac{w_\infty - q}{w_\infty - p} \\ (z_\infty - p)(w_\infty - p) &= (w_\infty - q)(z_\infty - q) \\ p^2 - pw_\infty - pz_\infty &= q^2 - qw_\infty - qz_\infty \\ p^2 - q^2 &= p(z_\infty + w_\infty) - q(z_\infty + w_\infty) \\ (p-q)(p+q) &= (p-q)(z_\infty + w_\infty) \\ p + q &= z_\infty + w_\infty \qquad \text{(since } p \neq q). \end{aligned}$$

This completes the proof. □

Theorem 3.5.8 *If T is a Möbius transformation that fixes two distinct, finite points p and q, sends z_∞ to ∞, and sends ∞ to w_∞, then*

$$T(z) = \frac{w_\infty z - pq}{z - z_\infty}.$$

PROOF. In the proof of Lemma 3.5.7, p. 64, we found that the constant λ in the normal form of T is

$$\lambda = \frac{z_\infty - p}{z_\infty - q}.$$

It follows that T has the normal form

$$\frac{z-p}{z-q} = \left(\frac{z_\infty - p}{z_\infty - q}\right) \cdot \frac{T(z)-p}{T(z)-q}.$$

Solve this expression for $T(z)$ and reduce it using the fact that $p+q = z_\infty + w_\infty$ to get the expression for T that appears in the statement of the theorem. The details are left to the reader. □

Example 3.5.9 Fix -1 and 1 and send $i \mapsto \infty$.

By Lemma 3.5.7, p. 64, the Möbius transformation sends ∞ to $-i$, so by Theorem 3.5.8, p. 65,

$$T(z) = \frac{-iz - (1)(-1)}{z - i} = \frac{-iz + 1}{z - i}.$$

Example 3.5.10 Analyze a Möbius transformation.

Consider the Möbius transformation

$$T(z) = \frac{(6+3i)z + (2-3i)}{z+3}.$$

First we find the fixed points and the normal form of T. To find the fixed points we solve $T(z) = z$ for z.

$$\begin{aligned} \frac{(6+3i)z + (2-3i)}{z+3} &= z \\ (6+3i)z + (2-3i) &= z^2 + 3z \\ z^2 - (3+3i)z - (2-3i) &= 0. \end{aligned}$$

Hey! Wait a moment! This looks familiar. Let's see ... yes! We showed in Example 2.4.4, p. 24 that this quadratic equation has solutions $z = i$ and $z = 3 + 2i$.

So the map has these two fixed points, and the normal form of T is

$$\frac{T(z) - i}{T(z) - (3+2i)} = \lambda \frac{z - i}{z - (3+2i)}.$$

To find the value of λ, plug into the normal form a convenient value of z. For instance, $T(-3) = \infty$, so

$$1 = \lambda \frac{-3 - i}{-3 - (3+2i)}.$$

It follows that $\lambda = 2$, so T is a hyperbolic map that pushes points along clines through i and $3+2i$. Below is a schematic for how the map pushes points around in $\mathbb{C}^+$. Notice $T(0) = \frac{2}{3} - i$, $T(1) = 2$, and $T(4i) = 2.16 + 4.12i$. Points are moving along type I clines of i and $3+2i$ away from i and toward $3+2i$.

From the original description of T we observe that the pole of the map is $z_\infty = -3$, and the inverse pole of the map is $w_\infty = 6+3i$. Notice that z_∞, w_∞, and the two fixed points all lie on the same Euclidean line. This will always be the case for a hyperbolic Möbius transformation (Exercise 3.5.9, p. ??).

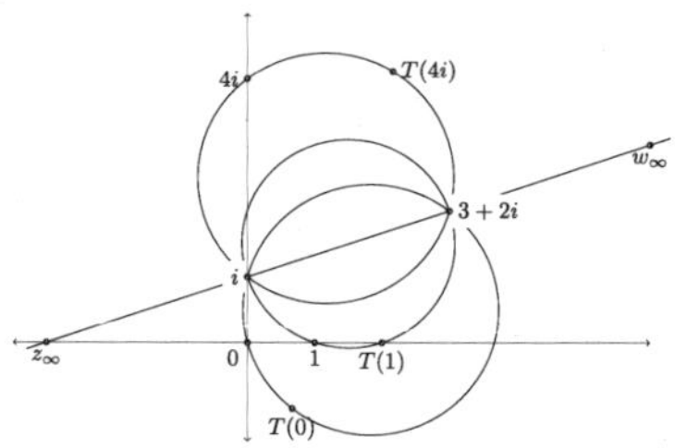

Example 3.5.11 Fix i and 0 and send $1 \mapsto 2$.

The normal form of this map is

$$\frac{T(z) - i}{T(z) - 0} = \lambda \frac{z - i}{z - 0}.$$

Since $T(1) = 2$ we know that

$$\frac{2 - i}{2} = \lambda(1 - i).$$

Solving for λ we have

$$\lambda = \frac{3}{4} + \frac{1}{4}i,$$

and the map is loxodromic.

Expressing λ in polar form, $\lambda = re^{i\theta}$, gives $r = \frac{\sqrt{10}}{4}$ and $\theta = \arctan(1/3)$. So T pushes points along type I clines of i and 0 according to the scale factor r and along type II clines of i and 0 according to the angle θ.

Now we consider Möbius transformations that fix just one point. One such Möbius transformation comes to mind immediately. For any complex number d, the translation $T(z) = z + d$ fixes just ∞. In the exercises, you prove that translations are the *only* Möbius transformations that fix ∞ and no other point.

Now suppose T fixes $p \neq \infty$ (and no other point). Let $S(z) = \frac{1}{z-p}$ be a Möbius transformation taking p to ∞, and let $U = S \circ T \circ S^{-1}$. Then $U(\infty) = S(T(S^{-1}(\infty))) = S(T(p)) = S(p) = \infty$, and U fixes no other point. Thus, $U(z) = z + d$ for some complex constant d.

The composition equation $S \circ T = U \circ S$ gives the following equation called the **normal form of a Möbius transformation T fixing** $p \neq \infty$ (and no other point):

Normal form, one fixed point $p \neq \infty$.

$$\frac{1}{T(z) - p} = \frac{1}{z - p} + d$$

Observe that $U(z) = z + d$ pushes points along lines parallel to one another in the direction of d (as in the right of Figure 3.5.12, p. 67). All of these parallel lines meet at ∞ and are mutually tangent at this point. The map S^{-1} takes this system of clines to a system of clines that meet just at p, and are tangent to one another at p, as pictured. The slope of the single line in this system depends on the value of the constant d. In fact, the single line in the system of clines is the line through p and $T(\infty)$ (see Exercise 3.5.12, p. ?? for details).

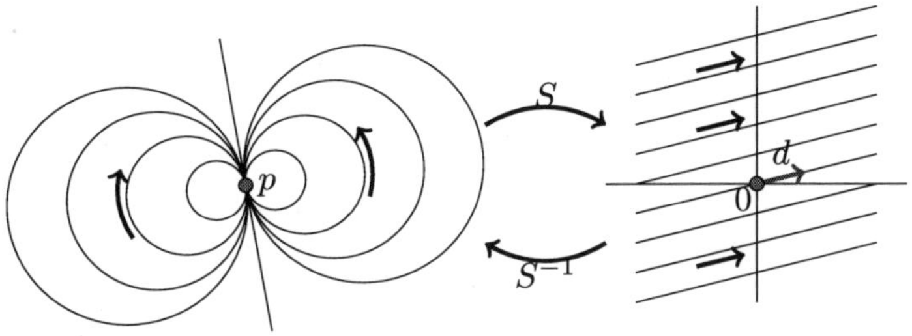

Figure 3.5.12 A parabolic map fixing p pushes points along clines that are mutually tangent at p.

A map that fixes just p will push points along such a system of clines that are mutually tangent at p. Such a map is called **parabolic**. In a sense, a parabolic map sends points both toward and away from p along these clines, just as any translation pushes points along a line toward ∞ and also away from ∞.

Example 3.5.13 Normal form, one fixed point..

Consider $T(z) = (7z - 12)/(3z - 5)$. To find its normal form we start by finding its fixed points.

$$\begin{aligned} z &= T(z) \\ z(3z-5) &= 7z - 12 \\ 3z^2 - 12z + 12 &= 0 \\ z^2 - 4z + 4 &= 0 \\ (z-2)^2 &= 0 \\ z &= 2. \end{aligned}$$

So T is parabolic and has normal form

$$\frac{1}{T(z) - 2} = \frac{1}{z - 2} + d.$$

To find d plug in the image of another point. Using the original description of the map, we know $T(0) = 2.4$, so

$$\frac{1}{0.4} = \frac{1}{-2} + d$$

so that $d = 3$. The normal form is then

$$\frac{1}{T(z) - 2} = \frac{1}{z - 2} + 3.$$

Exercises

1. Complete the proof of Theorem 3.5.8, p. 65.

2. Analyze each of the Möbius transformations below by finding the fixed points, finding the normal form, and sketching the appropriate coordinate system of clines, being sure to indicate the motion of the transformation.

a. $T(z) = \dfrac{z}{2z - 1}$

b. $T(z) = \dfrac{-z}{(1 + i)z - i}$

c. $T(z) = \dfrac{3iz - 5}{z - i}$

3. A transformation T is called an **involution** if it is its own inverse. If this is the case, then $T \circ T$ is the identity transformation. Prove that if a Möbius transformation T is an involution and not the identity transformation, it must be elliptic.

4. Suppose a Möbius transformation T has the following property: There are distinct points a, b, c in the complex plane $\mathbb{C}$ such that $T(a) = b, T(b) = c, T(c) = a$.

a. What is the image of the unique cline through a, b, and c under T?

b. Explain why the triple composition $T \circ T \circ T$ is the identity transformation.

c. Prove that T is elliptic.

5. Prove that if the Möbius transformation T fixes just ∞, then $T(z) = z + d$ for some complex constant d.

6. Find the Möbius transformation that fixes 2 and 4 and sends $2 + i$ to ∞.

7. Use the normal form to build and classify a Möbius transformation that fixes 4 and 8 and sends i to 0.

8. Suppose T is an elliptic Möbius transformation that fixes the distinct, finite points p and q.

a. Prove that the points z_∞ and w_∞ as defined in Lemma 3.5.7, p. 64 lie on the perpendicular bisector of segment pq.

b. Show that T is the composition of two inversions about clines that contain p and q.

9. Suppose the Möbius transformation T fixes the distinct, finite points p and q and sends z_∞ to ∞ and ∞ to w_∞. By Lemma 3.5.7, p. 64 we know $p + q = z_\infty + w_\infty$. Use the normal form of T to prove the following facts.

(a) If T is elliptic then the four points p, q, z_∞, and w_∞ form a rhombus. Under what conditions is this rhombus actually a square?

(b) If T is hyperbolic then these 4 points all lie on the same Euclidean line.

(c) If T is loxodromic, then under what conditions do these four points determine a rectangle?

10. Prove that any pair of nonintersecting clines in $\mathbb{C}$ may be mapped by a Möbius transformation to concentric circles.

11. Suppose $T = i_{C_1} \circ i_{C_2}$ where C_1 and C_2 are clines that do not intersect. Prove that T has two fixed points and these points are on all clines perpendicular to both C_1 and C_2.

12. Suppose $T(z)$ is parabolic with normal form

$$\frac{1}{T(z) - p} = \frac{1}{z - p} + d.$$

Prove that the line through p and $p + \frac{1}{d}$ gets sent to itself by T.

13. Analyze $T(z) = [(1+3i)z - 9i]/[iz + (1-3i)]$ by finding the fixed points, finding the normal form, and sketching the appropriate system of clines indicating the motion of the transformation.

14. Find a parabolic transformation with fixed point $2 + i$ for which $T(\infty) = 8$.

15. Given distinct points p, q, and z in $\mathbb{C}$, prove there exists a type II cline of p and q that goes through z.

4

Geometry

Recall the two paragraphs from Section 1.2 that we intended to spend time making sense of and working through:

> Whereas Euclid's approach to geometry was additive (he started with basic definitions and axioms and proceeded to build a sequence of results depending on previous ones), Klein's approach was subtractive. He started with a space and a group of allowable transformations of that space. He then threw out all concepts that did not remain unchanged under these transformations. Geometry, to Klein, is the study of objects and functions that remain unchanged under allowable transformations.
>
> Klein's approach to geometry, called the *Erlangen Program* after the university at which he worked at the time, has the benefit that all three geometries (Euclidean, hyperbolic and elliptic) emerge as special cases from a general space and a general set of transformations.

We now have both the space ($\mathbb{C}^+$) and the transformations (Möbius transformations), and are just about ready to embark on non-Euclidean adventures. Before doing so, however, one more phrase needs defining: *group of transformations*. This phrase has a precise meaning. Not every collection of transformations is lucky enough to form a group.

4.1 The Basics

Definition 4.1.1 A collection G of transformations of a set A is called a **group of transformations** if G has the following three properties:

1. *Identity*: G contains the identity transformation $T : A \to A$ defined by $T(a) = a$ for all $a \in A$.
2. *Closure*: If T and S are two transformations in G, then the composition $T \circ S$ is in G.
3. *Inverses*: If T is in G, then the inverse T^{-1} is in G.

◊

The reader who has seen group theory will know that in addition to the three properties listed in our definition, the group operation must satisfy a property called associativity. In the context of transformations, the group operation is composition of transformations, and this operation is always associative: if R, S, and T are transformations of a set A, then the transformation $(R \circ S) \circ T$ equals the transformation $R \circ (S \circ T)$. So, in the present context of transformations, we omit associativity as a property that needs checking.

Example 4.1.2 Group of translations.

Let $\mathcal{T}$ denote the collection of all translations of the plane $\mathbb{C}$. In particular, for each $b \in \mathbb{C}$, let $T_b : \mathbb{C} \to \mathbb{C}$ denote the translation $T_b(z) = z + b$. The set $\mathcal{T}$ consists of all T_b, for all $b \in \mathbb{C}$. That is,

$$\mathcal{T} = \{T_b \mid b \in \mathbb{C}\}.$$

Show that $\mathcal{T}$ is a group of transformations.

Solution. To verify $\mathcal{T}$ forms a group, we must check the three properties.

1. $\mathcal{T}$ contains the identity: Since $0 \in \mathbb{C}$, $\mathcal{T}$ contains $T_0(z) = z + 0 = z$, which is the identity transformation of $\mathbb{C}$.

2. $\mathcal{T}$ has closure: Suppose T_b and T_c are in $\mathcal{T}$. Then $T_b \circ T_c(z) = T_b(z + c) = (z + c) + b = z + (b + c)$. But this map is exactly the translation T_{b+c}, which is in $\mathcal{T}$ since $b + c \in \mathbb{C}$. Thus, the composition of two translations is again a translation. Notationally, we have shown that $T_b \circ T_c(z) = T_{b+c}(z)$.

3. $\mathcal{T}$ contains inverses: Suppose T_b is in $\mathcal{T}$, and consider T_{-b}, which is in $\mathcal{T}$ since $-b \in \mathbb{C}$. Note that $T_b \circ T_{-b}(z) = T_b(z - b) = (z - b) + b = z$, and $T_{-b} \circ T_b(z) = T_{-b}(z + b) = (z + b) - b = z$. Thus, T_{-b} is the inverse of T_b, and this inverse is in $\mathcal{T}$. Notationally, $T_b^{-1} = T_{-b}$: the inverse of translation by b is translation back by $-b$.

Definition 4.1.3 Let S be any set, and G a group of transformations on S. The pair (S, G) is called a **geometry**. A **figure** in the geometry is any subset A of S. An element of S is called a **point** in the geometry. Two figures A and B are called **congruent**, denoted $A \cong B$, if there exists a transformation T in G such that $T(A) = B$. ◊

Although a figure in a geometry (S, G) is defined to be a subset of S, we make one abuse of notation and sometimes treat points as figures. For instance, we might write $a \cong b$ for two points a and b in S when, formally, we mean $\{a\} \cong \{b\}$. Incidentally, $a \cong b$ in the geometry (S, G) means there exists a transformation $T \in G$ such that $T(a) = b$.

Let's look at some examples now to help sort through these definitions.

Example 4.1.4 Finite group of rotations.

Consider the set $H = \{R_0, R_{\pi/2}, R_\pi, R_{3\pi/2}\}$ consisting of four rotations of $\mathbb{C}$ about the origin (by 0, $\pi/2$, π, and $3\pi/2$ radians). We observe first that H forms a group. Since $R_0(z) = e^{i0}z = z$, H contains the identity transformation on $\mathbb{C}$. The set also satisfies closure, and the reader can check all possible compositions. For instance, $R_{3\pi/2} \circ R_\pi = R_{\pi/2}$. Finally, the inverse of each transformation in H is again in H. Check that $R_0^{-1} = R_0$, $R_{\pi/2}^{-1} = R_{3\pi/2}$, $R_\pi^{-1} = R_\pi$, and $R_{3\pi/2}^{-1} = R_{\pi/2}$. Thus, H is a group and we may study the geometry $(\mathbb{C}, H)$. For instance, is the circle C given by $|z - i| = .5$ congruent to the circle D given by $|z| = .5$? Well, is there a transformation in H that maps C onto D? No! The only four circles congruent to C are pictured below. These are found by rotating C about the origin by 0, $\pi/2$, π, or $3\pi/2$ radians, the only allowable transformations in this geometry.

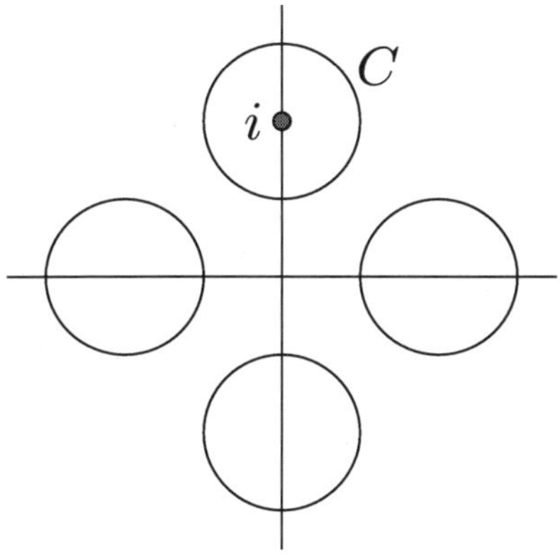

Notice also that any point $z \neq 0$ is congruent to four points: z, $e^{i\pi/2}z$, $e^{i\pi}z$, and $e^{i3\pi/2}z$. How many points are congruent to $z = 0$? Are all lines congruent in this geometry? Nope. We are only allowed these few rotations, so we have no way to map the line $y = x$, say, to the line $y = x + 1$.

Example 4.1.5 A two-element group.

Consider reflection of $\mathbb{C}$ across the real axis, given by $r(z) = \overline{z}$. Since $r \circ r$ is the identity map, the set $G = \{1, r\}$ is a group of transformations on $\mathbb{C}$, and we may define the geometry $(\mathbb{C}, G)$. Notice that while $3 + i$ is congruent to $3 - i$ in this geometry, it is not congruent to $-3 + i$. Also, the circle $|z - 2i| = 1$ is congruent to the circle $|z + 2i| = 1$ but not the circle $|z - 3i| = 1$.

Example 4.1.6 Translational geometry.

Let $\mathcal{T}$ denote the group of translations in Example 4.1.2, p. 72, and consider the geometry $(\mathbb{C}, \mathcal{T})$. We call this geometry **translational geometry**. Which figures in Figure 4.1.7, p. 74 are congruent in this geometry?

Remember, two figures are congruent if we can find a transformation that "moves" one figure on top of the other. Since our allowable moves here are translations, we cannot change the radius of a circle (that's a dilation), and we cannot rotate objects. So, in translational geometry the only figures congruent in Figure 4.1.7, p. 74 are H and L.

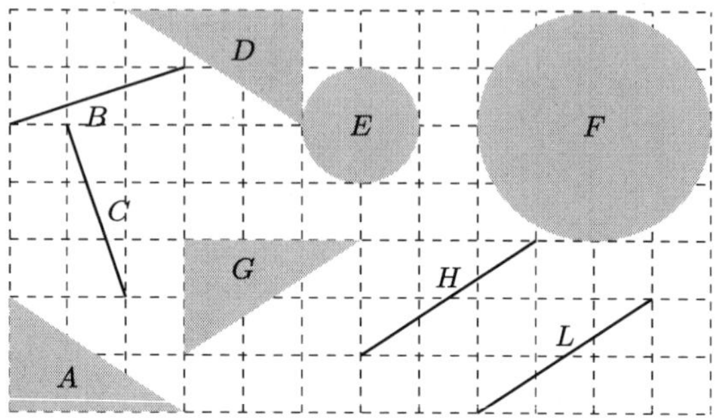

Figure 4.1.7 Figures in the plane.

Definition 4.1.8 A collection $\mathcal{D}$ of figures in a geometry (S, G) is called an **invariant set** if, for any figure A in $\mathcal{D}$ and any transformation T in G, $T(A)$ is also in $\mathcal{D}$. A function f defined on $\mathcal{D}$ is called an **invariant function** if $f(B) = f(T(B))$ for any figure B in $\mathcal{D}$ and any transformation T in G. ◊

For instance, suppose $\mathcal{D}$ is the set of all lines in $\mathbb{C}$. Let f be the function that takes a line to its slope. In translational geometry, $(\mathbb{C}, \mathcal{T})$, the set $\mathcal{D}$ of all lines is an invariant set because if A is any line, then so is its image, $T(A)$, under any translation T in $\mathcal{T}$. Furthermore, f is an invariant function because any translation of any line preserves the slope of that line.

Of course, two figures in an invariant set need not be congruent. For instance, in translational geometry the set $\mathcal{D}$ of all lines is an invariant set, although if lines A and B in $\mathcal{D}$ have different slopes then they are not congruent. This feature of the set $\mathcal{D}$ makes it seem too big, in some sense. Can invariant sets be more exclusive, containing only members that are congruent to one another? You bet they can.

Definition 4.1.9 A set of figures $\mathcal{D}$ in a geometry is called **minimally invariant** if no proper subset of it is also an invariant set. ◊

For instance, the set of all lines is not a minimally invariant set in translational geometry because it has proper subsets that are also invariant sets. One such subset consists of all lines with slope 8.

Theorem 4.1.10 *An invariant set $\mathcal{D}$ of figures in a geometry (S, G) is minimally invariant if and only if any two figures in $\mathcal{D}$ are congruent.*

PROOF. First assume $\mathcal{D}$ is a minimally invariant set in the geometry (S, G), and suppose A and B are arbitrary figures in $\mathcal{D}$. We must show that $A \cong B$.

We begin by constructing a new set of figures, the one consisting of A and all transformations of A. In particular, define

$$\mathcal{A} = \{T(A) \mid T \in G\}.$$

Notice that for any $T \in G$, $T(A)$ is in the set $\mathcal{D}$ since $\mathcal{D}$ is invariant. This means that $\mathcal{A}$ is a subset of $\mathcal{D}$.

Furthermore, $\mathcal{A}$ itself is an invariant set, thanks to the *group* nature of G. In particular, if C is any member of $\mathcal{A}$, then $C = T_0(A)$ for some particular T_0 in G. Thus, applying any transformation T to C,

$$T(C) = T(T_0(A)) = T \circ T_0(A)$$

and since $T \circ T_0$ is again a transformation in G, $T \circ T_0(A)$ lives in $\mathcal{A}$.

So we've established two facts: (1) $\mathcal{A}$ is a subset of $\mathcal{D}$, and (2) $\mathcal{A}$ is an invariant set. Since $\mathcal{D}$ is a *minimally* invariant set it follows by definition that $\mathcal{A} = \mathcal{D}$. This means that the given set B, which is in $\mathcal{D}$, is also in $\mathcal{A}$. That is, $A \cong B$.

The proof of the other direction is left as an exercise for the reader. □

The proof of Theorem 4.1.10, p. 74 illustrates a convenient way to find minimally invariant sets: If A is a figure in (S, G), then $\mathcal{A} = \{T(A) \mid T \in G\}$ is a minimally invariant set.

Example 4.1.11 Euclidean geometry.

Euclidean geometry is the geometry $(\mathbb{C}, \mathcal{E})$, where $\mathcal{E}$ consists of all transformations of the form $T(z) = e^{i\theta}z + b$, where θ is a real number and b is in $\mathbb{C}$. Note that $\mathcal{E}$ consists of precisely those general linear transformations of the form $T(z) = az+b$ in which $|a| = 1$. In the exercises, you check that this collection is indeed a group of transformations.

The group $\mathcal{E}$ includes rotations and translations, but not dilations. Let's take a look at some familiar properties of objects that should be invariant in Euclidean geometry.

The **Euclidean distance** between two points z_1 and z_2 is defined to be $|z_1 - z_2|$. To show that this is an invariant function of $(\mathbb{C}, \mathcal{E})$, we need to show that for any T in the group $\mathcal{E}$, the distance between z_1 and z_2 equals the distance between $T(z_1)$ and $T(z_2)$:

$$\begin{aligned} |T(z_1) - T(z_2)| &= |(e^{i\theta}z_1 + b) - (e^{i\theta}z_2 + b)| \\ &= |e^{i\theta}(z_1 - z_2)| \\ &= |e^{i\theta}||z_1 - z_2| \\ &= |z_1 - z_2| \qquad \text{(since } |e^{i\theta}| = 1\text{).} \end{aligned}$$

Thus, Euclidean distance is preserved in $(\mathbb{C}, \mathcal{E})$.

Angles are preserved as well. We have already proved that general linear transformations preserve angles (Theorem 3.1.12, p. 34), and Euclidean transformations are general linear transformations, so angles are preserved in $(\mathbb{C}, \mathcal{E})$.

Definition 4.1.12 A geometry (S, G) is called **homogeneous** if any two points in S are congruent, and **isotropic** if the transformation group contains rotations about each point in S. ◊

Example 4.1.13 Homogeneous geometry.

Translational geometry $(\mathbb{C}, \mathcal{T})$ is homogeneous because there is a translation that will map any point of $\mathbb{C}$ to any other point of $\mathbb{C}$. That is, any two points of $\mathbb{C}$ are congruent. Of course, without rotations, translational geometry is not isotropic. Here's a formal argument that $(\mathbb{C}, \mathcal{T})$ is homogeneous:

Suppose p and q are arbitrary points in $\mathbb{C}$. We must find a translation T in $\mathcal{T}$ such that $T(p) = q$. Let $w = q - p$, and consider the translation T_w in $\mathcal{T}$. Then $T_w(p) = p + w = p + (q - p) = q$. Thus $T_w(p) = q$ and $p \cong q$. Since p and q are arbitrary points in $\mathbb{C}$ it follows that $(\mathbb{C}, \mathcal{T})$ is homogeneous.

Euclidean geometry $(\mathbb{C}, \mathcal{E})$ is homogeneous since it contains all translations, but the geometries of Example 4.1.4, p. 73 and Example 4.1.5, p. 73 are not.

Definition 4.1.14 **A metric** for a geometry (S, G) is an invariant function $d : S \times S \to \mathbb{R}$ mapping each ordered pair (x, y) of elements from S to a real number such that

1. $d(x, y) \geq 0$ for all $x, y \in S$ and $d(x, y) = 0$ if and only if $x = y$.
2. $d(x, y) = d(y, x)$ for all $x, y \in S$.
3. (Triangle inequality) $d(x, z) \leq d(x, y) + d(y, z)$ for all $x, y, z \in S$.

◊

Example 4.1.15 Euclidean metric.

The Euclidean metric is defined by $d(z, w) = |z - w|$. We have already shown that d is preserved under Euclidean transformations, and the first two conditions of being a metric follow directly from the definition of modulus. We establish the triangle inequality by direct computation in the following lemma.

Lemma 4.1.16 *For any points z, w, v in $\mathbb{C}$,*

$$|z - w| \leq |z - v| + |v - w|.$$

PROOF. If $v = w$ then the the result holds, so we assume $v \neq w$. Since d is invariant under Euclidean transformations, we may assume that $v = 0$ and $w = r > 0$ is a point on the positive real axis. (Translate the plane by $-v$ to send v to 0, and then rotate about 0 until the image of w under the translation lands on the positive real axis.) Thus, it's enough to show that for any complex number z and any positive real number r,

$$|z - r| \leq |z| + r.$$

Notice that

$$\begin{aligned} |z - r| \leq |z| + r &\iff |z - r|^2 \leq (|z| + r)^2 \\ &\iff (z - r)(\overline{z} - r) \leq |z|^2 + 2r|z| + r^2 \end{aligned}$$

$$\iff |z|^2 - r(z+\overline{z}) + r^2 \le |z|^2 + 2r|z| + r^2$$
$$\iff -(z+\overline{z}) \le 2|z|$$
$$\iff -2Re(z) \le 2|z|$$
$$\iff -Re(z) \le |z|.$$

By letting $z = a + bi$, we may restate the last inequality as

$$-a \le \sqrt{a^2+b^2},$$

which is true since $-a \le |a| = \sqrt{a^2} \le \sqrt{a^2+b^2}$. □

Exercises

1. Find a particular translation to prove that in Figure 4.1.7, p. 74 $H \cong L$ in translational geometry.

2. Let $\mathcal{A}$ be the set of all circles in $\mathbb{C}$ centered at the origin, and let G be the set of all inversions about circles in $\mathcal{A}$. That is,

$$G = \{i_C \mid C \in \mathcal{A}\}.$$

Is G a group of transformations of $\mathbb{C}^+$? Explain.

3. Prove that the group $\mathcal{E}$ of Euclidean transformations of $\mathbb{C}$ is indeed a group.

4. Let G be the set of all dilations of $\mathbb{C}^+$. That is

$$G = \{T(z) = kz \mid k \in \mathbb{R}, k > 0\}.$$

Is G a group of transformations of $\mathbb{C}^+$? Explain.

5. True or False? Determine whether the statement is true or false, and support your answer with an argument.

a. Any two lines are congruent in Euclidean geometry $(\mathbb{C}, \mathcal{E})$.

b. Any two circles are congruent in Euclidean geometry $(\mathbb{C}, \mathcal{E})$.

6. Prove that if a set of figures $\mathcal{D}$ is invariant in a geometry (S, G), and any two figures in $\mathcal{D}$ are congruent, then $\mathcal{D}$ is minimally invariant.

7. Describe a minimally invariant set of translational geometry that contains the figure D from Figure 4.1.7, p. 74.

8. **Rotational geometry** is the geometry $(\mathbb{C}, \mathcal{R})$ where $\mathcal{R}$ is the group of rotations about the origin. That is

$$\mathcal{R} = \{R_\theta(z) = e^{i\theta}z \mid \theta \in \mathbb{R}\}.$$

a. Prove that $\mathcal{R}$ is a group of transformations.

b. Is $\mathcal{D} = \{\text{all lines in } \mathbb{C}\}$ an invariant set in rotational geometry? Is it a minimally invariant set?

c. Find a minimally invariant set of rotational geometry that contains the circle $|z - (2+i)| = 4$.

d. Is $(\mathbb{C}, \mathcal{R})$ homogeneous? Isotropic?

9. Prove that the function $v(z_1, z_2) = z_1 - z_2$ is invariant in translational geometry $(\mathbb{C}, \mathcal{T})$ but not rotational geometry $(\mathbb{C}, \mathcal{R})$.

10. Prove that the following function is a metric for any geometry (S, G).

$$d(x,y) = \begin{cases} 0 & \text{if } x = y; \\ 1 & \text{if } x \neq y \end{cases}.$$

11. Prove that $(\mathbb{C}, \mathcal{E})$ is isotropic. That is, show the group $\mathcal{E}$ contains all rotations about all points in $\mathbb{C}$.

12. Which figures from Figure 4.1.7, p. 74 are congruent in $(\mathbb{C}, \mathcal{E})$?

13. Let's create a brand new geometry, using the set of integers $\mathbb{Z} = \{\ldots, -2, -1, 0, 1, 2, \ldots\}$ For each integer n, we define the transformation $T_n : \mathbb{C} \to \mathbb{C}$ by $T_n(z) = z + ni$. Let G denote the set of all transformations T_n for all integers n. That is, $G = \{T_n \mid n \in \mathbb{Z}\}$.

a. Prove that $(\mathbb{C}, G)$ is a geometry.

b. Consider the set of figures $\mathcal{D}$ consisting of all lines in the plane with slope 4. Is $\mathcal{D}$ an invariant set of $(\mathbb{C}, G)$? Is it minimally invariant? Explain.

c. My favorite line, for clear and personal reasons, is $y = x + 8$. Please describe a minimally invariant set of figures containing this line.

d. Determine the set of points in $\mathbb{C}$ congruent to i in this geometry. Is $\mathbb{C}$ homogeneous?

4.2 Möbius Geometry

We spent a fair amount of time studying Möbius transformations in Chapter 3, and this will pay dividends now.

Definition 4.2.1 Möbius Geometry is the geometry $(\mathbb{C}^+, \mathcal{M})$, where $\mathcal{M}$ denotes the group of all Möbius transformations. ◊

Without actually stating it, we essentially proved that $\mathcal{M}$ is a group of transformations. Namely, we proved that the inverse of a Möbius transformation is again a Möbius transformation, and that the composition of two Möbius transformations is a Möbius transformation. We remark that the identity map on $\mathbb{C}^+$, $T(z) = z$, is a Möbius transformation (of the form $T(z) = (az + b)/(cz + d)$, where $a = d = 1$, and $b = c = 0$), so $\mathcal{M}$ is a group.

Below we recast the key results from Chapter 3 in geometric terms:

- Any two clines are congruent in Möbius Geometry (Theorem 3.4.15, p. 59).
- The set of all clines is a minimally invariant set of Möbius Geometry (Theorems 3.4.5, p. 55 and Theorem 3.4.15, p. 59).
- The cross ratio is an invariant of Möbius Geometry (Theorem 3.4.12, p. 58).

- Angle measure is an invariant of Möbius Geometry (Theorem 3.4.5, p. 55).

While we're at it, let's restate three other facts about Möbius transformations:

- Any transformation in $\mathcal{M}$ is uniquely determined by the image of three points.
- If T in $\mathcal{M}$ is not the identity map, then T fixes exactly 1 or 2 points.
- Möbius transformations preserve symmetry points.

What else? Euclidean distance is not an invariant function of Möbius Geometry. To see this, one need look no further than the map $T(z) = 1/z$. If $p = 2$ and $q = 3$ (two points on the real axis) then $d(p, q) = |p - q| = 1$. However, their image points $T(p) = 1/2$ and $T(q) = 1/3$ have a Euclidean distance between them of $1/6$. So our old-fashioned notion of distance goes out the window in Möbius geometry.

We emphasize that angles *are preserved* in Möbius geometry, which is a good thing. Why is this a good thing? Remember that in the distant past, humanity set out looking for a geometry in which Euclid's first 4 postulates hold true, but the 5th one fails. The 4th postulate states that all right angles equal one another. This means that if Ralph is holding a right angle over in the corner, and Randy is holding one down the block somewhere, we ought to be able to transform one onto the other and see that the angles are the same. Transformations do not change angles.

Rather than pursue the very general Möbius geometry, we take the preceeding facts and apply them straight away to two of its special "subgeometries," hyperbolic geometry and elliptic geometry.

Exercises

1. Which figures in Figure 4.2.2, p. 80 are congruent in $(\mathbb{C}^+, \mathcal{M})$.

2. Describe a minimally invariant set in $(\mathbb{C}^+, \mathcal{M})$ containing the "triangle" comprised of the three vertices 0, 1, and i and the three Euclidean line segments connecting them. Be as specific as possible about the members of this set.

3. Suppose p and q are distinct, finite points in $\mathbb{C}^+$. Let G consist of all elliptic Möbius transformations that fix p and q. We consider the geometry $(\mathbb{C}^+, G)$.

a. Show that G is a group of transformations.

b. Determine a minimally invariant set in $(\mathbb{C}^+, G)$ that contains the Euclidean line through p and q.

c. Determine a minimally invariant set in $(\mathbb{C}^+, G)$ that contains the perpendicular bisector of segment pq.

d. For any point $z \neq p, q$ in $\mathbb{C}^+$, characterize all points in $\mathbb{C}^+$ congruent to z.

e. Is $(\mathbb{C}^+, G)$ homogeneous?

4. Repeat the previous exercise for the set G consisting of all hyperbolic Möbius transformations that fix p and q.

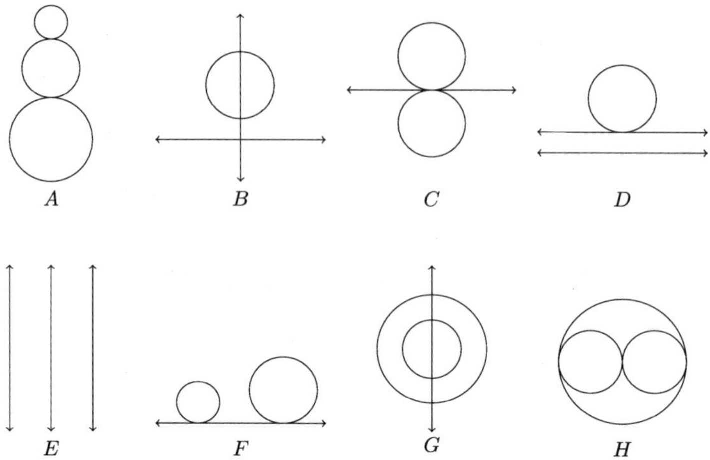

Figure 4.2.2 Which of these figures are congruent in $(\mathbb{C}^+, \mathcal{M})$?

5

Hyperbolic Geometry

Hyperbolic geometry can be modelled in many different ways. We will focus here on the Poincaré disk model, developed by Henri Poincaré (1854-1912) in around 1880. Poincaré did remarkable work in mathematics, though he was never actually a professor of mathematics. He was particularly interested in the relationship between mathematics, physics, and psychology. He began studying non-Euclidean geometry in detail after it appeared in his study of two apparently unrelated disciplines: differential equations and number theory.[1] Poincaré took Klein's view that geometries are generated by sets and groups of transformations on them. We consider a second model of hyperbolic geometry, the upper half-plane model, in Section 5.5.

5.1 The Poincaré Disk Model

Definition 5.1.1 The **Poincaré disk model for hyperbolic geometry** is the pair $(\mathbb{D}, \mathcal{H})$ where $\mathbb{D}$ consists of all points z in $\mathbb{C}$ such that $|z| < 1$, and $\mathcal{H}$ consists of all Möbius transformations T for which $T(\mathbb{D}) = \mathbb{D}$. The set $\mathbb{D}$ is called the **hyperbolic plane**, and $\mathcal{H}$ is called the **transformation group in hyperbolic geometry.** ◊

We note that $\mathcal{H}$ does indeed form a group of transformations, a fact that is worked out in the exercises. Throughout this chapter the unit circle will be called **the circle at infinity**, denoted by $\mathbb{S}^1_\infty$. Of course, the circle at infinity is not included in the hyperbolic plane $\mathbb{D}$ but bounds it. The circle at infinity will be used extensively in our investigations. We note here that any Möbius transformation that sends $\mathbb{D}$ to itself also sends $\mathbb{S}^1_\infty$ to itself.

[1] See Arthur Miller's chapter in [13] for a discussion of Poincaré's diverse interests.

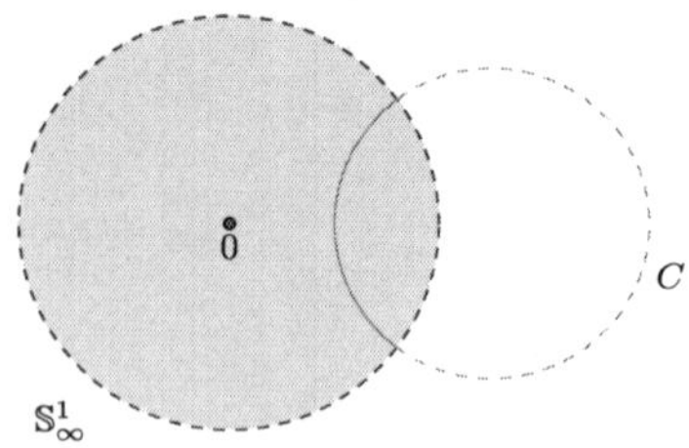

Figure 5.1.2 Inversion about a cline orthogonal to the unit circle takes $\mathbb{D}$ to $\mathbb{D}$.

Consider a cline C that is orthogonal to the circle at infinity $\mathbb{S}^1_\infty$, as in Figure 5.1.2, p. 82. If we invert about C, $\mathbb{S}^1_\infty$ is inverted to itself. Moreover, this inversion takes the interior of $\mathbb{S}^1_\infty$, namely the hyperbolic plane $\mathbb{D}$, to itself as well, (Exercise 3.2.10, p. **??**). It follows that compositions of two such inversions is a Möbius transformation that sends $\mathbb{D}$ to itself, and is thus in the group $\mathcal{H}$. These inversions play an important role in hyperbolic geometry, and we give them a name.

An inversion in a cline C that is orthogonal to $\mathbb{S}^1_\infty$ is called a **reflection of the hyperbolic plane**, or, a **hyperbolic reflection**.

It turns out that these reflections generate all the maps in $\mathcal{H}$. For instance, rotation about the origin is a Möbius transformation that sends $\mathbb{D}$ to itself, so it is in $\mathcal{H}$. But rotation about the origin is also the composition of two reflections about lines that intersect at the origin. Since any line through the origin meets the unit circle at right angles, reflection about such a line is a reflection of the hyperbolic plane, so rotation about the origin is the composition of two such reflections. We now prove the following general result.

Theorem 5.1.3 *Any Möbius transformation in $\mathcal{H}$ is the composition of two reflections of the hyperbolic plane.*

PROOF. Suppose T is a Möbius transformation that sends $\mathbb{D}$ to itself. This means some point in $\mathbb{D}$, say z_0, gets sent to the origin, 0. Let z_0^* be the point symmetric to z_0 with respect to $\mathbb{S}^1_\infty$. Since T sends the unit circle to itself, and Möbius transformations preserve symmetry points, it follows that T sends z_0^* to ∞. Furthermore, some point z_1 on $\mathbb{S}^1_\infty$ gets sent to the point 1.

If $z_0 = 0$, then $z_0^* = \infty$, and T fixes 0 and ∞. Then by Example 3.5.3, p. 61, $T(z) = re^{i\theta}z$ is a dilation followed by a rotation. However, since T also sends $\mathbb{D}$ onto $\mathbb{D}$, the dilation factor must be $r = 1$. So T is simply a rotation about the origin, which is the composition of two hyperbolic reflections about Euclidean lines through the origin.

Now assume $z_0 \neq 0$. In this case, by using z_0, z_0^*, and z_1 as anchors, we may achieve T via two hyperbolic reflections, as follows:

First, invert about a circle C orthogonal to $\mathbb{S}^1_\infty$ that sends z_0 to the origin.

Such a circle does indeed exist, and we will construct it now. As in Figure 5.1.4, p. 83, draw circle C_1 with diameter $0z_0^*$. Let p be a point of intersection of C_1 and the unit circle $\mathbb{S}^1_\infty$. Construct the circle C through p centered at z_0^*. Since $\angle 0pz_0^*$ is right, $\mathbb{S}^1_\infty$ is orthogonal to C, so inversion about C sends $\mathbb{S}^1_\infty$ to itself. Furthermore, since z_0^* gets sent to ∞ and symmetry points must be preserved, inversion in C sends z_0 to 0.

Thus, the first inversion takes z_0 to 0 and z_0^* to ∞. To build T we must also send z_1 to 1. Note that inversion in circle C will have sent z_1 to some point z_1' on the unit circle (since $\mathbb{S}^1_\infty$ is sent to itself). Now reflect across the line through the origin that bisects angle $\angle 10z_1'$. This sends z_1' to 1, sends $\mathbb{D}$ to $\mathbb{D}$, and leaves 0 and ∞ fixed. Composing these two inversions yields a Möbius transformation that sends z_0 to 0, z_0^* to ∞ and z_1 to 1. Since a Möbius transformation is uniquely determined by the image of three points, this Möbius transformation is T. □

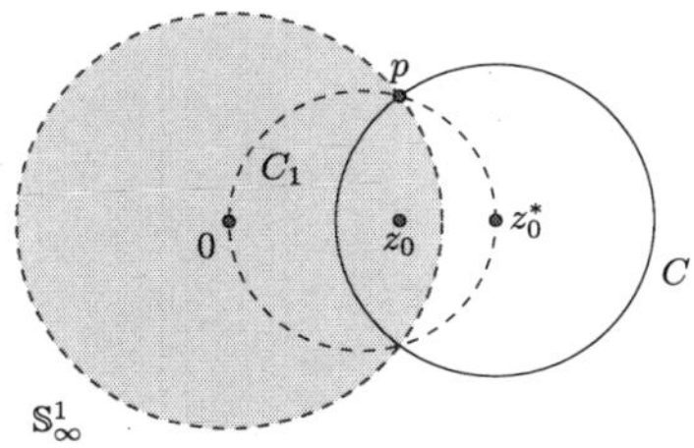

Figure 5.1.4 Constructing a circle C orthogonal to $\mathbb{S}^1_\infty$ about which z_0 is inverted to 0.

Notice that in proving Theorem 5.1.3, p. 82 we proved the following useful fact.

Lemma 5.1.5 *Given z_0 in $\mathbb{D}$ and z_1 on $\mathbb{S}^1_\infty$ there exists a transformation in $\mathcal{H}$ that sends z_0 to 0 and z_1 to* 1.

Therefore, one may view any transformation in $\mathcal{H}$ as the composition of two inversions about clines orthogonal to $\mathbb{S}^1_\infty$. Moreover, these maps may be categorized according to whether the two clines of inversion intersect zero times, once, or twice. In Figure 5.1.6, p. 84 we illustrate these three cases. In each case, we build a transformation T in $\mathcal{H}$ by inverting about the solid clines in the figure (first about L_1, then about L_2). The figure also tracks the journey of a point z under these inversions, first to z' by inverting about L_1, then onto $T(z)$ by inverting z' about L_2. The dashed clines in the figure represent some of the clines of motion, the clines along which points are moved by the transformation. Notice these clines of motion are orthogonal to *both* clines of inversion. Let's work through the three cases in some detail.

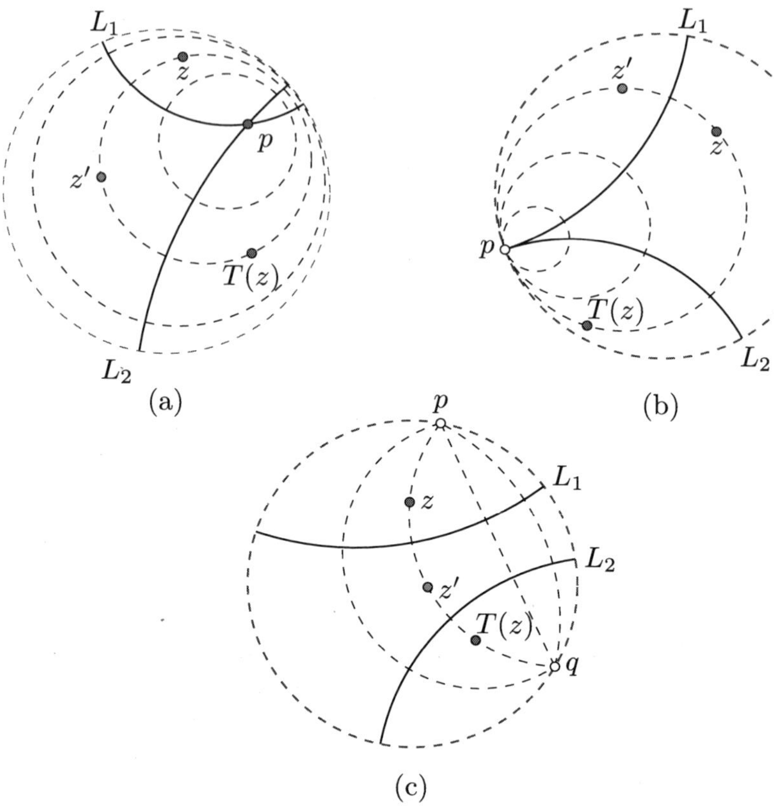

Figure 5.1.6 The three types of transformations in $\mathcal{H}$: (a) hyperbolic rotation (b) parallel displacement (c) hyperbolic translation.

If the two clines of inversion, L_1 and L_2, intersect inside $\mathbb{D}$, say at the point p, then they also intersect outside $\mathbb{D}$ at the point p^* symmetric to p with respect to the unit circle since both clines are orthogonal to $\mathbb{S}^1_\infty$. This scene is shown in Figure 5.1.6, p. 84(a). The resulting Möbius transformation will fix p (and p^*), causing a rotation of points in $\mathbb{D}$ around p along type II clines of p and p^*. Not surprisingly, we will call this type of map in $\mathcal{H}$ a **rotation of the hyperbolic plane** about the point p; or, if the context is clear, we call such a map a rotation about p.

If the clines of inversion intersect just once, then it must be at a point p on the unit circle. Otherwise the symmetric point p^*, which would be distinct from p, would also belong to both clines, giving us two points of intersection. The resulting map moves points along circles in $\mathbb{D}$ that are tangent to the unit circle at this point p. Circles in $\mathbb{D}$ that are tangent to the unit circle are called **horocycles**, and this type of map is called a **parallel displacement.** See Figure 5.1.6, p. 84(b).

If the clines of inversion do not intersect, then at least one of the clines must be a circle; and according to Theorem 3.2.16, p. 46, there are two points p and q symmetric with respect to both clines. These two points will be fixed by the resulting Möbius transformation, since each inversion sends p to q and q to p. Furthermore, these two fixed points must live on the unit circle by a symmetric points argument (the details of which are left as an exercise). In other words, if the clines of inversion L_1 and L_2 do not intersect, then they are type II clines of the fixed points p and q of the resulting transformation in $\mathcal{H}$. Moreover, this transformation will push points along type I clines of p and q. We call such a Möbius transformation in $\mathcal{H}$ a **translation of the hyperbolic plane** or, simply, a *translation*. See Figure 5.1.6, p. 84(c).

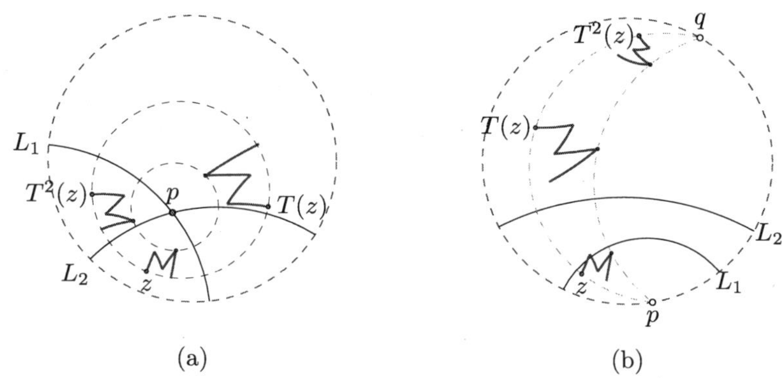

Figure 5.1.7 Moving an 'M' about the hyperbolic plane, by (a) rotation about p; and (b) translation fixing ideal points p and q.

Example 5.1.8 Moving an 'M' around in $(\mathbb{D}, \mathcal{H})$.

Figure 5.1.7, p. 85(a) depicts the image of the figure M (resembling the letter 'M') under two applications of a rotation T of the hyperbolic plane about point p. This rotation is generated by two inversions about clines L_1 and L_2 that intersect at p (and meet $\mathbb{S}^1_\infty$ at right angles). The figure M is pictured, as is $T(M)$ and $T(T(M))$. The figure also tracks successive images of a point z on M: z gets mapped to $T(z)$ which gets mapped to $T^2(z) = T(T(z))$. By this map T, any point z in $\mathbb{D}$ rotates around p along the unique type II cline of p and p^* that contains z.

Figure 5.1.7, p. 85(b) depicts the image of M under two applications of a translation of the hyperbolic plane. The translation is generated by two inversions about non-intersecting clines L_1 and L_2 (that meet $\mathbb{S}^1_\infty$ at right angles). The fixed points of the map are the points p and q on the circle at infinity. Under this translation, any point z in $\mathbb{D}$ heads away from p and toward q on the unique cline through the three points p, q, and z.

We now derive the following algebraic description of transformations in $\mathcal{H}$:

Transformations in $\mathcal{H}$.

Any transformation T in the group $\mathcal{H}$ has the form

$$T(z) = e^{i\theta}\frac{z - z_0}{1 - \overline{z}_0 z}$$

where θ is some angle, and z_0 is the point inside $\mathbb{D}$ that gets sent to 0.

Assume z_0 is in $\mathbb{D}$, z_1 is on the unit circle $\mathbb{S}^1_\infty$, and that the map T in $\mathcal{H}$ sends $z_0 \mapsto 0$, $z_0^* \mapsto \infty$ and $z_1 \mapsto 1$. Using the cross ratio,

$$T(z) = (z, z_1; z_0, z_0^*) = \frac{z_1 - z_0^*}{z_1 - z_0} \cdot \frac{z - z_0}{z - z_0^*}.$$

But $z_0^* = \frac{1}{\overline{z_0}}$, so

$$T(z) = \frac{z_1 - 1/\overline{z_0}}{z_1 - z_0} \cdot \frac{z - z_0}{z - 1/\overline{z_0}} = \frac{\overline{z_0}z_1 - 1}{z_1 - z_0} \cdot \frac{z - z_0}{\overline{z_0}z - 1}.$$

Now, the quantity

$$\frac{\overline{z_0}z_1 - 1}{z_1 - z_0}$$

is a complex constant, and it has modulus equal to 1. To see this, observe that since $1 = |z_1|^2 = z_1\overline{z_1}$,

$$\begin{aligned} \frac{\overline{z_0}z_1 - 1}{z_1 - z_0} &= \frac{\overline{z_0}z_1 - z_1\overline{z_1}}{z_1 - z_0} \\ &= \frac{-z_1(\overline{z_1 - z_0})}{z_1 - z_0}. \end{aligned}$$

Since $|z_1| = 1$ and, in general $|\beta| = |\overline{\beta}|$ we see that this expression has modulus 1, and can be expressed as $e^{i\theta}$ for some θ. Thus, if T is a transformation in $\mathcal{H}$ it may be expressed as

$$T(z) = e^{i\theta}\frac{z - z_0}{1 - \overline{z}_0 z}$$

where θ is some angle, and z_0 is the point inside $\mathbb{D}$ that gets sent to 0.

Is the converse true? Is every transformation in the form above actually a member of $\mathcal{H}$? The answer is yes, and the reader is asked to work through the details in the exercises.

Exercises

1. Prove that $(\mathbb{D}, \mathcal{H})$ is homogeneous.

2. Suppose T is a Möbius transformation of the form

$$T(z) = e^{i\theta}\frac{z - z_0}{1 - \overline{z}_0 z},$$

where z_0 is in $\mathbb{D}$. Prove that T maps $\mathbb{D}$ to $\mathbb{D}$ by showing that if $|z| < 1$ then $|T(z)| < 1$.

3. Construct the fixed points of the hyperbolic translation defined by the inversion of two nonintersecting clines that intersect $\mathbb{S}^1_\infty$ at right angles, as shown in the following diagram.

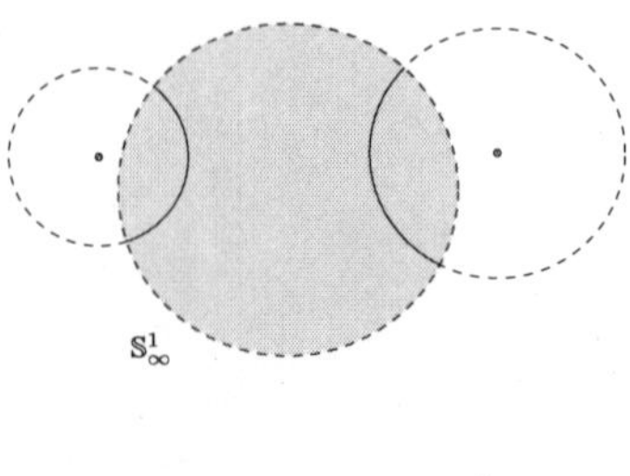

4. Suppose p and q are two points in $\mathbb{D}$. Construct two clines orthogonal to $\mathbb{S}^1_\infty$ that, when inverted about in composition, send p to 0 and q to the positive real axis.

5. Prove that any two horocycles in $(\mathbb{D}, \mathcal{H})$ are congruent.

6. Prove that $\mathcal{H}$ is a group of transformations.

5.2 Figures of Hyperbolic Geometry

The Euclidean transformation group, $\mathcal{E}$, consisting of all (Euclidean) rotations and translations, is generated by reflections about Euclidean lines. Similarly, the transformations in $\mathcal{H}$ are generated by hyperbolic reflections, which are inversions about clines that intersect the unit circle at right angles. This suggests that these clines ought to be the lines of hyperbolic geometry.

Definition 5.2.1 A **hyperbolic line** in $(\mathbb{D}, \mathcal{H})$ is the portion of a cline inside $\mathbb{D}$ that is orthogonal to the circle at infinity $\mathbb{S}^1_\infty$. A point on $\mathbb{S}^1_\infty$ is called an **ideal point**. Two hyperbolic lines are **parallel** if they share one ideal point. ◊

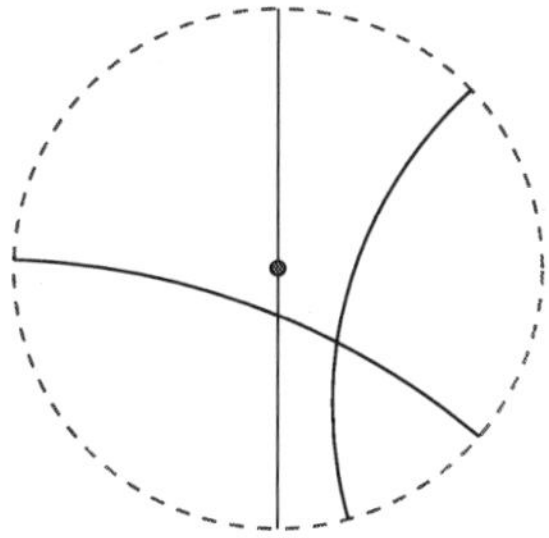

Figure 5.2.2 A few hyperbolic lines in the Poincaré disk model.

Theorem 5.2.3 *There exists a unique hyperbolic line through any two distinct points in the hyperbolic plane.*

Proof. Let p and q be arbitrary points in $\mathbb{D}$. Construct the point p^* symmetric to p with respect to the unit circle, $\mathbb{S}^1_\infty$. Then there exists a cline through p, q and p^*, and this cline will be orthogonal to $\mathbb{S}^1_\infty$, so it gives a hyperbolic line through p and q. Since there is just one cline through p, q and p^*, this hyperbolic line is unique. □

Which hyperbolic lines happen to be portions of Euclidean lines (instead of Euclidean circles)? A Euclidean line intersects a circle at right angles if and only if it goes through the center of the circle. Thus, the only hyperbolic lines that also happen to be Euclidean lines are those that go through the origin.

One may also use a symmetric points argument to arrive at this last fact. Any Euclidean line goes through ∞. To be a hyperbolic line (i.e., to be orthogonal to $\mathbb{S}^1_\infty$), the line must also pass through the point symmetric to ∞ with respect to the unit circle. This point is 0. Thus, to be a *hyperbolic* line in $(\mathbb{D}, \mathcal{H})$, a Euclidean line must go through the origin.

Theorem 5.2.4 *Any two hyperbolic lines are congruent in hyperbolic geometry.*

PROOF. We first show that any given hyperbolic line L is congruent to the hyperbolic line on the real axis. Suppose p is a point on L, and v is one of its ideal points. By Lemma 5.1.5, p. 83 there is a transformation T in $\mathcal{H}$ that maps p to 0, v to 1, and p^* to ∞. Thus $T(L)$ is the portion of the real axis inside $\mathbb{D}$, and L is congruent to the hyperbolic line on the real axis. Since any hyperbolic line is congruent to the hyperbolic line on the real axis, the group nature of $\mathcal{H}$ ensures that any two hyperbolic lines are congruent. □

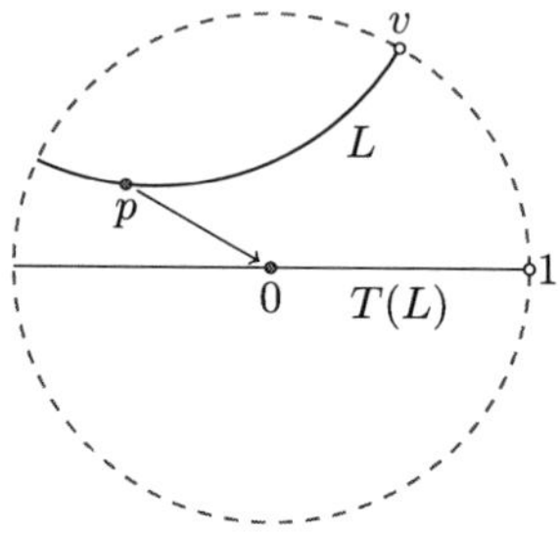

Figure 5.2.5 Any hyperbolic line is congruent to the hyperbolic line on the real axis.

Theorem 5.2.6 *Given a point z_0 and a hyperbolic line L not through z_0, there exist two distinct hyperbolic lines through z_0 that are parallel to L.*

PROOF. Consider the case where z_0 is at the origin. The line L has two ideal points, call them u and v, as in Figure 5.2.7, p. 88. Moreover, since L does not go through the origin, Euclidean segment uv is not a diameter of the unit circle. Construct one Euclidean line through 0 and u, and a second Euclidean line through 0 and v. (These lines will be distinct because uv is not a diameter of the unit circle.) Each of these lines is a hyperbolic line through 0, and each shares exactly one ideal point with L. Thus, each is parallel to L. The fact that the result holds for general z_0 is left as an exercise. □

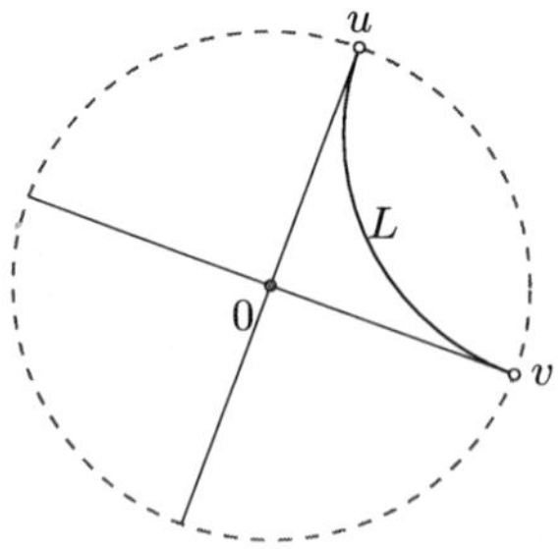

Figure 5.2.7 Through a point not on a given hyperbolic line L there exist two hyperbolic lines parallel to L.

Figure 5.2.7, p. 88 illustrates an unusual feature of parallel lines in hyperbolic geometry: there is no notion of *transitivity*. In Euclidean geometry we know that if line L is parallel to line M, and line M is parallel to line N, then line L is parallel to line N. This is not the case in hyperbolic geometry.

Example 5.2.8 Hyperbolic triangles.

Three points in the hyperbolic plane $\mathbb{D}$ that are not all on a single hyperbolic line determine a hyperbolic triangle. The hyperbolic triangle Δpqr is pictured below. The sides of the triangle are portions of hyperbolic lines.

Are all hyperbolic triangles congruent? No. Since transformations in $\mathcal{H}$ are Möbius transformations they preserve angles, so triangles with different angles are not congruent.

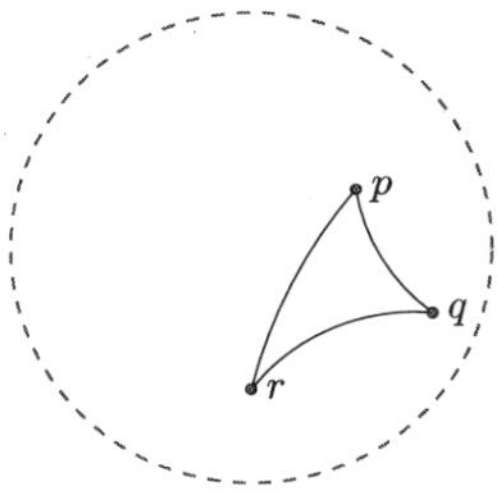

The next section develops a distance function for the hyperbolic plane. As in Euclidean geometry, we want to be able to compute the distance between two points, the length of a path, the area of a region, and so on. Moreover, the distance function should be an invariant; the distance between points should not change under a transformation in $\mathcal{H}$. With this in mind, consider again a hyperbolic rotation about a point p, as in Figure 5.1.6, p. 84(a). It fixes the point p and moves points around type II clines of p and p^*. If the distance between points is unchanged under transformations in $\mathcal{H}$, then all points on a given type II cline of p and p^* will be the same distance away from p. This leads us to define a hyperbolic circle as follows.

Definition 5.2.9 Suppose p is any point in $\mathbb{D}$, and p^* is the point symmetric to p with respect to the unit circle. A **hyperbolic circle centered at *p*** is a Euclidean circle C inside $\mathbb{D}$ that is a type II circle of p and p^*. ◊

Figure 5.2.10, p. 89 shows a typical hyperbolic circle. This circle is centered at point p and contains point q. Construction of such a circle may be achieved with compass and ruler as in Exercise 5.2.5, p. ??.

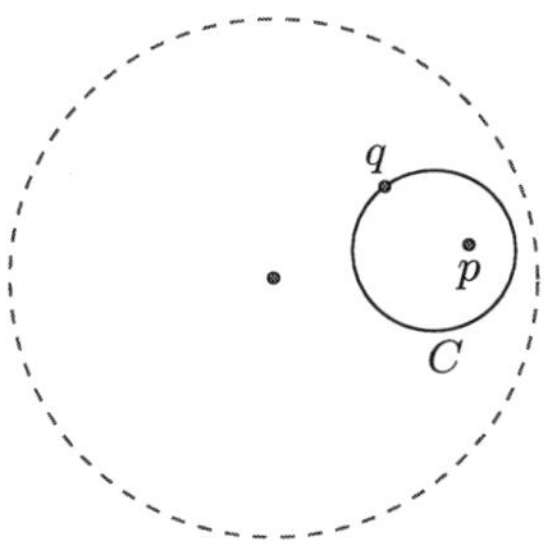

Figure 5.2.10 A hyperbolic circle centered at p through q.

Theorem 5.2.11 *Given any points p and q in $\mathbb{D}$, there exists a hyperbolic circle centered at p through q.*

PROOF. Given $p, q \in \mathbb{D}$, construct p^*, the point symmetric to p with respect to $\mathbb{S}^1_\infty$. Then by Exercise 3.5.15, p. ?? there exists a type II cline of p and p^* that goes through q. This type II cline lives within $\mathbb{D}$ because $\mathbb{S}^1_\infty$ is also a type II cline of p and p^*, and distinct type II clines cannot intersect. This type II cline is the hyperbolic circle centered at p through q. □

Exercises

1. Suppose C is a hyperbolic circle centered at z_0 through point p. Show that there exists a hyperbolic line L tangent to C at p, and that L is perpendicular to hyperbolic segment z_0p.

2. *Constructing a hyperbolic line through two given points.*

   a. Given a point p in $\mathbb{D}$, construct the point p^* symmetric to p with respect to the unit circle (see Figure 3.2.18, p. 48).

   b. Suppose q is a second point in $\mathbb{D}$. Construct the cline through p, q, and p^*. Call this cline C. Explain why C intersects the unit circle at right angles.

   c. Consider the portion of cline C you constructed in part (b) that lies in $\mathbb{D}$. This is the unique hyperbolic line through p and q. Mark the ideal points of this hyperbolic line.

3. Can two distinct hyperbolic lines be tangent at some point in $\mathbb{D}$? Explain.

4. Suppose L is a hyperbolic line that is part of a circle C. Can the origin of the complex plane be in the interior of C? Explain.

5. *Constructing a hyperbolic circle centered at a point p through a point q.*

   Suppose p and q are two points in $\mathbb{D}$, and that q is not on the line through p and p^* - the point symmetric to p with respect to the unit circle.

   a. Find the center of the Euclidean circle through p, p^*, and q. Call the center point o.

   b. Construct the segment oq.

   c. Construct the perpendicular to oq at q. This perpendicular intersects the Euclidean line through p and p^*. Call the intersection point o'.

   d. Construct the Euclidean circle centered at o' through q.

   e. Prove that this circle is the hyperbolic circle through q centered at p.

6. Explain why Theorem 5.2.6, p. 88 applies in the general case, when z_0 is not at the origin.

7. Given a point and a hyperbolic line not passing through it, prove that there is a hyperbolic line through the point that is perpendicular to the given line. Is this perpendicular unique?

5.3 Measurement in Hyperbolic Geometry

In this section we develop a notion of distance in the hyperbolic plane. If someone is standing at point p and wants to get to point q, he or she should be able to say how far it is to get there, whatever the route taken.

The distance formula is derived following the approach given in Section 30 of Boas' text [2]. We first list features our distance function ought to have, and use the notation that $d_H(p,q)$ represents the hyperbolic distance from p to q in the hyperbolic plane $\mathbb{D}$.

1. The distance between 2 distinct points should be positive.

2. The shortest path between 2 points should be on the hyperbolic line connecting them.

3. If p, q, and r are three points on a hyperbolic line with q between the other two then $d_H(p,q) + d_H(q,r) = d_H(p,r)$.

4. Distance should be preserved by transformations in $\mathcal{H}$. (A lunch pail shouldn't shrink if it is moved to another table.) In other words, the distance formula should satisfy

$$d_H(p,q) = d_H(T(p), T(q))$$

   for any points p and q in $\mathbb{D}$, and any transformation T in $\mathcal{H}$.

5. In the limit for small distances, hyperbolic distance should be proportional to Euclidean distance.

Perhaps the least obvious of the features listed is the last one. One theme of this text is that locally, on small scales, non-Euclidean geometry behaves much like Euclidean geometry. A small segment in the hyperbolic plane is approximated to the first order by a Euclidean segment. Small hyperbolic triangles look like Euclidean triangles and hyperbolic angles correspond to Euclidean angles; the hyperbolic distance formula will fit with this theme.

To find the distance function, start with a point's distance from the origin. Given a point z in $\mathbb{D}$, rotate about 0 so that z gets sent to the point $x = |z|$ on the positive real axis.

We may find a hyperbolic line L about which x gets reflected to the origin. Such a hyperbolic line is constructed in the proof of Theorem 5.1.3, p. 82. Recall, the line L is on the circle centered at x^* (the point symmetric to x with respect to to $\mathbb{S}^1_\infty$) that goes through the points at which $\mathbb{S}^1_\infty$ intersects the circle with diameter $0x^*$. Let $x+h$ be a point near x on the positive real axis, and suppose $x+h$ gets inverted to the point w, as depicted in Figure 5.3.1, p. 92. One can show (in Exercise 5.3.1, p. ??) that

$$w = \frac{-h}{1 - x^2 - hx}.$$

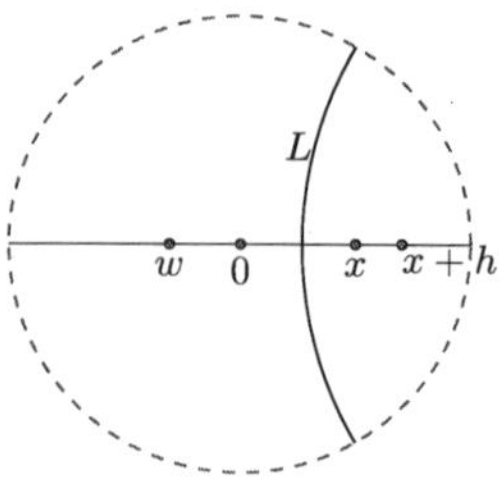

Figure 5.3.1 Reflection of the hyperbolic plane sending x to 0 and $x + h$ to w.

If distance is to be preserved by transformations in $\mathcal{H}$,

$$d_H(x, x + h) = d_H(0, w). \tag{1}$$

Also, $0, x$, and $x + h$ are all on the same hyperbolic line (the real axis), so assuming $h > 0$

$$d_H(0, x) + d_H(x, x + h) = d_H(0, x + h). \tag{2}$$

For $x \in \mathbb{R}$ define the function $d(x) = d_H(0, x)$ which is the hyperbolic distance of x to the origin. Then (2) and (1) may be combined to give

$$d(x + h) - d(x) = d(w).$$

Divide both sides by h to get

$$\frac{d(x + h) - d(x)}{h} = \frac{d(w)}{h}.$$

As $h \to 0$ we obtain

$$d'(x) = \lim_{h \to 0} \frac{d(w)}{h}.$$

We now interrupt this derivation with an important point. In the limit for small w, the hyperbolic distance of w from 0, $d(w)$, is proportional to the Euclidean distance $|w - 0| = |w|$. Since w is the image of $x + h$ under the inversion and x gets inverted to 0, it follows that $w \to 0$ as $h \to 0$. So, we assume that

$$\lim_{h \to 0} \frac{d(w)}{|w|} = k$$

for some constant k. Following convention, we set the constant of proportionality to $k = 2$, as this makes length and area formulas look very nice later on. Now, back to the derivation.

$$\begin{aligned} d'(x) &= \lim_{h \to 0} \frac{d(w)}{h} \\ &= \lim_{h \to 0} \frac{d(w)}{|w|} \frac{|w|}{h} \\ &= \lim_{h \to 0} \left[2 \cdot \frac{h}{(1 - x^2 - hx)h} \right] \\ &= \frac{2}{1 - x^2}. \end{aligned}$$

To get back to the distance function $d(x)$ we integrate:

$$\int \frac{2}{1 - x^2}\, dx = \int \left(\frac{1}{1 - x} + \frac{1}{1 + x} \right) dx \qquad \text{(partial fractions)}$$

$$
\begin{aligned}
&= -\ln(1-x) + \ln(1+x) \\
d(x) &= \ln\left(\frac{1+x}{1-x}\right),
\end{aligned}
$$

so we arrive at the following distance formula.

The hyperbolic distance from 0 to z.

The hyperbolic distance from 0 to a point z in $\mathbb{D}$ is

$$d_H(0,z) = \ln\left(\frac{1+|z|}{1-|z|}\right).$$

Notice that if z inches its way in $\mathbb{D}$ out toward the circle at infinity (i.e., $|z| \to 1$), the hyperbolic distance from 0 to z approaches ∞. This is a good thing. Thinking of Euclid's postulates, this notion of distance satisfies one of our fundamental requirements: *One can produce a hyperbolic segment to any finite length.*

To arrive at a general distance formula $d_H(p,q)$, observe something curious. The hyperbolic line through 0 and x has ideal points -1 and 1. Furthermore, the expression $(1+x)/(1-x)$ corresponds to the cross ratio of the points 0, x, 1, and -1. In particular,

$$(0, x; 1, -1) = \frac{0-1}{0+1} \cdot \frac{x+1}{x-1} = \frac{1+x}{1-x}.$$

Thus,

$$d_H(0,x) = \ln((0,x;1,-1)).$$

We can now derive a general distance formula, assuming the invariance of distance under transformations in $\mathcal{H}$. There is a transformation T in $\mathcal{H}$ that takes p to the origin and q to some spot on the positive real-axis, call this spot x (see Figure 5.3.2, p. 94). Thus,

$$
\begin{aligned}
d_H(p,q) &= d_H(T(p), T(q)) && \text{(invariance of distance)} \\
&= d_H(0,x) \\
&= \ln((0,x;1,-1)) \\
&= \ln((p,q;u,v)), && \text{(invariance of cross ratio)}
\end{aligned}
$$

where u and v are the ideal points of the hyperbolic line through p and q. To be precise, u is the ideal point you would head toward as you went from p to q, and v is the ideal point you would head toward as you went from q to p.

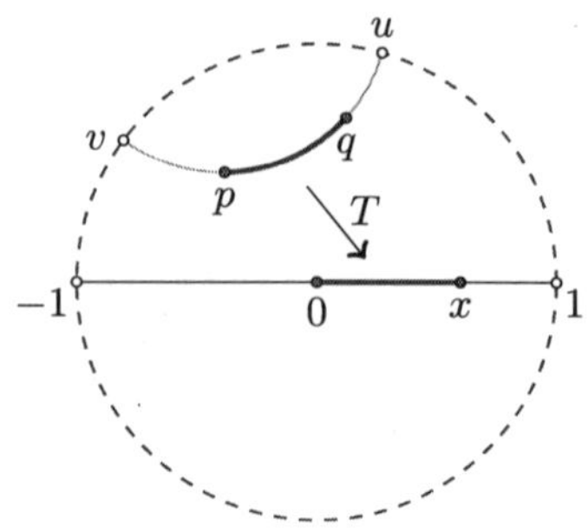

Figure 5.3.2 To find the distance between p and q, we may first transform p to 0 and q to the positive real axis.

A working formula for $\mathbf{d_H(p, q)}$

One may compute the hyperbolic distance between p and q by first finding the ideal points u and v of the hyperbolic line through p and q and then using the formula $d_H(p,q) = \ln((p,q;u,v))$. In practice, finding coordinates for these ideal points can be a difficult task, and it is often simpler to compute the distance between points by first moving one of them to the origin. (This simpler approach uses the fact that hyperbolic distance is preserved under transformations in $\mathcal{H}$. This fact will be proved shortly.)

One transformation in $\mathcal{H}$ that sends p to 0 has the form

$$T(z) = \frac{z - p}{1 - \overline{p}z}.$$

The map T sends q to some other point, $T(q)$, in $\mathbb{D}$. Assuming again that T preserves distance, it follows that $d_H(p,q) = d_H(0, T(q))$, and

$$d_H(p,q) = \ln\left(\frac{1 + |T(q)|}{1 - |T(q)|}\right).$$

Making the substitution $T(q) = \dfrac{q - p}{1 - \overline{p}q}$ provides us with the following working formula for the hyperbolic distance between two points.

Theorem 5.3.3 *Given two points p and q in $\mathbb{D}$, the hyperbolic distance between them is*

$$d_H(p,q) = \ln\left[\frac{|1 - \overline{p}q| + |q - p|}{|1 - \overline{p}q| - |q - p|}\right].$$

Example 5.3.4 The distance between two points.

For instance, suppose $p = \frac{1}{2}i$, $q = \frac{1}{2} + \frac{1}{2}i$, $z = .95e^{i5\pi/6}$ and $w = -.95$. Then $d_H(p,q) \approx 1.49$ units, while $d_H(z,w) \approx 4.64$ units.

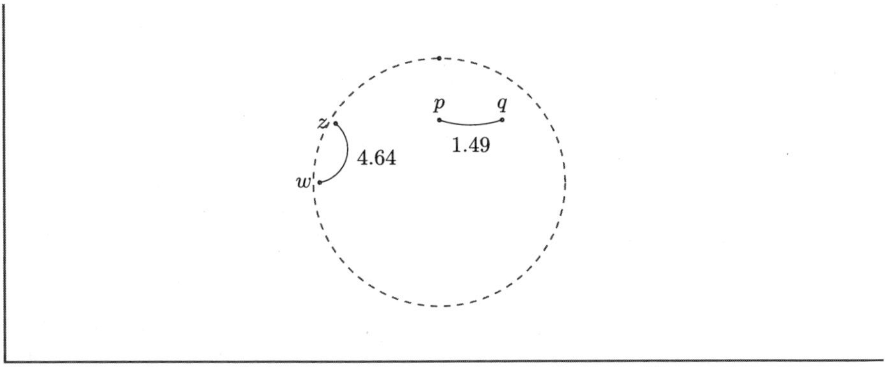

The arc-length differential

Now that we can compute the distance between two points in the hyperbolic plane, we turn our attention to measuring the length of *any path* that takes us from p to q.

Definition 5.3.5 **A smooth curve** is a differentiable map from an interval of real numbers to the plane

$$\boldsymbol{r} : [a, b] \to \mathbb{C}$$

such that $\boldsymbol{r}'(t)$ exists for all t and never equals 0. ◊

In the spirit of this text, we write $\boldsymbol{r}(t) = x(t) + iy(t)$, in which case $\boldsymbol{r}'(t) = x'(t) + iy'(t)$.

Recall that in calculus we first approximate the Euclidean length of a given smooth curve $\boldsymbol{r}(t) = x(t) + iy(t)$ by summing the contributions of small straight line segments having Euclidean length

$$\begin{aligned}
\Delta s &= |\boldsymbol{r}(t + \Delta t) - \boldsymbol{r}(t)| \\
&= \sqrt{[x(t + \Delta t) - x(t)]^2 + [y(t + \Delta t) - y(t)]^2} \\
&= \sqrt{\left[\frac{x(t + \Delta t) - x(t)}{\Delta t}\right]^2 + \left[\frac{y(t + \Delta t) - y(t)}{\Delta t}\right]^2} |\Delta t|.
\end{aligned}$$

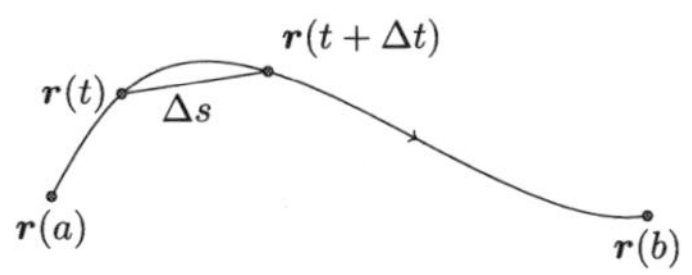

As $\Delta t \to 0$ we obtain the Euclidean arc-length differential

$$ds = \sqrt{(dx/dt)^2 + (dy/dt)^2}\, dt,$$

which may be expressed as

$$ds = |\boldsymbol{r}'(t)|\, dt.$$

For instance, we may compute the (Euclidean) circumference of a circle with radius a as follows. Consider $\boldsymbol{r} : [0, 2\pi] \to \mathbb{C}$ by $\boldsymbol{r}(t) = a\cos(t) + ia\sin(t)$. This map traces a circle of radius a centered at the origin. To find the length of this curve, which we denote as $\mathcal{L}(\boldsymbol{r})$, compute the integral

$$\mathcal{L}(\boldsymbol{r}) = \int_0^{2\pi} |\boldsymbol{r}'(t)|\, dt$$

$$\begin{aligned}&= \int_0^{2\pi} |-a\sin(t) + ia\cos(t)|\ dt \\ &= \int_0^{2\pi} \sqrt{a^2\sin^2(t) + a^2\cos^2(t)}\ dt \\ &= \int_0^{2\pi} a\ dt \\ &= 2\pi a.\end{aligned}$$

In the hyperbolic plane, we may deduce the arc-length differential by a similar argument. Suppose $\boldsymbol{r}$ is a smooth curve in $\mathbb{D}$ given by $\boldsymbol{r}(t) = x(t) + iy(t)$, for $a \leq t \leq b$. One may approximate the length of a tiny portion of the curve, say from $\boldsymbol{r}(t)$ to $\boldsymbol{r}(t + \Delta t)$, by the hyperbolic distance between these two points, $d_H(\boldsymbol{r}(t), \boldsymbol{r}(t + \Delta t))$. To compute this distance, we first send the point $\boldsymbol{r}(t)$ to 0 by the transformation

$$T(z) = \frac{z - \boldsymbol{r}(t)}{1 - \overline{\boldsymbol{r}(t)}z},$$

so that

$$d_H(\boldsymbol{r}(t), \boldsymbol{r}(t + \Delta t)) = \ln[1 + |T(\boldsymbol{r}(t + \Delta t))|] - \ln[1 - |T(\boldsymbol{r}(t + \Delta t))|].$$

To arrive at an arc-length differential, we want to let Δt approach 0. As this happens, $T(\boldsymbol{r}(t + \Delta t))$ approaches $T(\boldsymbol{r}(t))$, which is 0. From calculus we also know that $\ln(1 + x) \approx x$ for x very close to 0. Thus, for small Δt, we have

$$\begin{aligned}d_H(\boldsymbol{r}(t), \boldsymbol{r}(t + \Delta t)) &\approx |T(\boldsymbol{r}(t + \Delta t))| + |T(\boldsymbol{r}(t + \Delta t))| \\ &= 2 \cdot \left| \frac{\boldsymbol{r}(t + \Delta t) - \boldsymbol{r}(t)}{1 - \overline{\boldsymbol{r}(t)}\boldsymbol{r}(t + \Delta t)} \right| \\ &= 2 \cdot \frac{\left| \frac{\boldsymbol{r}(t+\Delta t) - \boldsymbol{r}(t)}{\Delta t} \right|}{|1 - \overline{\boldsymbol{r}(t)}\boldsymbol{r}(t + \Delta t)|} \cdot |\Delta t|.\end{aligned}$$

Now, as $\Delta t \to 0$, the numerator in the above quotient goes to $|\boldsymbol{r}'(t)|$ and the denominator goes to $1 - |\boldsymbol{r}(t)|^2$, and we arrive at the following hyperbolic arc-length differential.

Definition 5.3.6 If $\boldsymbol{r} : [a, b] \to \mathbb{D}$ is a smooth curve in the hyperbolic plane, define the **length of $\boldsymbol{r}$**, denoted $\mathcal{L}(\boldsymbol{r})$, to be

$$\mathcal{L}(\boldsymbol{r}) = \int_a^b \frac{2}{1 - |\boldsymbol{r}(t)|^2}\ |\boldsymbol{r}'(t)| dt.$$

◇

One can immediately check that the hyperbolic distance between two points in $\mathbb{D}$ corresponds to the length of the hyperbolic line segment connecting them.

Theorem 5.3.7 *The arc-length defined above is an invariant of hyperbolic geometry. That is, if $\boldsymbol{r}$ is a smooth curve in $\mathbb{D}$, and T is any transformation in $\mathcal{H}$, then $\mathcal{L}(\boldsymbol{r}) = \mathcal{L}(T(\boldsymbol{r}))$.*

The proof of this theorem is left as an exercise. One can prove that hyperbolic reflections preserve arc-length as well. This should come as no surprise, given the construction of the distance formula at the start of this section. Still, one can prove this fact from our definition of arc-length (Exercise 5.3.6, p. **??**). Thus, all hyperbolic reflections and all transformations in $\mathcal{H}$ are **hyperbolic isometries**: they preserve the hyperbolic distance between points in $\mathbb{D}$.

Another consequence of the invariance of distance, when applied to hyperbolic rotations, is the following:

Corollary 5.3.8 *All points on a hyperbolic circle centered at p are equidistant from p.*

PROOF. Suppose u and v are on the same hyperbolic circle centered at p. That is, these points are on the same type II cline with respect to p and p^*, so there exists a hyperbolic rotation that fixes p and maps u to v. Thus, $d_H(p,u) = d_H(T(p),T(u)) = d_H(p,v)$. It follows that any two points on the hyperbolic circle centered at p are equidistant from p. □

We are now in a position to argue that in the hyperbolic plane, the *shortest path* (geodesic) connecting two points p and q is along the hyperbolic line through them.

Theorem 5.3.9 *Hyperbolic lines are geodesics; that is, the shortest path between two points in $(\mathbb{D},\mathcal{H})$ is along the hyperbolic segment between them.*

Proof Sketch: We first argue that the geodesic from 0 to a point c on the positive real axis is the real axis itself.

Suppose $\boldsymbol{r}(t) = x(t) + iy(t)$ for $a \leq t \leq b$, is an arbitrary smooth curve from 0 to c (so $\boldsymbol{r}(a) = 0$ and $\boldsymbol{r}(b) = c$).

Suppose further that $x(t)$ is nondecreasing (if our path backtracks in the x direction, we claim the path cannot possibly be a geodesic). Then

$$\mathcal{L}(\boldsymbol{r}) = \int_a^b \frac{2}{1-[(x(t))^2+(y(t))^2]}\sqrt{(x'(t))^2+(y'(t))^2}\,dt.$$

The hyperbolic line segment from 0 to c can be parameterized by $\boldsymbol{r}_0(t) = x(t) + 0i$ for $a \leq t \leq b$, which has length

$$\mathcal{L}(\boldsymbol{r}_0) = \int_a^b \frac{2}{1-[x(t)]^2}\sqrt{(x'(t))^2}\,dt.$$

The curve $\boldsymbol{r}_0$ is essentially the shadow of $\boldsymbol{r}$ on the real axis.

One can compare the integrands directly to see that $\mathcal{L}(\boldsymbol{r}) \geq \mathcal{L}(\boldsymbol{r}_0)$.

Since transformations in $\mathcal{H}$ preserve arc-length and hyperbolic lines, it follows that the shortest path between any two points in $\mathbb{D}$ is along the hyperbolic line through them.

Corollary 5.3.10 *The hyperbolic distance function is a metric on the hyperbolic plane. In particular, for any points p, q, u in $\mathbb{D}$*

1. $d_H(p,q) \geq 0$, *and* $d_H(p,q) = 0$ *if and only if* $p = q$;

2. $d_H(p,q) = d_H(q,p)$; *and*

3. $d_H(p,q) + d_H(q,u) \geq d_H(p,u)$.

PROOF. Recall our formula for the hyperbolic distance between two points in Theorem 5.3.3, p. 94:

$$d_H(p,q) = \ln\left[\frac{|1-\overline{p}q| + |q-p|}{|1-\overline{p}q| - |q-p|}\right].$$

This expression is always non-negative because the quotient inside the natural log is always greater than or equal to 1. In fact, the expression equals 1 (so that the distance equals 0) if and only if $p = q$.

Note further that this formula is symmetric. Interchanging p and q leaves the distance unchanged.

Finally, the hyperbolic distance formula satisfies the triangle inequality because hyperbolic lines are geodesics. □

Example 5.3.11 Two paths from p to q.

Two paths from $p = .5i$ to $q = .5 + .5i$ are shown below: the (solid) hyperbolic segment from p to q, and the (dashed) path $\boldsymbol{r}$ that looks like a Euclidean segment. Which path is shorter?

We may compute the length of the hyperbolic segment connecting p and q with the distance formula from Theorem 5.3.3, p. 94. This distance is approximately 1.49 units.

By contrast, consider the path in $\mathbb{D}$ corresponding to the Euclidean line segment from p to q. This path may be described by $\boldsymbol{r}(t) = t + \frac{1}{2}i$ for $0 \le t \le \frac{1}{2}$. Then $\boldsymbol{r}'(t) = 1$ and

$$\begin{aligned}\mathcal{L}(\boldsymbol{r}) &= \int_0^{\frac{1}{2}} \frac{2}{1-(t^2+\frac{1}{4})}dt \\ &\approx 1.52.\end{aligned}$$

It is no surprise that the hyperbolic segment connecting p to q is a shorter path in $(\mathbb{D}, \mathcal{H})$ than the Euclidean line segment connecting them.

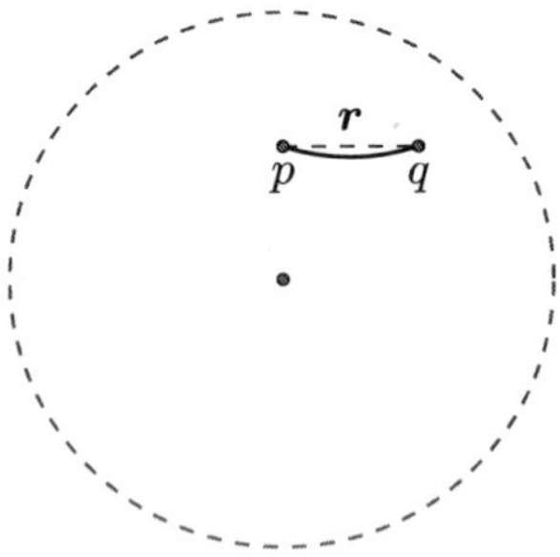

Example 5.3.12 Perpendicular bisectors in $(\mathbb{D}, \mathcal{H})$.

For any two points p and q in $\mathbb{D}$, we may construct the perpendicular bisector to hyperbolic segment pq by following the construction in Euclidean geometry. Construct both the hyperbolic circle centered at p that goes through q and the hyperbolic circle centered at q that goes through p. The hyperbolic line through the two points of intersection of these circles is the perpendicular bisector to segment pq, labeled L in the following diagram.

Hyperbolic reflection about L maps p to q and q to p. Since hyperbolic reflections preserve hyperbolic distances, each point on L is hyperbolic equidistant from p and q. That is, for each z on L, $d_H(z,p) = d_H(z,q)$.

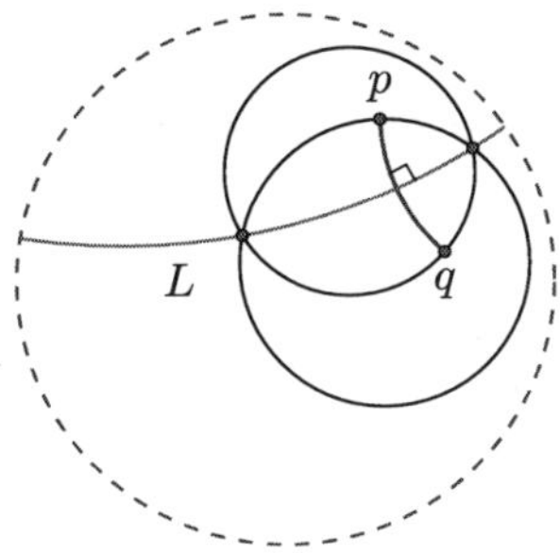

In Euclidean geometry one uses perpendicular bisectors to construct the circle through three noncollinear points. This construction can break down in hyperbolic geometry. Consider the three points p, q, and r in Figure 5.3.13, p. 99. The corresponding perpendicular bisectors do not intersect. There is no point in $\mathbb{D}$ hyperbolic equidistant from all three of these points. In particular, in hyperbolic geometry, there need not be a hyperbolic circle through three noncollinear points.

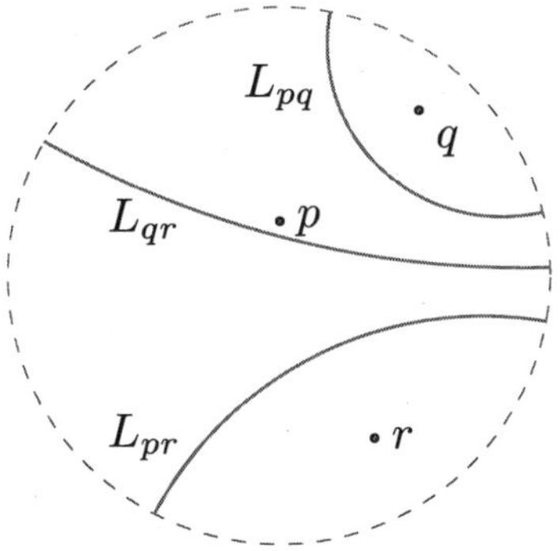

Figure 5.3.13 Three noncollinear points need not determine a circle in hyperbolic geometry.

Exercises

1. Suppose $0 < x < 1$ and L is a hyperbolic line about which x gets inverted to the origin. (Such an inversion was constructed in Theorem 5.1.3, p. 82.) For a real number h, let w be the image of $x + h$ under this inversion. Prove that $w = \frac{-h}{1-x^2-hx}$.

2. Determine a point in $\mathbb{D}$ whose hyperbolic distance from the origin is 2,003,007.4 units.

3. Suppose L is any hyperbolic line, and C is any cline through the ideal points of L. For any point z on L, its perpendicular distance to C is the length of the hyperbolic segment from z to C that meets C at right angles. Prove that the perpendicular distance from C to L is the same at every point of L. Hint: Use the fact that distance is an invariant of hyperbolic geometry.

4. Determine the hyperbolic distance from the point $p = 0.5$ to the point $q = 0.25 + 0.5i$.

5. Prove Theorem 5.3.7, p. 96.

6. Hyperbolic reflections preserve distance in $(\mathbb{D}, \mathcal{H})$

a. Use the definition of arc-length to prove that hyperbolic reflection about the real axis preserves arc-length.

b. Use part (a) and Theorem 5.3.7, p. 96 to argue that hyperbolic reflection about any hyperbolic line preserves arc-length in $(\mathbb{D}, \mathcal{H})$.

7. Suppose z_0 is in the hyperbolic plane and $r > 0$. Prove that the set C consisting of all points z in $\mathbb{D}$ such that $d_H(z, z_0) = r$ is a Euclidean circle.

5.4 Area and Triangle Trigonometry

The arc-length differential determines an area differential and the area of a region will also be an invariant of hyperbolic geometry. The area of a region will not change as it moves about the hyperbolic plane. We express the area formula in terms of polar coordinates.

Definition 5.4.1 Suppose a region R in $\mathbb{D}$ is described in polar coordinates. The **area** of R in $(\mathbb{D}, \mathcal{H})$, denoted $A(R)$, is given by

$$A(R) = \iint_R \frac{4r}{(1-r^2)^2} dr d\theta.$$

◊

The integral in this formula is difficult to evaluate directly in all but the simplest cases. Following is one such case.

Example 5.4.2 The area of a circle in $(\mathbb{D}, \mathcal{H})$.

Suppose our region is given by a circle whose hyperbolic radius is a. Since area is an invariant, we may as well assume the circle is centered at the origin. Let x be the point at which the circle intersects the positive real axis (so $0 < x < 1$), as pictured below. Then, by the distance formula

$$a = \ln\left(\frac{1+x}{1-x}\right).$$

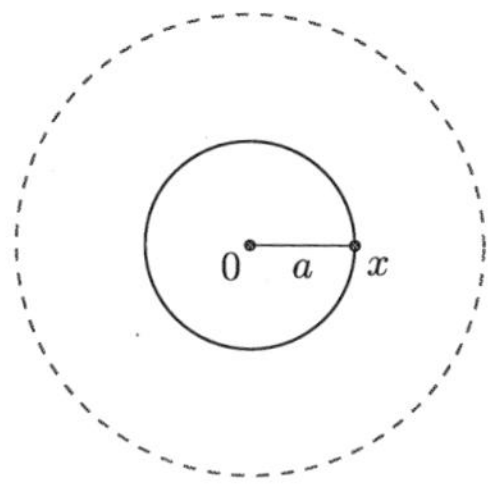

Solving for x, we have

$$x = \frac{e^a - 1}{e^a + 1}.$$

This circular region may be described in polar coordinates by $0 \leq \theta \leq 2\pi$ and $0 \leq r \leq x$. The area of the region is then given by the following integral, which we compute with the u-substitution $u = 1 - r^2$:

$$\begin{aligned}
&\int_0^{2\pi} \int_0^x \frac{4r}{(1-r^2)^2}\, dr d\theta \\
&= \left(\int_0^{2\pi} d\theta\right)\left(\int_1^{1-x^2} \frac{-2}{u^2}\, du\right) \\
&= 2\pi \left[\left.\frac{2}{u}\right|_1^{1-x^2}\right] \\
&= 2\pi \left[\frac{2}{1-x^2} - 2\right] \\
&= 4\pi \frac{x^2}{1-x^2}.
\end{aligned}$$

Replace x in terms of a to obtain

$$\begin{aligned}
4\pi \frac{(e^a-1)^2}{(e^a+1)^2} \cdot \frac{(e^a+1)^2}{(e^a+1)^2 - (e^a-1)^2} &= 4\pi \frac{(e^a-1)^2}{4e^a} \\
&= 4\pi \left(\frac{e^a - 1}{2e^{a/2}}\right)^2 \\
&= 4\pi \left(\frac{e^{a/2} - e^{-a/2}}{2}\right)^2.
\end{aligned}$$

This last expression can be rewritten using the hyperbolic sine function, evaluated at $a/2$. We investigate the hyperbolic sine and cosine functions in the exercises but note their definitions here.

Definition 5.4.3 The **hyperbolic sine function**, denoted $\sinh(x)$, and the **hyperbolic cosine function**, denoted $\cosh(x)$, are functions of real numbers defined by

$$\sinh(x) = \frac{e^x - e^{-x}}{2} \text{ and } \cosh(x) = \frac{e^x + e^{-x}}{2}.$$

◊

The area derivation in Example 5.4.2, p. 100 may then be summarized as follows.

Theorem 5.4.4 *The area of a hyperbolic circle with hyperbolic radius r is* $4\pi\sinh^2(r/2)$.

Other regions are not as simple to describe in polar coordinates. An important area for us will be the area of a $\frac{2}{3}$**-ideal triangle**, the figure that results if two of the three vertices of a hyperbolic triangle are moved to ideal points. See Figure 5.4.6, p. 102.

Theorem 5.4.5 *The area of a $\frac{2}{3}$-ideal triangle having interior angle α is equal to $\pi - \alpha$.*

The proof of this theorem is given in the following section. The proof there makes use of a different model for hyperbolic geometry, the so-called upper half-plane model.

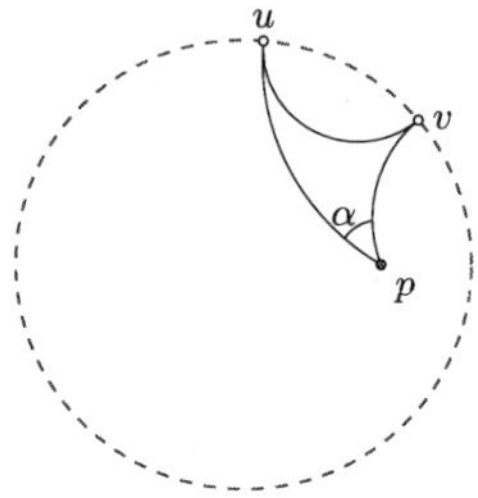

Figure 5.4.6 A $\frac{2}{3}$-ideal triangle having interior angle α has area equal to $\pi - \alpha$.

An **ideal triangle** consists of three ideal points and the three hyperbolic lines connecting them. It turns out that all ideal triangles are congruent (a fact proved in the exercises); the set of all ideal triangles is minimally invariant in $(\mathbb{D}, \mathcal{H})$.

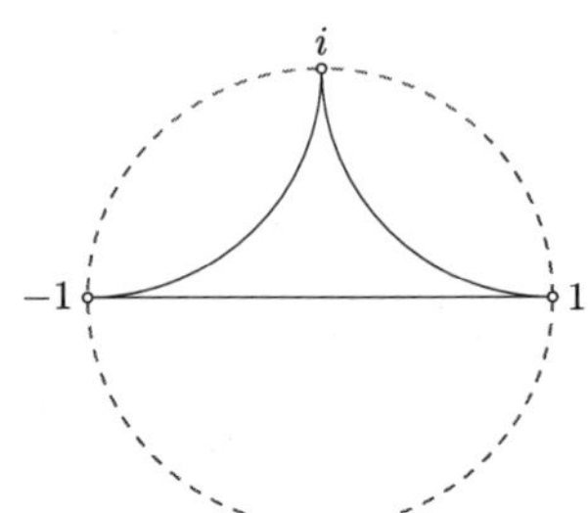

Figure 5.4.7 All ideal triangles are congruent to this one.

Theorem 5.4.8 *Any ideal triangle has area equal to π.*

PROOF. Since all ideal triangles are congruent, assume our triangle Δ is the ideal triangle shown in Figure 5.4.7, p. 102.

But then Δ can be partitioned into two $\frac{2}{3}$-ideal triangles by drawing the vertical hyperbolic line from 0 along the imaginary axis to ideal point i. Each $\frac{2}{3}$-ideal triangle has interior angle $\pi/2$, so Δ has area $\pi/2 + \pi/2 = \pi$. □

It is a remarkable fact that π is an upper bound for the area of any triangle in $(\mathbb{D}, \mathcal{H})$. No triangle in $(\mathbb{D}, \mathcal{H})$ can have area as large as π, even though side lengths can be arbitrarily large!

Theorem 5.4.9 *The area of a hyperbolic triangle in* $(\mathbb{D}, \mathcal{H})$ *having interior angles* α, β, *and* γ *is*

$$A = \pi - (\alpha + \beta + \gamma).$$

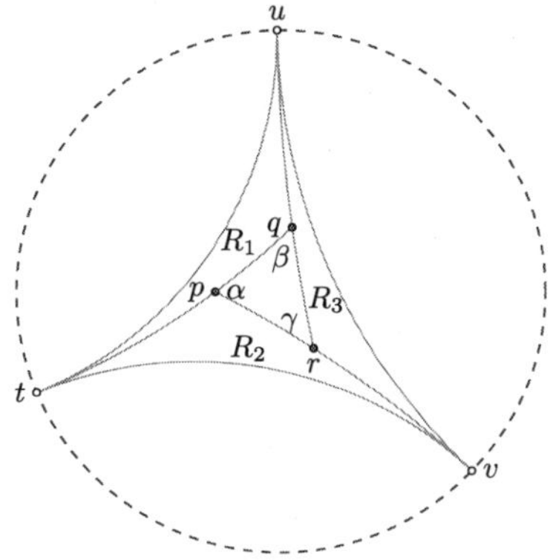

Figure 5.4.10 Determining the area of a hyperbolic triangle.

PROOF. Consider Figure 5.4.10, p. 103 containing triangle Δpqr. We have extended segment qp to the ideal point t, u is an ideal point of line rq, and v is an ideal point of line pr. The area of the ideal triangle Δtuv is π. Notice that regions R_1, R_2, and R_3 are all $\frac{2}{3}$-ideal triangles contained within the ideal triangle. Consider R_1, whose ideal points are u and t, and whose interior angle is $\angle uqt$. Since the line through q and r has ideal point u, the interior angle of R_1 is $\angle uqt = \pi - \beta$. Similarly, R_2 has interior angle $\pi - \alpha$ and R_3 has interior angle $\pi - \gamma$.

Let R denote the triangle region Δpqr whose area $A(R)$ we want to compute. We then have the following relationships among areas:

$$\begin{aligned}\pi &= A(R) + A(R_1) + A(R_2) + A(R_3) \\ &= A(R) + [\pi - (\pi - \alpha)] + [\pi - (\pi - \beta)] + [\pi - (\pi - \gamma)].\end{aligned}$$

Solving for $A(R)$,

$$A(R) = \pi - (\alpha + \beta + \gamma),$$

and this completes the proof. □

In Euclidean geometry trigonometric formulas relate the angles of a triangle to its side lengths. There are hyperbolic trigonometric formulas as well.

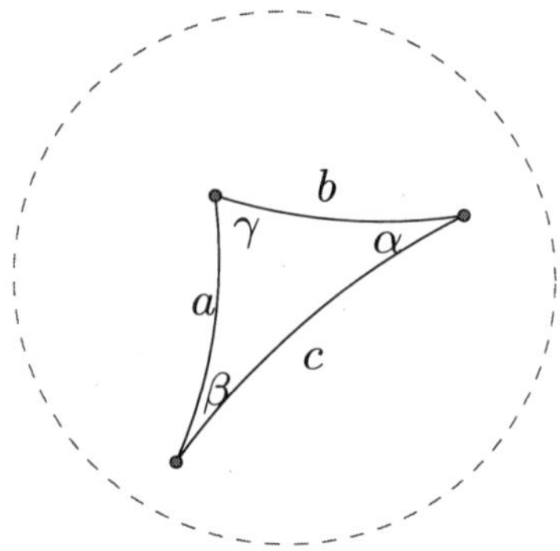

Figure 5.4.11 Relating angles and lengths in a hyperbolic triangle.

Theorem 5.4.12 *Suppose a hyperbolic triangle in $\mathbb{D}$ has angles α, β, and γ and opposite hyperbolic side lengths a, b, c, as pictured in Figure 5.4.11, p. 104. Then the following laws hold.*

a. *First hyperbolic law of cosines.*

$$\cosh(c) = \cosh(a)\cosh(b) - \sinh(a)\sinh(b)\cos(\gamma).$$

b. *Second hyperbolic law of cosines.*

$$\cosh(c) = \frac{\cos(\alpha)\cos(\beta) + \cos(\gamma)}{\sin(\alpha)\sin(\beta)}.$$

c. *Hyperbolic law of sines.*

$$\frac{\sinh(a)}{\sin(\alpha)} = \frac{\sinh(b)}{\sin(\beta)} = \frac{\sinh(c)}{\sin(\gamma)}.$$

The proofs of these laws are left as exercises for the interested reader. The following result follows from the first hyperbolic law of cosines.

Corollary 5.4.13 Hyperbolic hypotenuse theorem. *In a right hyperbolic triangle with hyperbolic side lengths a and b, and hypotenuse c,*

$$\cosh(c) = \cosh(a)\cosh(b).$$

The second hyperbolic law of cosines also leads to an interesting result. In the hyperbolic plane, if we find ourselves at point z, we may infer our distance c to a point w by estimating a certain angle, called the angle of parallelism of z to the line L through w that is perpendicular to segment zw. The following is a picture of this scene:

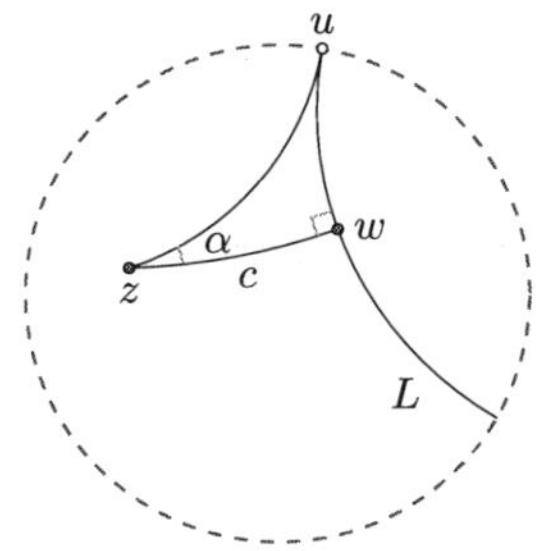

In this setting, Δzwu is a $\frac{1}{3}$-ideal triangle, and the second hyperbolic law of cosines applies with $\gamma = 0$ and $\beta = \pi/2$ to yield the following result.

Corollary 5.4.14 *Suppose z and w are points in $\mathbb{D}$, and L is a hyperbolic line through w that is perpendicular to hyperbolic segment zw. Suppose further that u is an ideal point of L. Let $\alpha = \angle wzu$ and $c = d_H(z, w)$. Then*

$$\cosh(c) = \frac{1}{\sin(\alpha)}.$$

The angle of parallelism is pursued further in Section 7.4.

Example 5.4.15 Flying around in $(\mathbb{D}, \mathcal{H})$.

Suppose a two-dimensional ship is plopped down in $\mathbb{D}$. What would the pilot see? How would the ship move? How would the pilot describe the world? Are all points equivalent in this world? Could the pilot figure out whether the universe adheres to hyperbolic geometry as opposed to, say, Euclidean geometry?

Recall what we know about hyperbolic geometry. First of all, any two points in the hyperbolic plane are congruent, so the geometry *is* homogeneous. The pilot could not distinguish between any two points, geometrically.

Second, the shortest path between two points is the hyperbolic line between them, so light would travel along these hyperbolic lines, assuming light follows geodesics. The pilot's line of sight would follow along these lines, and the ship would move along these lines to fly as quickly as possible from p to q, assuming no pesky asteroid fields block the path. To observe a galaxy at point q from the point p (as in the diagram below), the pilot would point a telescope in the direction of line L, the line along which the light from the galaxy travels to reach the telescope.

With a well-defined metric, we can say more. The pilot will view the hyperbolic plane as infinite and without boundary. In theory, the pilot can make an orbit of arbitrary radius about an asteroid located anywhere in the space.

To test for hyperbolic geometry, perhaps the pilot can turn to triangles. The angles of a triangle in the hyperbolic plane sum to less than 180°, but only noticeably so for large enough triangles. In our disk model of hyperbolic geometry, we can easily observe this angle deficiency. In the figure below, triangle Δzuw has angle sum about 130°, and Δpqr has angle sum of about 22°! Whether an intrepid 2-D explorer could map out such a large triangle depends on how much ground she could cover relative to the size of her universe. We will have more to say about such things in Chapters 7 and 8.

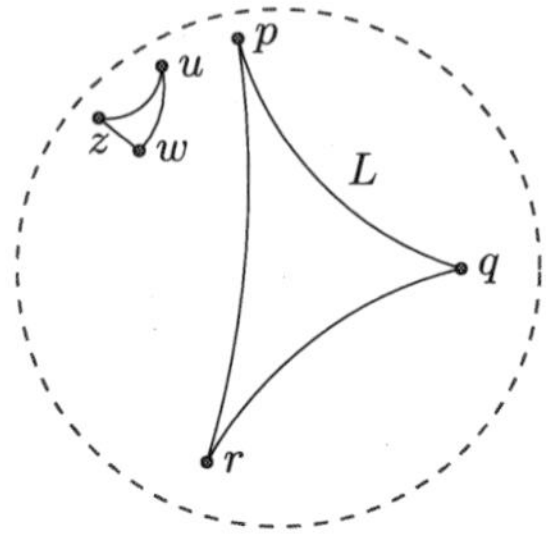

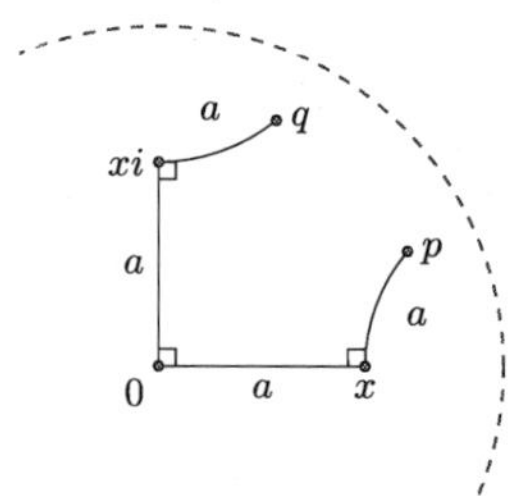

Figure 5.4.16 A journey that would trace a square in the Euclidean plane does not get you home in $(\mathbb{D}, \mathcal{H})$.

Example 5.4.17 Hyperbolic squares?

Simply put, hyperbolic squares don't exist. In fact, no four-sided figures with four right angles exist, *if we assume the sides are hyperbolic segments.* If such a figure existed, its angle sum would be 2π. But such a figure could be divided along a diagonal into two triangles whose total angle sum must then be 2π as well. This means that one of the triangles would have angle sum at least π, which cannot happen.

On the other hand, there is no physical obstruction to a two-dimensional explorer making the following journey in the hyperbolic plane: Starting at a point such as p in Figure 5.4.16, p. 106, head along a line in a certain direction for a units, turn right (90°) and proceed in a line for a more units, then turn right again and proceed in a line a units, and then turn right one more time and proceed in a line for a units. Let q denote the point at which the explorer arrives at the end of this journey. In the Euclidean plane, q will equal p, because the journey traces out a square built from line segments. However, this is not the case in $(\mathbb{D}, \mathcal{H})$ (though if we connect p and q with a hyperbolic line we obtain a geodesic pentagon with (at least) three right angles!). In the exercises we investigate the distance between p and q as a function of the length a.

However, we *can* build a four-sided figure closely resembling a rectangle, if we drop the requirement that the legs be hyperbolic line segments.

Through any point $0 < a < 1$ on the positive real axis, we may construct a hyperbolic line L_1 through a that is perpendicular to the real axis. Also construct a hyperbolic line L_2 through $-a$ that is perpendicular to the real axis. Now pick a point z on L_1 and construct the cline arc C_1 through $z, 1$ and -1. Also construct the cline arc C_2 through $\overline{z}, 1$ and -1. This creates a four sided figure, which we call a **block**. We claim that each angle in the figure is right, and that opposite sides have equal length. Moreover, z and a can be chosen so that all four sides have the same length. This figure isn't a rectangle, however, in the sense that not all four sides are hyperbolic segments. The arcs C_1 and C_2 are not hyperbolic lines.

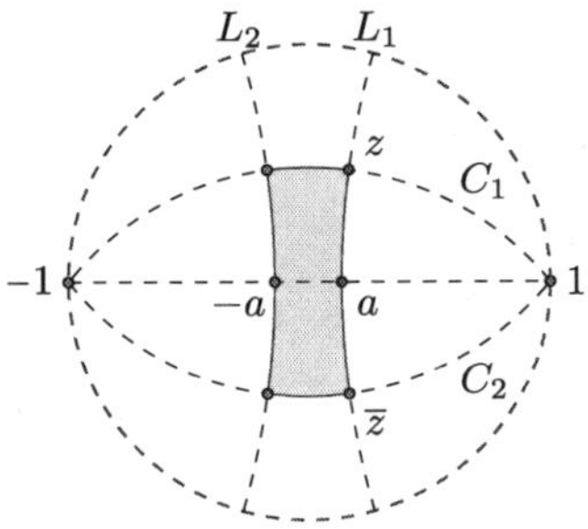

Figure 5.4.18 Blocks in $\mathbb{D}$: Four-sided, right-angled figures whose opposite sides have equal length.

While squares don't exist in the hyperbolic plane, we may build right-angled regular polygons with more than four sides using hyperbolic line segments. In fact, for each triple of positive real numbers (a, b, c) we may build a right-angled hexagon in the hyperbolic plane with alternate side lengths a, b, and c. We encourage the reader to work carefully through the construction of this hexagon in the proof of Theorem 5.4.19, p. 107. We use all our hyperbolic constructions to get there.

Theorem 5.4.19 *For any triple (a, b, c) of positive real numbers there exists a right-angled hexagon in $(\mathbb{D}, \mathcal{H})$ with alternate side lengths a, b, and c. Moreover, all right-angled hexagons with alternate side lengths a, b, and c are congruent.*

PROOF. We prove the existence of a right-angled hexagon with vertices $v_0, v_1, \ldots, v_5$ such that $d_H(v_0, v_1) = a$, $d_H(v_2, v_3) = b$, and $d_H(v_4, v_5) = c$.

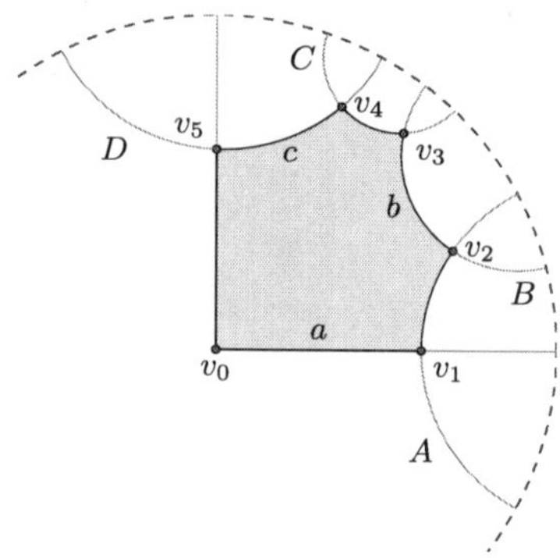

Figure 5.4.20 Building a right hexagon in the hyperbolic plane that has alternate side lengths (a, b, c).

First, let v_0 be the origin in the hyperbolic plane, and place v_1 on the positive real axis so that $d_H(v_0, v_1) = a$. Note that

$$v_1 = \frac{e^a - 1}{e^a + 1}.$$

Next, construct the hyperbolic line A perpendicular to the real axis at the point v_1. This line is part of the cline that has diameter $v_1 v_1^*$.

Pick any point v_2 on the line A. For the sake of argument, assume that v_2 lies above the real axis, as in Figure 5.4.20, p. 108.

Next, construct the hyperbolic line B perpendicular to A at the point v_2. This line is part of the cline through v_2 and v_2^* with center on the line tangent to A at v_2.

Next, construct the point v_3 on line B that is a distance b away from v_2. This point is found by intersecting B with the hyperbolic circle centered at v_2 with radius b. (To construct this circle, we first find the scalar k so that the hyperbolic distance between kv_2 and v_2 is b.)

Next, draw the perpendicular C to line B at v_3.

Then construct the common perpendicular of C and the imaginary axis, call this perpendicular D. We construct this common perpendicular as follows. First find the two points p and q symmetric to both C and the imaginary axis (see Theorem 3.2.16, p. 46). The points p and q will live on the circle at infinity. The common perpendicular of C and the imaginary axis will be the cline through p and q that is also a hyperbolic line (i.e., orthogonal to the circle at infinity).

If C and the imaginary axis intersect, no such perpendicular exists (think triangle angles), so drag v_2 away from v_1 until these lines do not intersect. Then construct D as in the preceeding paragraph. Let v_4 and v_5 be the points of intersection of D with C and the imaginary axis, respectively.

This construction gives us a right angled hexagon such that $d_H(v_0, v_1) = a$ and $d_H(v_2, v_3) = b$. We also want $d_H(v_4, v_5) = c$. Notice that this last distance is a function of the position of vertex v_2 on line A. As v_2 goes along A to v_1 there is a point beyond which D no longer exists, and as v_2 goes along A to the circle at infinity, the length of segment v_4v_5 takes on all positive real values. So, by the intermediate value theorem, there is some point at which the segment has length c. Finally, all right-angled hexagons with alternate side lengths a, b, and c

are congruent to the one just constructed because angles, hyperbolic lines, and distances are preserved under transformations in $\mathcal{H}$. □

Example 5.4.21 Inscribe a circle in an ideal triangle.

We show that if one inscribes a circle in any ideal triangle, its points of tangency form an equilateral triangle with side lengths equal to $2\ln(\varphi)$ where φ is the golden ratio $(1+\sqrt{5})/2$.

Since all ideal triangles are congruent, we choose one that is convenient to work with. Consider the ideal triangle with ideal points -1, 1, and i.

The hyperbolic line L_1 joining -1 and i is part of the circle C_1 with radius 1 centered at $-1+i$. The hyperbolic line L_2 joining i and 1 is part of the circle C_2 with radius 1 centered at $1+i$. Let C denote the circle with radius 2 centered at $-1+2i$, as pictured below.

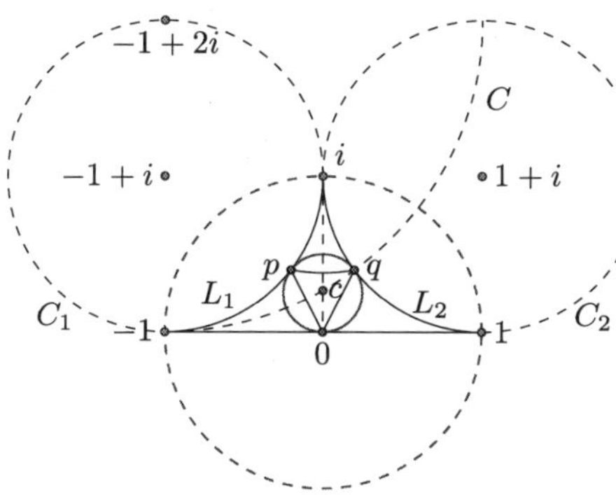

Inversion about C gives a hyperbolic reflection of $\mathbb{D}$ that maps L_1 onto the real axis. Indeed, the circle C_1, since it passes through the center of C, gets mapped to a line - the real axis, in fact. Moreover, hyperbolic reflection across the imaginary axis maps L_1 onto L_2. Let c be the point of intersection of these two hyperbolic lines of reflection, as pictured. The hyperbolic circle with hyperbolic center c that passes through the origin will be tangent to the real axis, and will thus inscribe the ideal triangle. Let the points of tangency on L_1 and L_2 be p and q, respectively.

The point q can be found analytically as the point of intersection of circles C and C_2. Working it out, one finds $q = \frac{1}{5} + \frac{2}{5}i$. Thus,

$$\begin{aligned}
d_H(0,q) &= \ln\left(\frac{1+|q|}{1-|q|}\right) \\
&= \ln\left(\frac{1+\frac{1}{\sqrt{5}}}{1-\frac{1}{\sqrt{5}}}\right) \\
&= \ln\left(\frac{\sqrt{5}+1}{\sqrt{5}-1}\right) \\
&= \ln\left(\frac{(\sqrt{5}+1)^2}{(\sqrt{5}-1)(\sqrt{5}+1)}\right) \\
&= \ln\left(\frac{(\sqrt{5}+1)^2}{4}\right)
\end{aligned}$$

$$= \ln(\varphi^2)$$
$$= 2\ln(\varphi).$$

Exercises

1. *Properties of* $\sinh(x) = (e^x - e^{-x})/2$ *and* $\cosh(x) = (e^x + e^{-x})/2$.

a. Verify that $\sinh(0) = 0$ and $\cosh(0) = 1$.

b. Verify that $\frac{d}{dx}[\sinh(x)] = \cosh(x)$ and $\frac{d}{dx}[\cosh(x)] = \sinh(x)$.

c. Verify that $\cosh^2(x) - \sinh^2(x) = 1$.

d. Verify that the power series expansions for $\cosh(x)$ and $\sinh(x)$ are

$$\cosh(x) = 1 + \frac{x^2}{2} + \frac{x^4}{4!} + \cdots$$
$$\sinh(x) = x + \frac{x^3}{3!} + \frac{x^5}{5!} + \cdots.$$

2. Prove that the circumference of a hyperbolic circle having hyperbolic radius r is $C = 2\pi\sinh(r)$.

3. *The hyperbolic plane looks Euclidean on small scales.*

a. Prove

$$\lim_{r\to 0+} \frac{4\pi\sinh^2(r/2)}{\pi r^2} = 1.$$

Thus, for small r, the Euclidean formula for the area of a circle is a good approximation to the true area of a circle in the hyperbolic plane.

b. Prove

$$\lim_{r\to 0+} \frac{2\pi\sinh(r)}{2\pi r} = 1.$$

Thus, for small r, the Euclidean formula for the circumference of a circle is a good approximation to the true circumference of a circle in the hyperbolic plane.

4. Prove that all ideal triangles are congruent in hyperbolic geometry.

5. An intrepid tax collector lives in a country in the hyperbolic plane. For collection purposes, the country is divided into triangular grids. The collector is responsible for collection in a triangle having angles 12°, 32°, and 17°. What is the area of the collector's triangle? Can the entire space $\mathbb{D}$ be subdivided into a finite number of triangles?

6. Consider the hyperbolic triangle with vertices at 0, $\frac{1}{2}$, and $\frac{1}{2} + \frac{1}{2}i$. Calculate the area of this triangle by determining the angle at each vertex.

7. Recall the block constructed in Example 5.4.17, p. 106. Prove that all four angles are 90°, and that for any choice of z, opposite sides have equal hyperbolic length.

8. Find a formula for the area of an n-gon, comprised of n hyperbolic line segments in terms of its n interior angles $\alpha_1, \alpha_2, \cdots, \alpha_n$. Hint: Decompose the n-gon into triangles.

9. *Building a hyperbolic octagon with interior angles* $45°$. Let r be a real number such that $0 < r < 1$. The eight points $v_k = re^{i\frac{\pi}{4}k}$ for $k = 0, 1, \cdots, 7$ determine a regular octagon in the hyperbolic plane, as shown in Figure 5.4.22, p. 111. Note that v_0 is the real number r. The interior angle of each corner is a function of r. We find the value of r for which the interior angle is $45°$.

a. Prove that the center of the circle containing the hyperbolic line through v_0 and v_1 is

$$z_0 = \frac{1+r^2}{2r} + \frac{1+r^2}{2r}\tan(\pi/8)i.$$

b. Let $b = \frac{1+r^2}{2r}$ be the midpoint of segment $v_0v_0^*$ and show that $\angle v_0 z_0 b = \pi/8$ precisely when the interior angles of the octagon equal $\pi/4$.

c. Using $\Delta v_0 b z_0$ and part (b), show that the interior angles of the octagon equal $\pi/4$ precisely when

$$\tan(\pi/8) = \frac{|b - v_0|}{|z_0 - b|} = \frac{\frac{1+r^2}{2r} - r}{\frac{1+r^2}{2r} \cdot \tan(\pi/8)}.$$

d. Solve the equation in (c) for r to obtain $r = (1/2)^{(1/4)}$.

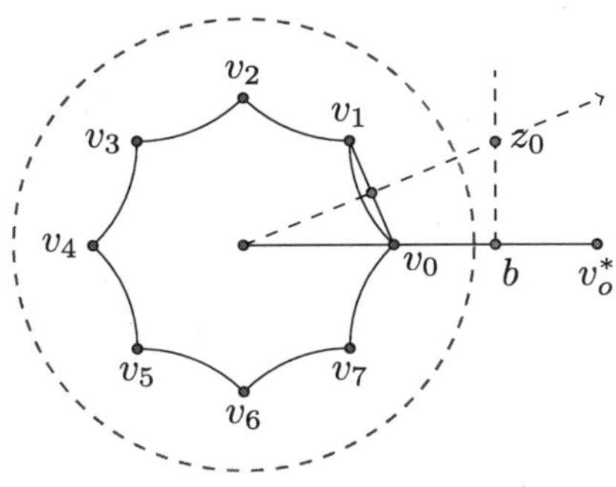

Figure 5.4.22 Building an octagon with interior angles equal to $45°$.

10. Suppose we construct a regular n-gon in the hyperbolic plane from the corner points $r, re^{\frac{1}{n}2\pi i}, re^{\frac{2}{n}2\pi i}, \cdots, re^{\frac{n-1}{n}2\pi i}$ where $0 < r < 1$. Calculate the hyperbolic length of any of its sides.

11. Prove the first hyperbolic law of cosines by completing the following steps.

a. Show that for any positive real numbers x and y,

$$\cosh(\ln(x/y)) = \frac{x^2+y^2}{2xy} \quad \text{and} \quad \sinh(\ln(x/y)) = \frac{x^2-y^2}{2xy}.$$

b. Given two points p and q in $\mathbb{D}$, let $c = d_H(p,q)$. Use the hyperbolic distance formula from Theorem 5.3.3, p. 94 and part (a) to show

$$\cosh(c) = \frac{(1+|p|^2)(1+|q|^2) - 4\text{Re}(p\overline{q})}{(1-|p|^2)(1-|q|^2)}.$$

c. Now suppose our triangle has one vertex at the origin, and one point on the positive real axis. In particular, suppose $p = r$ $(0 < r < 1)$ and $q = ke^{i\gamma}$ $(0 < k < 1)$, with angles α, β, γ and hyperbolic side lengths a, b, and c as in Figure 5.4.23, p. 112.

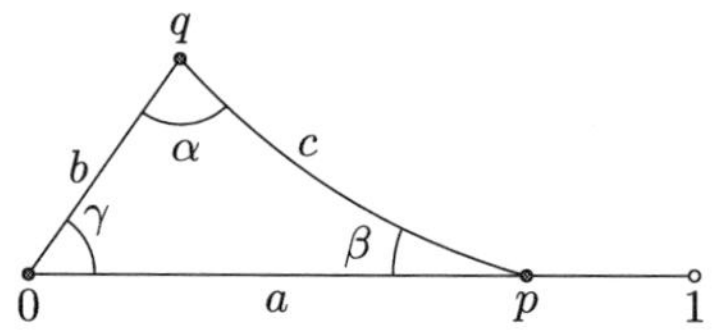

Figure 5.4.23 A hyperbolic triangle with one corner at the origin and one leg on the positive real axis.

Show

$$\cosh(a) = \frac{1+r^2}{1-r^2} \quad ; \quad \sinh(a) = \frac{2r}{1-r^2};$$

$$\cosh(b) = \frac{1+k^2}{1-k^2} \quad ; \quad \sinh(b) = \frac{2k}{1-k^2}.$$

d. Show that for the triangle in part (c),

$$\cosh(c) = \cosh(a)\cosh(b) - \sinh(a)\sinh(b)\cos(\gamma).$$

e. Explain why this formula works for any triangle in $\mathbb{D}$.

12. In this exercise we prove the hyperbolic law of sines. We assume our triangle is as in Figure 5.4.24, p. 113. Thus, $q = ke^{i\gamma}$ for some $0 < k < 1$ and $p = r$ for some real number $0 < r < 1$. Suppose further that the circle containing side c has center z_0 and Euclidean radius R, shown in the figure, and that m_q is the midpoint of segment qq^* and m_p is the midpoint of segment pp^*, so that $\Delta z_0 m_q q$ and $\Delta p m_p z_0$ are right triangles.

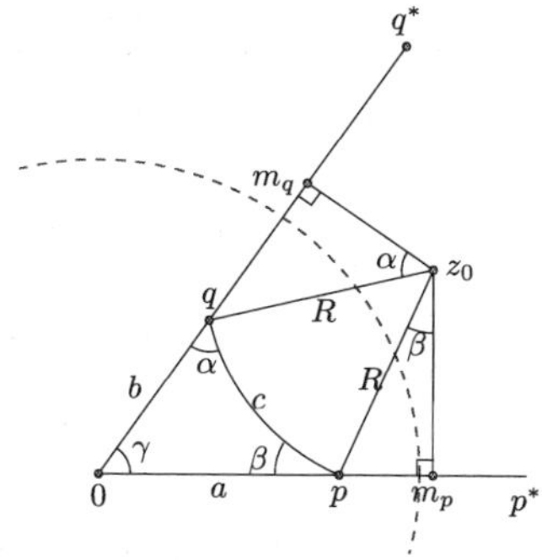

Figure 5.4.24 Deriving the hyperbolic law of sines.

a. Verify that the triangle angles α and β correspond to angles $\angle m_q z_0 q$ and $\angle p z_0 m_p$, respectively.

b. Notice that $\sin(\alpha) = |m_q - q|/R$ and $\sin(\beta) = |m_p - p|/R$. Verify that $|m_q - q| = \frac{1/k-k}{2} = \frac{1-k^2}{2k}$ and that $|m_p - p| = \frac{1-r^2}{2r}$.

c. Verify that

$$\frac{\sinh(a)}{\sin(\alpha)} = \frac{\sinh(b)}{\sin(\beta)}.$$

d. Explain why we may conclude that for any hyperbolic triangle in $\mathbb{D}$,

$$\frac{\sinh(a)}{\sin(\alpha)} = \frac{\sinh(b)}{\sin(\beta)} = \frac{\sinh(c)}{\sin(\gamma)}.$$

13. Prove the second law of hyperbolic cosines.

14. Recall the journey in Example 5.4.17, p. 106 in which a bug travels a path that would trace a square in the Euclidean plane. For convenience, we assume the starting point p is such that the first right turn of 90° occurs at the point x on the positive real axis and the second turn occurs at the origin. (This means that $x = (e^a - 1)/(e^a + 1)$.) The third corner must then occur at xi. We have reproduced the journey with some more detail in Figure 5.4.25, p. 114. In this exercise we make use of hyperbolic triangle trig to measure some features of this journey from p to q in terms of the length a of each leg.

a. Determine the hyperbolic distance between p and the origin (corner two of the journey). In particular, show that $\cosh(d_H(0,p)) = \cosh^2(a)$. Note that if this journey had been done in the Euclidean plane, the corresponding distance would be $\sqrt{2}a$. How do these distances compare for small positive values of a? Is $\cosh^2(a)$ close to $\cosh(\sqrt{2}a)$?

b. Let $\theta = \angle x0p$. Show that $\tan(\theta) = \frac{1}{\cosh(a)}$. What is the corresponding angle if this journey is done in the Euclidean plane? What does θ approach as $a \to 0^+$?

c. Show that $\angle x0p = \angle 0px$.

d. Show that $\cosh(d_H(p,q)) = \cosh^4(a)[1 - \sin(2\theta)] + \sin(2\theta)$.

e. Let $\alpha = \angle qp0$, $b = d_H(0,p)$ and $c = d_H(p,q)$. Show that

$$\sin(\alpha) = \frac{\sinh(b)}{\sinh(c)} \cos(2\theta).$$

f. Determine the area of the pentagon enclosed by the journey if, after reaching q we return to p along the geodesic. In particular, show that the area of this pentagon equals $\frac{3\pi}{2} - 2(\theta + \alpha)$. What is the corresponding area if the journey had been done in the Euclidean plane?

g. Would any of these measurements change if we began at a different point in the hyperbolic plane and/or headed off in a different direction initially than the ones in Figure 5.4.25, p. 114?

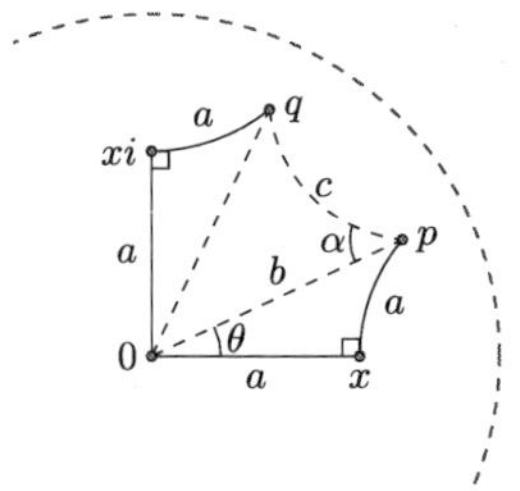

Figure 5.4.25 A journey that would trace a square in the Euclidean plane does not get you home in $(\mathbb{D}, \mathcal{H})$. But how close will the finish point q be to the starting point p?

5.5 The Upper Half-Plane Model

The Poincaré disk model is one way to represent hyperbolic geometry, and for most purposes it serves us very well. However, another model, called the upper half-plane model, makes some computations easier, including the calculation of the area of a triangle.

Definition 5.5.1 The **upper half-plane model of hyperbolic geometry** has space $\mathbb{U}$ consisting of all complex numbers z such that $\text{Im}(z) > 0$, and transformation group $\mathcal{U}$ consisting of all Möbius transformations that send $\mathbb{U}$ to itself. The space $\mathbb{U}$ is called the upper half-plane of $\mathbb{C}$. ◊

The Poincaré disk model of hyperbolic geometry may be transferred to the upper half-plane model via a Möbius transformation built from two inversions as follows:

1. Invert about the circle C centered at i passing through -1 and 1 as in Figure 5.5.2, p. 115.

2. Reflect about the real axis.

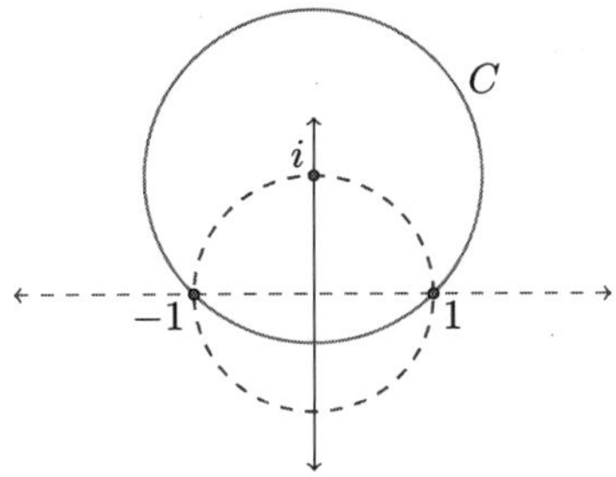

Figure 5.5.2 Inversion in C maps the unit disk to the upper-half plane.

Notice that inversion about the circle C fixes -1 and 1, and it takes i to ∞. Since reflection across the real axis leaves these image points fixed, the composition of the two inversions is a Möbius transformation that takes the unit circle to the real axis. The map also sends the interior of the disk into the upper half plane. Notice further that the Möbius transformation takes ∞ to $-i$; therefore, by Theorem 3.5.8, p. 65, the map can be written as

$$V(z) = \frac{-iz+1}{z-i}.$$

This Möbius transformation is the key to transferring the disk model of the hyperbolic plane to the upper half-plane model. In fact, when treading back and forth between these models it is convenient to adopt the following convention for this section: Let z denote a point in $\mathbb{D}$, and w denote a point in the upper half-plane $\mathbb{U}$, as in Figure 5.5.3, p. 115. We record the transformations linking the spaces below.

Going between $(\mathbb{D}, \mathcal{H})$ and $(\mathbb{U}, \mathcal{U})$.

The Möbius transformation V mapping $\mathbb{D}$ to $\mathbb{U}$, and its inverse V^{-1}, are given by:

$$w = V(z) = \frac{-iz+1}{z-i} \quad \text{and} \quad z = V^{-1}(w) = \frac{iw+1}{w+i}.$$

Some features of the upper half-plane model immediately come to light. Since V is a Möbius transformation, it preserves clines and angles. This means that the ideal points in the disk model, namely the points on the circle at infinity, $\mathbb{S}^1_\infty$, have moved to the real axis and that hyperbolic lines in the disk model have become clines that intersect the real axis at right angles.

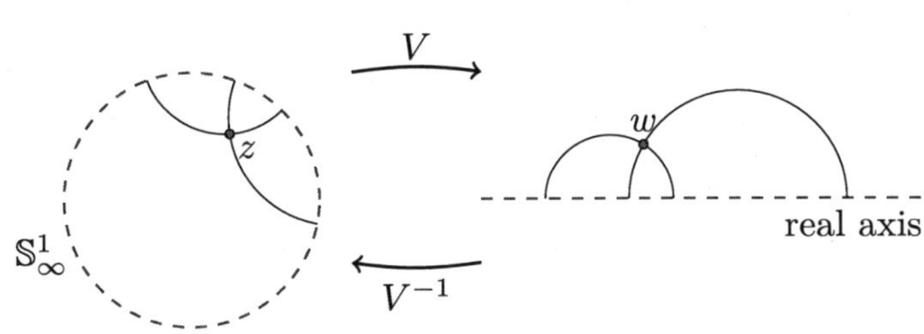

Figure 5.5.3 Mapping the disk to the upper half-plane.

Define the hyperbolic distance between two points w_1, w_2 in the upper half-plane model, denoted $d_U(w_1, w_2)$, to be the hyperbolic distance between their pre-images in the disk model.

Suppose w_1 and w_2 are two points in V whose pre-images in the unit disk are z_1 and z_2, respectively. Then,

$$d_U(w_1, w_2) = d_H(z_1, z_2) = \ln((z_1, z_2; u, v)),$$

where u and v are the ideal points of the hyperbolic line through z_1 and z_2. But, since the cross ratio is preserved under Möbius transformations,

$$d_U(w_1, w_2) = \ln((w_1, w_2; p, q)),$$

where p, q are the ideal points of the hyperbolic line in the upper half-plane through w_1 and w_2. In particular, going from w_1 to w_2 we're heading toward ideal point p.

Example 5.5.4 The distance between ri and si.

For $r > s > 0$ we compute the distance between ri and si in the upper half-plane model.

The hyperbolic line through ri and si is the positive imaginary axis, having ideal points 0 and ∞. Thus,

$$\begin{aligned} d_U(ri, si) &= \ln((ri, si; 0, \infty)) \\ &= \frac{ri - 0}{ri - \infty} \cdot \frac{si - \infty}{si - 0} \\ &= \ln\left(\frac{r}{s}\right). \end{aligned}$$

Example 5.5.5 The distance between any two points.

To find the distance between any two points w_1 and w_2 in $\mathbb{U}$, we first build a map in the upper half-plane model that moves these two points to the positive imaginary axis. To build this map, we work through the Poincaré disk model.

By the transformation V^{-1} we send w_1 and w_2 back to $\mathbb{D}$. We let $z_1 = V^{-1}(w_1)$ and $z_2 = V^{-1}(w_2)$. Then, let $S(z) = e^{i\theta}\frac{z - z_1}{1 - \overline{z_1}z}$ be the transformation in $(\mathbb{D}, \mathcal{H})$ that sends z_1 to 0 with θ chosen carefully so that z_2 gets sent to the positive imaginary axis. In fact, z_2 gets sent to the point ki where $k = |S(z_2)| = |S(V^{-1}(w_2))|$ (and $0 < k < 1$). Then, applying V to the situation, 0 gets sent to i and ki gets sent to $\frac{1+k}{1-k}i$. Thus, $V \circ S \circ V^{-1}$ sends w_1 to i and w_2 to $\frac{1+k}{1-k}i$, where by the previous example the distance between the points is known:

$$d_U(w_1, w_2) = \ln(1 + k) - \ln(1 - k).$$

Describing k in terms of w_1 and w_2 is left for the adventurous reader. We do not need to pursue that here.

We now derive the hyperbolic arc-length differential for the upper half-plane model working once again through the disk model. Recall the arc-length differential in the disk model is

$$ds = \frac{2|dz|}{1-|z|^2}.$$

Since $z = V^{-1}(w) = \frac{iw+1}{w+i}$ we may work out the arc-length differential in terms of dw. We will need to take the derivative of a complex expression, which can be done just as if it were a real valued expression. Here we go:

$$\begin{aligned}
ds &= \frac{2|dz|}{1-|z|^2} \\
&= \frac{2\left|d\left(\frac{iw+1}{w+i}\right)\right|}{1-\left|\frac{iw+1}{w+i}\right|^2} && (z = \tfrac{iw+1}{w+i}) \\
&= \frac{2|i(w+i)dw-(iw+1)dw|}{|w+i|^2} \Bigg/ \left[1-\frac{|iw+1|^2}{|w+i|^2}\right] && \text{(chain rule)} \\
&= \frac{4|dw|}{|w+i|^2-|iw+1|^2} \\
&= \frac{4|dw|}{(w+i)(\overline{w}-i)-(iw+1)(-i\overline{w}+1)} \\
&= \frac{4|dw|}{2i(\overline{w}-w)} \\
&= \frac{|dw|}{Im(w)}.
\end{aligned}$$

This leads us to the following definition:

Definition 5.5.6 The length of a smooth curve $\boldsymbol{r}(t)$ for $a \leq t \leq b$ in the upper half-plane model $(\mathbb{U}, \mathcal{U})$, denoted $\mathcal{L}(\boldsymbol{r})$, is given by

$$\mathcal{L}(\boldsymbol{r}) = \int_a^b \frac{|\boldsymbol{r}'(t)|}{\text{Im}(\boldsymbol{r}(t))}\, dt.$$

◊

Example 5.5.7 The length of a curve.

To find the length of the horizontal curve $\boldsymbol{r}(t) = t + ki$ for $a \leq t \leq b$, note that $\boldsymbol{r}'(t) = 1$ and $\text{Im}(\boldsymbol{r}(t)) = k$. Thus,

$$\mathcal{L}(\boldsymbol{r}) = \int_a^b \frac{1}{k}\, dt = \frac{b-a}{k}.$$

From the arc-length differential $ds = \frac{dw}{\text{Im}(w)}$ comes the area differential:

Definition 5.5.8 In the upper half-plane model $(\mathbb{U}, \mathcal{U})$ of hyperbolic geometry, the area of a region R described in cartesian coordinates, denoted $A(R)$, is given by

$$A(R) = \iint_R \frac{1}{y^2}\, dxdy.$$

◊

Example 5.5.9 The area of a $\frac{2}{3}$-ideal triangle.

Suppose $w \in \mathbb{U}$ is on the unit circle, and consider the $\frac{2}{3}$-ideal triangle $1w\infty$ as pictured.

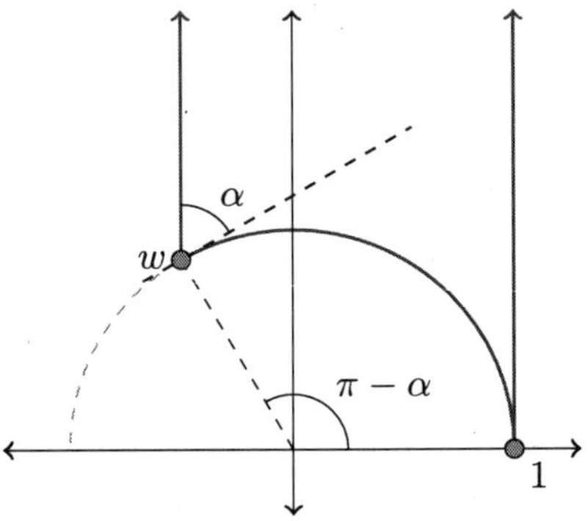

In particular, suppose the interior angle at w is α, so that $w = e^{i(\pi-\alpha)}$ where $0 < \alpha < \pi$.

The area of this $\frac{2}{3}$-ideal triangle is thus

$$\begin{aligned} A &= \int_{\cos(\pi-\alpha)}^{1} \int_{\sqrt{1-x^2}}^{\infty} \frac{1}{y^2}\, dydx \\ &= \int_{\cos(\pi-\alpha)}^{1} \frac{1}{\sqrt{1-x^2}}\, dx. \end{aligned}$$

With the trig substituion $\cos(\theta) = x$, so that $\sqrt{1-x^2} = \sin(\theta)$ and $-\sin(\theta)d\theta = dx$, the integral becomes

$$\begin{aligned} &= \int_{\pi-\alpha}^{0} \frac{-\sin(\theta)}{\sin(\theta)}\, d\theta \\ &= \pi - \alpha. \end{aligned}$$

It turns out that any $\frac{2}{3}$-ideal triangle is congruent to one of the form $1w\infty$ where w is on the upper half of the unit circle (Exercise 5.5.3, p. ??), and since our transformations preserve angles and area, we have proved the area formula for a $\frac{2}{3}$-ideal triangle.

Theorem 5.5.10 *The area of a $\frac{2}{3}$-ideal triangle having interior angle α is equal to $\pi - \alpha$.*

Exercises

1. What becomes of horocycles when we transfer the disk model of hyperbolic geometry to the upper half-plane model?

2. What do hyperbolic rotations in the disk model look like over in the upper half-plane model? What about hyperbolic translations?

3. Give an explicit description of a transformation that takes an arbitrary $\frac{2}{3}$-ideal triangle in the upper half-plane to one with ideal points 1 and ∞ and an interior vertex on the upper half of the unit circle.

4. Determine the area of the "triangular" region pictured below. What is the image of this region under V^{-1} in the disk model of hyperbolic geometry? Why doesn't this result contradict Theorem 5.4.9, p. 103?

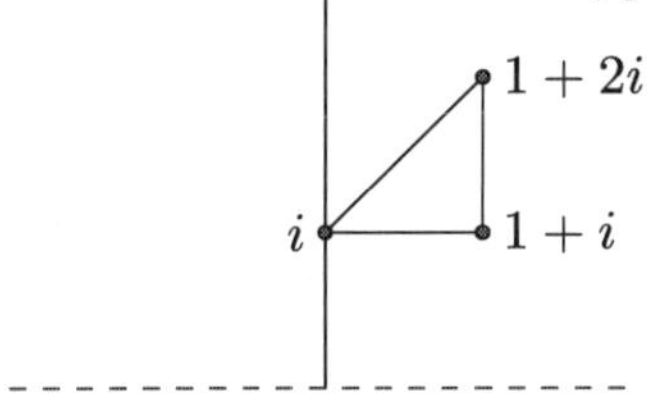

5. *Another type of block.* Consider the four-sided figure $pqst$ in $(\mathbb{D}, \mathcal{H})$ shown in the following diagram. This figure is determined by two horocycles C_1 and C_2, and two hyperbolic lines L_1 and L_2 all sharing the same ideal point. Note that the lines are orthogonal to the horocycles, so that each angle in the four-sided figure is 90°.

a. By rotation about the origin if necessary, assume the common ideal point is i and use the map V to transfer the figure to the upper half-plane. What does the transferred figure look like in $\mathbb{U}$? Answer parts (b)-(d) by using this transferred version of the figure.

b. Prove that the hyperbolic lengths of sides pq and st are equal.

c. Let c equal the hyperbolic length of the leg pt along the larger radius horocycle C_1, and let d equal the hyperbolic length of the leg sq on C_2. Show that $c = e^x d$ where x is the common length found in part (b).

d. Prove that the area of the four-sided figure is $c - d$.

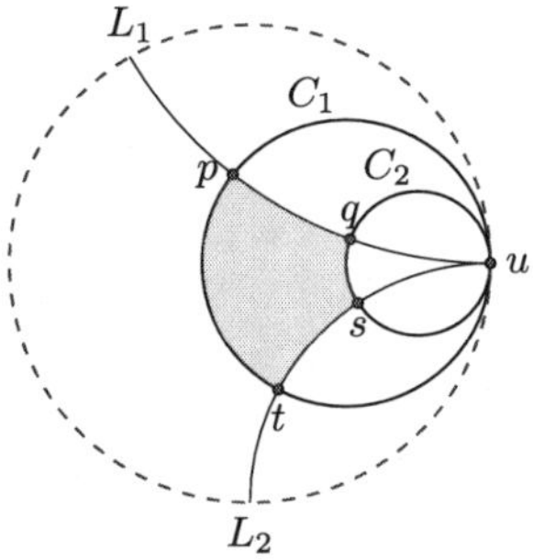

6

Elliptic Geometry

Elliptic geometry is the second type of non-Euclidean geometry that might describe the geometry of the universe. In this chapter we focus our attention on two-dimensional elliptic geometry, and the sphere will be our guide. The chapter begins with a review of stereographic projection, and how this map is used to transfer information about the sphere onto the extended plane. We develop elliptic geometry in Sections 6.2 and 6.3, and then pause our story in Section 6.4 to reflect on what we have established, geometry-wise, before moving on to geometry on surfaces in Chapter 7.

6.1 Antipodal Points

Recall, the unit 2-sphere $\mathbb{S}^2$ consists of all points (a, b, c) in $\mathbb{R}^3$ for which $a^2 + b^2 + c^2 = 1$, and $\mathbb{S}^2$ may be mapped onto the extended plane by the stereographic projection map $\phi : \mathbb{S}^2 \to \mathbb{C}^+$ defined by

$$\phi(a, b, c) = \begin{cases} \frac{a}{1-c} + \frac{b}{1-c}i & \text{if } c \neq 1; \\ \infty & \text{if } c = 1 \end{cases}.$$

Two distinct points on a sphere are called **diametrically opposed points** if they are on the same line through the center of the sphere. Diametrically opposed points on the sphere are also called antipodal points. If $P = (a, b, c)$ is on $\mathbb{S}^2$ then the point diametrically opposed to it is $-P = (-a, -b, -c)$. It turns out that ϕ maps diametrically opposed points of the sphere to points in the extended plane that satisfy a particular equation.

Definition 6.1.1 Two points z and w in $\mathbb{C}^+$ are called **antipodal points** if they satisfy the equation

$$z \cdot \overline{w} = -1.$$

Furthermore, we set 0 and ∞ to be antipodal points in $\mathbb{C}^+$. If z and w are antipodal points, we say w is antipodal to z, and vice versa. $\diamondsuit$

Each z in $\mathbb{C}^+$ has a unique antipodal point, z_a, given as follows:

$$z_a = \begin{cases} -1/\overline{z} & \text{if } z \neq 0, \infty; \\ \infty & \text{if } z = 0; \\ 0 & \text{if } z = \infty \end{cases} .$$

Since $-\frac{1}{\overline{z}} = -\frac{1}{|z|^2} z$, we note that z_a is a scaled version of z, so that z and z_a live on the same Euclidean line through the origin. Again, since 0 and ∞ are antipodal points, this notion extends to all points $z \in \mathbb{C}^+$.

Lemma 6.1.2 *Given two diametrically opposed points on the unit sphere, their image points under stereographic projection are antipodal points in* $\mathbb{C}^+$.

PROOF. First note that the north pole $N = (0, 0, 1)$ and the south pole $S = (0, 0, -1)$ are diametrically opposed points and they get sent by ϕ to ∞ and 0, respectively, in $\mathbb{C}^+$; so the lemma holds in this case.

Now suppose $P = (a, b, c)$ is a point on the sphere with $|c| \neq 1$, and $Q = (-a, -b, -c)$ is diametrically opposed to P. The images of these two points under stereographic projection are

$$\phi(P) = \frac{a}{1-c} + \frac{b}{1-c}i \text{ and } \phi(Q) = \frac{-a}{1+c} - \frac{b}{1+c}i.$$

If we expand the following product

$$\phi(P) \cdot \overline{\phi(Q)} = \left[\frac{a}{1-c} + \frac{b}{1-c}i\right] \cdot \left[\frac{-a}{1+c} + \frac{b}{1+c}i\right],$$

we obtain

$$\phi(P) \cdot \overline{\phi(Q)} = -\frac{a^2 + b^2}{1 - c^2}$$

which reduces to -1 since $a^2 + b^2 + c^2 = 1$.

Thus, diametrically opposed points on the sphere get mapped via stereographic projection to antipodal points in the extended plane. □

A cline C in $\mathbb{C}^+$ is called a **great circle** if whenever z is on C, so is its antipodal point z_a. Some great circles are drawn in Figure 6.1.3, p. 122. We note that the unit circle is a great circle in $\mathbb{C}^+$ as is any line through the origin.

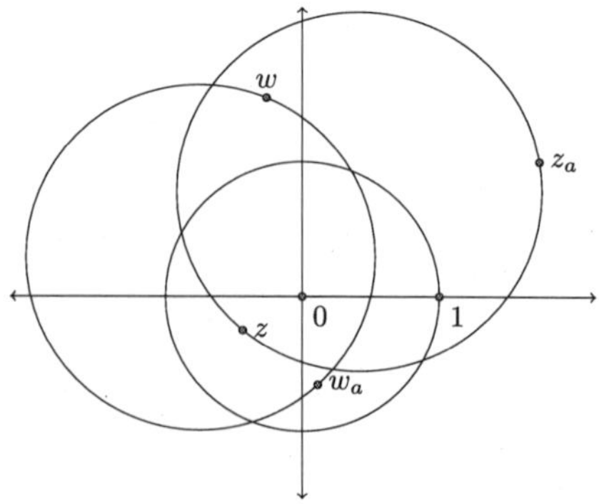

Figure 6.1.3 Five great circles in $\mathbb{C}^+$.

To construct a great circle in the extended plane, it is enough to ensure that it passes through one particular pair of antipodal points. This can be proved with the aid of stereographic projection, but an alternative proof is given below, one that does not leave the plane, but rather uses a proposition from Book III of Euclid's *Elements.*

Lemma 6.1.4 *If a cline in* $\mathbb{C}^+$ *contains two antipodal points then it is a great circle.*

PROOF. Suppose C is a cline in $\mathbb{C}^+$ containing antipodal points p and p_a, and suppose q is any other point on C. We show q_a is also on C.

If C is a line, it must go through the origin since p and p_a are on the same line through the origin. Since q and q_a are also on the same line through the origin, if q is on C then q_a is too.

If C is a circle, then the origin of the plane is in the interior of C and the chord pp_a contains the origin, as pictured in Figure 6.1.5, p. 123. The line through q and the origin intersects C at another point, say w. We show $w = q_a$.

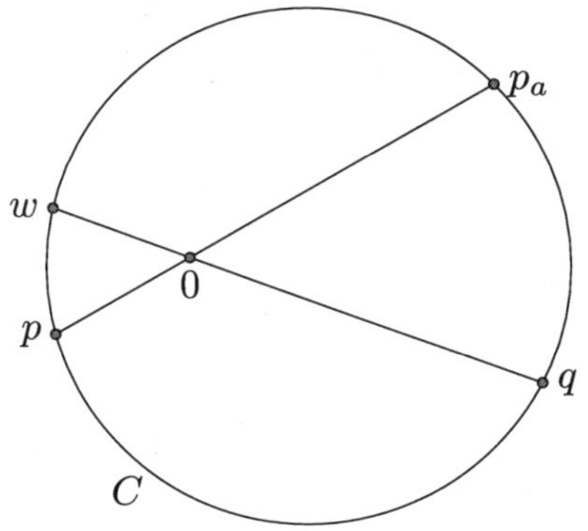

Figure 6.1.5 A cline C containing a pair of antipodal points p and p_a must be a great cirlce. In the figure, $w = q_a$.

The intersecting chords theorem (Book III, Proposition 35 of Euclid's *Elements*) applied to this figure tells us that $|p| \cdot |p_a| = |q| \cdot |w|$. (We leave the proof to Exercise 6.1.7, p. ??. The proof essentially follows that of Lemma 3.2.7, p. 42, except we consider a point inside the given circle.) As antipodal points, $|p| \cdot |p_a| = 1$, and it follows that $|w| = 1/|q|$. Since the segment wq contains the origin, it follows that w is the point antipodal to q. □

The following theorem tells us that inversions will play a central role in elliptic geometry, just as they do in hyperbolic geometry.

Theorem 6.1.6 *Reflection of* $\mathbb{S}^2$ *about a great circle corresponds via stereographic projection to inversion about a great circle in* $\mathbb{C}^+$.

We work through the relationship in one case, and refer the interested reader to [10] for the general proof.

Example 6.1.7 Reflection of $\mathbb{S}^2$ about the equator.

We argue that reflection of $\mathbb{S}^2$ about the equator corresponds to inversion about the unit circle.

First of all, stereographic projection sends the equator of $\mathbb{S}^2$ to the unit circle in $\mathbb{C}^+$. Now, reflection of $\mathbb{S}^2$ across the equator sends the point $P = (a, b, c)$ to the point $P^* = (a, b, -c)$. We must argue that $\phi(P)$ and $\phi(P^*)$ are symmetric with respect to the unit circle.

If $|c| = 1$ then P and P^* correspond to the north and south poles, and their image points are 0 and ∞, and these points are symmetric with respect to the unit circle. So, assume $|c| \neq 1$. Notice that

$$\phi(P) = \frac{a}{1-c} + \frac{b}{1-c}i \text{ and } \phi(P^*) = \frac{a}{1+c} + \frac{b}{1+c}i$$

are on the same ray beginning at the origin. Indeed, one is the positive scalar multiple of the other:

$$\phi(P^*) = \frac{1-c}{1+c}\phi(P).$$

Moreover,

$$\begin{aligned}
|\phi(P)| \cdot |\phi(P^*)| &= \frac{1-c}{1+c} \cdot |\phi(P)|^2 \\
&= \frac{1-c}{1+c} \cdot \frac{a^2+b^2}{(1-c)^2} \\
&= \frac{a^2+b^2}{1-c^2} \\
&= 1.
\end{aligned}$$

Again, the last equality holds because $a^2 + b^2 + c^2 = 1$. Thus, $\phi(P)$ and $\phi(P^*)$ are symmetric with respect to the unit circle. It follows that inversion in the unit circle, $i_{\mathbb{S}^1}$, corresponds to reflection of $\mathbb{S}^2$ across the equator, call this map R, by the equation

$$i_{\mathbb{S}^1} \circ \phi = \phi \circ R.$$

We end the section with one more feature of the stereographic projection map. The proof can be found in [10].

Theorem 6.1.8 *The image of a circle on $\mathbb{S}^2$ via stereographic projection is a cline in $\mathbb{C}^+$. Moreover, the pre-image of a circle in $\mathbb{C}^+$ is a circle on $\mathbb{S}^2$. The pre-image of a line in $\mathbb{C}^+$ is a circle on $\mathbb{S}^2$ that goes through $N = (0, 0, 1)$.*

In fact, one can offer a constructive proof of this theorem. A circle on $\mathbb{S}^2$ can be represented as the intersection of $\mathbb{S}^2$ with a plane $Ax + By + Cz + D = 0$ in 3-dimensional space. One can show that the circle in $\mathbb{S}^2$ defined by $Ax+By+Cz+D = 0$ gets mapped by ϕ to the cline $(C+D)(u^2+v^2)+2Au+2Bv+(D-C) = 0$ in the plane (described via u, v cartesian coordinates); conversely the circle $|w - w_0| = r$ in $\mathbb{C}$ gets mapped by the inverse function ϕ^{-1} to the circle in $\mathbb{S}^2$

given by the plane $-2x_0x - 2y_oy + (1 - |w_0|^2 + r^2)z + (1 + |w_0|^2 - r^2) = 0$ where $w_0 = x_0 + y_0i$.

Example 6.1.9 The image of a circle under ϕ.

Consider the circle on $\mathbb{S}^2$ defined by the vertical plane $x = -\frac{1}{2}$. In standard form, this plane has constants $A = 2, B = C = 0$, and $D = 1$, so the image under ϕ is the circle

$$(u^2 + v^2) + 4u + 1 = 0.$$

Completing the square we obtain the circle

$$(u + 2)^2 + v^2 = 3$$

having center $(-2, 0)$ and radius $\sqrt{3}$.

Example 6.1.10 The pre-image of a circle under ϕ.

The pre-image of the circle $|w - (3 + 2i)| = 4$ in $\mathbb{C}$ is the circle on $\mathbb{S}^2$ defined by the plane

$$-2 \cdot 3x - 2 \cdot 2y + (1 - 13 + 4)z + (1 + 13 - 4) = 0$$

or

$$-3x - 2y - 4z + 5 = 0.$$

Exercises

1. *Constructing an antipodal point.* Suppose z is a point inside the unit circle. Prove that the following construction, which is depicted in Figure 6.1.11, p. 125, gives z_a, the point antipodal to z: (1) Draw the line through z and the origin; (2) draw the line through the origin perpendicular to line (1), and let T be on line (2) and the unit circle; (3) construct the segment zT; (4) construct the perpendicular to segment (3) at point T. Line (4) intersects line (1) at the point z_a. Use similar triangles to prove that $z_a = -\frac{1}{|z|^2}z$.

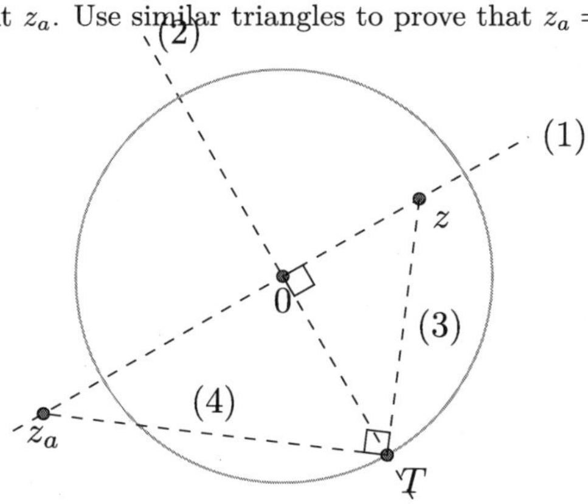

Figure 6.1.11 Constructing the antipodal point to z.

2. Explain why any great circle in $\mathbb{C}^+$ either contains 0 or has 0 in its interior.

3. Characterize those great circles in $\mathbb{C}^+$ that are actually Euclidean lines.

4. Prove that reflection of $\mathbb{S}^2$ across the great circle through $(0,0,1)$, $(0,0,-1)$, and $(1,0,0)$ corresponds via stereographic projection to reflection of $\mathbb{C}^+$ across the real axis.

5. Determine the image under ϕ of the circle $z = 1/2$ on the unit sphere.

6. Explain why reflection of $\mathbb{S}^2$ across any longitudinal great circle (i.e. a great circle through the north and south poles) corresponds to reflection of $\mathbb{C}^+$ across a line through the origin.

7. Prove the intersecting chords theorem in two parts.

a. Suppose C is a circle with radius r centered at o. Suppose p is a point inside C and a line through p intersects C at points m and n, as pictured below. If we let $s = |p - o|$ prove that $|p - m| \cdot |p - n| = r^2 - s^2$.

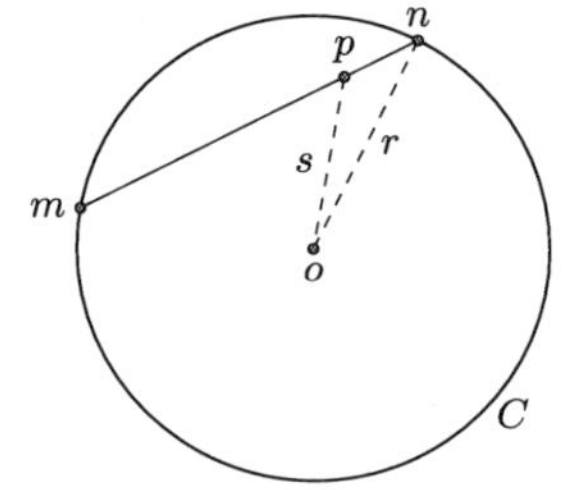

b. Prove the intersecting chords theorem: If mn and ab are any two chords of C passing through a given interior point p, then

$$|m - p| \cdot |a - p| = |m - p| \cdot |b - p|.$$

6.2 Elliptic Geometry

As was the case in hyperbolic geometry, the space in elliptic geometry is derived from $\mathbb{C}^+$, and the group of transformations consists of certain Möbius transformations. We first consider the transformations.

Definition 6.2.1 Let $\mathcal{S}$ consist of all Möbius transformations T that preserve antipodal points. In other words, $\mathcal{S}$ consists of all Möbius transformations T with the property that if z and z_a are antipodal points in $\mathbb{C}^+$ then $T(z)$ and $T(z_a)$ are antipodal points in $\mathbb{C}^+$. ◊

We leave it to the reader to verify that $\mathcal{S}$ actually forms a group. Considering the antipodal point construction in Figure 6.1.11, p. 125, it seems clear that rotation of $\mathbb{C}^+$ about the origin should preserve antipodal points. So, these rotations should be in $\mathcal{S}$. Let's run through this.

Example 6.2.2 Rotations about 0 are in $\mathcal{S}$.

Suppose $R(z) = e^{i\theta}z$ is a rotation about the origin and z and z_a are antipodal points. If $z = \infty$ or 0, then rotation about the origin fixes z, and it also fixes its antipodal point, so the map R preserves antipodal points in these cases. Now suppose $z \neq 0, \infty$. Then $z_a = -\frac{1}{\bar{z}}$. Since $\overline{R(z_a)} = -\frac{e^{-i\theta}}{z}$, it follows that

$$R(z) \cdot \overline{R(z_a)} = -e^{i\theta}z \cdot \frac{e^{-i\theta}}{z} = -1.$$

Thus, the image points $R(z)$ and $R(z_a)$ are still antipodal points. Rotations about the origin belong to the group $\mathcal{S}$.

Now we consider what a typical transformation in $\mathcal{S}$ looks like.

Suppose the Möbius transformation T is in $\mathcal{S}$, and that z and w are antipodal points. Then $T(z) \cdot \overline{T(w)} = -1$. Since z and w are antipodal points, $w = -\frac{1}{\bar{z}}$, so $T(z) \cdot \overline{T(-1/\bar{z})} = -1$, or

$$T(z) = \frac{-1}{\overline{T(-1/\bar{z})}}. \tag{1}$$

Assume $T(z) = (az+b)/(cz+d)$, and that it has determinant $ad - bc = 1$. (Recall, from Exercise 3.4.4, p. ?? that we can always write a Möbius transformation in a form with determinant 1, and this form is unique up to sign.) Now,

$$\begin{aligned} \overline{T(-1/\bar{z})} &= \overline{\left[\frac{-a/\bar{z}+b}{-c/\bar{z}+d}\right]} \\ &= \frac{-\bar{a}/z+\bar{b}}{-\bar{c}/z+\bar{d}} \\ &= \frac{\bar{b}z-\bar{a}}{\bar{d}z-\bar{c}}. \end{aligned}$$

Substituting into equation (1) of this derivation yields

$$\frac{az+b}{cz+d} = \frac{-\bar{d}z+\bar{c}}{\bar{b}z-\bar{a}}.$$

The transformation on the right also has determinant one, so these two transformations are identical up to sign. We can assume that $d = -\bar{a}$ and that $c = \bar{b}$, so that T may be expressed as follows:

$$T(z) = \frac{az+b}{\bar{b}z-\bar{a}}.$$

We can make this general form look a lot like the general form for a transformation in $\mathcal{H}$. To do so, first multiply each term by $-1/\bar{a}$, assuming $a \neq 0$. (If $a = 0$, what would the transformation look like?)

$$\begin{aligned} T(z) &= \frac{-\frac{a}{\bar{a}}z - \frac{b}{\bar{a}}}{-\frac{\bar{b}}{\bar{a}}z+1} \\ &= \frac{-\frac{a}{\bar{a}}(z+\frac{b}{a})}{-\frac{\bar{b}}{\bar{a}}z+1} \end{aligned}$$

$$= e^{i\theta} \cdot \frac{z - z_0}{\overline{z}_0 z + 1},$$

where $e^{i\theta} = -a/\bar{a}$ and $z_0 = -b/a$. Thus, we have derived the following algebraic description of transformations in $\mathcal{S}$.

Transformations in $\mathcal{S}$.

Any transformation T in the group $\mathcal{S}$ has the form

$$T(z) = e^{i\theta} \frac{z - z_0}{1 + \overline{z}_0 z}$$

for some angle θ and some z_0 in $\mathbb{C}^+$.

One can show that the following converse holds: Any transformation having the form above preserves antipodal points. It follows that for any point $z_0 \in \mathbb{C}^+$, there exists a transformation T in $\mathcal{S}$ such that $T(z_0) = 0$, and since rotations about the origin live in $\mathcal{S}$ we can prove the following useful result (see Exercise 6.2.1, p. ??).

Lemma 6.2.3 *Given distinct points z_0 and z_1 in $\mathbb{C}^+$, there exists a transformation in $\mathcal{S}$ that sends z_0 to 0 and z_1 to the real axis.*

We now prove a theorem that helps us visualize the maps in $\mathcal{S}$.

Theorem 6.2.4 *If a Möbius transformation preserves antipodal points, then it is an elliptic Möbius transformation.*

PROOF. Suppose T is a Möbius transformation that preserves antipodal points. If T is not the identity map then it must fix one or two points. However, if T preserves antipodal points and fixes a point p, then it must fix its antipodal point p_a. Thus, T must have two fixed points and T has normal form

$$\frac{T(z) - p}{T(z) - p_a} = \lambda \frac{z - p}{z - p_a}.$$

To show T is an elliptic Möbius transformation, we must show that $|\lambda| = 1$. Setting $z = 0$ the normal form reduces to

$$\frac{T(0) - p}{T(0) - p_a} = \lambda \frac{p}{p_a}.$$

Solve for $T(0)$ to obtain

$$T(0) = \frac{pp_a - \lambda pp_a}{p_a - \lambda p}.$$

On the other hand, setting $z = \infty$ and solving for $T(\infty)$, one checks that

$$T(\infty) = \frac{p - \lambda p_a}{1 - \lambda}.$$

Since T preserves antipodal points, $T(0) \cdot \overline{T(\infty)} = -1$; therefore, we have

$$\frac{pp_a - \lambda pp_a}{p_a - \lambda p} \cdot \frac{\overline{p} - \overline{\lambda}\overline{p_a}}{1 - \overline{\lambda}} = -1.$$

If we expand this expression and solve it for $\lambda\overline{\lambda}$ (using the fact that $p \cdot \overline{p_a} = -1$, and $p \neq p_a$), we obtain $\lambda\overline{\lambda} = 1$, from which it follows that $|\lambda| = 1$. Thus T is an elliptic Möbius transformation. □

In Exercise 3.5.8, p. ?? we showed that any elliptic Möbius transformation is the composition of two inversions about clines that intersect at the two fixed points. In the case of a Möbius transformation that preserves antipodal points, these two fixed points must be antipodal to each other. It follows by Lemma 6.1.4, p. 123 that the two clines of inversion are great circles in $\mathbb{C}^+$. Thus, we may view each transformation of $\mathcal{S}$ as the composition of two inversions about great circles. This is reassuring. By Theorem 6.1.6, p. 123, these inversions correspond to reflections of the sphere about great circles, and composing two of these reflections of the sphere yields a rotation of the sphere. The transformation group $\mathcal{S}$, then, consists of Möbius transformations that correspond via stereographic projection to rotations of the sphere. We summarize these facts below.

Theorem 6.2.5 *Any transformation in $\mathcal{S}$ is the composition of two inversions about great circles in $\mathbb{C}^+$, and it corresponds via stereographic projection to a rotation of the unit 2-sphere.*

Before turning to the space in elliptic geometry, we make one more comment about the group $\mathcal{S}$. The reader may have noticed a strong similarity, algebraically, between the maps in $\mathcal{S}$ and the maps in $\mathcal{H}$, the transformation group in hyperbolic geometry. Recall, transformations in $\mathcal{H}$ have the form

$$T(z) = e^{i\theta}\frac{z - z_0}{1 - \overline{z}_0 z}. \qquad \text{(transformation in } \mathcal{H}\text{)}$$

The single sign difference between the algebraic desciption of maps in $\mathcal{S}$ from the maps in $\mathcal{H}$ is not a coincidence. We could have defined the transformations in hyperbolic geometry as those Möbius transformations that preserve symmetric points with respect to the unit circle. That is, we *could* have defined the group $\mathcal{H}$ to consist of all Möbius transformations satisfying this property: If $z \cdot \bar{w} = 1$ then $T(z) \cdot \overline{T(w)} = 1$. If we had then asked what such a T would look like, we would have gone through the argument as we did in this section, with a +1 initially instead of a -1. This sign difference propagates to the sign difference in the final form of the description of the map.

The space for elliptic geometry

One could let the space be all of $\mathbb{C}^+$. If we take this tack, then we are reproducing the geometry of the sphere in $\mathbb{C}^+$. We call the geometry $(\mathbb{C}^+, \mathcal{S})$ **spherical geometry**. Distance can be defined to match distance on the unit sphere, and great cirlces in $\mathbb{C}^+$ will be geodesics. Rather than develop these details with this choice of spaces, we will focus instead on a different space. We do so because we want to build a geometry in which there is a *unique* line between any two points. This is not quite true on the sphere, and so not quite true in $(\mathbb{C}^+, \mathcal{S})$. If two points in $\mathbb{C}^+$ are antipodal points, such as 0 and ∞, then there are infinitely many lines (great circles) through these points.

So, we choose to work primarily with a space in which this feature of many distinct lines through two points vanishes. The trick is to *identify antipodal points.* That is, the space we will consider is actually the space $\mathbb{C}^+$ *with antipodal points identified.* What does this space look like?

Remember the flat torus from Chapter 1? Each point on the boundary of the rectangle is identified with the corresponding point on the opposite edge. The two points are fused together into a single point.

In elliptic space, *every* point gets fused together with another point, its antipodal point. So, for instance, the point $2+i$ gets identified with its antipodal point $-\frac{2}{5}-\frac{i}{5}$. In elliptic space, these points are one and the same.

With the flat torus, we could visualize the space after identifying points by wrapping it up in three-dimensional space. This was possible since we were only identifying the edges of the rectangle. In the present case every point in $\mathbb{C}^+$ gets paired up. To help visualize the space here we look at a region in the plane that contains one representative from each pair.

Consider the closed unit disk, consisting of all complex numbers z such that $|z| \leq 1$. For each point w outside this disk, its antipodal point w_a is inside the disk. Thus, the closed unit disk contains a representative from each pair of antipodal points. However, there is some redundancy: for a point w on the boundary of the disk ($|w| = 1$), its antipodal point w_a is also on the boundary. To account for this redundancy, we identify each point on the boundary of the closed unit disk with its antipodal point.

This will be our model for the space in elliptic geometry, and this space is called the projective plane.

Definition 6.2.6 The **projective plane**, denoted $\mathbb{P}^2$, consists of all complex numbers z such that $|z| \leq 1$ with the additional feature that antipodal points on the unit circle are identified. ◊

We can think of this space as the closed unit disk with its two edges (top-half circle and bottom-half circle) identified according to the arrows in Figure 6.2.7, p. 130. Notice the pleasant journey a bug has taken from p to q in this figure. From p she heads off toward point c, which appears on the boundary of our model. When she arrives there she simply keeps walking, though in our model we see her leave the "screen" and reappear at the antipodal point c_a. She has her sights set on point d and saunters down there, continues on (reappearing at d_a), and heads on to q, hungry but content.

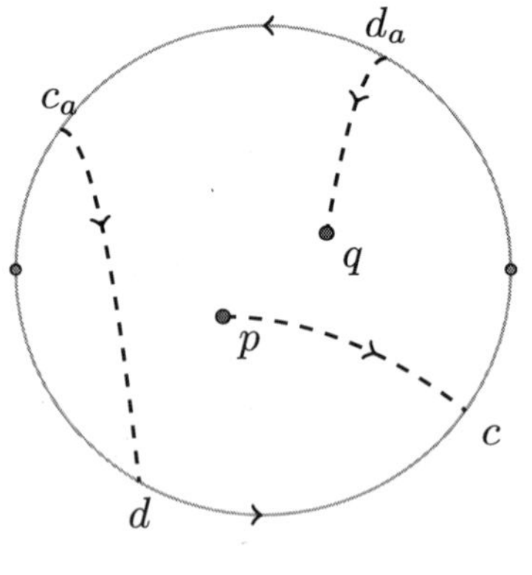

Figure 6.2.7 A leisurely stroll from p to q in the projective plane $\mathbb{P}^2$.

Definition 6.2.8 The **disk model for elliptic geometry**, $(\mathbb{P}^2, \mathcal{S})$, is the geometry whose space is $\mathbb{P}^2$ and whose group of transformations $\mathcal{S}$ consists of all Möbius transformations that preserve antipodal points. ◊

Because the transformations of $\mathcal{S}$ are generated by inversions about great circles, these circles ought to determine the lines in elliptic geometry.

Definition 6.2.9 An **elliptic line** in $(\mathbb{P}^2, \mathcal{S})$ is the portion of a great circle in $\mathbb{C}^+$ that lives in the closed unit disk. ◊

Two elliptic lines have been constructed in Figure 6.2.10, p. 131.

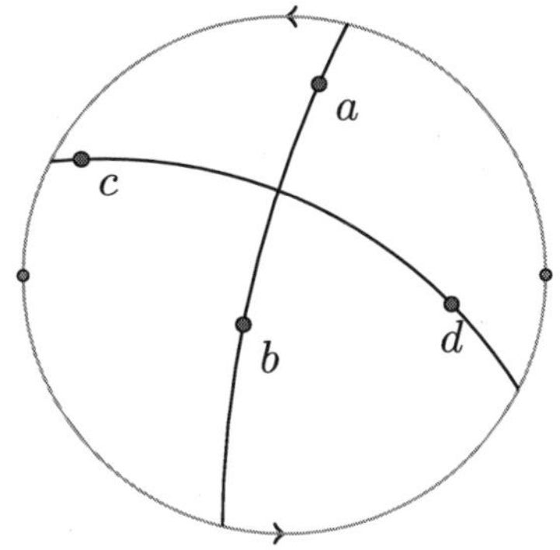

Figure 6.2.10 Elliptic lines go through antipodal points.

Theorem 6.2.11 *There is a unique elliptic line connecting two points p and q in $\mathbb{P}^2$.*

PROOF. Suppose p and q are distinct points in $\mathbb{P}^2$. This means $q \neq p_a$ as points in $\mathbb{C}^+$. Construct the antipodal point p_a, which gives us three distinct points in $\mathbb{C}^+$: p, q and p_a. There exists a unique cline through these three points. Since this cline goes through p and p_a, it is an elliptic line by Lemma 6.1.4, p. 123. □

Note that elliptic lines through the origin are Euclidean lines, just as was the case in the Poincaré model of hyperbolic geometry. As a result, to prove facts about elliptic geometry, it can be convenient to transform a general picture to the special case where the origin is involved.

Theorem 6.2.12 *The set of elliptic lines is a minimally invariant set of elliptic geometry.*

PROOF. By definition, any transformation T in $\mathcal{S}$ preserves antipodal points. Thus, if L is an elliptic line, then $T(L)$ is as well, and the set of elliptic lines is an invariant set of elliptic geometry.

To show the set is minimally invariant, we appeal to Theorem 4.1.10, p. 74, and prove that any two elliptic lines are congruent. To see this, notice that any elliptic line L is congruent to the elliptic line on the real axis. Indeed, for any points z_0 and z_1 on L, Lemma 6.2.3, p. 128 ensures the existence of a transformation T in $\mathcal{S}$ that sends z_0 to the origin, and z_1 to the real axis. It follows that $T(L)$ is the real axis. Since all elliptic lines are congruent to the real axis, any two elliptic lines are congruent. □

Theorem 6.2.13 *Any two elliptic lines intersect in $\mathbb{P}^2$.*

PROOF. Given any two elliptic lines, apply a transformation T in $\mathcal{S}$ that sends one of them to the real axis. It is enough to prove that any elliptic line in $\mathbb{P}^2$ must intersect the real axis. Suppose M is an arbitrary elliptic line in $\mathbb{P}^2$ and z is a point on M. If $\text{Im}(z) = 0$ then z is on the real axis and we are done.

If $\text{Im}(z) > 0$, then z lies above the real axis. It follows that $\text{Im}(z_a) < 0$ by the definition of the antipodal point z_a. Since M contains both z and z_a it intersects the real axis at some point.

If $\text{Im}(z) < 0$, then $\text{Im}(z_a) > 0$ and M must intersect the real axis as before. In either case, M must intersect the real axis, and it follows that any two elliptic lines must intersect. □

As an immediate consequence of this theorem, there is no notion of parallel lines in elliptic geometry.

Corollary 6.2.14 *If p in $\mathbb{P}^2$ is not on the elliptic line L, then every elliptic line through p intersects L.*

Exercises

1. *The transformation group in elliptic geometry.*

a. Prove that $\mathcal{S}$ is a group of transformations.

b. For each $\theta \in \mathbb{R}$ and $z_0 \in \mathbb{C}$, prove that the following Möbius transformation is in $\mathcal{S}$:

$$T(z) = e^{i\theta}\frac{z - z_0}{1 + \overline{z_0}z}.$$

c. For each $\theta \in \mathbb{R}$, prove that $T(z) = e^{i\theta}\frac{1}{z}$ is in $\mathcal{S}$.

d. Use (b) and (c) to prove that for any distinct points $p, q \in \mathbb{C}^+$ there exists a transformation in $\mathcal{S}$ that sends p to 0 and q to a point on the positive real axis, thus proving Lemma 6.2.3, p. 128.

2. Prove that the disk model for elliptic geometry is homogeneous.

3. Given a point z not on an elliptic line L, prove there exists an elliptic line through z that intersects L at right angles.

4. Is there a nonidentity transformation in $\mathcal{S}$ that fixes two distinct points in $\mathbb{P}^2$? If so, find one, otherwise explain why no such transformation exists.

5. Find a transformation in $\mathcal{S}$ that sends the point $\frac{1}{2}$ to the point $\frac{1}{2} + \frac{1}{2}i$.

6.3 Measurement in Elliptic Geometry

Rather than derive the arc-length formula here as we did for hyperbolic geometry, we state the following definition and note the single sign difference from the hyperbolic case. This sign difference is consistent with the sign difference in the algebraic descriptions of the transformations in the respective geometries.

Definition 6.3.1 If $\boldsymbol{r} : [a, b] \to \mathbb{P}^2$ is a smooth curve in $(\mathbb{P}^2, \mathcal{S})$, the **length of $\boldsymbol{r}$**, denoted $\mathcal{L}(\boldsymbol{r})$, is given by

$$\mathcal{L}(\boldsymbol{r}) = \int_a^b \frac{2|\boldsymbol{r}'(t)|}{1 + |\boldsymbol{r}(t)|^2}\, dt.$$

The **area** of a figure R described in polar coordinates in the elliptic space $\mathbb{P}^2$, denoted $A(R)$, is given by

$$A(R) = \iint_R \frac{4r}{(1+r^2)^2} dr d\theta.$$

$\diamond$

Theorem 6.3.2 *Arc-length is an invariant of elliptic geometry.*

The proof of this theorem is left as an exercise, and is essentially the same as the proof that hyperbolic arc-length is an invariant of hyperbolic geometry, from which it follows that area is invariant. One can also prove that the shortest path between two points is along the elliptic line between them. That is, geodesics follows elliptic lines.

However, one must be careful when measuring the shortest path between points in the projective plane. If p and q are two points in $\mathbb{P}^2$ then there is exactly one elliptic line through them both, but we may view this line as consisting of two elliptic segments, both of which connect p to q. That is, if a bug finds herself at point p and wants to walk along an elliptic line to point q, she can do so by proceeding in either direction along the line, as shown in Figure 6.3.3, p. 133. The **elliptic distance between** p **and** q, which we denote by $d_S(p,q)$, is then the minimum value of the two segment lengths.

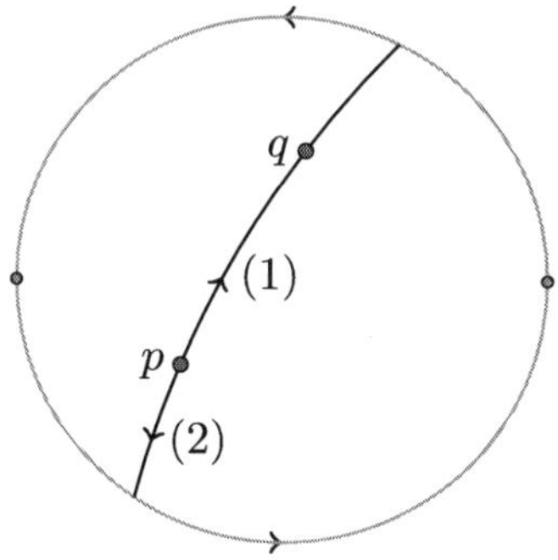

Figure 6.3.3 There is a single elliptic line joining points p and q, but two elliptic line segments. The distance from p to q is the shorter of these two segments.

Theorem 6.3.4 *The distance between two points p and q in $(\mathbb{P}^2, \mathcal{S})$ is*

$$d_S(p,q) = \ min\left\{2\arctan\left(\left|\frac{q-p}{1+\overline{p}q}\right|\right), 2\arctan\left(\left|\frac{1+\overline{p}q}{q-p}\right|\right)\right\}.$$

PROOF. We first determine the elliptic distance between the origin and a point x (with $0 < x \leq 1$) on the positive real axis.

The elliptic line through 0 and x lives on the real axis, and we may parameterize the "eastbound" segment connecting 0 to x by $\boldsymbol{r}(t) = t$ for $0 \leq t \leq x$. (The "westbound" segment from 0 to x is clearly not shorter than the eastbound segment.) The length of this segment is

$$\int_0^x \frac{2|\boldsymbol{r}'(t)|}{1+|\boldsymbol{r}(t)|^2}\, dt = \int_0^x \frac{2|1|}{1+|t|^2}\, dt$$

$$= 2\int_0^x \frac{1}{1+t^2}\,dt$$
$$= 2\arctan(x).$$

Thus, $d_S(0,x) = 2\arctan(x)$, for $0 < x \leq 1$.

To determine the distance $d_S(p,q)$ between arbitrary points in $\mathbb{P}^2$, we may first apply a transformation in $\mathcal{S}$ that sends p to the origin, and q to a point on the positive real axis. By an appropriate choice of θ, the transformation

$$T(z) = e^{i\theta}\frac{z-p}{1+\overline{p}z}$$

will do the trick. Now, T is a Möbius transformation of the entire extended plane, and it may take q outside the unit disk, in which case q_a will be mapped to a point on the real axis inside the unit disk. So, either $|T(q)|$ or $|T(q_a)|$ will be a real number between 0 and 1. If we call this number x, then $d_S(p,q) = d_S(0,x)$, since transformations in $\mathcal{S}$ preserve distance between points.

Now,

$$|T(q)| = \left|\frac{q-p}{1+\overline{p}q}\right|,$$

and the reader can check, using the fact that $q_a = -1/\overline{q}$, that

$$|T(q_a)| = \left|\frac{1+\overline{p}q}{q-p}\right|.$$

It follows that

$$d_S(p,q) = \min\left\{2\arctan\left(\left|\frac{q-p}{1+\overline{p}q}\right|\right), 2\arctan\left(\left|\frac{1+\overline{p}q}{q-p}\right|\right)\right\}.$$

This completes the proof. □

With the sphere as our model, we can check our formulas against measurements on the sphere. For instance, $d_S(0,1) = 2\arctan(1) = \pi/2$. The elliptic segment from 0 to 1 corresponds via stereographic projection to one-quarter of a great circle on the unit sphere. Any great circle on the unit sphere has circumference 2π, so one-quarter of a great circle has length $\pi/2$ on the sphere. We also note that the distance formula $d_S(0,x) = 2\arctan(x)$ applies to spherical geometry $(\mathbb{C}^+, \mathcal{S})$ for all positive real numbers x, and this distance matches the corresponding distances of the points on the unit 2-sphere, see Exercise 6.3.12, p. ??.

We emphasize that $\pi/2$ is an upper bound for the distance between two points in $(\mathbb{P}^2, \mathcal{S})$. However, there is no upper bound on how long a journey along an elliptic line can be. If Bormit the bug wants to head out from point p and travel r units along any line, Bormit can do it, without obstruction, for any $r > 0$. Of course, if r is large enough, Bormit will do "laps" on this journey. We say a path is a geodesic path if it follows along an elliptic line.

Definition 6.3.5 In $(\mathbb{P}^2, \mathcal{S})$, the **elliptic circle** centered at z_0 with radius r consists of all points $z \in \mathbb{P}^2$ such that there exists a geodesic path of length r from z_0 to z. ◊

Each transformation T in $\mathcal{S}$ is an elliptic Möbius transformation by Theorem 6.2.4, p. 128 that fixes two antipodal points, say p and p_a. So T pushes points along type II clines of p and p_a, and since transformations preserve distance between points, these type II clines of p and p_a determine elliptic circles; all points on these type II clines are equidistant from p.

Now, suppose p and q are any distinct points in $\mathbb{P}^2$. There exists a type II cline of p and p_a that goes through q. If this cline lives entirely inside the closed unit disk it represents the elliptic circle centered at p through q. Of course, this cline may not live entirely inside the disk, as is the case in Figure 6.3.6, p. 135. But each point on the type II cline of p and p_a through q has antipodal point on the type II cline of p and p_a through q_a. So, in $\mathbb{P}^2$ we may represent the elliptic circle centered at p through q by the portions of these two type II clines of p and p_a that live in the closed unit disk.

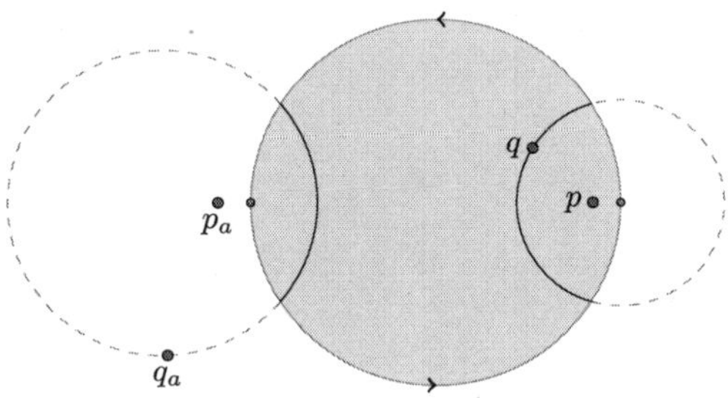

Figure 6.3.6 The elliptic circle centered at p through q in $\mathbb{P}^2$ may consist of portions of two distinct clines.

We note also that elliptic circles centered at the origin correpond to Euclidean circles centered at the origin. In particular, a Euclidean circle centered at the origin with Euclidean radius a (with $0 < a < 1$) corresponds to an elliptic circle centered at the origin with elliptic radius $2\arctan(a)$.

Theorem 6.3.7 *An elliptic circle in* $\mathbb{P}^2$ *with elliptic radius* $r < \pi/2$ *has circumference* $C = 2\pi\sin(r)$.

The proof of this theorem is left as an exercise. Circles with elliptic radius greater than or equal to $\pi/2$ are also investigated in the exercises. They may not look like circles!

The area of a triangle. We now turn our attention to finding a formula for the area of a triangle in elliptic geometry. We begin with lunes. A **lune** is the region in $\mathbb{P}^2$ bounded between two elliptic lines. How do two elliptic lines bound a region? Two lines trap a region because we are identifying antipodal points on the unit circle. A bug living in the shaded region of $\mathbb{P}^2$ pictured in Figure 6.3.8, p. 136 would be able to visit all shaded points without crossing the boundary walls determined by the two elliptic lines. The shaded region is a single, connected region bounded by two lines. So what is the area of this region?

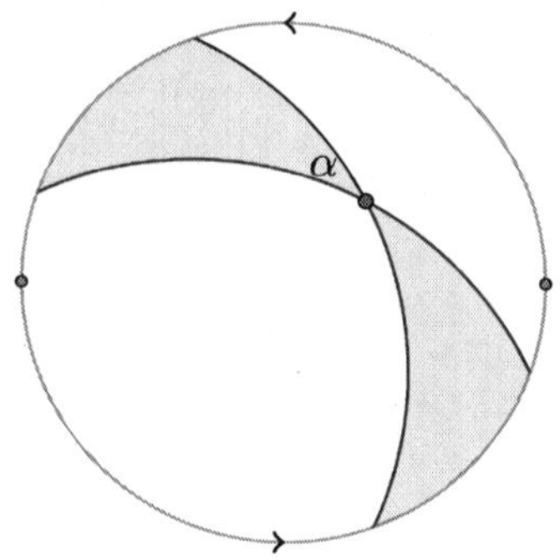

Figure 6.3.8 A lune in $\mathbb{P}^2$ with angle α.

Lemma 6.3.9 The area of a lune. *In* $(\mathbb{P}^2, \mathcal{S})$, *the area of a lune with angle* α *is* 2α.

PROOF. To compute the area of a lune, first move the vertex of the lune to the origin in such a way that one leg of the lune lies on the real axis, as in Figure 6.3.10, p. 136. Then half of the lunar region can be described in polar coordinates by $0 \leq r \leq 1$ and $0 \leq \theta \leq \alpha$.

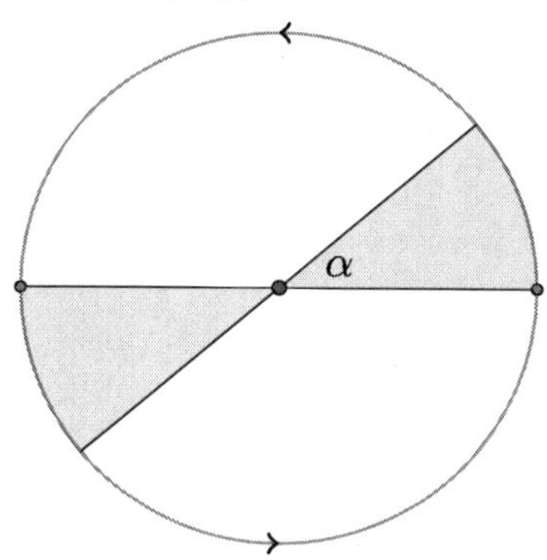

Figure 6.3.10 A lune whose elliptic lines intersect at the origin.

So the area of a lune having angle α is given by

$$\begin{aligned} A &= 2\int_0^\alpha \int_0^1 \frac{4r}{(1+r^2)^2} dr d\theta && \text{(Let } u = 1+r^2\text{)} \\ &= 2\int_0^\alpha \left[\frac{-2}{1+r^2}\bigg|_0^1 \right] d\theta \\ &= 2\int_0^\alpha 1 \, d\theta \\ &= 2\alpha. \end{aligned}$$

□

Example 6.3.11 Triangle area in $(\mathbb{P}^2, \mathcal{S})$.

Triangle Δpqr below is formed from 3 elliptic lines. Notice that each corner of the triangle determines a lune, and that the three lunes cover the entire projective plane, with some overlap. In particular, the three lunes in sum cover the triangle three times, so the sum of the three lune areas equals the area of the entire projective plane plus two times the area of the triangle.

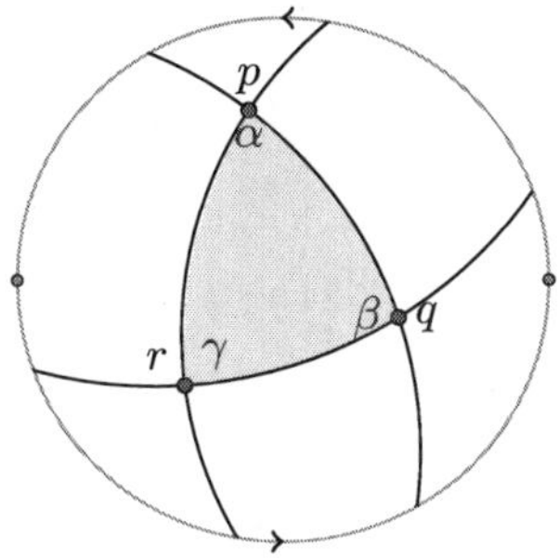

The area of the entire projective plane is 2π (see Exercise 6.3.9, p. ??), so we have the following relation:

$$\begin{aligned} 2\pi + 2 \cdot A(\Delta pqr) &= A(\text{Lune } p) + A(\text{Lune } q) + A(\text{Lune } r) \\ 2\pi + 2 \cdot A(\Delta pqr) &= (2\alpha + 2\beta + 2\gamma) \\ A(\Delta pqr) &= (\alpha + \beta + \gamma) - \pi. \end{aligned}$$

We summarize the result of this example with the following theorem.

Theorem 6.3.12 *In elliptic geometry $(\mathbb{P}^2, \mathcal{S})$, the area of a triangle with angles α, β, γ is*

$$A = (\alpha + \beta + \gamma) - \pi.$$

From this theorem it follows that the angles of any triangle in elliptic geometry sum to more than $180°$.

We close this section with a discussion of trigonometry in elliptic geometry. We derive formulas analogous to those in Theorem 5.4.12, p. 104 for hyperbolic triangles. We assume here that the triangle determined by distinct points p, q and z in $(\mathbb{P}^2, \mathcal{S})$ is formed by considering the shortest paths connecting these three points. So triangle side lenghths will not exceed $\pi/2$ in what follows.

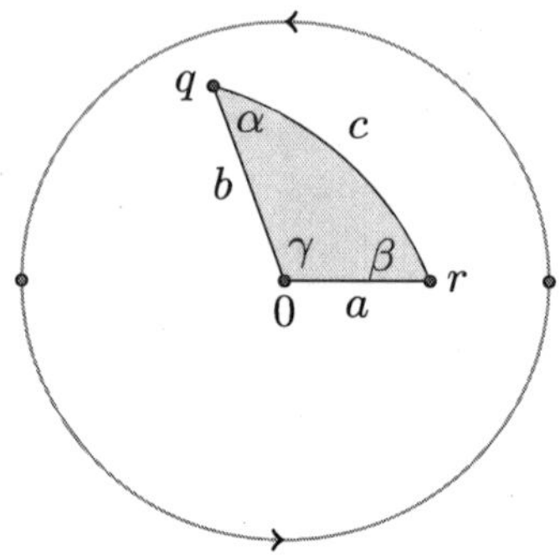

Figure 6.3.13 An elliptic triangle with side lengths and angles marked.

Theorem 6.3.14 *Suppose we have an elliptic triangle with elliptic side lengths a, b, and c, and angles α, β, and γ as in Figure 6.3.13, p. 138. Then the following laws hold:*

a. Elliptic law of cosines

$$\cos(c) = \cos(a)\cos(b) + \sin(a)\sin(b)\cos(\gamma).$$

b. Elliptic law of sines

$$\frac{\sin(a)}{\sin(\alpha)} = \frac{\sin(b)}{\sin(\beta)} = \frac{\sin(c)}{\sin(\gamma)}.$$

PROOF. a. Position our triangle conveniently, with one corner at the origin, one on the positive real axis at the point r $(0 < r \leq 1)$, and one at the point $q = ke^{i\gamma}$ (with $0 < k \leq 1$) as in Figure 6.3.13, p. 138. Then $a = d_S(0, r) = 2\arctan(r)$, so that

$$\begin{aligned}\cos(a) &= \cos(2\arctan(r)) \\ &= \cos^2(\arctan(r)) - \sin^2(\arctan(r))\end{aligned}$$

by the cosine double angle formula. If we set $\theta = \arctan(r)$ we may use the following right triangle to rewrite the above description of $\cos(a)$ as follows:

$$\begin{aligned}\cos(a) &= \frac{1}{1+r^2} - \frac{r^2}{1+r^2} \\ &= \frac{1-r^2}{1+r^2}\end{aligned}$$

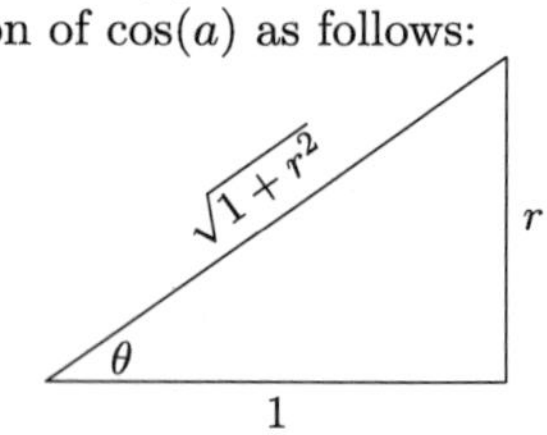

On the other hand,

$$\begin{aligned}\sin(a) &= \sin(2\arctan(r)) \\ &= 2\sin(\arctan(r))\cos(\arctan(r)),\end{aligned}$$

from which it follows that

$$\sin(a) = \frac{2r}{1+r^2}.$$

Turning our attention to the side with length b, $b = d_S(0, q) = 2\arctan(|q|) = 2\arctan(k)$, since $q = ke^{i\gamma}$ with $k > 0$. It follows that

$$\cos(b) = \frac{1-k^2}{1+k^2} \quad \text{and} \quad \sin(b) = \frac{2k}{1+k^2}.$$

And the third side? Theorem 6.3.4, p. 133 tells us

$$c = d_S(r, ke^{i\gamma}) = 2\arctan\left(\left|\frac{ke^{i\gamma} - r}{1 + rke^{i\gamma}}\right|\right).$$

Since in general $\cos(2\arctan(x)) = (1-x^2)/(1+x^2)$, it follows that

$$\cos(c) = \frac{|1 + rke^{i\gamma}|^2 - |ke^{i\gamma} - r|^2}{|1 + rke^{i\gamma}|^2 + |ke^{i\gamma} - r|^2},$$

which can be expanded using $|z|^2 = z \cdot \overline{z}$, and then reduced to obtain

$$\cos(c) = \frac{1 + r^2k^2 - k^2 - r^2 + 2rk(e^{i\gamma} + e^{-i\gamma})}{1 + r^2 + k^2 + r^2k^2}.$$

Now, $e^{i\gamma} + e^{-i\gamma} = 2\cos(\gamma)$, so we have

$$\begin{aligned}
\cos(c) &= \frac{(1-r^2)(1-k^2) + 2rk2\cos(\gamma)}{(1+r^2)(1+k^2)} \\
&= \frac{1-r^2}{1+r^2} \cdot \frac{1-k^2}{1+k^2} + \frac{2r}{1+r^2} \cdot \frac{2k}{1+k^2}\cos(\gamma) \\
&= \cos(a)\cos(b) + \sin(a)\sin(b)\cos(\gamma).
\end{aligned}$$

Though we worked out the formula for a conveniently located triangle, it holds for any triangle in elliptic geometry because angles and distances are preserved by transformations in elliptic geometry, and there is a transformation that takes any triangle to this convenient location.

b. To prove the elliptic law of sines, first construct the circle containing side c. This circle goes through r and q and their antipodal points $-1/r$ and q_a as pictured in Figure 6.3.15, p. 139. We let p denote the center of the circle, and R its Euclidean radius.

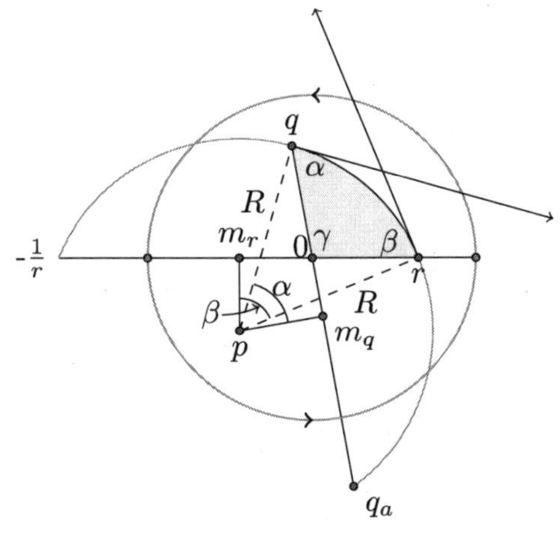

Figure 6.3.15 Deriving the elliptic law of sines.

Let m_r be the midpoint of the segment connecting r and $-1/r$, and let m_q be the midpoint of the segment connecting q and q_a. So,

$$|m_r - r| = \frac{1}{2}\left(r + \frac{1}{r}\right) = \frac{1+r^2}{2r},$$

and

$$|m_q - q| = \left|\frac{1}{2}\left(k + \frac{1}{k}\right)e^{i\gamma}\right| = \frac{1+k^2}{2k}.$$

Note further that $\Delta p m_r r$ is right, and $\angle m_r r p = \pi/2 - \beta$ so that $\angle r p m_r = \beta$. From this right triangle we see $\sin(\beta) = (1+r^2)/(2rR)$.

Similarly, $\Delta p m_q q$ is right, and we have $\angle m_q p q = \alpha$, and $\sin(\alpha) = (1 + k^2)/(2kR)$.

Comparing ratios,

$$\begin{aligned}\frac{\sin(a)}{\sin(\alpha)} &= \frac{2r}{1+r^2} \cdot \frac{2kR}{1+k^2}\\ &= \frac{2k}{1+k^2} \cdot \frac{2rR}{1+r^2}\\ &= \frac{\sin(b)}{\sin(\beta)}.\end{aligned}$$

To see that the ratio $\sin(c)/\sin(\gamma)$ must match the preceding common ratio, note that transformations in elliptic geometry preserve distances and angles, so we may transform our triangle above to one in which the length c is now on the real axis with one end at the origin. The argument above ensures that the ratio $\sin(c)/\sin(\gamma)$ then matches one of the other ratios, and so all three agree. □

Corollary 6.3.16 Elliptic hypotenuse theorem. *In a right triangle in* $(\mathbb{P}^2, \mathcal{S})$ *with elliptic side lengths a and b, and hypotenuse c,*

$$\cos(c) = \cos(a)\cos(b).$$

Exercises

1. Prove Theorem 6.3.7, p. 135. Namely, prove that the circumference of a circle in elliptic geometry is $C = 2\pi\sin(r)$, where $r < \pi/2$ is the elliptic radius.

2. Prove

$$\lim_{r\to 0^+} \frac{2\pi\sin(r)}{2\pi r} = 1.$$

Thus, for small r, the Euclidean formula for the circumference of a circle is a good approximation to the true circumference of a circle in elliptic geometry.

3. *Circles with large radius.*

a. Give a careful sketch of the circle centered at 0 with elliptic radius $\pi/2$.

b. Give a careful sketch of the circle centered at 0 with elliptic radius $2\pi/3$.

c. Give a careful sketch of the circle centered at 0 with elliptic radius π.

d. Give a careful sketch of the circle centered at 0 with elliptic radius 2π.

4. Let C be an elliptic circle with center z_0 and elliptic radius $r > 0$. For what value(s) of r is C an elliptic line? For what value(s) of r is C a single point?

5. Determine the elliptic distance between $\frac{1}{2}$ and $\frac{1}{2}i$.

6. Prove that the area of a circle in elliptic geometry with radius $r < \pi/2$ is

$$A = 4\pi \sin^2(r/2).$$

7. Prove

$$\lim_{r \to 0+} \frac{4\pi \sin^2(r/2)}{\pi r^2} = 1.$$

Thus, for small r, the Euclidean formula for the area of a circle is a good approximation to the true area of a circle in elliptic geometry.

8. Prove that arc-length is an invariant of elliptic geometry.

9. Prove that the area of $\mathbb{P}^2$ is 2π. Thus, unlike the hyperbolic case, the space in elliptic geometry has finite area.

10. An intrepid tax collector lives in a country in the elliptic space $\mathbb{P}^2$. For collection purposes, the country is divided into triangular grids. The collector observes that the angles of the triangle she collects in are 92°, 62°, and 27°. What is the area of her triangle? (Be sure to convert the angles to radians.) Can the entire space $\mathbb{P}^2$ be subdivided into a finite number of triangles?

11. Find a formula for the area of an n-gon in elliptic geometry $(\mathbb{P}^2, \mathcal{S})$, given that its n angles are $\alpha_1, \alpha_2, \cdots, \alpha_n$.

12. In this exercise we show the distance between any two points p and q in spherical geometry $(\mathbb{C}^+, \mathcal{S})$ is

$$d_{\mathcal{S}}(p, q) = 2 \arctan\left(\left|\frac{q - p}{1 + \overline{p}q}\right|\right),$$

and that $d_{\mathcal{S}}(p, q)$ corresponds to the distance on the sphere between $\phi^{-1}(p)$ and $\phi^{-1}(q)$.

a. The definition of arc-length in spherical geometry $(\mathbb{C}^+, \mathcal{S})$ is the same as the one for $(\mathbb{P}^2, \mathcal{S})$. Using this definition, follow the proof of Theorem 6.3.4, p. 133 to show that for any positive real number x in $\mathbb{C}^+$, $d_{\mathcal{S}}(0, x) = 2 \arctan(x)$.

b. Use invariance of arc-length to explain why, for arbitrary p and q in $\mathbb{C}^+$,

$$d_{\mathcal{S}}(p, q) = 2 \arctan\left(\left|\frac{q - p}{1 + \overline{p}q}\right|\right).$$

c. Suppose $x > 0$ is a real number. Determine $\phi^{-1}(x)$, the point on the unit sphere corresponding to x via stereographic projection. What is $\phi^{-1}(0)$?

d. Determine the distance between $\phi^{-1}(0)$ and $\phi^{-1}(x)$ on the sphere. In particular, show that this distance equals $\arccos((1 - x^2)/(1 + x^2))$. Hint: the distance between these points will equal the angle between the vectors to these points, and this angle can be found using the formula $\cos(\theta) = \vec{v} \cdot \vec{w}$ for two unit vectors.

e. Show that for $x > 0$, $\arccos((1-x^2)/(1+x^2)) = 2\arctan(x)$. Hint: You may find the following half-angle formula useful: $\tan(\theta/2) = \tan(\theta)/(\sec(\theta)+1)$.

13. Prove that $(\mathbb{P}^2, \mathcal{S})$ is isotropic.

6.4 Revisiting Euclid's Postulates

Without much fanfare, we have shown that the geometry $(\mathbb{P}^2, \mathcal{S})$ satisfies the first four of Euclid's postulates, but fails to satisfy the fifth. This is also the case with hyperbolic geometry $(\mathbb{D}, \mathcal{H})$. Moreover, the elliptic version of the fifth postulate differs from the hyperbolic version. It is the purpose of this section to provide the proper fanfare for these facts.

Recall Euclid's five postulates:

1. One can draw a straight line from any point to any point.
2. One can produce a finite straight line continuously in a straight line.
3. One can describe a circle with any center and radius
4. All right angles equal one another.
5. Given a line and a point not on the line, there is exactly one line through the point that does not intersect the given line.

That the first postulate is satisfied in $(\mathbb{P}^2, \mathcal{S})$ is Theorem 6.2.11, p. 131.

The second postulate holds here even though our elliptic space is finite. We can extend line segments indefinitely because the space has no boundary. If we are at a point in the space, and decide to head off in a certain direction along an elliptic straight line, we can walk for as long and far as we want (though we would eventually return to our starting point and continue making laps along the elliptic line).

The third postulate follows by a similar argument. In the previous section we defined a circle about *any* point in $\mathbb{P}^2$. And since we can walk an arbitrarily long distance from any point, we can describe a circle of any radius about the point.

The fourth postulate follows since Möbius transformations preserve angles and the maps in $\mathcal{S}$ are special Möbius transformations.

The fifth postulate fails because any two elliptic lines intersect (Theorem 6.2.13, p. 131). Thus, given a line and a point not on the line, there is *not a single line* through the point that does not intersect the given line.

Recall that in our model of hyperbolic geometry, $(\mathbb{D}, \mathcal{H})$, we proved that given a line and a point not on the line, there *are two lines* through the point that do not intersect the given line.

So we have three different, equally valid geometries that share Euclid's first four postulates, but each has its own parallel postulate. Furthermore, on a small scale, the three geometries all behave similarly. A tiny bug living on the surface of a sphere might reasonably suspect Euclid's fifth postulate holds, given his limited perspective. A tiny bug in the hyperbolic plane would reasonably conclude the same. Small triangles have angles adding up nearly to 180°, and small circles have areas and circumferences that are accurately described by the Euclidean formulas πr^2 and $2\pi r$. We explore geometry on surfaces in more detail in the next chapter.

7

Geometry on Surfaces

In hyperbolic geometry $(\mathbb{D}, \mathcal{H})$ and elliptic geometry $(\mathbb{P}^2, \mathcal{S})$, the area of a triangle is determined by the sum of its angles. This is a significant difference from Euclidean geometry, in which a triangle with three given angles can be built to have any desired area. Does this mean that if a bug lives in a world adhering to elliptic geometry, it can never stumble upon a triangle with three right angles having area 3π? Yes and no. In the elliptic geometry as defined in Chapter 6, no such triangle exists because a triangle with 3 right angles must have area $(\frac{\pi}{2} + \frac{\pi}{2} + \frac{\pi}{2}) - \pi = \frac{\pi}{2}$. So the answer appears to be yes. However, the elliptic geometry $(\mathbb{P}^2, \mathcal{S})$ models the geometry of the *unit* sphere, and this choice of sphere radius is somewhat arbitrary. What if the radius of the sphere changes? Imagine a triangle with three right angles having one vertex at the north pole and two vertices on the equator. If the sphere uniformly expands, the angles of the triangle will stay the same, but the area of the triangle will increase. So, if a bug is convinced she lives in a world with elliptic geometry, but is also convinced she has found a triangle with three right angles and area 3π, the bug might be drawn to conclude she lives in a world modeled on a larger sphere than the unit 2-sphere.

The key geometrical property of a space dictating the relationship between the angles of a triangle and its area is called curvature. Curvature also dictates the relationship between the circumference of a circle and its radius.

7.1 Curvature

Consider the smooth curve in Figure 7.1.1, p. 146. The curvature of the curve at a point is a measure of how drastically the curve bends away from its tangent line, and this curvature is often studied in a multivariable calculus course. The radius of curvature at a point corresponds to the radius of the circle that best approximates the curve at this point. The radius r of this circle is the reciprocal of the curvature k of the curve at the point: $k = 1/r$.

Figure 7.1.1 The curvature of a curve.

The curvature of a surface (such as the graph of a function $z = f(x, y)$) at a particular point is a measure of how drastically the surface bends away from its tangent plane at the point. There are three fundamental types of curvature. A surface has positive curvature at a point if the surface lives entirely on one side of the tangent plane, at least near the point of interest. The surface has negative curvature at a point if it is saddle-shaped, in the sense that the tangent plane cuts through the surface. Between these two cases is the case of zero curvature. In this case the surface has a line along which the surface agrees with the tangent plane. For instance, a cylinder has zero curvature, as suggested in Figure 7.1.2, p. 146(c).

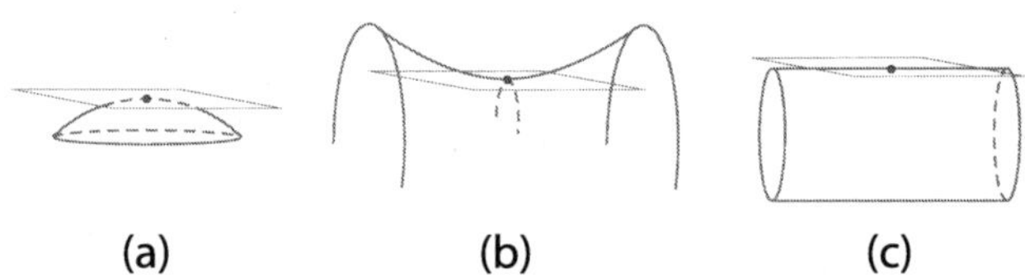

Figure 7.1.2 The curvature of a surface at a point can be (a) positive; (b) negative; or (c) zero.

This informal description of curvature makes use of how the surface is embedded in space. One of Gauss' great theorems, one he called his *Theorem Egregium*, states that the curvature of a surface is an intrinsic property of the surface. The curvature doesn't change if the surface is bent without stretching, and our tireless two-dimensional inhabitant living in the space can determine the curvature by taking measurements.

A two-dimensional bug living in the hyperbolic plane, the projective plane, or the Euclidean plane would notice that a small circle's circumference is related to its radius by the Euclidean formula $c \approx 2\pi r$. In Euclidean geometry this formula applies to all circles, but in the non-Euclidean cases, the observant bug might notice in large circles a significant difference between the actual circumference of a circle and the circumference predicted by $c = 2\pi r$. Large circles about a cup-shaped point with positive curvature will have circumference less than that predicted by Euclidean geometry. This fact explains why a large chunk of orange peel fractures if pressed flat onto a table. Large circles drawn around a saddle-shaped point with negative curvature will have circumference greater than that predicted by the Euclidean formula.

Calculus may be used to precisely capture this deviation between the Euclidean-predicted circumference $2\pi r$ and the actual circumference c for circles of radius r in the different geometries.

Recall that in the hyperbolic plane, $c = 2\pi \sinh(r)$; in the Euclidean plane $c = 2\pi r$; and in the elliptic plane $c = 2\pi \sin(r)$. In Figure 7.1.3, p. 147 we have graphed the ratio $\frac{c}{2\pi r}$ where c is the circumference of a circle with radius r in (a) the hyperbolic plane; (b) the Euclidean plane; and (c) the elliptic plane.

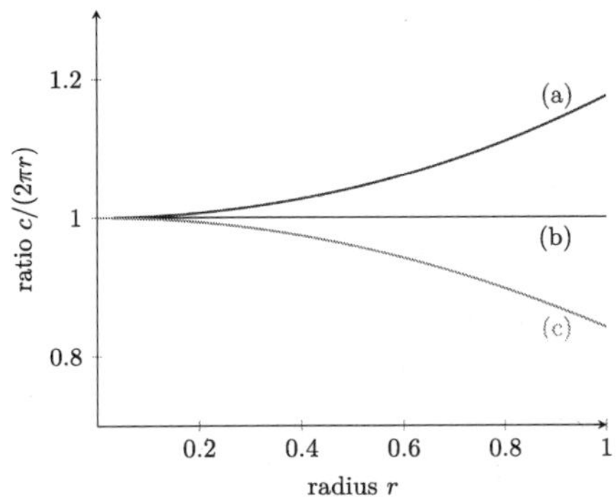

Figure 7.1.3 Plotting the ratio $c/2\pi r$ against r in (a) hyperbolic geometry, (b) Euclidean geometry, and (c) elliptic geometry.

In all three cases, the ratio $c/2\pi r$ approaches 1 as r shrinks to 0. Furthermore, in all three cases the *derivative* of the ratio approaches 0 as $r \to 0^+$. But with the *second* derivative of the ratio we may distinguish these geometries. It can be shown that the curvature at a point is proportional to this second derivative evaluated in the limit as $r \to 0^+$. We will not derive this formula for curvature, but will use this working definition as it appears in Thurston's book [11].

Definition 7.1.4 Suppose a circle of radius r about a point p is drawn in a space[1], and its circumference is c. The **curvature of the space at** p is

$$k = -3 \lim_{r \to 0^+} \frac{d^2}{dr^2}\left[\frac{c}{2\pi r}\right].$$

◊

Since we are interested in worlds that are homogeneous and isotropic, we will focus our attention on worlds in which the curvature is the same at all points. That is, we investigate surfaces of constant curvature.

Example 7.1.5 The curvature of a sphere.

Consider the sphere with radius s in the following diagram, and note the circle centered at the north pole N having surface radius r. The circle is parallel to the plane $z = 0$, has Euclidean radius x, and hence circumference $2\pi x$.

[1] the term 'space' is intentionally vague here. Our space needs to have a well-defined metric, so that it makes sense to talk about radius and circumference. The space might be the Euclidean plane, the hyperbolic plane or the sphere. Other spaces are discussed in Section 7.5.

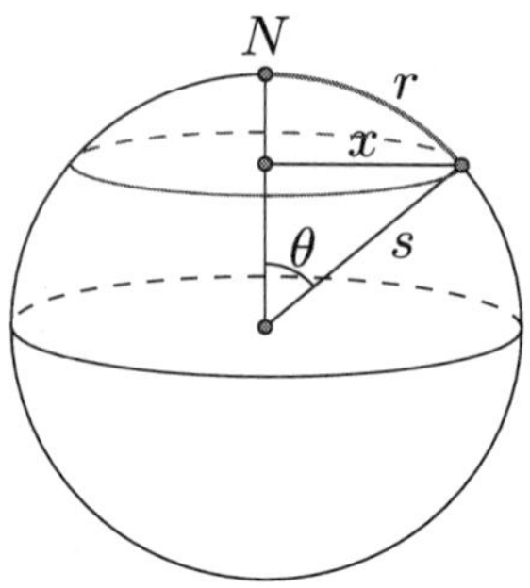

But $x = s\sin(\theta)$ and $r = \theta \cdot s$, from which we deduce $x = s\sin(\frac{r}{s})$, and in terms of the surface radius r of the circle, its circumference is

$$c = 2\pi s \sin\left(\frac{r}{s}\right).$$

The curvature of the sphere at N is thus

$$k = -3 \lim_{r\to 0+} \frac{d^2}{dr^2}\left[\frac{2\pi s\sin(r/s)}{2\pi r}\right].$$

Cancelling the 2π terms and replacing $\sin(r/s)$ with its power series expansion, we have

$$\begin{aligned} k &= -3 \lim_{r\to 0+} \frac{d^2}{dr^2}\left[\frac{s(\frac{r}{s} - \frac{r^3}{6s^3} + \frac{r^5}{120s^5} - \cdots)}{r}\right] \\ &= -3 \lim_{r\to 0+} \frac{d^2}{dr^2}\left[1 - \frac{r^2}{6s^2} + \frac{r^4}{120s^4} - \cdots\right] \\ &= -3 \lim_{r\to 0+} \left[\frac{-1}{3s^2} + \frac{12r^2}{120s^4} - \cdots\right]. \end{aligned}$$

Note that all the terms of the second derivative after the first have powers of r in the numerator, so these terms go to 0 as $r \to 0^+$, and the curvature of the sphere at the north pole is $1/s^2$. In fact because the sphere is homogeneous, the curvature at any point is

$$k = \frac{1}{s^2}.$$

Example 7.1.6 Curvature of the hyperbolic plane.

Because hyperbolic geometry is homogeneous and its transformations preserve circles and lengths, the curvature is the same at all points in the hyperbolic plane. We choose to compute the curvature at the origin.

Recall, the circumference of a circle in $(\mathbb{D}, \mathcal{H})$ is $c = 2\pi \sinh(r)$. To compute the curvature, use the power series expansion

$$\sinh(r) = r + \frac{r^3}{3!} + \frac{r^5}{5!} + \cdots.$$

$$\begin{aligned} k &= -3 \lim_{r \to 0^+} \frac{d^2}{dr^2} \left[\frac{2\pi \sinh(r)}{2\pi r} \right] \\ &= -3 \lim_{r \to 0^+} \frac{d^2}{dr^2} \left[1 + \frac{r^2}{3!} + \frac{r^4}{5!} + \cdots \right] \\ &= -3 \lim_{r \to 0^+} \left[\frac{1}{3} + \frac{12r^2}{5!} + \cdots \right]. \end{aligned}$$

Again, each term of the second derivative after the first has a power of r in its numerator, so in the limit as $r \to 0^+$, each of these terms vanishes. Thus, the curvature of the hyperbolic plane in $(\mathbb{D}, \mathcal{H})$ is $k = -1$.

Exercises

1. Use our working definition to show that the curvature of the projective plane in elliptic geometry is 1. Recall, $c = 2\pi \sin(r)$ in this geometry.

2. Use our working definition to explain why the curvature of the Euclidean plane is $k = 0$.

7.2 Elliptic Geometry with Curvature $k > 0$

One may model elliptic geometry on spheres of varying radii, and a change in radius will cause a change in the curvature of the space as well as a change in the relationship between the area of a triangle and its angle sum.

For any real number $k > 0$, we may construct a sphere with constant curvature k. According to Example 7.1.5, p. 147, the sphere centered at the origin with radius $1/\sqrt{k}$ works. Geometry on this sphere can be modeled down in the extended plane via stereographic projection. This geometry will be called elliptic geometry with curvature $k > 0$.

Consider the sphere $\mathbb{S}^2_k$ centered at the origin of $\mathbb{R}^3$ with radius $1/\sqrt{k}$. Define stereographic projection $\phi_k : \mathbb{S}^2_k \to \mathbb{C}^+$, just as we did in Section 3.3, to obtain the formula

$$\phi_k(a, b, c) = \begin{cases} \frac{a}{1 - c\sqrt{k}} + \frac{b}{1 - c\sqrt{k}} i & \text{if } c \neq \frac{1}{\sqrt{k}}; \\ \infty & \text{if } c = \frac{1}{\sqrt{k}} \end{cases}.$$

Diametrically opposed points on $\mathbb{S}^2_k$ get mapped via ϕ_k to points z and z_a that satisfy the equation $z_a = \frac{-1}{k\bar{z}}$, by analogy with Lemma 6.1.2, p. 122. We call two such points in $\mathbb{C}^+$ antipodal with respect to $\mathbb{S}^2_k$, or just antipodal points if the value of k is understood.

Our model for elliptic geometry with curvature k has space $\mathbb{P}^2_k$ equal to the closed disk in $\mathbb{C}$ of radius $1/\sqrt{k}$, with antipodal points of the boundary identified. This space is simply a scaled version of the projective plane from Chapter 6.

The group of transformations, denoted $\mathcal{S}_k$, consists of those Möbius transformations that preserve antipodal points with respect to $\mathbb{S}^2_k$. That is, $T \in \mathcal{S}_k$ if and only if the following holds:

$$\text{if } z_a = -\frac{1}{k\bar{z}} \text{ then } T(z_a) = -\frac{1}{k\overline{T(z)}}.$$

The geometry $(\mathbb{P}^2_k, \mathcal{S}_k)$ with $k > 0$ is called **elliptic geometry with curvature** k. Note that $(\mathbb{P}^2_1, \mathcal{S}_1)$ is precisely the geometry we studied in Chapter 6.

The transformations of $\mathbb{C}^+$ in the group $\mathcal{S}_k$ correspond precisely with rotations of the sphere $\mathbb{S}^2_k$. One can show that transformations in $\mathcal{S}_k$ have the form

$$T(z) = e^{i\theta}\frac{z - z_0}{1 + k\overline{z_0}z}.$$

We define lines in elliptic geometry with curvature k to be clines with the property that if they go through z then they go through $z_a = -\frac{1}{k\bar{z}}$. These lines correspond precisely to great circles on the sphere $\mathbb{S}^2_k$.

The arc-length and area formulas also slip gently over from Chapter 6 to this more general setting.

The arc-length of a smooth curve $\boldsymbol{r}$ in $\mathbb{P}^2_k$ is

$$\mathcal{L}(\boldsymbol{r}) = \int_a^b \frac{2|\boldsymbol{r}'(t)|}{1 + k|\boldsymbol{r}(t)|^2}\, dt.$$

As before, arc-length is an invariant, and the shortest path between two points is along the elliptic line through them. In the exercises we derive a formula for the distance between points in this geometry. The greatest possible distance between two points in $(\mathbb{P}^2_k, \mathcal{S}_k)$ turns out to be $\pi/(2\sqrt{k})$.

The area of a region R given in polar form is computed by the formula

$$A(R) = \iint_R \frac{4r}{(1 + kr^2)^2} dr d\theta.$$

To compute the area of a triangle, proceed as in Chapter 6. First, tackle the area of a **lune**, a 2-gon whose sides are elliptic lines in $(\mathbb{P}^2_k, \mathcal{S}_k)$.

Lemma 7.2.1 *Assume $k > 0$. A lune in $(\mathbb{P}^2_k, \mathcal{S}_k)$ with interior angle α has area $2\alpha/k$.*

PROOF. Without loss of generality, we may consider the vertex of our lune to be the origin. As before, elliptic lines through the origin must also pass through ∞, so our two lines forming the lune are Euclidean lines. After a convenient rotation, we may further assume one of these lines is the real axis, so that the lune resembles the one in Figure 6.3.10, p. 136. To compute the area of the lune, compute the integral

$$A = 2\int_0^{\alpha}\int_0^{1/\sqrt{k}} \frac{4r}{(1 + kr^2)^2} dr d\theta.$$

Letting $u = 1 + kr^2$ so that $du = 2krdr$, the bounds of integration change from $[0, 1/\sqrt{k}]$ to $[1, 2]$. Then,

$$A = 2\int_0^\alpha \frac{2}{k}\int_1^2 \frac{du}{u^2}d\theta = \frac{4}{k}\int_0^\alpha \frac{1}{2}d\theta = \frac{2\alpha}{k}.$$

Thus, the angle of a lune with interior angle α is $2\alpha/k$. □

We remark that the lune with angle π actually covers the entire disk of radius $1/\sqrt{k}$. Thus, the area of the entire space $\mathbb{P}^2_k$ is $2\pi/k$, which matches half the surface area of a sphere of radius $1/\sqrt{k}$. We often call $s = 1/\sqrt{k}$ the **radius of curvature** for the geometry; it is the radius of the disk on which we model the geometry.

Also, the integral computation in the proof of Lemma 7.2.1, p. 150 reveals the following useful antiderivative:

$$\int \frac{4r}{(1+kr^2)^2}dr = \frac{-2}{k(1+kr^2)} + C.$$

This fact may speed up future integral computations.

Lemma 7.2.2 *In elliptic geometry with curvature k, the area of a triangle with angles α, β, and γ is*

$$A = \frac{1}{k}(\alpha + \beta + \gamma - \pi).$$

PROOF. As in the case $k = 1$, the area of any triangle may be determined from the area of three lunes and the total area of $\mathbb{P}^2_k$, as depicted in Example 6.3.11, p. 137. □

Example 7.2.3 Triangles on the Earth.

The surface of the Earth is approximately spherical with radius about 6375 km. Therefore, the geometry on the surface of the Earth can be reasonably modeled by $(\mathbb{P}^2_k, \mathcal{S}_k)$ where $k = 1/6375^2$ km^{-2}. The area of a triangle on the Earth's surface having angles α, β, and γ is

$$A = \frac{1}{k}(\alpha + \beta + \gamma - \pi).$$

Can you find the area of the triangle formed by Paris, New York, and Rio? Use a globe, a protractor, and some string. The string follows a geodesic between two points when it is pulled taut.

Exercises

1. Prove that for $k > 0$, any transformation in $\mathcal{S}_k$ has the form

$$T(z) = e^{i\theta}\frac{z - z_0}{1 + k\overline{z_0}z},$$

where θ is any real number and z_0 is a point in $\mathbb{P}^2_k$.

2. Verify the formula for the stereographic projection map ϕ_k.

3. Assume $k > 0$ and let $s = 1/\sqrt{k}$. Derive the following measurement formulas in $(\mathbb{P}^2_k, \mathcal{S}_k)$.

a. The length of a line segment from 0 to x, where $0 < x \leq s$ is

$$d_k(0, x) = 2s\arctan(x/s).$$

b. The circumference of the circle centered at the origin with elliptic radius $r < \pi/(2\sqrt{k})$ is $C = 2\pi s\sin(r/s)$.

c. The area of the circle centered at the origin with elliptic radius $r < \pi/(2\sqrt{k})$ is $A = 4\pi s^2 \sin^2\left(\frac{r}{2s}\right)$.

4. In this exercise we investigate the idea that the elliptic formulas in Exercise 7.2.3, p. **??** for distance, circumference, and area approach Euclidean formulas when $k \to 0^+$.

a. Show that the elliptic distance $d_k(0, x)$ from 0 to x, where $0 < x \leq s$, approaches $2x$ as $k \to 0^+$ (twice the usual notion of Euclidean distance).

b. Show that the elliptic circumference of a circle with elliptic radius r approaches $2\pi r$ as $k \to 0^+$.

c. Show that the elliptic area of this circle approaches πr^2 as $k \to 0^+$.

5. *Triangle trigonometry in* $(\mathbb{P}^2_k, \mathcal{S}_k)$.

Suppose we have a triangle in $(\mathbb{P}^2_k, \mathcal{S}_k)$ with side lengths a, b, c and angles α, β, γ as pictured in Figure 6.3.13, p. 138.

a. Prove the elliptic law of cosines in $(\mathbb{P}^2_k, \mathcal{S}_k)$:

$$\cos(\sqrt{k}c) = \cos(\sqrt{k}a)\cos(\sqrt{k}b) + \sin(\sqrt{k}a)\sin(\sqrt{k}b)\cos(\gamma).$$

b. Prove the elliptic law of sines in $(\mathbb{P}^2_k, \mathcal{S}_k)$:

$$\frac{\sin(\sqrt{k}a)}{\sin(\alpha)} = \frac{\sin(\sqrt{k}b)}{\sin(\beta)} = \frac{\sin(\sqrt{k}c)}{\sin(\gamma)}.$$

7.3 Hyperbolic Geometry with Curvature $k < 0$

We may do the same gentle scaling of the Poincaré model of hyperbolic geometry as we did in the previous section to the disk model of elliptic geometry. In particular, for each negative number $k < 0$ we construct a model for hyperbolic geometry with curvature k.

We define the space $\mathbb{D}_k$ to be the open disk of radius $1/\sqrt{|k|}$ centered at the origin in $\mathbb{C}$. That is, $\mathbb{D}_k$ consists of all z in $\mathbb{C}$ such that $|z| < 1/\sqrt{|k|}$. In this setting, the circle at infinity is the boundary circle $|z| = 1/\sqrt{|k|}$.

The group $\mathcal{H}_k$ consists of all Möbius transformations that send $\mathbb{D}_k$ to itself. The geometry $(\mathbb{D}_k, \mathcal{H}_k)$ with $k < 0$ is called **hyperbolic geometry with curvature k.** Pushing analogy with the elliptic case, we may define the group of transformations to consist of all Möbius transformations with this property: if z

and z^* are symmetric with respect to the circle at infinity then $T(z)$ and $T(z^*)$ are also symmetric with respect to the circle at infinity. Noting that the point symmetric to z with respect to this circle is $z^* = \frac{1}{|k|\overline{z}} = -\frac{1}{k\overline{z}}$, we draw the satisfying conclusion that $T \in \mathcal{H}_k$ if and only if the following holds:

$$\text{if } z^* = -\frac{1}{k\overline{z}} \text{ then } T(z^*) = -\frac{1}{k\overline{T(z)}}.$$

Thus, the group $\mathcal{H}_k$ in the hyperbolic case has been defined precisely as the group $\mathcal{S}_k$ in the elliptic case. Furthermore, one can show that transformations in $\mathcal{H}_k$ have the form

$$T(z) = e^{i\theta}\frac{z - z_0}{1 + k\overline{z_0}z},$$

where z_0 is a point in $\mathbb{D}_k$.

Straight lines in this geometry are the clines in $\mathbb{C}^+$ orthogonal to the circle at infinity. By Theorem 3.2.8, p. 43, a straight line in $(\mathbb{D}_k, \mathcal{H}_k)$ is precisely a cline with the property that if it goes through z then it goes through its symmetric point $\frac{-1}{k\overline{z}}$.

The arc-length and area formulas also get tweaked by the scale factor, and now look identical to the formulas for elliptic geometry with curvature k.

The arc-length of a smooth curve $\boldsymbol{r}$ in $\mathbb{D}_k$ is

$$\mathcal{L}(\boldsymbol{r}) = \int_a^b \frac{2|\boldsymbol{r}'(t)|}{1 + k|\boldsymbol{r}(t)|^2}\,dt.$$

The area of a region R given in polar coordinates is computed by the formula

$$A(R) = \iint_R \frac{4r}{(1 + kr^2)^2}\,dr\,d\theta.$$

As in Chapter 5 when k was fixed at -1, the area formula is a bear to use, and one may convert to an upper half-plane model to determine the area of a $\frac{2}{3}$-ideal triangle in $\mathbb{D}_k$. The ambitious reader might follow the methods of Section 5.5 to show that the area of a $\frac{2}{3}$-ideal triangle in $(\mathbb{D}_k, \mathcal{H}_k)$ $(k < 0)$ with interior angle α is $-\frac{1}{k}(\pi - \alpha)$.

With this formula in hand, we can derive the area of any triangle in $\mathbb{D}_k$ in terms of its angles, exactly as we did in Chapter 5.

Lemma 7.3.1 *In hyperbolic geometry with curvature k, the area of a triangle with angles α, β, and γ is*

$$A = \frac{1}{k}(\alpha + \beta + \gamma - \pi).$$

Observing negative curvature

Suppose we are located at a point z in a hyperbolic universe with curvature k. We see in the distance a hyperbolic line L that seems to extend indefinitely. We might intuitively see the point w on the line that is closest to us, as suggested in Figure 7.3.2, p. 154. Now suppose we look down the road a bit to a point v. If v is close to w the angle $\angle wzv$ will be close to 0. As v gets further and further away from w, the angle will grow, getting closer and closer to the angle $\theta = \angle wzu$, where u is an ideal point of the line L.

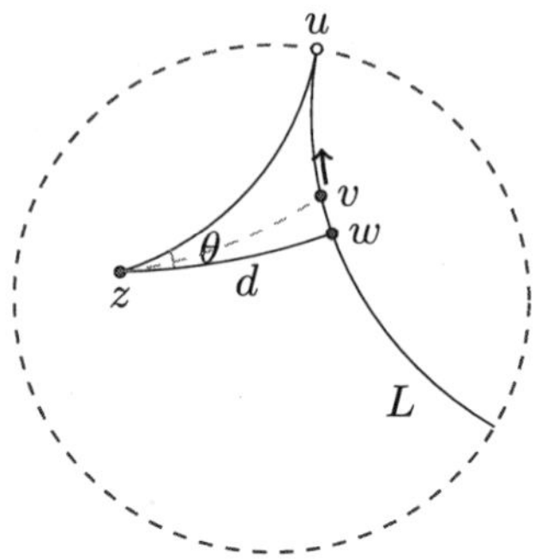

Figure 7.3.2 The angle of parallelism θ of a point z to a line L.

A curious fact about hyperbolic geometry is that this angle θ, which is called the **angle of parallelism of z to L**, is a function of z's distance d to L. In Section 5.4 we saw that $\cosh(d) = 1/\sin(\theta)$ in $(\mathbb{D}, \mathcal{H})$. In particular, one may deduce the distance d to the line L by computing θ. No such analogy exists in Euclidean geometry. In a Euclidean world, if one looks farther and farther down the line L, the angle will approach 90°, no matter one's distance d from the line. The following theorem provides another formula relating the angle of parallelism to a point's distance to a line.

Theorem 7.3.3 Lobatchevsky's formula. *In hyperbolic geometry with curvature k, the hyperbolic distance d of a point z to a hyperbolic line L is related to the angle of parallelism θ by the formula*

$$\tan(\theta/2) = e^{-\sqrt{|k|}d}.$$

PROOF. For this proof, let $s = \frac{1}{\sqrt{|k|}}$. Note that s is the Euclidean radius of the circle at infinity in the disk model for hyperbolic geometry with curvature k. Since angles and lines and distances are preserved, assume z is the origin and L is orthogonal to the positive real axis, intersecting it at the point x (with $0 < x < s$).

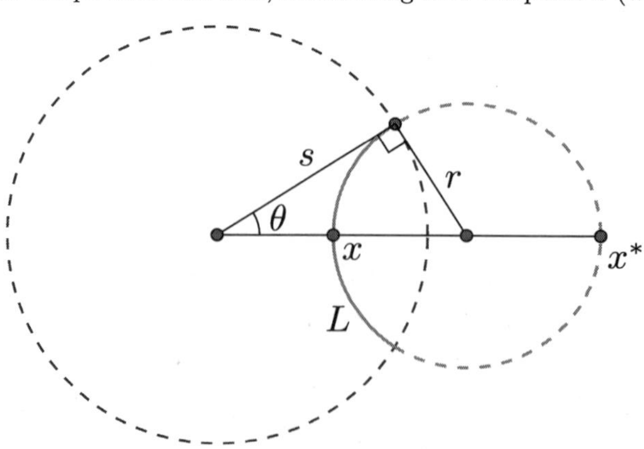

Figure 7.3.4 Deriving Lobatchevsky's formula.

Recall the half-angle formula

$$\tan(\theta/2) = \frac{\tan(\theta)}{\sec(\theta)+1}.$$

According to Figure 7.3.4, p. 154, $\tan(\theta) = r/s$, where r is the Euclidean radius of the circle containing the hyperbolic line L. Furthermore, $\sec(\theta) = (x+r)/s$, so

$$\tan(\theta/2) = \frac{r}{x+r+s}. \tag{1}$$

We may express x and r in terms of the hyperbolic distance d from 0 to x. In Exercise 7.3.2, p. ?? we prove the hyperbolic distance from 0 to x in $(\mathbb{D}_k, \mathcal{H}_k)$ is

$$d = s\ln\left(\frac{s+x}{s-x}\right)$$

so that

$$x = s\cdot\frac{e^{d/s}-1}{e^{d/s}+1}.$$

Express r in terms of d by first expressing it in terms of x. Note that segment xx^* is a diameter of the circle containing L, where $x^* = \frac{-1}{kx}$ is the point symmetric to x with respect to the circle at infinity. Thus, r is half the distance from x to x^*:

$$r = -\frac{1+kx^2}{2kx}.$$

Replacing k with $-1/s^2$, we have

$$r = \frac{s^2-x^2}{2x}.$$

One checks that after writing x in terms of d, r is given by

$$r = \frac{2se^{d/s}}{e^{2d/s}-1}.$$

Substitute this expression for r into the equation labeled (1) in this proof, and after a dose of satisfactory simplifying one obtains the desired result:

$$\tan(\theta/2) = e^{-d/s}.$$

Since $s = 1/\sqrt{|k|}$ this completes the proof. □

Parallax. If a star is relatively close to the Earth, then as the Earth moves in its annual orbit around the Sun, the star will appear to move relative to the backdrop of the more distant stars. In the idealized picture that follows, e_1 and e_2 denote the Earth's position at opposite points of its orbit, and the star s is orthogonal to the plane of the Earth's orbit. The angle p is called the **parallax**, and in a Euclidean universe, p determines the star's distance from the Sun, D, by the equation $D = d/\tan(p)$, where d is the Earth's distance from the Sun.

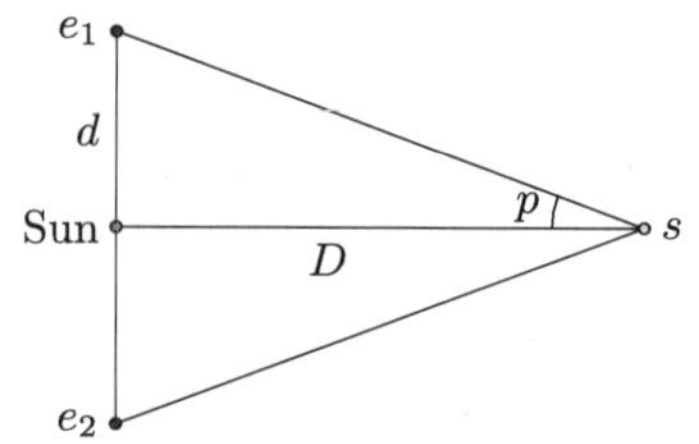

We may determine p by observation, and d is the radius of Earth's orbit around the Sun (d is about 8.3 light-minutes.) In practice, p is quite small, so a working formula is $D = \frac{d}{p}$. The first accurate measurement of parallax was recorded in 1837 by Friedrich Bessel (1784-1846) . He found the stellar parallax of 0.3 arc seconds (1 arc second $= 1/3600°$) for star 61 Cygni, which put the star at about 10.5 light-years away.

If we live in a hyperbolic universe with curvature k, a detected parallax puts a bound on how curved the universe can be. Consider Figure 7.3.5, p. 156. As before, e_1 and e_2 represent the position of the Earth at opposite points of its orbit, so that the distance between them is $2d$, or about 16.6 light-minutes. Assume star s is on the positive real axis and we have detected a parallax p, so that angle $\angle e_2 s e_1 = 2p$.

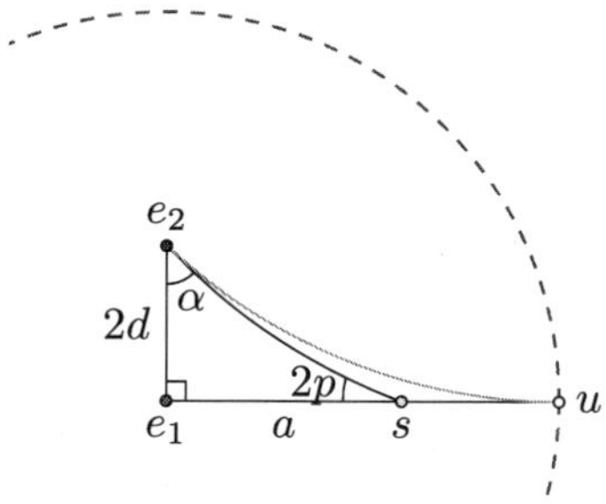

Figure 7.3.5 A detected parallax in a hyperbolic universe puts a bound on its curvature

The angle $\alpha = \angle e_1 e_2 s$ in Figure 7.3.5, p. 156 is less than the angle of parallelism $\theta = \angle e_1 e_2 u$. Noting that $\tan(x)$ is an increasing function and applying Lobatchevsky's formula it follows that

$$\tan(\alpha/2) < \tan(\theta/2) = e^{-\sqrt{|k|}2d}.$$

We may solve this inequality for $|k|$:

$$\begin{aligned} \tan(\alpha/2) &< e^{-\sqrt{|k|}2d} \\ \ln(\tan(\alpha/2)) &< -\sqrt{|k|}2d && \ln(x) \text{ is increasing} \\ \left[\frac{\ln(\tan(\alpha/2))}{2d}\right]^2 &> |k|. && x^2 \text{ is decreasing for } x < 0 \end{aligned}$$

To get a bound for $|k|$ in terms of p, note that $\alpha \approx \pi/2 - 2p$ (the triangles used in stellar parallax have no detectable angular deviation from 180°), so

$$|k| < \left[\frac{\ln(\tan(\pi/4 - p))}{2d}\right]^2.$$

We remark that for values of p near 0, the expression $\ln(\tan(\pi/4 - p))$ has linear approximation equal to $-2p$, so a working bound for k, which appeared in Schwarzschild's 1900 paper [27], is $|k| < (p/d)^2$.

Exercises

1. Prove that for $k < 0$, any transformation in $\mathcal{H}_k$ has the form

$$T(z) = e^{i\theta}\frac{z - z_0}{1 + k\overline{z_0}z},$$

where θ is any real number and z_0 is a point in $\mathbb{D}_k$.

2. Assume $k < 0$ and let $s = 1/\sqrt{|k|}$. Derive the following measurement formulas in $(\mathbb{D}_k, \mathcal{H}_k)$.

a. The length of a line segment from 0 to x, where $0 < x < s$ is

$$d_k(0, x) = s \ln\left(\frac{s + x}{s - x}\right).$$

Hint: Evaluate the integral by partial fractions.

b. The circumference of the circle centered at the origin with hyperbolic radius r is $c = 2\pi s \sinh(r/s)$.

c. The area of the circle centered at the origin with hyperbolic radius r is $A = 4\pi s^2 \sinh^2(\frac{r}{2s})$.

3. Let's investigate the idea that the hyperbolic formulas in Exercise 7.3.2, p. ?? for distance, circumference, and area approach Euclidean formulas when $k \to 0^-$.

a. Show that the hyperbolic distance $d_k(0, x)$ from 0 to x, where $0 < x < s$, approaches $2x$ as $k \to 0^-$.

b. Show that the hyperbolic circumference of a circle with hyperbolic radius r approaches $2\pi r$ as $k \to 0^-$.

c. Show that the hyperbolic area of this circle approaches πr^2 as $k \to 0^-$.

4. *Triangle trigonometry in* $(\mathbb{D}_k, \mathcal{H}_k)$.

Suppose we have a triangle in $(\mathbb{D}_k, \mathcal{H}_k)$ with side lengths a, b, c and angles α, β, and γ as pictured in Figure 5.4.11, p. 104. Suppose further that $s = 1/\sqrt{|k|}$.

a. Prove the hyperbolic law of cosines in $(\mathbb{D}_k, \mathcal{H}_k)$:

$$\cosh(c/s) = \cosh(a/s)\cosh(b/s) - \sinh(a/s)\sinh(b/s)\cos(\gamma).$$

b. Prove the hyperbolic law of sines in $(\mathbb{D}_k, \mathcal{H}_k)$:

$$\frac{\sinh(a/s)}{\sin(\alpha)} = \frac{\sinh(b/s)}{\sin(\beta)} = \frac{\sinh(c/s)}{\sin(\gamma)}.$$

5. As $k < 0$ approaches 0, the formulas of hyperbolic geometry $(\mathbb{D}_k, \mathcal{H}_k)$ approach those of Euclidean geometry. What happens to Lobatchevsky's formula as k approaches 0? What must be the angle of parallelism θ in the limiting case? Is this value of θ independent of d?

6. Bessel determined a parallax of $p = .3$ arcseconds for the star 61 Cygni. Convert this angle to radians and use it to estimate a bound for the curvature constant k if the universe is hyperbolic. The units for this bound should be light years^{-2} (convert the units for the Earth-Sun distance to light-years).

7. The smallest detectable parallax is determined by the resolving power of our best telescopes. Search the web to find the smallest detected parallax to date, and use it to estimate a bound on k if the universe is hyperbolic.

7.4 The Family of Geometries (X_k, G_k)

A strong connection exists between the family $(\mathbb{P}^2_k, \mathcal{S}_k)$ of elliptic geometries with curvature $k > 0$ and the family $(\mathbb{D}_k, \mathcal{H}_k)$ of hyperbolic geometries with curvature $k < 0$. The two families sport identical descriptions of the transformation group, identical descriptions of straight lines, identical arc-length and area formulas, as well as identical formulas for the area of a triangle.

We may symbolize this connection with the following description of an infinite family of geometries, one for each real number k. This general description will allow us to elegantly express some important features common to hyperbolic, Euclidean, and elliptic geometry.

Definition 7.4.1 For each real number k the **geometry (X_k, G_k)** has space

$$X_k = \begin{cases} \mathbb{D}_k & \text{if } k < 0; \\ \mathbb{C} & \text{if } k = 0; \\ \mathbb{P}^2_k & \text{if } k > 0, \end{cases}$$

and group of transformations G_k consisting of all Möbius transformations of the form

$$T(z) = e^{i\theta}\frac{z - z_0}{1 + k\overline{z_0}z},$$

where $\theta \in \mathbb{R}$ and z_0 is a point in X_k. Moreover, the unique line through two points p and q in (X_k, G_k) is the unique cline through the points p, q, and $-1/(k\overline{p})$. A smooth curve $\boldsymbol{r} : [a, b] \to X_k$ has arc-length given by

$$\mathcal{L}(\boldsymbol{r}) = \int_a^b \frac{2|\boldsymbol{r}'(t)|}{1 + k|\boldsymbol{r}(t)|^2}\, dt.$$

The area of a polar region R in (X_k, G_k) is given by

$$A(R) = \iint_R \frac{4r}{(1 + kr^2)^2} dr d\theta.$$

◇

As we have seen, these geometries manifest themselves in strikingly different ways. If $k > 0$, the sum of the angles of a triangle must be greater than π; and if $k < 0$ the sum of the angles of a triangle must be less than π. If $k > 0$ the space $X_k = \mathbb{P}_k^2$ has finite area; if $k < 0$, $X_k = \mathbb{D}_k$ has infinite area. If $k > 0$ the circumference of a circle with radius r is less than $2\pi r$; if $k < 0$ the circumference is greater than $2\pi r$.

What about when $k = 0$? We may check that (X_0, G_0) corresponds to Euclidean geometry, though with a scaled metric. In particular, lines in (X_0, G_0) correspond to Euclidean lines (since $k = 0$, $-1/(k\overline{p}) = \infty$, so the unique line through p and q is the Euclidean line), and when $k = 0$ the arc-length is simply twice the usual Euclidean arc-length. So while we are scaling distances in (X_0, G_0), Euclidean geometry applies: triangles are Euclidean triangles and have angle sum equal to 180°. Triangles with a right angle are Euclidean right triangles and satisfy the Pythagorean theorem.

Thus, we treat (X_k, G_k) as one big family of geometries. The *sign* of k dictates the *type* of geometry we have, and the magnitude of k dictates the radius of the disk in which we model the geometry (unless $k = 0$ in which case the space is $\mathbb{C}$). Morevoer, Euclidean geometry (X_0, G_0) marks the edge of the knife from which we move into a hyperbolic world is k drops below 0, and into an elliptic world if k rises above 0.

We now summarize some results established in the previous sections and emphasize key features common to all (X_k, G_k).

First and foremost, we note that arc-length is an invariant function of (X_k, G_k) and that the arc-length ensures that the shortest path from p to q in (X_k, G_k) is along the line between them. We have discussed these facts in the cases $k = -1, 0, 1$, and the result holds for arbitrary k. So, the arc-length formula provides a metric on (X_k, G_k): Given $p, q \in X_k$, we define $d_k(p, q)$ to be the length of the shortest path from p to q. The circle in (X_k, G_k) centered at p through q consists of all points in X_k whose distance from p equals $d_k(p, q)$.

Theorem 7.4.2 *For all real numbers k, (X_k, G_k) is homogeneous and isotropic.*

PROOF. Given any point p in X_k, the transformation $T(z) = \frac{z-p}{1+k\overline{p}z}$ in G_k maps p to the origin. So all points in X_k are congruent to 0. By the group structure of G_k it follows that any two points in X_k are congruent, so the geometry is homogeneous.

To show (X_k, G_k) is isotropic we consider three cases.

If $k < 0$ then (X_k, G_k) models hyperbolic geometry on the open disk with radius $s = 1/\sqrt{|k|}$. As such, G_k contains the sorts of Möbius transformations discussed in Chapter 5 and pictured in Figure 5.1.6, p. 84. In particular, for any point $p \in \mathbb{D}_k$, G_k contains all elliptic Möbius transformations that swirl points around type II clines of p and $-1/(k\overline{p})$, the point symmetric to p with respect to the circle at infinity. These maps are preciley the rotations about the point p in this geometry: they rotate points in X_k around cicles centered at p.

If $k = 0$, then transformations in G_0 have the form $T(z) = e^{i\theta}(z - z_0)$. Now, rotation by angle θ about the point p in the Euclidean plane is given by $T(z) = e^{i\theta}(z - p) + p$. Setting $z_0 = p - pe^{-i\theta}$ we see that this rotation indeed lives in G_0.

If $k > 0$ then (X_k, G_k) models elliptic geometry on the projective plane with radius $s = 1/\sqrt{k}$. As such, for each $p \in X_k$, G_k contains all elliptic Möbius transformations that fix p and p_a, the point antipodal to p with respect to the circle with radius s. Such a map rotates points around type II clines with respect to p and p_a. Since these type II clines correspond to circles in X_k centered at the fixed point, it follows that G_k contains all rotations.

Thus, for all $k \in \mathbb{R}$, (X_k, G_k) is isotropic. □

Theorem 7.4.3 *Suppose k is any real number, and we have a triangle in (X_k, G_k) whose angles are α, β, and γ and whose area is A. Then*

$$kA = (\alpha + \beta + \gamma - \pi).$$

Proof of this tidy result has already appeared in pieces (see Exercise 1.2.2, p. **??**, Lemma 7.2.2, p. 151, and Lemma 7.3.1, p. 153); we emphasize that this triangle area formula reveals the locally Euclidean nature of all the geometries (X_k, G_k): a small triangle (one with area close to 0) will have an angle sum close to 180°. Observe also that the closer $|k|$ is to 0, the larger a triangle needs to be in order to detect an angle sum different from 180°. Of course, if $k = 0$ the theorem tells us that the angles of a Euclidean triangle sum to π radians.

Theorem 7.4.4 *Suppose a convex n-sided polygon ($n \geq 3$) in (X_k, G_k) has interior angles α_i for $i = 1, 2, \ldots, n$. The area A of the n-gon is related to its interior angles by*

$$kA = \left(\sum_{i=1}^{n} \alpha_i\right) - (n-2)\pi.$$

PROOF. A convex n-gon can be divided into $n - 2$ triangles as in Figure 7.4.5, p. 160. Observe that the area of the n-gon equals the sum of the areas of these triangles.

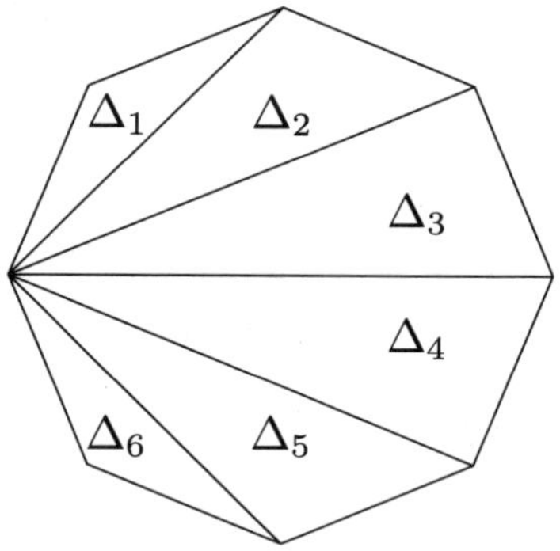

Figure 7.4.5 Splitting an n-gon into $n - 2$ triangles in the case $n = 8$.

By Theorem 7.4.3, p. 160, the area A_i of the ith triangle Δ_i is related to its angle sum by

$$kA_i = (\sum \text{angles in } \Delta_i) - \pi.$$

Thus,

$$\begin{aligned} kA &= \sum_{i=1}^{n-2} kA_i \\ &= \sum_{i=1}^{n-2} (\sum \text{angles in } \Delta_i - \pi). \end{aligned}$$

Now, the total angle sum of the $n-2$ triangles equals the interior angle sum of the n-gon, so it follows that

$$kA = \left(\sum_{i=1}^{n} \alpha_i\right) - (n-2)\pi.$$

This completes the proof. □

Lemma 7.4.6 *Suppose $k \in \mathbb{R}$, $s = \frac{1}{\sqrt{|k|}}$ and $0 < x < s$ is a real number (if $k = 0$, we just assume $0 < x$). In (X_k, G_k), the circle centered at 0 through x has area*

$$\frac{4\pi x^2}{1+kx^2}.$$

PROOF. Consider the circle centered at the origin that goes through the point x on the positive real axis, where $0 < x < s$. The circular region matches the polar rectangle $0 < \theta < 2\pi$ and $0 < r < x$, so the area is given by

$$\int_0^{2\pi}\int_0^{x} \frac{4r}{(1+kr^2)^2}\,dr\,d\theta.$$

Evaluating this integral gives the result, and the details are left as an exercise. □

Theorem 7.4.7 Unified Pythagorean Theorem. *Suppose $k \in \mathbb{R}$, and we have a geodesic right triangle in (X_k, G_k) whose legs have length a and b and whose hypotenuse has length c. Then*

$$A(c) = A(a) + A(b) - \frac{k}{2\pi}A(a)A(b),$$

where $A(r)$ denotes the area of a circle with radius r as measured in (X_k, G_k).

PROOF. Suppose $k \in \mathbb{R}$. If $k = 0$ the equation reduces to $c^2 = a^2 + b^2$, which is true by the Pythagorean Theorem 1.2.1, p. 5! Otherwise, assume $k \neq 0$ and let $s = \frac{1}{\sqrt{|k|}}$, as usual. Without loss of generality we may assume our right triangle is defined by the points $z = 0$, $p = x$, and $q = yi$, where $0 < x, y < s$. By construction, the legs zp and zq are Euclidean segments, and $\angle pzq$ is right.

Let $a = d_k(z,p), b = d_k(z,q)$, and $c = d_k(p,q)$. By Lemma 7.4.6, p. 161,

$$A(a) = \frac{4\pi x^2}{1+kx^2}, \quad \text{and} \quad A(b) = \frac{4\pi y^2}{1+ky^2}.$$

To find $A(c)$, we first find $d_k(p,q)$. By invariance of distance,

$$d_k(p,q) = d_k(0, |T(q)|),$$

where $T(z) = \frac{z-p}{1+k\bar{p}z}$. Let $t = |T(q)| = \frac{|yi-x|}{|1+kxyi|}$, which is a real number.

Now, $A(c)$ is the area of a circle with radius c, and the circle centered at 0 through t has this radius, so

$$A(c) = \frac{4\pi t^2}{1+kt^2}.$$

Using the fact that $t^2 = \frac{x^2+y^2}{1+k^2x^2y^2}$, one can now check by direct substitution that

$$A(c) = A(a) + A(b) - \frac{k}{2\pi}A(a)A(b).$$

□

While we have proved the theorem, it feels a bit like we have missed the best part - discovery of the relationship. For more on this, we encourage the reader to consult [20].

Example 7.4.8 Detecting curvature with triangles.

Suppose a two-dimensional bug in (X_k, G_k) walks along a line for $a > 0$ units, turns left $90°$, and walks on a line for another a units, thus creating a right triangle with legs of equal length. Let c denote the hypotenuse of this triangle. The diagram below depicts such a route, in each of the three geometry types. For convenience, we assume the journey begins at the origin and proceeds first along the positive real axis.

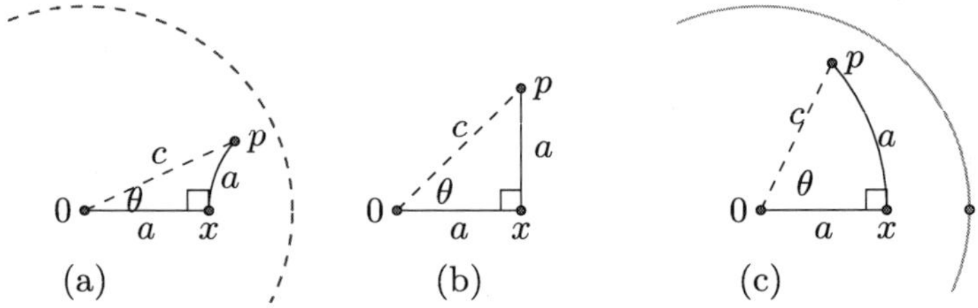

It turns out the value of c as a function of a can reveal the curvature k of the geometry. If $k = 0$ the Pythagorean theorem tells us that $c^2 = 2a^2$. For $k < 0$, the hyperbolic law of cosines (Exercise 7.3.4, p. ??) tells us that $\cosh(\sqrt{|k|}c) = \cosh^2(\sqrt{|k|}a)$. For $k > 0$, the elliptic law of cosines (Exercise 7.2.5, p. ??) tells us that $\cos(\sqrt{k}c) = \cos^2(\sqrt{k}a)$. We may solve each of these equations for c, using the fact that a and c are positive, to give us c as a function of a and the curvature k. We have plotted these functions for $k = -1, 0, 1$ below. When $k < 0$ the length of the hypotenuse of such a triangle is slightly longer than that predicted by the Euclidean formula (the Pythagorean theorem); when $k > 0$ the length is smaller than the length predicted by the Euclidean formula.

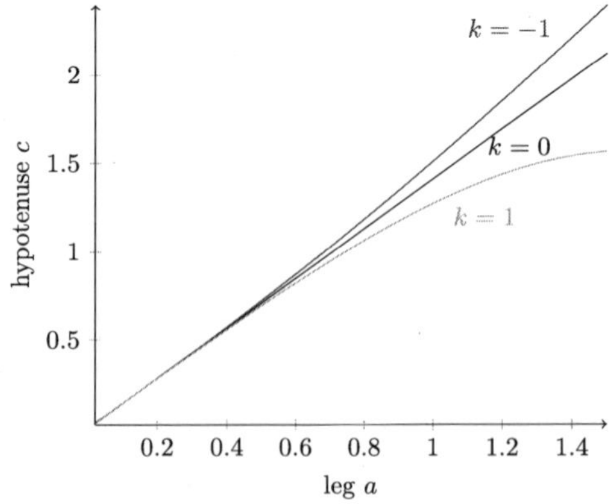

We close by summarizing measurement formulas for these geometries. Except for the case $k = 0$ these formulas were proved in the exercises of the previoius two sections. The case $k = 0$ is tackled in Exercise 7.4.1, p. ??.

Measurement Formulas in (X_k, G_k).

Suppose $k \in \mathbb{R}$, $s = \frac{1}{\sqrt{|k|}}$ and $0 < x < s$ is a real number (with the convention that if $k = 0$ we simply require $0 < x$).

- In (X_k, G_k), the distance from 0 to x is given by

$$d_k(0, x) = \begin{cases} s \ln\left(\frac{s+x}{s-x}\right) & \text{if } k < 0; \\ 2x & \text{if } k = 0; \\ 2s \arctan(x/s) & \text{if } k > 0. \end{cases}$$

- A circle with radius r as measured in (X_k, G_k) has area $A(r)$ given by

$$A(r) = \begin{cases} 4\pi s^2 \sinh^2(\frac{r}{2s}) & \text{if } k < 0; \\ \pi r^2 & \text{if } k = 0; \\ 4\pi s^2 \sin^2(\frac{r}{2s}) & \text{if } k > 0, \end{cases}$$

- A circle with radius r as measured in (X_k, G_k) has circumference $C(r)$ given by

$$C(r) = \begin{cases} 2\pi s \sinh(r/s) & \text{if } k < 0; \\ 2\pi r & \text{if } k = 0; \\ 2\pi s \sin(r/s) & \text{if } k > 0. \end{cases}$$

Exercises

1. Check that the measurement formulas in (X_k, G_k) are correct when $k = 0$. In particular, show that $d_0(0, x) = 2x$ for any $x > 0$ on the real axis, and that a circle with radius r as measured in (X_0, G_0) has area $A(r) = \pi r^2$ and circumference $C(r) = 2\pi r$.

2. Complete the proof of Lemma 7.4.6, p. 161.

3. Use Definition 7.1.4, p. 147 to prove that for all real numbers k, the curvature of (X_k, G_k) is indeed equal to k. Hint: Tackle three cases: $k < 0, k = 0$, and $k > 0$.

4. Suppose an intrepid team of two-dimensional explorers sets out to determine which 2-dimensional geometry is theirs. Their cosmologists have told them there world is homogeneous, isotropic, and metric, so they believe that the geometry of their universe is modeled by (X_k, G_k) for some real number k. They carefully measure the angles and area of a triangle. They find the angles to be 29.2438°, 73.4526°, and 77.2886°, and the area is 8.81 km^2. Which geometry is theirs? What is the curvature of their universe?

5. Prove that in (X_k, G_k) the derivative of area with respect to r is circumference: $\frac{d}{dr}[A(r)] = C(r)$.

6. Suppose a two-dimensional bug in (X_k, G_k) traces the right triangle route from 0 to p as depicted in Example 7.4.8, p. 162. Argue that for a given value of a, the hyperbolic hypotenuse length exceeds the Euclidean hypotenuse length, which exceeds the elliptic hypotenuse length. Hint: One might prove that for all k, when $a = 0$, $c = 0$ and $\frac{dc}{da}|_{a=0} = \sqrt{2}$; and then show that for $a > 0$, $\frac{d^2c}{da^2}$ is positive for negative values of k, and it is negative for positive values of k.

7. Suppose a team of two-dimensional explorers living in (X_k, G_k) travels 8 units along a line. Then they turn right (90°) and travel 8 units along a line. At this point they find they are 12 units from their starting point. Which type of geometry applies to their universe? Can they determine the value of k from this measurement? If so, what is it?

8. Repeat the previous exercise using the measurements $a = 8$ units and $c = 11.2$ units.

9. Suppose a team of two-dimensional explorers living in (X_k, G_k) finds themselves at point p. They travel 8 units along a line to a point z, turn right (90°) and travel another 8 units along a line to the point q. At this point they measure $\angle pqz = .789$ radians. Which type of geometry applies to their universe? Can they determine the value of k from this measurement? If so, what is it?

10. Suppose a team of two-dimensional explorers living in (X_k, G_k) tethers one of their team to a line 18 scrambles long (a scramble is the standard unit for measuring length in this world - and 24 scrambles equals one tubablast). They swing the volunteer around in a circle, and though he laughs maniacally, he is able to record with confidence that he traveled 113.4 scrambles. Assuming these measurements are correct, which type of geometry applies to their universe? Can they determine the value of k from these measurements? If so, what is it?

7.5 Surfaces

Back in Chapter 1 we motivated the study of non-Euclidean geometry with a question in cosmology: What is the shape of the universe? We discussed the idea that different shapes inherit different types of geometry. Indeed, the rules of geometry are different on a sphere than on a flat plane. In this section we take a break from geometry in order to discuss the shapes themselves.

In topology one studies those features of a space that remain unchanged if the space is stretched or otherwise continuously deformed. Such features of a space are called topological features.

The features of a space that *do* change under such deformations are geometric features. For instance, as a ball is inflated its volume, curvature, and surface area change; these are geometric properties. On the other hand, no matter how big or lumpy the ball gets, or how it is stretched (unless it pops!), a loop drawn on the surface of the ball separates the surface into two disjoint pieces. This is a topological property of the ball. A second topological property of a space is whether any loop drawn on it can be continuously contracted (while staying in the space) to a point. The sphere also has this feature. Nothing about the sphere's shape prevents a loop from shrinking on the surface to a point.

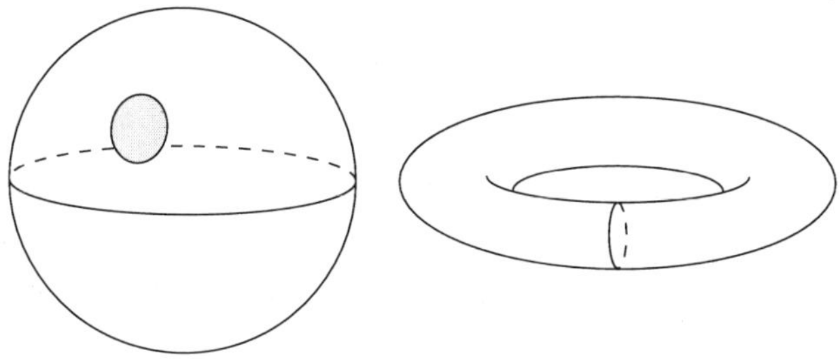

Figure 7.5.1 The sphere and torus are topologically distinct.

On the surface of a donut there are loops one can draw that do *not* separate the surface into disjoint pieces. The loop that goes around the donut like an armband in Figure 7.5.1, p. 165 is one such loop. Furthermore, this loop cannot be continuously contracted to a point while staying on the surface. This suggests the surface of a ball and the surface of a donut are topologically different shapes.

The sphere is an example of a **simply connected space** because any loop drawn on the surface can be contracted to a point. The torus is an example of a **multiconnected space** because there exist loops in the torus that cannot be contracted to a point.

Roughly speaking, two spaces are topologically equivalent, or **homeomorphic**, if one can be continuously deformed to look like the other. For instance, a circle is topologically equivalent to a square. One can be mapped onto the other via a **homeomorphism**: a continuous bijection between the objects that has a continuous inverse. One homeomorphism is suggested in the following example.

Example 7.5.2 A circle is homeomorphic to a square.

Construct a homeomorphism as follows. Assume the square and circle are concentric as shown below, and that z_0 is the center of the circle. Then, for each point z on the square, define $T(z)$ to be the point on the circle through which the ray $\overrightarrow{z_0 z}$ passes. One can show that T is a homeomorphism: it is a 1-1 and onto function that is continuous, and its inverse is continuous as well.

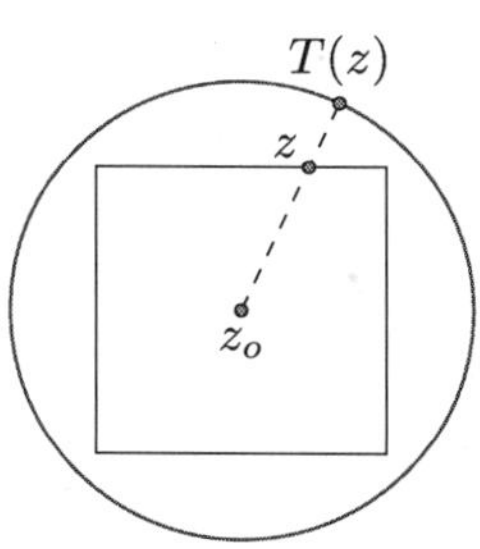

We are quickly heading into the realm of topology, and must resist the temptation to dive headlong and formally into this rich subject. In this text we restrict our focus to a whirlwind tour of topological tools that are used to investigate possible shapes for two- and three-dimensional universes. We encourage the reader interested in a more formal approach to the subject to consult any number of good texts, including [9].

Our candidate universes are examples of manifolds. A topological n-manifold is a space with the feature that each point in the space has a neighborhood that looks like a patch of $\mathbb{R}^n$. In cosmology, the spatial section of space-time is assumed to be a 3-manifold, and when we ask about the shape of the universe, we are asking about the shape of this 3-manifold. In this section we focus on 2-manifolds.

A bit more formally, $\mathbb{R}^n$ consists of all n-tuples of real numbers $\boldsymbol{p} = (x_1, x_2, \ldots, x_n)$. The **open n-ball** centered at a point $\boldsymbol{p}$ in $\mathbb{R}^n$ with radius $r > 0$, denoted $B_n(\boldsymbol{p}, r)$, is the set

$$B_n(\boldsymbol{p}, r) = \{\boldsymbol{x} \in \mathbb{R}^n \mid |\boldsymbol{x} - \boldsymbol{p}| < r\},$$

where $|\boldsymbol{x} - \boldsymbol{p}|$ is the Euclidean distance between the points $\boldsymbol{x}$ and $\boldsymbol{p}$.

For instance, an open 1-ball is an open interval in $\mathbb{R}$. The open 2-ball $B_2(z_0, r)$ consists of all points z in $\mathbb{C}$ such that $|z - z_0| < r$. The open 3-ball $B_3(\boldsymbol{p}, r)$ consists of all points in $\mathbb{R}^3$ inside the sphere centered at $\boldsymbol{p}$ with radius r.

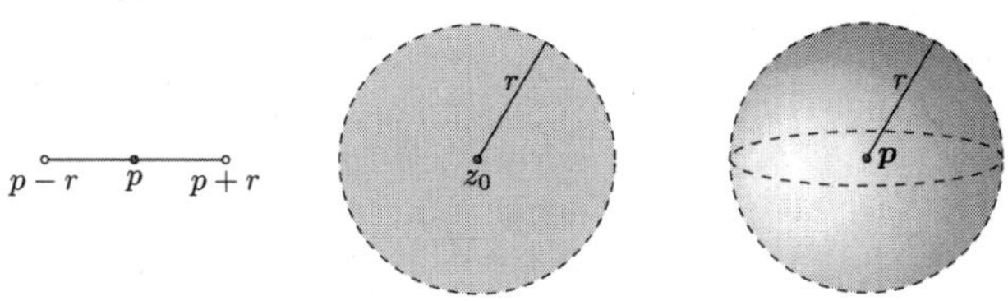

Figure 7.5.3 Open n-balls for $n = 1, 2, 3$.

A **topological n-manifold** is a space X with the feature that each point in X has a neighborhood that is homeomorphic to an open n-ball.

A circle is an example of a 1-manifold: each point on a circle has a neighborhood homeomorphic to an open interval. The surface of a sphere is a 2-manifold: each point on the sphere has a neighborhood that is homeomorphic to an open 2-ball.

Example 7.5.4 Some 2-manifolds.

a. Let S consist of parallel planes in $\mathbb{R}^3$. In particular, let $S = \{(x, y, z) \in \mathbb{R}^3 \mid z = 0 \text{ or } z = 1\}$ as in part (a) of the following diagram. Each point in S has a neighborhood of points that is an open 2-ball.

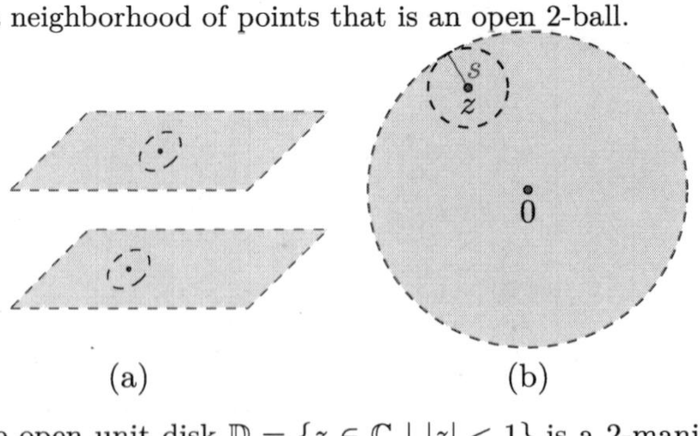

(a) (b)

b. The open unit disk $\mathbb{D} = \{z \in \mathbb{C} \mid |z| < 1\}$ is a 2-manifold. Each point in $\mathbb{D}$ has a neighborhood that is an open 2-ball in the plane. In particular, if $|z| = r < 1$, let $s = 1 - r$. Then $B_2(z, s)$ does the trick.

c. *The flat torus.* Consider the flat torus of chapter 1, which has been redrawn in Figure 7.5.5, p. 167. It consists of all points in a rectangle drawn in the Euclidean plane, with the additional feature that each point on the top edge is identified with the point on the bottom edge having the same x-coordinate; and each point on the left edge is identified with the point on the right edge having the same y-coordinate. In Figure 7.5.5, p. 167 we indicate this edge identification with oriented labels: the a edges get identified by matching the arrow orientations, as do the b edges.

Each point in the flat torus has a neighborhood homeomorphic to an open 2-ball.

If a point p is not on an edge, as in Figure 7.5.5, p. 167, then by choosing a radius small enough, there is an open 2-ball about the point that misses the edges.

If a point q is on an edge but not at a corner, then by choosing a radius small enough, there is an open 2-ball about the point that misses the corners. This open 2-ball consists of parts of two open 2-balls from $\mathbb{R}^2$. Because of the edge identification, these open 2-ball halves come together to form a perfect open 2-ball about the point.

If a point u is at a corner of the rectangle, there is an open 2-ball about the point that consists of parts of four different open 2-balls from $\mathbb{R}^2$. Because of the edge identification, these four "quarter balls" come together to form a single open 2-ball of points around the corner point.

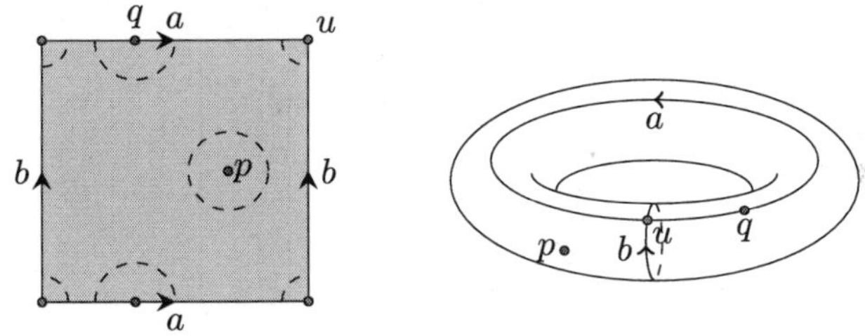

Figure 7.5.5 The flat torus is a 2-manifold as well as a surface

Definition 7.5.6 A **surface** is a closed, bounded, and connected topological 2-manifold. ◊

Of the 2-manifolds in Example 7.5.4, p. 166, only the third is a surface according to this definition. A set in $\mathbb{R}^n$ is **bounded** if it lives entirely within some open n-ball of finite radius. The parallel planes manifold extends infinitely far away from the origin in $\mathbb{R}^3$ so this manifold is not bounded. This manifold is not connected either. Informally, a space is connected if it has just one piece. The parallel planes manifold has two distinct pieces (the two planes) that are separated in space, so it is not connected. The open unit disk $\mathbb{D}$ is bounded and connected, but not closed as a set in $\mathbb{R}^2$. A set S in $\mathbb{R}^n$ is **closed** if it has the following feature: if $\{z_k\}$ is a sequence of points in S that converges to a point z, then z is also in S.

To see that $\mathbb{D}$ is not closed, consider the sequence $\{\frac{1}{2}, \frac{2}{3}, \frac{3}{4}, \frac{4}{5}, \ldots\}$. Each point in this sequence lives in $\mathbb{D}$, but the limit of the sequence, which is 1, does not. The torus, on the other hand, is closed, bounded, and connected, so we call it a surface. We note that another topological term, compactness, is often used when discussing surfaces. A space living in $\mathbb{R}^n$ is *compact* if and only if it is closed and bounded. Thus, for us, a surface is a compact, connected 2-manifold.

Rather than concern ourselves with a formal development of these topological concepts, we take with us this informal introduction to help us to pursue the construction of surfaces. It turns out that all surfaces can be built from the three venerable surfaces in Figure 7.5.7, p. 168 by a process called the connected sum.

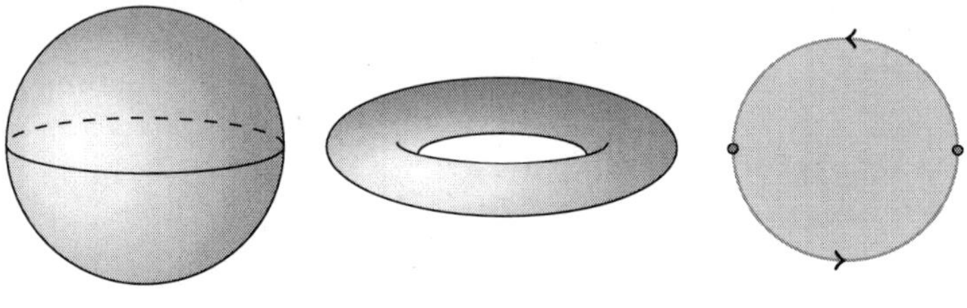

Figure 7.5.7 The sphere $\mathbb{S}^2$, the torus $\mathbb{T}^2$, and the projective plane $\mathbb{P}^2$.

Connected Sum. If X_1 and X_2 are surfaces, the **connected sum** surface, denoted $X_1\#X_2$, is obtained as follows:

1. Remove an open 2-ball from X_1 and an open 2-ball from X_2;

2. Connect the boundaries of these open 2-balls with a cylinder.

Note that since X_i is a surface, each point in each space has a neighborhood homeomorphic to an open 2-ball, so we may always achieve the connected sum of two surfaces. The result is a new surface: it is still closed, bounded, and connected, and each point still has an open neighborhood homeomorphic to an open 2-ball.

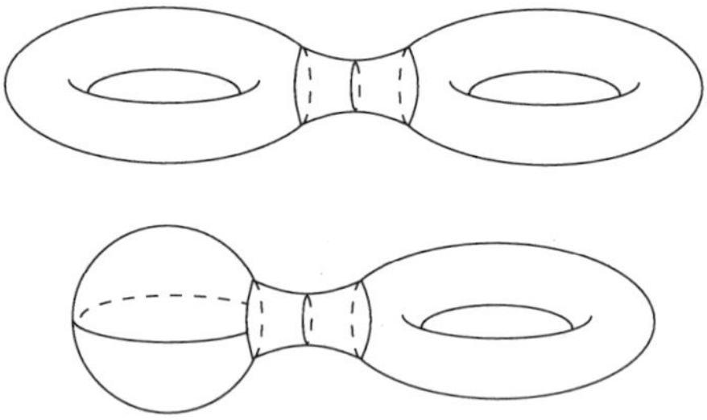

Figure 7.5.8 Some connected sums.

Example 7.5.9 Some connected sums.

Let $\mathbb{T}^2$ denote the torus surface in $\mathbb{R}^3$ and $\mathbb{S}^2$ denote the sphere, as usual. Figure 7.5.8, p. 168 depicts two connected sums: $\mathbb{T}^2\#\mathbb{T}^2$, and $\mathbb{S}^2\#\mathbb{T}^2$. The surface $\mathbb{T}^2\#\mathbb{T}^2$ is called the two-holed torus, and it is topologically equivalent to the surface labeled H_2 in Figure 7.5.10, p. 169. One can shrink the length dimension of the connecting cylinder to make the one look like the other. The surface $\mathbb{S}^2\#\mathbb{T}^2$ is homeomorphic to the torus $\mathbb{T}^2$. To see this, observe that if one removes an open-2 ball from a sphere and attaches one end of a cylinder to the sphere along the boundary of the removed disk, the result is homeomorphic to a closed disk, as suggested in the following diagram. So, if one removes an open 2-ball from a surface X and then caps the hole with this sphere-with-cylinder shape, the net effect is patching the hole. In the arithmetic of connected sums, the sphere plays the role of 0: $\mathbb{S}^2 \# X = X$ for any surface X.

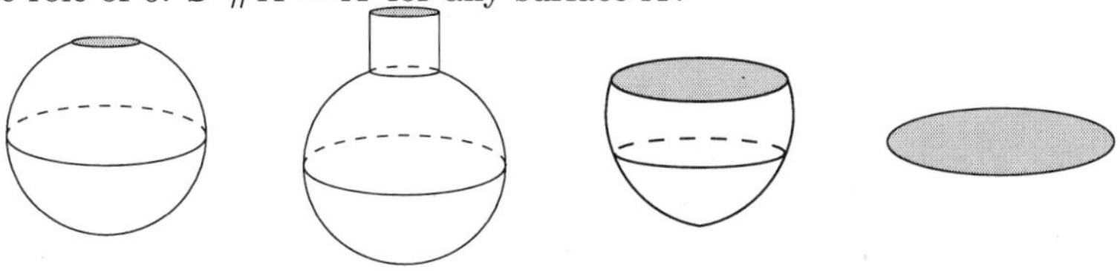

For each integer $g \geq 1$, the **handlebody surface of genus** g, denoted H_g, is defined as

$$H_g = \overbrace{\mathbb{T}^2 \# \mathbb{T}^2 \# \cdots \# \mathbb{T}^2}^{g \text{ copies}}.$$

The surface H_g gets its name from the fact that it is topologically equivalent to a sphere with g handles attached to it. For this reason, we set $H_0 = \mathbb{S}^2$. A few handlebody surfaces are pictured in Figure 7.5.10, p. 169.

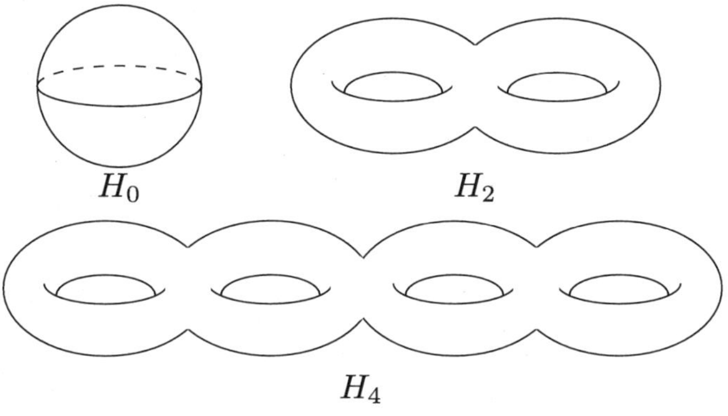

Figure 7.5.10 Some handlebody surfaces.

For each integer $g \geq 1$, define **the cross-cap surface of genus** g by

$$C_g = \overbrace{\mathbb{P}^2 \# \mathbb{P}^2 \# \cdots \# \mathbb{P}^2}^{g \text{ copies}}.$$

A **cross-cap** is the space obtained by removing an open 2-ball from the projective plane $\mathbb{P}^2$. The cross-cap surface C_g is topologically equivalent to a sphere with g open 2-balls removed and replaced with cross-caps.

The surface C_1 is the projective plane. This space does not embed in $\mathbb{R}^3$ as the handlebody surfaces do, but it can be represented as a disk with antipodal points identified, as we did in Chapter 6. Figure 7.5.11, p. 170 depicts the connected sum $C_1 \# C_1$. In Figure 7.5.11, p. 170(a), we have removed an open ball from each copy of C_1. The boundary circles of these open 2-balls must be joined, and we indicate this by orienting the boundary circles and giving each one the same label of c. In Figure 7.5.11, p. 170(b), we have sliced open each copy of C_1 at the vertex to which the c loops are joined. The c loops are now edges that we identify together in Figure 7.5.11, p. 170(c). Thus, we may view C_2 as the square with edge identifications as indicated in part (c) of the figure. It turns out this space C_2 is homeomorphic to the Klein bottle, a famous surface we consider shortly.

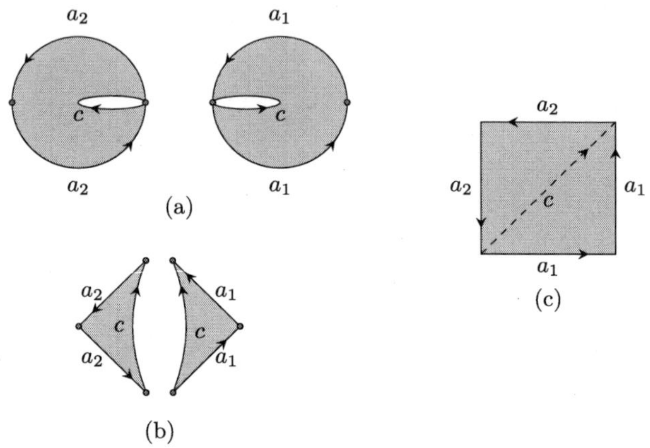

Figure 7.5.11 Constructing C_2.

Polygonal Surfaces

Our representation of C_2 is an example of a **polygonal surface**. To build a polygonal surface, start with a finite number of polygons having an even number of edges and then identify edges in pairs.

If the surface is built from a single polygon, the edge identifications of the polygon can be encoded in a **boundary label**. Each edge of the polygon gets assigned a letter and an orientation. Edges that are identified have the same letter, and we obtain a boundary label by traversing the boundary of our polygon in the counter-clockwise direction (by convention) and recording the letters we encounter, with an exponent of +1 if our walk is in the direction of the oriented edge, and an exponent of -1 if our walk is in the opposite direction of the oriented edge. For instance, a boundary label for the surface C_2 found in Figure 7.5.11, p. 170 is $a_1a_1a_2a_2$. Furthermore, we may inductively show that by repeating the connected sum operation of Figure 7.5.11, p. 170 to $C_{g-1}\#C_1$, the surface C_g can be represented as a $2g$-gon having boundary label

$$a_1a_1a_2a_2\cdots a_ga_g.$$

It turns out that *all* surfaces can be constructed this way, an important and useful result. We have seen that the torus can be constructed as a polygonal surface: take a rectangle and identify the edges according to the boundary label $aba^{-1}b^{-1}$. In Figure 7.5.13, p. 171 we demonstrate that the 2-holed torus can be represented as a regular octagon with boundary label

$$(a_1b_1a_1^{-1}b_1^{-1})(a_2b_2a_2^{-1}b_2^{-1}).$$

In general, for $g \geq 1$ the surface H_g can be represented by a regular $4g$-gon having boundary label

$$(a_1 b_1 a_1^{-1} b_1^{-1})(a_2 b_2 a_2^{-1} b_2^{-1}) \cdots (a_g b_g a_g^{-1} b_g^{-1}).$$

The remarkable theorem here is that the handlebody surfaces and the cross-cap surfaces account for all possible surfaces, without redundancy.

Theorem 7.5.12 *Any surface is homeomorphic to the sphere $\mathbb{S}^2$, a handlebody surface H_g with $g \geq 1$, or a crosscap surface C_g with $g \geq 1$. Moreover, no two surfaces in this list are homeomoprhic to each other.*

Two proofs of this theorem are floating around the literature now. The classic proof, which makes use of cell divisions, can be found, for instance, in [9]. The new proof, due to John Conway, bypasses the artificial constructs in the classic proof, and can be found in [12].

To summarize, we have two ways to think about surfaces. First, the classification theorem above can be restated as follows: any surface is homeomorphic to the sphere, the sphere with some number of handles attached, or the sphere with some number of cross-caps attached. Second, any surface can be constructed from a $2m$-gon with its edges identified in pairs, for some $m \geq 1$.

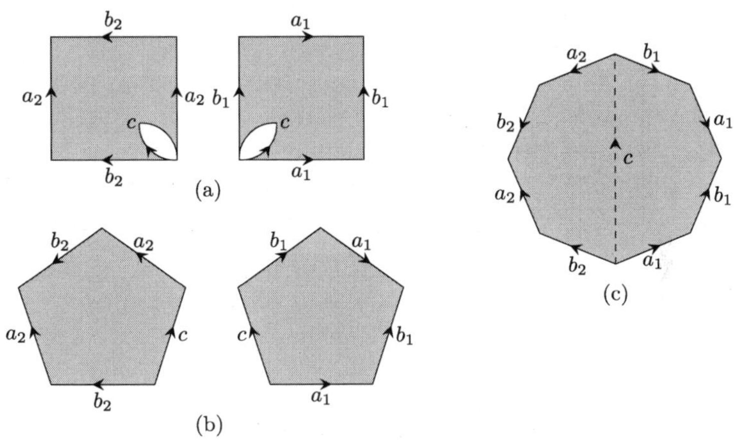

Figure 7.5.13 H_2 constructed from an octagon.

Characterizing a surface

If somebody throws a surface at us, how do we know which one we're catching? One way to characterize a surface is to determine two particular topological invariants: its orientability status and its Euler characteristic. Let's discuss what these features of a surface are.

Orientability status

The **Möbius strip** is obtained from a rectangle by identifying the left and right edges with a twist:

Figure 7.5.14 A Möbius strip.

Notice that a Möbius strip has an orientation-reversing path. A clock rotating clockwise, if it heads along the Möbius strip, will eventually return to its starting place to find that it is now rotating counterclockwise.

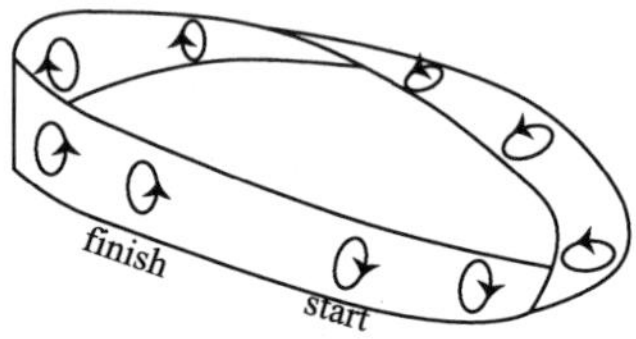

A surface is called **non-orientable** if it contains a Möbius strip. If a surface does not contain a Möbius strip then it is **orientable**. The Möbius strip itself is not a surface as we've defined it because it has an edge. Points on this edge don't have any neighborhoods that look like open 2-balls (they look more like half balls). But the Klein bottle in the following example is a non-orientable surface.

Example 7.5.15 The Klein bottle.

The Klein bottle looks a lot like the torus, but there's a twist. The top and bottom edges are identified as they were for the torus, but the left and right edges are oriented oppositely. More formally, it is the polygonal surface obtained from a square with boundary label $aba^{-1}b$, and the Klein bottle is denoted by $\mathbb{K}^2$.

Why is the Klein bottle non-orientable? A bug leaving the screen on the right near the top would reappear on the left near the bottom. But take a closer look, the bug has become mirror-reversed.

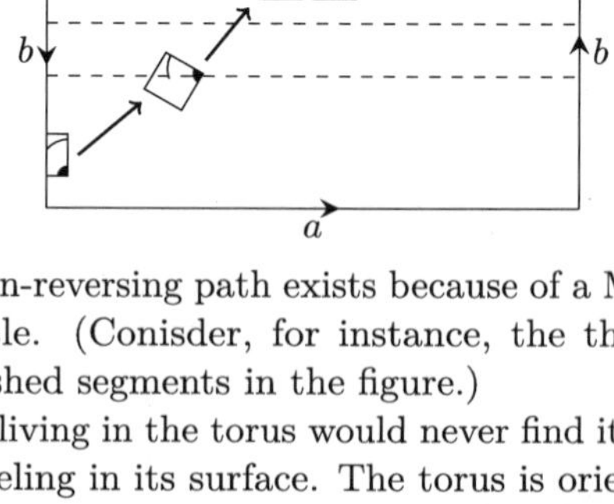

This orientation-reversing path exists because of a Möbius strip lurking in the Klein bottle. (Conisder, for instance, the thin horizontal strip formed by the dashed segments in the figure.)

The same bug living in the torus would never find itself mirror reversed as a result of traveling in its surface. The torus is orientable.

A surface's orientability status is a topological invariant. This means that if S and T are homeomorphic surfaces then they must have the same orientability status. Notice that there exists a Möbius strip in each C_g (take a thin strip from the middle of one a_1 edge to the middle of the other), so that all cross-cap surfaces are non-orientable. On the other hand, all the handlebody surfaces H_g $(g \geq 0)$ are orientable.

Euler Characteristic

In addition to an orientability status, each surface has attached to it an integer called the Euler characteristic. The Euler characteristic is a topological invariant, and it can be calculated from a cell division of a surface, which is a kind of tiling of the surface by planar faces. Let's make this more precise.

An **n-dimensional cell**, or **n-cell**, is a subset of a space whose interior is homeomorphic to an open n-ball in $\mathbb{R}^n$. For instance, a 1-cell, also called an *edge*, is a set whose interior is homeomorphic to an open interval; a 2-cell, or *face*, is a set whose interior is homeomorphic to an open 2-ball in the plane. We call points in a space 0-cells. A 0-cell is also called a *vertex* (plural *vertices*).

Definition 7.5.16 A **cell complex** C is a collection of cells in some space subject to these two conditions:

1. The interiors of any two cells in the complex are disjoint
2. The boundary of each cell is the union of lower-dimensional cells in C.

A cell complex C is called an **n-dimensional cell complex**, or n-complex, if it contains an n-cell, but no higher-dimensional cells. ◊

Example 7.5.17 Some cell complexes.

A 1-complex is commonly called a *graph*: it consists of vertices and edges. At each end of an edge is a vertex (possibly the same vertex at each end), and no two edges intersect in their interiors. The left side of the following diagram shows a 1-complex with seven 0-cells and five 1-cells. To the right is a 2-complex with one 0-cell and one 2-cell. The entire boundary of the 2-cell is attached to the single 0-cell, thus creating a well-known surface, the 2-sphere.

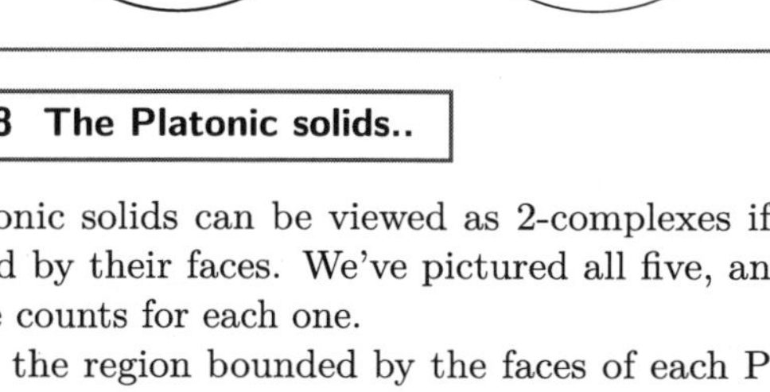

Example 7.5.18 The Platonic solids..

The five Platonic solids can be viewed as 2-complexes if we ignore the space bounded by their faces. We've pictured all five, and given vertex, edge, and face counts for each one.

Of course, the region bounded by the faces of each Platonic solid is homeomorphic to an open 3-ball, so the Platonic solids can also be viewed as 3-complexes; each solid having exactly one 3-cell.

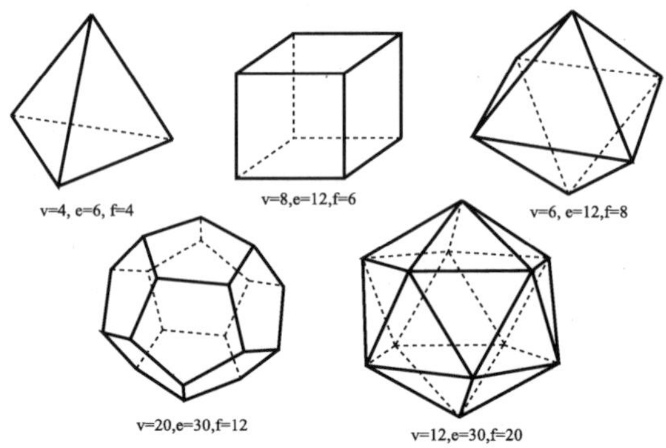

Definition 7.5.19 A **cell division** of a space X is a cell complex C that is homeomorphic to X. ◊

For instance, each Platonic solid (viewed as a 2-complex) is a cell division of $\mathbb{S}^2$. To construct a homeomorphism, map each point of the Platonic solid to a point on a sphere by projection as suggested in Figure 7.5.20, p. 174.

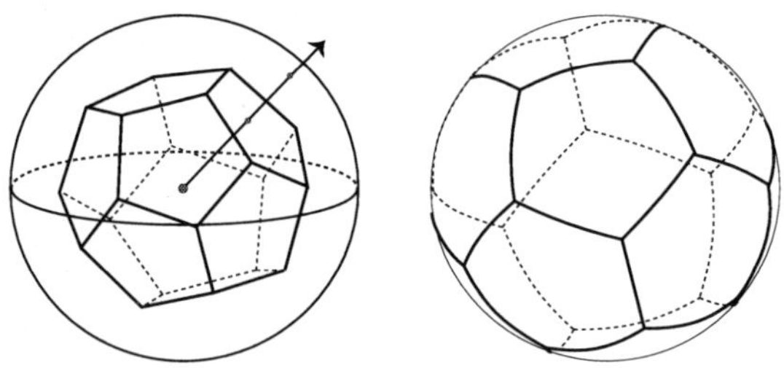

Figure 7.5.20 A dodecahedron and sphere are homeomorphic.

Example 7.5.21 Attempted cell divisions of H_1.

Three cell divisions of the torus are pictured below, along with one failed cell division. In each valid cell division, we count the number of faces, edges, and vertices of the cell division. To make an accurate count, one must take the edge identification into account.

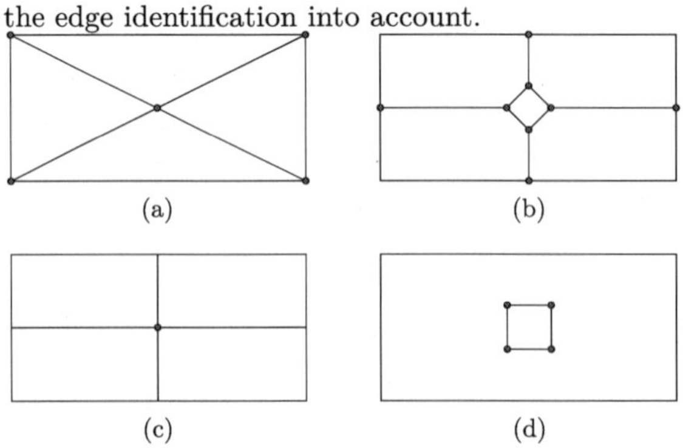

Cell division (a) has two vertices, six edges, and four faces. One vertex is in the center of the rectangle, and the other vertex is in the corner (remember, all four corners get identified to a single point). As for the edges, four emanate from the center vertex, and we have two others: the horizontal edge along the boundary of the rectangle (appearing twice), and the vertical edge along the boundary (also appearing twice). Thus, the edges of the rectangle are also edges of the cell division, so the faces in this cell division are triangles, and there are four of them.

Cell division (b) has six vertices, eight edges, and two faces. There are four vertices in the interior of the rectangle, one vertex on the horizontal boundary of the rectangle, and one vertex on the vertical boundary. Notice that the corner point of the rectangle is not a vertex of the cell division. To count the edges, observe that four edges form the inner diamond, and one edge leaves each vertex of the diamond, for a total of eight edges. The boundary edges of the rectangle do *not* form edges in this cell division. Counting faces, we have one inside the diamond and one outside the diamond. Convince yourself that the region outside the diamond makes just one face.

You can check that cell division (c) has one vertex in the center of the rectangle, two edges (one is horizontal, the other is vertical), and one face.

The attempt (d) fails to be a cell division of the torus. Why is this? At first glance, we have four vertices, four edges, and two faces. The trouble here is the "face" outside the inner square. It is not a 2-cell - that is, its interior is not homeomorphic to an open 2-ball. To see this, note that this region contains a loop that does not separate the "face" into two pieces. Can you find such a loop? Since no open 2-ball has this feature, the region in question is not homeomorphic to an open 2-ball.

Definition 7.5.22 The **Euler characteristic** of a surface S, denoted $\chi(S)$, is

$$\chi(S) = v - e + f$$

where v, e, and f denote the number of 0-cells (vertices), 1-cells (edges), and 2-cells (faces), respectively, of a cell division of the surface. ◊

The Euler characteristic is well-defined. This means that different cell divisions of the same surface will determine the same value of χ. Furthermore, this simple number is a powerful topological invariant: If two surfaces have different Euler characteristics then they are not homeomorphic. However, the Euler characteristic alone doesn't completely characterize a surface: if two surfaces have the same Euler characteristic, they need not be homeomorphic.

The Euler characteristic of the sphere is 2. Each Platonic solid in Example 7.5.18, p. 173 is a cell division of $\mathbb{S}^2$, and a count reveals $\chi(\mathbb{S}^2) = 2$.

The Euler characteristic of the torus $\mathbb{T}^2$ is 0. Each valid cell division in Example 7.5.21, p. 174 yields $v - e + f = 0$.

Each polygonal surface induces a cell division of the surface. This cell division has a single face, and after identifying the edges in pairs, the corners and edges of the underlying polygon correspond to vertices and edges in the cell division of the surface. To determine the Euler characteristic of a polygonal surface, be careful to make edge and vertex counts *after* the edge identifications.

Theorem 7.5.23 *The handlebody surface H_g has Euler characteristic $\chi(H_g) = 2-2g$, for all $g \geq 0$. The cross-cap surface C_g has Euler characteristic $\chi(C_g) = 2-g$, for all $g \geq 1$.*

PROOF. We have already seen that the Euler characteristic of the sphere is 2, so the result holds for H_0. For $g \geq 1$ consider the standard polygonal representation of H_g as a $4g$-gon with boundary label $(a_1 b_1 a_1^{-1} b_1^{-1}) \cdots (a_g b_g a_g^{-1} b_g^{-1})$. One checks that all the corners come together at a single point, so our cell division of H_g has a single vertex. For instance, consider the 2-holed torus in Figure 7.5.24, p. 176. Starting at the lower right-hand corner labeled (1), begin traversing the corner point in a clockwise direction. After hitting the b_1 edge near its initial point, one reappears on the other b_1 edge near its initial point. Keep circling the corner (according to the sequence indicated) until you return to the starting point. Notice that all eight corners are traversed before returning to the starting point. So the cell division determined by the polygon will have a single vertex. Since the $4g$ edges are identified in pairs, the cell division has $2g$ edges, and there is one face, the interior of the polygon. Thus, $\chi(H_g) = 1 - 2g + 1 = 2 - 2g$.

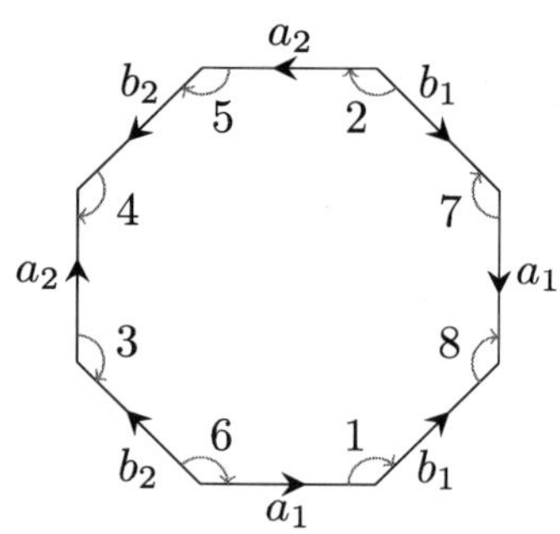

Figure 7.5.24 This cell division of H_2 has a single vertex.

The cross-cap surface C_g can be represented by the polygonal surface obtained by identifying the edges of a $2g$-gon according to the boundary label $(a_1 a_1) \cdots (a_g a_g)$. Once again, all the corners come together at a single point in the edge identification, and the number of edges in the cell division is half the number of edges in the $2g$-gon. So the cell division determined by the polygon has one vertex, g edges, and one face. Thus, $\chi(C_g) = 2 - g$. □

In light of the previous theorem and the surface classification theorem, a surface is uniquely determined by its orientability status and Euler characteristic. We summarize the classification in the table below.

Table 7.5.25 Classification of surfaces

χ	orientable	non-orientable
2	H_0	
1		C_1
0	H_1	C_2
-1		C_3
-2	H_2	C_4
-3		C_5
-4	H_3	C_6
$\vdots$	$\vdots$	$\vdots$

This completes our brief, somewhat informal foray into the topology of surfaces. Again, several good sources provide a rigorous development of these ideas, including [9]. In the next section we turn to the task of attaching geometry to a surface.

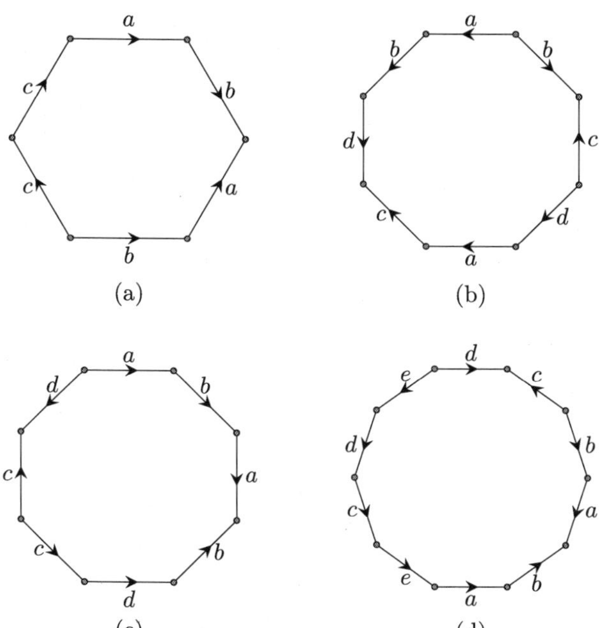

Figure 7.5.26 Four polygonal surfaces.

Exercises

1. Find the Euler characteristic of each surface in Figure 7.5.26, p. 177. Then determine whether each surface is orientable or non-orientable. Then classify the surface.
2. Classify the polygonal surface built from a hexagon having boundary label $abca^{-1}b^{-1}c^{-1}$.

3. With the aid of Figure 7.5.27, p. 178, convince yourself that the connected sum of two projective planes is homeomorphic to the Klein bottle as defined in Example 7.5.15, p. 172. At the top of Figure 7.5.27, p. 178 there are two projective planes (with boundary labels a_1a_1 and a_2a_2), each with a disk removed. In the connected sum, join the boundaries of the removed disks, which can be achieved by joining the s_1 arcs together and the s_2 arcs together. The b and c edges in the first projective plane (and the d and e edges in the second projective plane) indicate cuts we will make to the space, portrayed in the subsequent pictures. Thus, by removing a disk from each projective plane, and cutting as indicated by the b, c, d, and e edges, we obtain four rectangles (topologically), all of whose edges get identified as indicated. Convince yourself that by moving these rectangles around (either by rotation, or reflection about a vertical or horizontal axis) we produce the Klein bottle.

4. What surface in our catalog do we obtain from the connected sum of a torus and a projective plane? That is, what is $H_1\#C_1$? Explain your answer.

5. Show that in the polygonal representation of C_g, all corner points come together at a single point when the edges are identified.

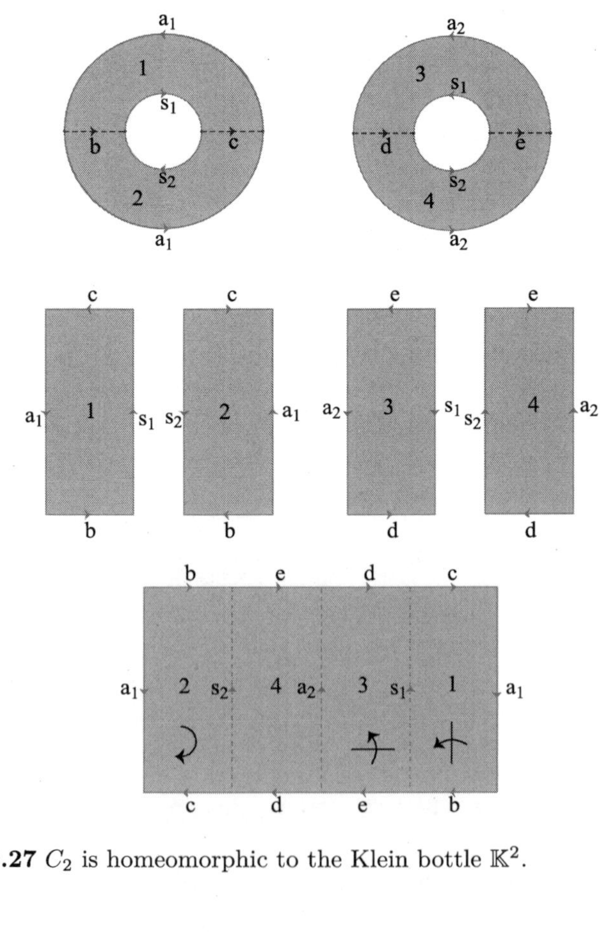

Figure 7.5.27 C_2 is homeomorphic to the Klein bottle $\mathbb{K}^2$.

7.6 Geometry of Surfaces

If you've got a surface in your hand, you can find a homeomorphic version of the surface on which to construct hyperbolic geometry, elliptic geometry, or Euclidean geometry. And the choice of geometry is unique: No surface admits more than one of these geometries. As we shall see, of the infinitely many surfaces, all but four admit hyperbolic geometry (two admit Euclidean geometry and two admit elliptic geometry). Thus, if you randomly generate a constant curvature surface for a two-dimensional bug named Bormit, Bormit will no doubt live in a world with hyperbolic geometry.

Chances are, too, that a constant curvature surface cannot be embedded in three-dimensional space. Only the sphere has this nice feature. In fact, if X is any surface that lives in $\mathbb{R}^3$, like the handlebody surfaces in Figure 7.5.10, p. 169, then it must have at least one point with positive curvature. Why is this? The surface in $\mathbb{R}^3$ is bounded, so there must be some sphere in $\mathbb{R}^3$ centered at the origin that contains the entire surface. Shrink this sphere until it just bumps into the surface at some point. The curvature of the surface at this point matches the curvature of the sphere, which is positive.

We have seen that any surface is homeomorphic to a polygonal surface representing H_g or C_g, for some g, and we now show that each of these may be given a homogeneous, isotropic and metric geometry (so that it has constant curvature). A polygonal surface can only run into trouble homogeneity-wise where the corners come together. Any point in the interior of the polygon has a nice 360° patch of space about it, as does any point in the interior of an edge. However, if the angles of the corners that come together at a point do not add up to 360°, then the surface has either a cone point or a saddle-point, depending on whether the angle sum is less than or more than 360°. As we saw in Chapter 1 (Exercises 1.3.5, p. 9 and Example 1.3.7, p. 10), in either case, we will not have a homogeneous geometry; a two-dimensional bug would be able to distinguish (with triangles or circles) a cone point from a flat point from a saddle point.

To smooth out such cone points or saddle points we change the angles at the corners so that the angles *do* add up to 360°. We now have the means for doing this. If we need to shrink the corner angles, we can put the polygon in the hyperbolic plane. If we need to expand the angles, we can put the polygon in the projective plane.

Example 7.6.1 C_3 **admits hyperbolic geometry.**

The standard polygonal representation of $C_3 = \mathbb{P}^2\#\mathbb{P}^2\#\mathbb{P}^2$, is a hexagon having boundary label $a_1a_1a_2a_2a_3a_3$, as in Figure 7.6.2, p. 180. All six corners of the hexagon come together at a single point. In the Euclidean plane, a regular hexagon has corner angles equal to 120°. To avoid a saddle point when joining the six corners together, shrink the corner angles to 60°. A tiny copy of a regular hexagon in the hyperbolic plane will have corner angles just under 120°. If the hexagon grows so that its vertices approach ideal points, its corner angles will approach 0°. At some point, then, the interior angles will be 60° on the nose. (We may construct this precise hexagon as well. See Exercise 7.6.4, p. ??.) If C_3 is built from this hexagon living in the hyperbolic plane, the surface inherits the geometry of the space in which it finds itself; that is, the surface C_3 *admits* hyperbolic geometry, a nice homogeneous, isotropic and metric geometry.

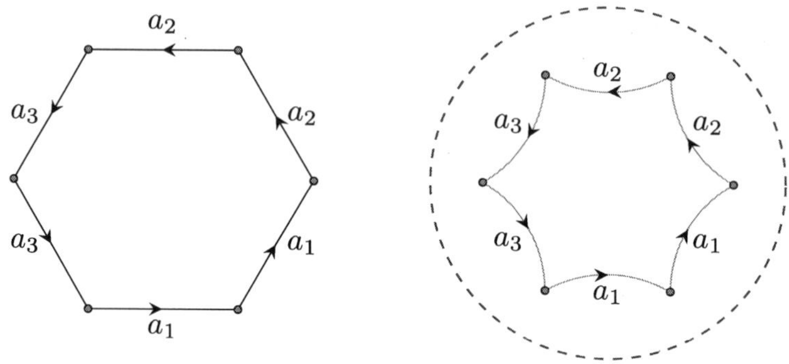

Figure 7.6.2 C_3 admits hyperbolic geometry.

Example 7.6.3 An elliptic polygonal surface.

Revisiting Example 1.3.9, p. 11, consider the hexagon with boundary label *abcabc*. The six corners of this polygonal surface come together in groups of two. These corners create cone points because the angle sum of the two corners coming together is less than 360° in the Euclidean plane. We can avoid cone points by putting the hexagon in $\mathbb{P}^2$. A small regular hexagon in the projective plane will have corner angles just slightly greater than 120°, but we need each corner angle to expand to 180°. We may achieve these angles by expanding the hexagon until it covers the entire projective plane. In fact, the surface of Example 1.3.9, p. 11 *is* the projective plane, and it admits elliptic geometry.

Theorem 7.6.4 *Each surface admits one homogeneous, isotropic, and metric geometry. In particular, the sphere (H_0) and projective plane (C_1) admit elliptic geometry. The torus (H_1) and Klein bottle (C_2) admit Euclidean geometry. All handlebody surfaces H_g with $g \geq 2$ and all cross-cap surfaces C_g with $g \geq 3$ admit hyperbolic geometry.*

The following section offers a more formal discussion of how any surface admits one of our three geometries but we present an intuitive argument here.

The sphere and projective plane admit elliptic geometry by construction: The space in elliptic geometry *is* the projective plane, and via stereographic projection, this is the geometry on $\mathbb{S}^2$.

The torus and Klein bottle are built from regular 4-gons (squares) whose edges are identified in such a way that all 4 corners come together at a point. In each case, if we place the square in the Euclidean plane all corner angles are $\pi/2$, so the sum of the angles is 2π, and our surfaces admit Euclidean geometry.

Each handlebody surfaces H_g for $g \geq 2$ and each cross-cap surfaces C_g for $g \geq 3$ can be built from a regular n-gon where $n \geq 6$. Again, all n corners come together at a single point. A regular n-gon in the Euclidean plane has interior angle $(n-2)\pi/n$ radians, so the corner angles sum to $(n-2)\pi$ radians. This angle sum exceeds 2π radians since $n \geq 6$. Placing a small version of this n-gon in the hyperbolic plane, the corner angle sum will be very nearly equal to $(n-2)\pi$ radians and will exceed 2π radians, but as we expand the n-gon the corners approach ideal points and the corner angles sum will approach 0 radians. Thus, at some point the angle sum will equal 2π radians on the nose, and the polygonal surface built from this precise n-gon admits hyperbolic geometry. Exercise 7.6.4, p. ?? works through how to construct this precise n-gon.

Of course, one need not build a surface from a regular polygon. For instance, the torus can be built from any rectangle in the Euclidean plane and it will inherit Euclidean geometry. So while the type of geometry our surface admits *is* determined, we have some flexibility where certain geometric measurements are concerned. For instance, there is no restriction on the total area of the torus, and the rectangle on which it is formed can have arbitrary length and width dimensions. These dimensions would have a simple, tangible meaning to a two-dimensional bug living in the surface (and might be experimentally determined). Each dimension corresponds to the length of a geodesic path that would return the bug to its starting point. A **closed geodesic path** in a surface is a path that follows along a straight line (in the underlying geometry) that starts and ends at the same point. Figure 7.6.5, p. 181 shows three closed geodesic paths, all starting and ending at a point near a bug's house. The length of one path equals the width of the rectangle, the length of another equals the length of the rectangle, and the third follows a path that is longer than the first two.

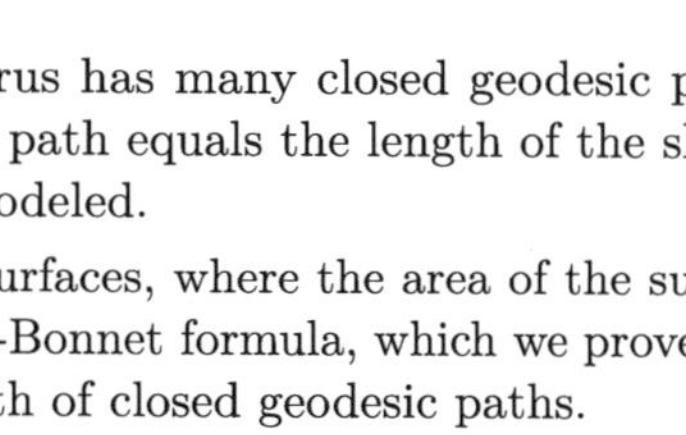

Figure 7.6.5 A flat torus has many closed geodesic paths. The length of the shortest closed geodesic path equals the length of the short side of the rectangle on which the torus is modeled.

Even in hyperbolic surfaces, where the area of the surface is fixed (for a given curvature) by the Gauss-Bonnet formula, which we prove shortly, there is freedom in determining the length of closed geodesic paths.

Example 7.6.6 Building hyperbolic surfaces from pants.

If we make three slices in the two-holed torus we obtain two pairs of pants, as indicated in the following figure.

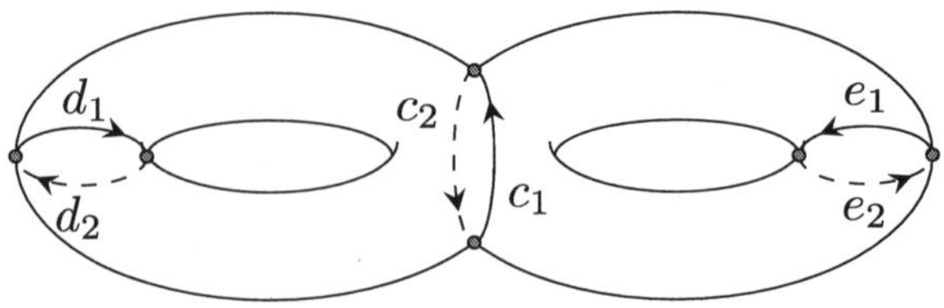

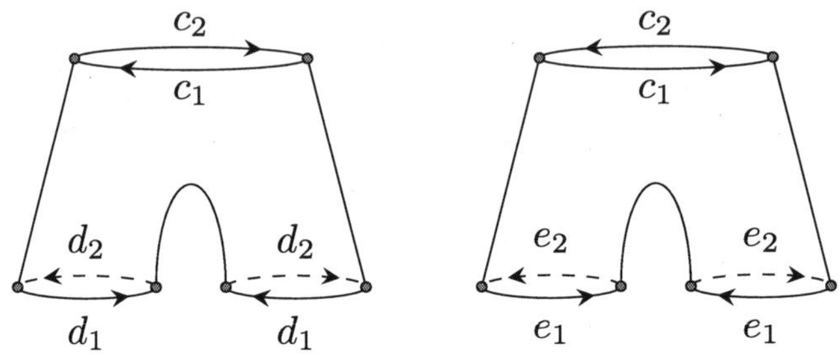

We label our cuts so that we can stitch up our surface later. Match the c_i, d_i, and e_i edges to recover the two-holed torus. Any pair of pants can be cut into two hexagons by cutting along the three vertical seams in the pants. It follows that the two-holed torus can be constructed from four hexagons, with edges identified in pairs as indicated below.

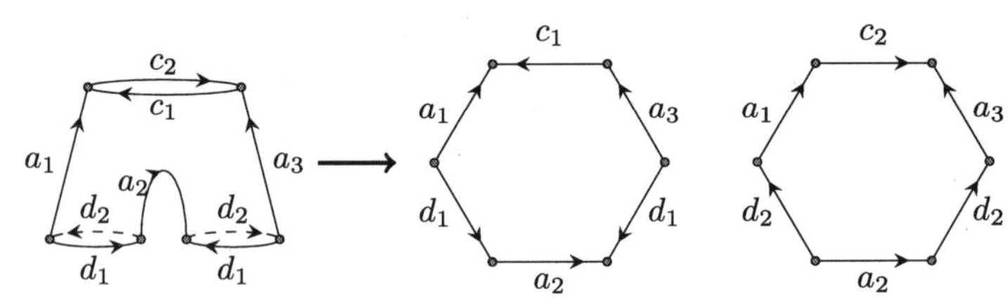

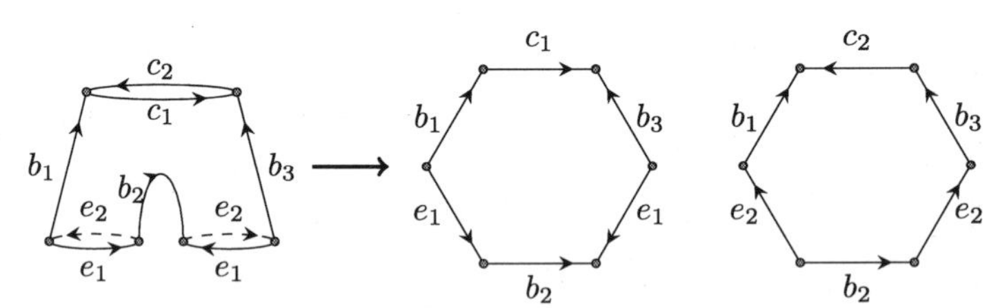

The four hexagons represent a cell division of H_2 having 6 vertices, 12 edges, and 4 faces. In the edge identification, corners come together in groups of 4, so we need each corner angle to equal 90° in order to endow it with a homogeneous geometry. We know we can do this in the hyperbolic plane. Moreover, according to Theorem 5.4.19, p. 107, there is freedom in choosing the dimensions of the hexagons. That is, for each triple of real numbers (a, b, c) there exists a right-angled hexagon in $\mathbb{D}$ with alternate lengths a, b, and c. So, there exists a two-holed torus for each combination of six seam lengths (a_1, a_2, a_3, b_1, b_2, and b_3).

A surface that admits one of our three geometries will have constant curvature. The reader might have already noticed that the *sign* of the curvature will equal the sign of the surface's Euler characteristic. Of course the *magnitude* of the curvature (if $k \neq 0$) can vary if we place a polygonal surface in a scaled version of $\mathbb{P}^2$ or $\mathbb{D}$. That is, while the type of homogeneous geometry a surface admits is determined by its Euler characteristic (which is determined by its shape), the curvature scale can vary if $k \neq 0$. By changing the radius of a sphere, we change its curvature (though it always remains positive). Similarly, the surface C_3 in Figure 7.6.2, p. 180 has constant curvature -1 if it is placed in the hyperbolic plane of Chapter 5. However, it can just as easily find itself in the hyperbolic plane with curvature $k = -8$. Recall, the hyperbolic plane with curvature $k < 0$ is modeled on the open disk in $\mathbb{C}$ centered at the origin with radius $1/\sqrt{|k|}$. Placing the hexagonal representation of C_3 into this space so that its corner angle sum is still 2π produces a surface with constant curvature k.

We have finally arrived at the elegant relationship between a surfacc's curvaturc k, its area, and its Euler characteristic. This relationship crystalizes the interaction between the topology and geometry of surfaces.

Theorem 7.6.7 Gauss-Bonnet. *The area of a surface with constant curvature k and Euler characteristic χ is given by the formula $kA = 2\pi\chi$.*

PROOF. The sphere with constant curvature k has radius equal to $1/\sqrt{k}$, and area equal to $4\pi/k$. Since the sphere has Euler characteristic 2, the Gauss-Bonnet formula holds in this case. The projective plane $\mathbb{P}^2$ with curvature k has area equal to $2\pi/k$, and Euler characteristic equal to 1, so the result holds in this case as well. The torus and the Klein bottle each have $k = 0$ and $\chi = 0$, so in this case the Gauss-Bonnet formula reduces to the true statement that $0 = 0$.

Any surface of constant negative curvature cam be represented by a regular n-sided polygon with $n \geq 6$. Furthermore, this polygon can be placed in the hyperbolic plane with curvature $k < 0$, so that its interior angles sum to 2π radians. According to Theorem 7.4.4, p. 160,

$$kA = 2\pi - (n-2)\pi = 2\pi\left(2 - \frac{n}{2}\right),$$

where A is the area of the n-gon.

Now, for $g \geq 2$, H_g is represented by a $4g$-gon so that

$$kA = 2\pi(2 - 2g) = 2\pi\chi(H_g).$$

For $g \geq 3$, C_g is represented by a $2g$-gon so that

$$kA = 2\pi(2 - g) = 2\pi\chi(C_g).$$

This completes the proof. □

Suppose a two-dimensional cosmologist believes she lives in a surface of constant curvature (because her universe looks homogeneous and isotropic). If she can deduce the curvature of the universe and its total area, she will know its Euler characteristic. That is, by measuring these geometric properties she can deduce the shape of her universe, or, at worst, narrow down the possibilities to two. If χ is 2 or an odd integer then the cosmologist will know the shape of the universe.

If $\chi < 2$ is even, her universe will have one of two possible shapes - one shape orientable, the other non-orientable.

Exercises

1. Suppose our intrepid team of two-dimensional explorers from Exercise 7.4.4, p. ??, after an extensive survey, estimates with high confidence that the area of their universe is between 800,000 km^2 and 900,000 km^2. Assuming their universe is homogeneous and isotropic, what shapes are possible for their universe? Can they deduce from this information the orientability status of their universe?

2. Suppose a certain constant curvature 3-holed torus H_3 has area 5.2 km^2. What must be the area of a constant curvature C_3 surface so that they have the same curvature?

3. *Building a hyperbolic surface from pairs of pants.* To construct H_g for $g \geq 2$ from pairs of pants, how many do we need? Express your answer in terms of g.

4. Suppose we want to build a regular n-gon in $(\mathbb{D}, \mathcal{H})$ from the vertices $v_k = re^{i\frac{k}{n}2\pi}$ for $k = 0, 1, \ldots, n-1$ so that the n interior angles sum to 2π. Prove that this is the case when $r = \sqrt{\cos(2\pi/n)}$. Hint: It may be helpful to refer to Exercise 5.4.9, p. ?? where we proved this result in the case $n = 8$.

7.7 Quotient Spaces

We may bend a sheet of paper and join its left and right edges together to obtain a cylinder. If we let $\mathbb{I}^2 = \{(x, y) \in \mathbb{R}^2 \mid 0 \leq x \leq 1, 0 \leq y \leq 1\}$ represent our square piece of paper, and $C = \{(x, y, z) \in \mathbb{R}^3 \mid x^2 + y^2 = 1, 0 \leq z \leq 1\}$ represent a cylinder, then the map

$$p : \mathbb{I}^2 \to C \text{ by } p((x, y)) = (\cos(2\pi x), \sin(2\pi x), y)$$

models this gluing process.

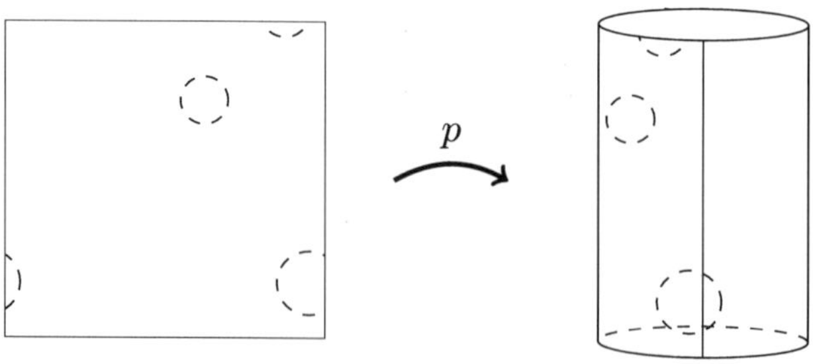

Figure 7.7.1 Bending a sheet of paper into a cylinder.

This map tries very hard to be a homeomorphism. The map is continuous, onto, and it is almost one-to-one with a continuous inverse. It fails in this endeavor only where we join the left and right edges: the points $(0, y)$ and $(1, y)$ in $\mathbb{I}^2$ both get sent by p to the point $(1, 0, y)$. But p is nice enough to *induce* a homeomorphism between the cylinder and a modified version of the domain $\mathbb{I}^2$, obtained by "dividing out" of $\mathbb{I}^2$ the mapping redundancies so that the result is one-to-one. The new version of $\mathbb{I}^2$ is called a quotient space. We develop quotient spaces in this section because all surfaces and candidate three-dimensional universes can be viewed as quotient spaces. We need the notion of an equivalence relation on a set. To get this, we need the notion of a relation.

A **relation on a set S** is a subset R of $S \times S$. In other words, a relation R consists of a set of ordered pairs of the form (a, b) where a and b are in S. If (a, b) is an element in the relation R, we may write aRb. It is common to describe equivalence relations, which we define shortly, with the symbol $\sim$ instead of R. So, when you see $a \sim b$ this means the ordered pair (a, b) is in the relation $\sim$, which is a subset of $S \times S$.

Definition 7.7.2 An **equivalence relation** on a set A is a relation $\sim$ that satisfies these three conditions:

1. Reflexivity: $x \sim x$ for all $x \in A$
2. Symmetry: If $x \sim y$ then $y \sim x$
3. Transitivity: If $x \sim y$ and $y \sim z$ then $x \sim z$.

For any element $a \in A$, the **equivalence class of a**, denoted $[a]$, is the subset of all elements in A that are related to a by $\sim$. That is,

$$[a] = \{x \in A \mid x \sim a\}.$$

$\Diamond$

Example 7.7.3 An equivalence relation.

Define $z \sim w$ in $\mathbb{C}$ if and only if $\text{Re}(z) - \text{Re}(w)$ is an integer and $\text{Im}(z) = \text{Im}(w)$. For instance, $(-1.6 + 4i) \sim (2.4 + 4i)$ since the difference of the real parts (-1.6 - 2.4 = -4) is an integer and the imaginary parts are equal. To show $\sim$ is an equivalence relation, we check the three requirements.

1. Reflexivity: Given $z = a + bi$, it follows that $z \sim z$ because $a - a = 0$ is an integer and $b = b$.

2. Symmetry: Suppose $z \sim w$. Then $\text{Re}(z) - \text{Re}(w) = k$ for some integer k and $\text{Im}(z) = \text{Im}(w)$. It follows that $\text{Re}(w) - \text{Re}(z) = -k$ is an integer and $\text{Im}(w) = \text{Im}(z)$. In other words, $w \sim z$.

3. Transitivity: Suppose $z \sim w$ and $w \sim v$. We must show $z \sim v$. Since $z \sim w$, $\text{Re}(z) - \text{Re}(w) = k$ for some integer k, and since $w \sim v$, $\text{Re}(w) - \text{Re}(v) = l$ for some integer l. Notice that

$$\begin{aligned} k + l &= [\text{Re}(z) - \text{Re}(w)] + [\text{Re}(w) - \text{Re}(v)] \\ &= \text{Re}(z) - \text{Re}(v). \end{aligned}$$

So, $\text{Re}(z) - \text{Re}(v)$ is an integer. Furthermore, we have $\text{Im}(z) = \text{Im}(w) = \text{Im}(v)$. Thus, $z \sim v$.

The equivalence class of a point $z = a+bi$ consists of all points $w = c+bi$ where $a - c$ is an integer. In other words, $c = a + n$ for some integer n, so $w = z+n$ and we may express the equivalence class as $[z] = \{z+n \mid n \in \mathbb{Z}\}$.

A **partition** of a set A consists of a collection of non-empty subsets of A that are mutually disjoint and have union equal to A. An equivalence relation on a set A serves to partition A by the equivalence classes. Indeed, each equivalence class is non-empty since each element is related to itself, and the union of all equivalence classes is all of A by the same reason. That equivalence classes are mutually disjoint follows from the following lemma.

Lemma 7.7.4 *Suppose $\sim$ is an equivalence relation on A, and a and b are any two elements of A. Then either $[a]$ and $[b]$ have no elements in common, or they are equal sets.*

PROOF. Suppose there is some element c that is in both $[a]$ and $[b]$. We show $[a] = [b]$ by arguing that each set is a subset of the other.

That $[a]$ is a subset of $[b]$: Suppose x is in $[a]$. We must show that x is in $[b]$ as well. Since x is in $[a]$, $x \sim a$. Since c is in $[a]$ and in $[b]$, $c \sim a$ and $c \sim b$. We may use these facts, along with transitivity and symmetry of the relation, to see that $x \sim a \sim c \sim b$. That is, x is in $[b]$. Therefore, everything in $[a]$ is also in $[b]$.

We may repeat the argument above to show that $[b]$ is a subset $[a]$. Thus, if $[a]$ and $[b]$ have any element in common, then they are entirely equal sets, and this completes the proof. □

In light of Lemma 7.7.4, p. 186, an equivalence relation on a set provides a natural way to divide its elements into subsets that have no points in common. An equivalence relation on A, then, determines a new set whose elements are the distinct equivalence classes.

Definition 7.7.5 If $\sim$ is an equivalence relation on a set A, the **quotient set** of A by $\sim$ is

$$A/_{\sim} = \{[a] \mid a \in A\}.$$

◊

We will be interested in quotients of three spaces: the Euclidean plane $\mathbb{C}$, the hyperbolic plane $\mathbb{D}$, and the sphere $\mathbb{S}^2$. If we build a quotient set from one of these spaces, we will call a region of the space a **fundamental domain** of the quotient set if it contains a representative of each equivalence class of the quotient and at most one representative in its interior.

Orbit Spaces

We may construct a natural quotient set from a geometry (X, G).

The group structure of G defines an equivalence relation $\sim_G$ on X as follows: For $x, y \in X$, let

$$x \sim_G y \text{ if and only if } T(x) = y \text{ for some } T \in G.$$

Indeed, for each $x \in X$, $x \sim_G x$ because the group G must contain the identity transformation, so the relation is reflexive. Next, if $x \sim_G y$ then $T(x) = y$ for some T in G. But the group contains inverses, so T^{-1} is in G and $T^{-1}(y) = x$.

Thus $y \sim_G x$, and so $\sim_G$ is symmetric. Third, transitivity of the relation follows from the fact that the composition of two maps in G is again in G.

Given geometry (X, G) we let X/G denote the quotient set determined by the equivalence relation $\sim_G$. In this setting we call the equivalence class of a point x in X, the **orbit** of x. So, the orbit of x consists of all points in the space X to which x can be mapped under transformations of the group G:

$$[x] = \{y \in X \mid T(x) = y \text{ for some } T \in G\}.$$

Put another way, the orbit of x is the set of points in X congruent to x in the geometry (X, G).

Note that if the geometry G is homogeneous, then any two points in X are congruent and, for any $x \in X$, the orbit of x is all of X. In this case the quotient set X/G consists of a single point, which is not so interesting. We typically want to consider orbit spaces X/G in which G is a "small" group of transformations.

We say that a group of transformations G of X is a **group of homeomorphisms of** X if each transformation in G is continuous. In this case, we call X/G an **orbit space**. If X has a metric, we say that a group of transformations of X is a **group of isometries** if each transformation of the group preserves distance between points.

Example 7.7.6 Building a topological cylinder.

Consider the horizontal translation $T_1(z) = z+1$ of $\mathbb{C}$. This transformation is a (Euclidean) isometry of $\mathbb{C}$ and it *generates* a group of isometries of $\mathbb{C}$ as follows. Put T_1 and T_1^{-1} in the group, along with any number of compositions of these transformations. Fortunately, any number of compositions of these two maps results in an isometry that is easy to write down. Any finite composition of copies of T_1 and T_1^{-1} indicates a series of instructions for a point z: at each step in the long composition z moves either one unit to the left if we apply T_1^{-1} or one unit to the right if we apply T_1. In the end, z has moved horizontally by some integer amount. That is, any such composition can be written as $T_n(z) = z + n$ for some integer n. We let $\langle T_1 \rangle$ denote the group generated by T_1, and we have

$$\langle T_1 \rangle = \{T_n(z) = z + n \mid n \in \mathbb{Z}\}.$$

The orbit of a point p under this group of isometries is

$$[p] = \{p + n \mid n \in \mathbb{Z}\}.$$

A fundamental domain for the orbit space $\mathbb{C}/\langle T_1 \rangle$ is the vertical strip consisting of all points z with $0 \leq \text{Re}(z) \leq 1$, as in the following figure. Every point in $\mathbb{C}$ is related to a point in this shaded vertical strip. Furthermore, no two points in the interior of the strip are related. By passing to the quotient, we are essentially "rolling" up the plane in to an infinitely tall cylinder. The rolling up process is described by the map $p : \mathbb{C} \to \mathbb{C}/\langle T_1 \rangle$ given by $p(z) = [z]$.

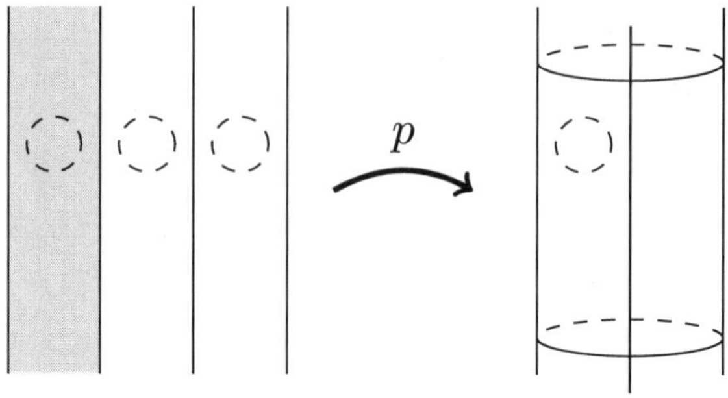

Example 7.7.7 A quotient space from rotations.

The rotation $R_{\frac{\pi}{2}}$ of $\mathbb{C}$ by $\pi/2$ about the origin generates a group of isometries of $\mathbb{C}$ consisting of four transformations. We generate the group as before, by considering all possible compositions of $R_{\frac{\pi}{2}}$ and $R_{\frac{\pi}{2}}^{-1}$. This group turns out to be finite: Any combination of these rotations produces a rotation by 0, $\pi/2$, π, or $3\pi/2$ radians, giving us

$$\langle R_{\frac{\pi}{2}} \rangle = \{1, R_{\frac{\pi}{2}}, R_{\pi}, R_{\frac{3\pi}{2}}\}.$$

The orbit of the point 0 is simply $\{0\}$ because each transformation in the group fixes 0, but the orbit of any other point in $\mathbb{C}$ is a four-element set. For instance, the orbit of 1 is $[1] = \{i, -1, -i, 1\}$.

It turns out that every surface can be viewed as a quotient space of the form M/G, where M is either the Euclidean plane $\mathbb{C}$, the hyperbolic plane $\mathbb{D}$, or the sphere $\mathbb{S}^2$, and G is a group of isometries in Euclidean geometry, hyperbolic geometry, or elliptic geometry, respectively. In topology terminology, the space M is called a **universal covering space** of the orbit space M/G.

Example 7.7.8 H_1 as quotient of $\mathbb{C}$.

Suppose a and b are positive real numbers. Let $\langle T_a, T_{bi} \rangle$ be the group of homeomorphisms *generated* by the horizontal translation $T_a(z) = z + a$ and the vertical translation $T_{bi}(z) = z + bi$.

This group contains all possible compositions of these two transformations and their inverses. Thus, the orbit of a point z consists of all complex numbers to which z can be sent by moving z horizontally by some integer multiple of a units, and vertically by some integer multiple of b units. An arbitrary transformation in $\Gamma = \langle T_a, T_{bi} \rangle$ has the form

$$T(z) = z + (ma + nbi)$$

where m and n are integers. A fundamental domain for the orbit space consists of the rectangle with corners $0, a, a + bi, bi$. The resulting quotient space is homeomorphic to the torus. Notice that points on the boundary of this rectangle are identified in pairs. In fact, the fundamental domain, with its boundary point redundancies, corresponds precisely to our polygonal surface representation of the torus.

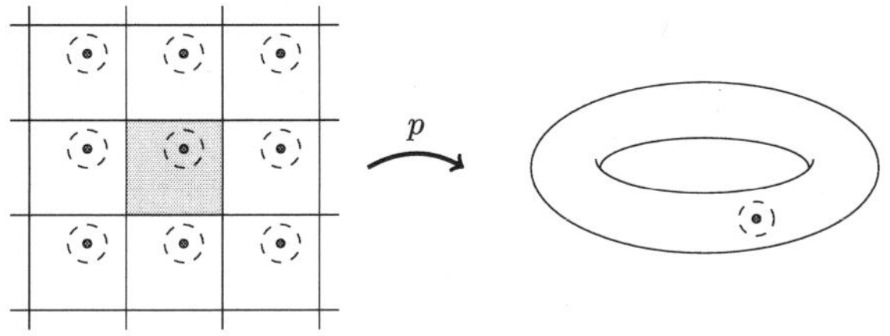

If the space M has a metric and our group of homeomorphisms is sufficiently nice, then the resulting orbit space inherits a metric from the universal covering space M. To be sufficiently nice, we first need our homeomorphisms to be isometries. The group of isometries must also be fixed-point free and properly discontinuous. The group G is **fixed-point free** if each isometry in G (other than the identity map) has no fixed points. The group G is **properly discontinuous** if every x in X has an open 2-ball U_x about it whose images under all isometries in G are pairwise disjoint. The interested reader is encouraged to see [10] or [9] for more detail. If our group G is a fixed-point free, properly discontinuous group of isometries, then the resulting orbit space inherits a metric from M.

Consider the quotient space in Example 7.7.7, p. 188. The group here is a group of isometries, since rotations preserve Euclidean distance, but it is not fixed-point free. All maps in G have fixed points (rotation about the origin fixes 0). This prevents the quotient space from inheriting the geometry of its mother space. Indeed, a circle centered at [0] with radius r would have circumference $\frac{2\pi r}{4}$, which doesn't correspond to Euclidean geometry.

The group of isometries in the torus example is fixed-point free and properly discontinuous, so the following formula for the distance between two points $[u]$ and $[v]$ in the orbit space $\mathbb{C}/\langle T_a, T_{bi}\rangle$ is well-defined:

$$d([u],[v]) = \min\{|z-w| \mid z \in [u], w \in [v]\}.$$

Figure 7.7.9, p. 190 depicts two points in the shaded fundamental domain, $[u]$ and $[v]$. The distance between them equals the Euclidean distance in $\mathbb{C}$ of the shortest path between any point in equivalence class $[u]$ and any point in equivalence class $[v]$. There are many such nearest pairs, and one such pair is labeled in Figure 7.7.9, p. 190 where z is in $[u]$ and w is in $[v]$. Also drawn in the figure is a solid line (in two parts) that corresponds to the shortest path one would take *within* the fundamental domain to proceed from $[u]$ to $[v]$. This path marks the shortest route a ship in the video game from Chapter 1 could take to get from $[u]$ to $[v]$.

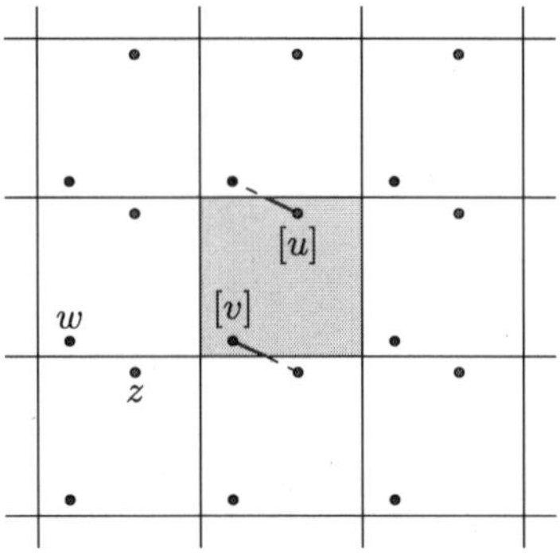

Figure 7.7.9 The distance between two points in the torus viewed as a quotient of $\mathbb{C}$.

Example 7.7.10 $\mathbb{P}^2$ as quotient of $\mathbb{S}^2$.

Let $T_a : \mathbb{S}^2 \to \mathbb{S}^2$ be the antipodal map $T_a(P) = -P$. This map is an isometry that sends each point on $\mathbb{S}^2$ to the point diametrically opposed to it, so it is fixed-point free. Since $T_a^{-1} = T_a$, the group generated by this map consists of just 2 elements: T_a and the identity map. The quotient space $\mathbb{S}^2/\langle T_a \rangle$ is the projective plane.

Example 7.7.11 H_2 as quotient of $\mathbb{D}^2$.

We may build a regular octagon in the hyperbolic plane whose interior angles equal $\pi/4$ radians. We may also find a hyperbolic transformation that takes an edge of this octagon to another edge. Labelling the edges as in the following diagram, let T_a be the hyperbolic isometry taking one a edge to the other, being careful to respect the edge orientations. We construct such a map by composing two hyperbolic reflections about hyperbolic lines: the hyperbolic line containing the first a edge, and the hyperbolic line m that bisects the b edge between the a edges. Since the two lines of reflection do not intersect, the resulting map in $\mathcal{H}$ is a translation in $\mathcal{H}$ and has no fixed points in $\mathbb{D}$ (the fixed points are ideal points).

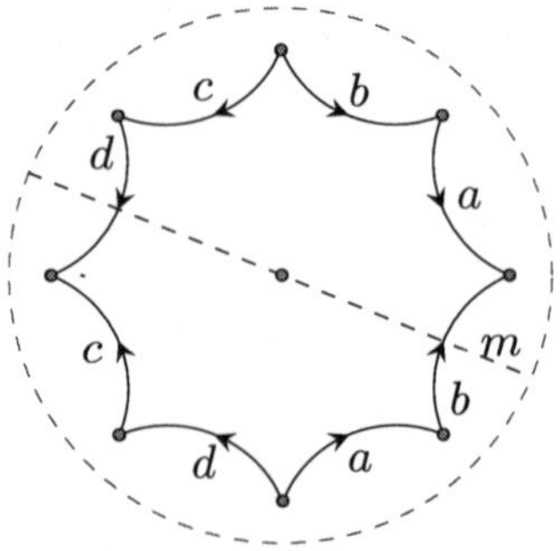

Define T_b, T_c, and T_d similarly and consider the group of isometries of $\mathbb{D}$ generated by these four maps. This group is a fixed-point free, properly discontinuous group of isometries of $\mathbb{D}$, so the resulting quotient space inherits hyperbolic geometry.

The distance between two points $[u]$ and $[v]$ in the quotient space is given by

$$d_H([u],[v]) = \min\{d_H(z,w) \mid z \in [u], w \in [v]\}.$$

Geodesics in the quotient space are determined by geodesics in the hyperbolic plane $\mathbb{D}$.

Topologically, the quotient space is homeomorphic to H_2, and the octagon pictured above serves as a fundamental domain of the quotient space. Moving copies of this octagon by isometries in the group produces a tiling of $\mathbb{D}$ by this octagon. Each copy of the octagon would serve equally well as a fundamental domain for the quotient space. Figure 7.7.12, p. 191 displays a portion of this tiling, including a geodesic triangle in the fundamental domain, and images of it in neighboring octagons.

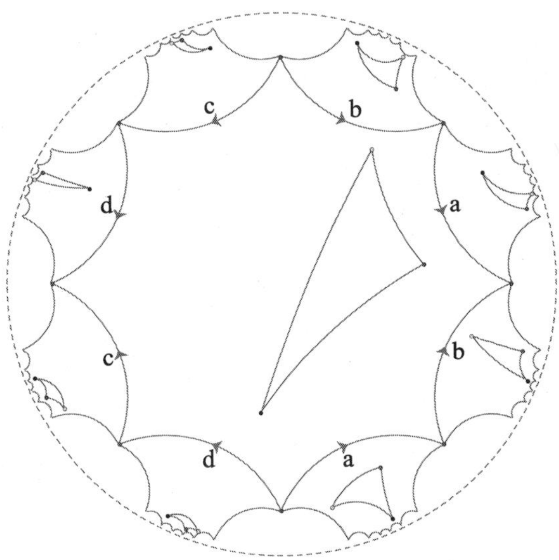

Figure 7.7.12 A triangle in H_2, with various images of it.

All surfaces H_g for $g \geq 2$ and C_g for $g \geq 3$ can be viewed as quotients of $\mathbb{D}$ by following the procedure in the previous example.

Start with a perfectly sized polygon in $\mathbb{D}$. The polygon must have corner angle sum equal to 2π radians, and the edges that get identified must have equal length so that an isometry can take one to the other. (In every example so far, we have used regular polygons in which all sides have the same length, but asymmetric polygons will also work.) Next, for each pair of oriented edges to be identified, find a hyperbolic isometry that maps one onto the other (respecting the orientation of the edges). The group generated by these isometries creates a quotient space homeomorphic to the space represented by the polygon, and it inherits hyperbolic geometry. Note also that the initial polygon can be moved by the isometries in the group to tile all of $\mathbb{D}$ without gaps or overlaps.

Dirichlet Domain

We end this section with a discussion of the Dirichlet domain, which is an important tool in the investigation of the shape of the universe. Suppose we live in a surface described as a quotient M/G where M is either $\mathbb{C}$, $\mathbb{D}$, or $\mathbb{S}^2$, and G is a fixed-point free and properly discontinuous group of isometries of the space. For each point x in M define the **Dirichlet domain with basepoint** x to consist of all points y in M such that

$$d(x, y) \leq d(x, T(y))$$

for all T in G, where it is understood that $d(x, y)$ is Euclidean distance, hyperbolic distance, or elliptic distance, depending on whether M is $\mathbb{C}$, $\mathbb{D}$, or $\mathbb{S}^2$, respectively.

At each basepoint x in M, the Dirichlet domain is itself a fundamental domain for the surface M/G, and it represents the fundamental domain that a two-dimensional inhabitant might build from his or her local perspective. It is a polygon in M (whose edges are lines in the local geometry) consisting of all points y that are as close to x or closer to x than any of its image points $T(y)$ under transformations in G.

We may visualize a Dirichlet domain with basepoint x as follows. Consider a small circle in M centered at x. Construct a circle of equal radius about all points in the orbit of x. Then, begin inflating the circle (and all of its images). Eventually the circles will touch one another, and as the circles continue to expand let them press into each other so that they form a geodesic boundary edge. When the circle has filled the entire surface, it will have formed a polygon with edges identified in pairs. This polygon is the Dirichlet domain.

At any basepoint in the torus of Example 7.7.8, p. 188 the Dirichlet domain will be a rectangle identical in proportions to the fundamental domain. In general, however, the shape of a Dirichlet domain may be different than the polygon on which the surface was built, and the shape of the Dirichlet domain may vary from point to point, which is rather cool.

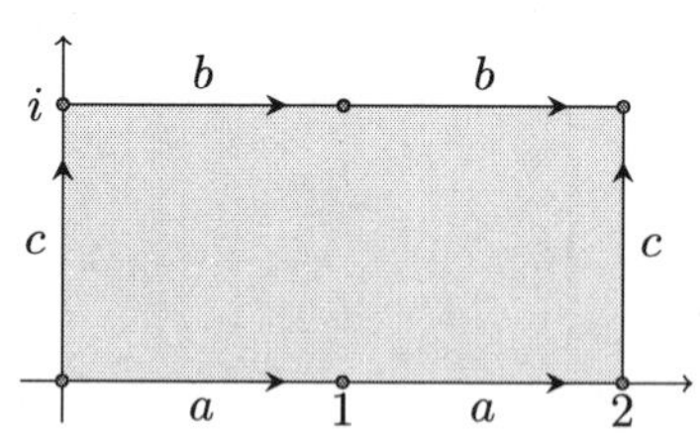

Figure 7.7.13 Building a Klein bottle from a hexagon.

Example 7.7.14 Dirichlet domains in a Klein bottle.

Consider the surface constructed from the hexagon in Figure 7.7.13, p. 192, which appeared in Levin's paper on cosmic topology [23]. Assume the hexagon is placed in $\mathbb{C}$ with its six corners at the points 0, 1, 2, $2+i$, $1+i$ and i.

This polygonal surface represents a cell division of a surface with three edges, two vertices, and one face. The Euler characteristic is thus 0, so the surface is either the torus or Klein bottle. In fact, it is a Klein bottle because it contains a Möbius strip. We may tile the Euclidean plane with copies of this hexagon using the transformations $T(z) = z + 2i$ (vertical translation) and $r(z) = \overline{z} + (1 + 2i)$ (a transformation that reflects a point about the horizontal axis $y = 1$ and then translates to the right by one unit). The following figure shows the shaded fundamental domain A and its images under various combinations of T and r.

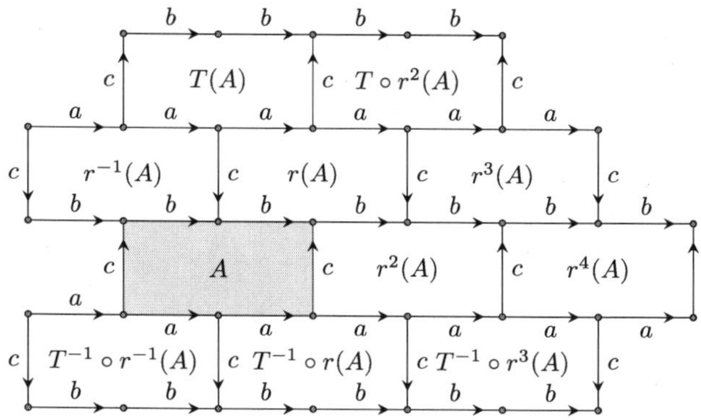

If Γ is the group of transformations generated by T and r, the quotient space $\mathbb{C}/\Gamma$ is the Klein bottle, and its geometry is Euclidean, inherited from the Euclidean plane $\mathbb{C}$.

It turns out that the Dirichlet domain at a basepoint in this space can vary in shape from point to point. Exercise 7.7.4, p. ?? investigates the shape of the Dirichlet domain at different points.

Exercises

1. Show that the Dirichlet domain at any point of the torus in Example 7.7.8, p. 188 is an a by b rectangle by completing the following parts.

a. Construct an a by b rectangle to be the fundamental domain, and place eight copies of this rectangle around the fundamental domain as in Figure 7.7.9, p. 190. Then plot a point x in the fundamental domain, and plot its image in each of the copies.

b. For each image x' of x, construct the perpendicular bisector of the segment xx'. The eight perpendicular bisectors enclose the Dirichlet domain based at x. Prove that the Dirichlet domain is also an a by b rectangle.

2. Construct C_3 as a quotient of $\mathbb{D}$ by a group of isometries of $\mathbb{D}$. Be as explicit as possible when defining the group of isometries.

3. Explain why the g-holed torus H_g can be viewed as a quotient of $\mathbb{D}$ by hyperbolic isometries for any $g \geq 2$.

4. Consulting Example 7.7.14, p. 192, show that the Dirichlet domain at any point z on the line $\text{Im}(z) = 1/2$, such as the one in Figure 7.7.15, p. 194, is a square. Show that the Dirichlet domain at any point z on the line $\text{Im}(z) = 0$ is a rectangle.

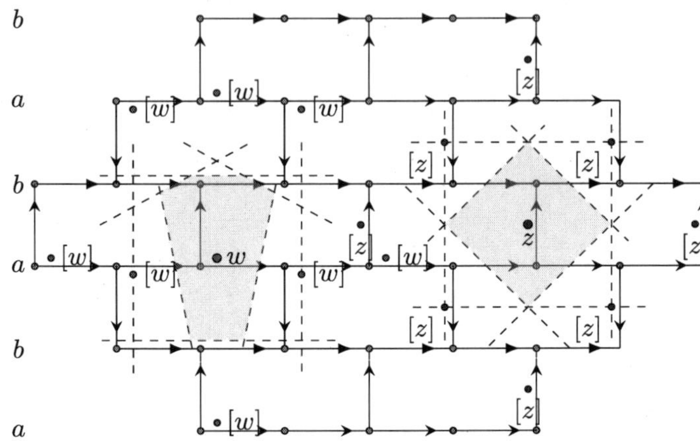

Figure 7.7.15 The Dirichlet domain at a point is obtained by considering perpendicular bisectors with its nearest images, and its shape can vary from point to point, as at points z and w. In the figure all vertically oriented edges are c edges. All horizontally oriented edges in a given row have the same label, either a or b as indicated.

8

Cosmic Topology

Cosmic topology can be described as the effort to determine the shape of our universe through observational techniques. In this chapter we discuss two programs of research in cosmic topology: the cosmic crystallography method and the circles-in-the-sky method. Both programs search for topology by assuming the universe is finite in volume without boundary. The chapter begins with a discussion of three-dimensional geometry and some 3-manifolds that have been given consideration as models for the shape of our universe.

8.1 Three-Dimensional Geometry and 3-Manifolds

Recall that $\mathbb{R}^3$ is the set of ordered triples of real numbers (x, y, z), and a 3-manifold is a space with the feature that every point has a neighborhood that is homeomorphic to an open 3-ball. We assume that the shape of the universe at any fixed time is a 3-manifold. Evidence points to a universe that is isotropic and homogeneous on the largest scales. If this is the case, then just as in the two-dimensional case, the universe admits one of three geometries: hyperbolic, elliptic, or Euclidean. This section offers a brief introduction to the three-dimensional versions of these geometries before turning to 3-manifolds. The reader is encouraged to see [12] for a broader intuitive discussion of these ideas, or [11] for a more rigorous approach.

Euclidean Geometry in Three Dimensions. Euclidean geometry is the geometry of our experience in three dimensions. Planes look like infinite tabletops, lines in space are Euclidean straight lines. Any planar slice of 3-space inherits two-dimensional Euclidean geometry.

The space for three-dimensional Euclidean geometry is $\mathbb{R}^3$, and we may use boldface notation $\boldsymbol{v}$ to represent a point in $\mathbb{R}^3$. The group of transformations in this geometry consists of all rotations of $\mathbb{R}^3$ about lines and all translations by vectors in $\mathbb{R}^3$. The distance between points $\boldsymbol{v} = (x_1, y_1, z_1)$ and $\boldsymbol{w} = (x_2, y_2, z_2)$ is given by the Euclidean distance formula

$$|\boldsymbol{v} - \boldsymbol{w}| = \sqrt{(x_1 - x_2)^2 + (y_1 - y_2)^2 + (z_1 - z_2)^2}.$$

Any transformation in the group can be expressed as a screw motion. A **screw motion** is a transformation of $\mathbb{R}^3$ consisting of a translation in the direction of a line followed by a rotation about that same line. Of course, rotations about lines and translations are special cases of this more general map.

Hyperbolic Geometry in Three Dimensions. The Poincaré disk model of hyperbolic geometry may be extended to three dimensions as follows. Let the space $\mathbb{H}^3$ consist of all points inside the unit ball in $\mathbb{R}^3$. That is, let

$$\mathbb{H}^3 = \{(x, y, z) \in \mathbb{R}^3 | x^2 + y^2 + z^2 < 1\}.$$

The unit 2-sphere $\mathbb{S}^2$ bounds $\mathbb{H}^3$, and is called the sphere at infinity. Points on the sphere at infinity are called ideal points and are not points in $\mathbb{H}^3$.

The group of transformations for three-dimensional hyperbolic geometry is generated by inversions about spheres that are orthogonal to the sphere at infinity. Inversion about a sphere is defined analogously to inversion in a circle. Suppose S is a sphere in $\mathbb{R}^3$ centered at $\boldsymbol{v_0}$ with radius r, and $\boldsymbol{v}$ is any point in $\mathbb{R}^3$. Define the point symmetric to $\boldsymbol{v}$ with respect to S to be the point $\boldsymbol{v}^*$ on the ray $\overrightarrow{\boldsymbol{v_0 v}}$ such that

$$|\boldsymbol{v} - \boldsymbol{v_0}||\boldsymbol{v}^* - \boldsymbol{v_0}| = r^2.$$

One may prove that inversion about a sphere S will send spheres orthogonal to S to themselves. So, composing two inversions about spheres orthogonal to $\mathbb{S}^2_\infty$ generates an orientation preserving transformation of hyperbolic three-space $\mathbb{H}^3$. The transformation group consists of all such compositions. Lines in this geometry correspond to arcs of clines in $\mathbb{H}^3$ that are orthogonal to the sphere at infinity (see line L in Figure 8.1.1, p. 196). These lines are geodesics in $\mathbb{H}^3$. As in the two-dimensional case, Euclidean lines through the origin of $\mathbb{H}^3$ are also hyperbolic lines. A plane in this geometry corresponds to the portion of a sphere or Euclidean plane inside $\mathbb{H}^3$ that meets the sphere at infinity at right angles, such as planes P_1 and P_2 in Figure 8.1.1, p. 196. If we restrict our attention to any plane in $\mathbb{H}^3$, we recover the two-dimensional hyperbolic geometry of Chapter 5.

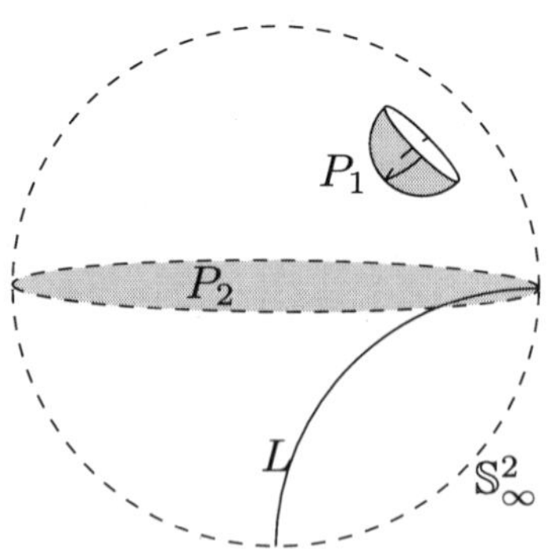

Figure 8.1.1 One model of hyperbolic space $\mathbb{H}^3$, the open unit 2-ball.

Elliptic Geometry in three dimensions. Three-dimensional elliptic geometry is derived from the geometry that the 3-sphere $\mathbb{S}^3$ inherits as a subspace of the Euclidean space $\mathbb{R}^4$. The 3-sphere consists of all points in 4-dimensional space one unit from the origin:

$$\mathbb{S}^3 = \{(x, y, z, w) \in \mathbb{R}^4 \mid x^2 + y^2 + z^2 + w^2 = 1\}.$$

Great circles in $\mathbb{S}^3$ are circles of maximum diameter drawn in the space. Great circles correspond to geodesics in the space. Similarly, a great 2-sphere in $\mathbb{S}^3$ is a 2-sphere of maximum diameter drawn in the space. As a subspace of $\mathbb{S}^3$, a great 2-sphere inherits the elliptic geometry of Chapter 6. The 3-sphere is discussed in more detail in Example 8.1.3, p. 199.

The transformation group for elliptic geometry in three dimensions is conveniently described by viewing $\mathbb{R}^4$ as the set of quaternions. A **quaternion** has the form $a + b\mathbf{i} + c\mathbf{j} + d\mathbf{k}$ where a, b, c, d are real numbers and $\mathbf{i}, \mathbf{j}$, and $\mathbf{k}$ are imaginary numbers with the feature that $\mathbf{i}^2 = \mathbf{j}^2 = \mathbf{k}^2 = -1$ and the additional property that the product $\mathbf{ijk} = -1$. The constant a is called the **scalar term** of the quaternion $q = a + b\mathbf{i} + c\mathbf{j} + d\mathbf{k}$. The **modulus** of q is $|q| = \sqrt{a^2 + b^2 + c^2 + d^2}$. A quaternion q is called a **unit quaternion**, if $|q| = 1$. The **conjugate** of q, denoted q^*, is the quaternion $q^* = a - b\mathbf{i} - c\mathbf{j} - d\mathbf{k}$. One can check that $q \cdot q^* = |q|^2$. The 3-sphere then consists of all unit quaternions.

The transformation group for the geometry on $\mathbb{S}^3$ is generated by multiplication on the left and/or right by unit quaternions. For fixed unit quaternions u and v, the map $T : \mathbb{S}^3 \to \mathbb{S}^3$ by $T(q) = uqv$ is a typical transformation in three-dimensional elliptic geometry. These transformations preserve antipodal points on the 3-sphere - distinct points on $\mathbb{S}^3$ that are on the same Euclidean line through the origin in $\mathbb{R}^4$.

As in the two-dimensional case, three-dimensional Euclidean, hyperbolic, and elliptic geometries are homogenous, isotropic and metric. Furthermore, triangles distinguish the geometries: in Euclidean space $\mathbb{R}^3$, a triangle has angle sum equal to π radians; in $\mathbb{S}^3$ any triangle angle sum exceeds π radians; in $\mathbb{H}^3$ any triangle angle sum is less than π radians. As a result, if we place a solid like a dodecahedron in $\mathbb{H}^3$ (so that the faces are portions of planes in $\mathbb{H}^3$), the angles at which the corners come together are smaller than the corner angles of the Euclidean dodecahedron. These angles shrink further as the corner points of the solid approach ideal points on the sphere at infinity. On the other hand, placing the dodecahedron in $\mathbb{S}^3$ will increase the angles at the corners.

This flexibility is very useful. Whereas surfaces can be constructed from polygons by identifying their edges in pairs, many 3-manifolds can be constructed from a 3-complex (such as the Platonic solids) by identifying its faces in pairs. A 3-manifold built in this way will admit either Euclidean geometry, hyperbolic geometry, or elliptic geometry depending on how, if at all, the corner angles need to change so that the corners come together to form a perfect patch of three-dimensional space. Now we investigate a few 3-manifolds and the geometry they admit.

Example 8.1.2 The 3-torus.

We may think of the 3-torus $\mathbb{T}^3$ as a cubical room with the following face (or wall) identifications: if we propel ourselves (with a jet pack) up through the ceiling, we reappear through the floor directly below where we had been. For instance, the elliptical points in the following figure are identified. Each point on the top face is identified with the corresponding point on the bottom face. If we fly through the left wall we reappear through the right wall at the corresponding spot (see the triangles in the figure). If we fly through the front wall we reappear through the back wall at the corresponding spot (see the squares in the figure).

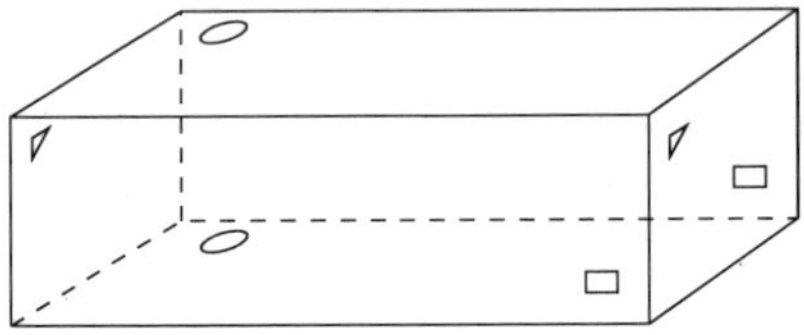

The 3-torus is the three-dimensional analogue of the torus video screen we saw on the first pages of this text. In fact, a slice of the 3-torus in a plane parallel to one of the faces *is* a torus. One checks that under the face identification, all eight corners come together in a single point. The angles at these corners are such that they form a perfect patch of three-dimensional space. We do not need to inflate the corner angles (in elliptic space) or shrink the angles (in hyperbolic space) in order for the corners to come together perfectly.

We can also view the 3-torus as an orbit space as discussed in Section 7.7. In particular, let T_x, T_y, T_z represent translations of $\mathbb{R}^3$ by one unit in the x-direction, y-direction, and z-direction, respectively. That is, $T_x(x, y, z) = (x+1, y, z)$, $T_y(x, y, z) = (x, y+1, z)$ and $T_z(x, y, z) = (x, y, z+1)$. These three transformations generate a group of transformations Γ of $\mathbb{R}^3$, and any transformation in the group has the form $T(x, y, z) = (x+a, y+b, z+c)$ where a, b, c are integers. A fundamental domain of the quotient space $\mathbb{R}^3/\Gamma$ is the unit cube

$$\mathbb{I}^3 = \{(x, y, z) \mid 0 \leq x, y, z \leq 1\},$$

and all the images of this cube under the transformations in Γ tile $\mathbb{R}^3$. The 3-torus is a quotient of $\mathbb{R}^3$ generated by Euclidean isometries, and it inherits Euclidean geometry.

The 3-torus is one of just ten compact and connected 3-manifolds admitting Euclidean geometry. Of these ten, six are orientable, and four are non-orientable. The 3-torus is orientable, and the other five orientable Euclidean manifolds are presented below in Example 8.1.7, p. 203 and Example 8.1.9, p. 204.

The elliptic 3-manifolds have also been classified. There are infinitely many different types, and it turns out they are all orientable. The 3-sphere is the simplest elliptic 3-manifold, and Albert Einstein assumed the universe had this shape when he first solved his equations for general relativity. He found a static, finite, simply connected universe without boundary appealing for aesthetic reasons, and it cleared up some paradoxes in physics that arise in an infinite universe. However, the equations of general relativity only tell us about the local nature of space, and do not fix the global shape of the universe. In 1917, the Dutch astronomer

Willem De Sitter (1872-1934) noticed that Einstein's solutions admitted a another, different global shape: namely three-dimensional elliptic space obtained from the 3-sphere by identifying antipodal points, just as we did in Chapter 6 in the two-dimensional case.

Example 8.1.3 The 3-sphere.

Recall, the 3-sphere consists of all points in 4-dimensional space 1 unit from the origin:

$$\mathbb{S}^3 = \{(x, y, z, w) \mid x^2 + y^2 + z^2 + w^2 = 1\}.$$

One model of $\mathbb{S}^3$ consists of two solid balls in $\mathbb{R}^3$ whose boundary 2-spheres are identified point for point, as in the following figure. The figure shows a path from point a to point b in $\mathbb{S}^3$ that goes through the point p on the boundary of the left-hand solid ball before entering the right-hand solid ball through the point on its boundary with which p has been identified (also called p).

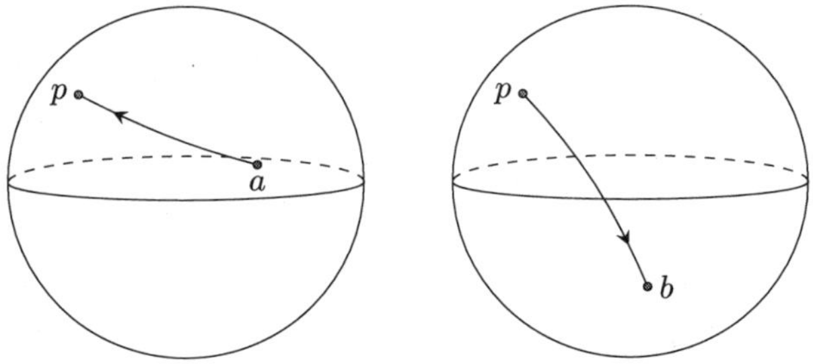

The 3-sphere has interesting features, often accessible by analogy with the 2-sphere. If you slice the 2-sphere with a plane in $\mathbb{R}^3$, the intersection is a circle (or a single point if the plane is tangent to the 2-sphere). Moreover, the circle of intersection is a geodesic on the 2-sphere if it is a great circle: a circle of maximum radius drawn on the 2-sphere. Bumped up a dimension, if you "slice" the 3-sphere with $\mathbb{R}^3$, the intersection is a 2-sphere (or a single point if the slice is tangent to $\mathbb{S}^3$). Moreover, the 2-sphere of intersection is a great 2-sphere if it is a 2-sphere of maximum diameter drawn in $\mathbb{S}^3$. The boundary 2-sphere common to both solid balls in the figure is a great 2-sphere of $\mathbb{S}^3$.

One may also view $\mathbb{S}^3$ by stereographically projecting it into the space obtained from $\mathbb{R}^3$ by adding a point at ∞, much as we identified $\mathbb{S}^2$ with the extended plane via stereographic projection in Section 3.3. Let $\widehat{\mathbb{R}^3}$ denote real 3-space with a point at infinity attached to it. To construct the stereographic projection map, it is convenient to first express $\mathbb{R}^3$ in terms of pure quaternions. A **pure quaternion** is a quaternion q whose scalar term is 0. That is, a pure quaternion has the form $q = b\mathbf{i} + c\mathbf{j} + d\mathbf{k}$. The point (x, y, z) in $\mathbb{R}^3$ is identified with the pure quaternion $q = x\mathbf{i} + y\mathbf{j} + z\mathbf{k}$.

Though we are working in four-dimensional space, Figure 3.3.4, p. 51 serves as a guide in the construction of the stereographic projection map. Let $N = (0, 0, 0, 1)$ be the north pole on $\mathbb{S}^3$. If $P = (a, b, c, d)$ is any point on $\mathbb{S}^3$ other than N, construct the Euclidean line through N and P. This line has parametric form

$$\mathcal{L}(t) = \langle 0, 0, 0, 1\rangle + t\langle a, b, c, d-1\rangle.$$

We define the image of P under stereographic projection to be the intersection of this line with the three-dimensional subspace consisting of all points $(x, y, z, 0)$ in $\mathbb{R}^4$. This intersection occurs when $1 + t(d-1) = 0$, or when

$$t = \frac{1}{1-d}.$$

Then the stereographic projection map $\phi : \mathbb{S}^3 \to \widehat{\mathbb{R}^3}$ is given by

$$\phi((a,b,c,d)) = \begin{cases} \frac{a}{1-d}\mathbf{i} + \frac{b}{1-d}\mathbf{j} + \frac{c}{1-d}\mathbf{k} & \text{if } d \neq 1; \\ \infty & \text{if } d = 1. \end{cases}$$

In this way, we can transfer the geometry of the 3-sphere into real 3-space with a point at infinity attached to it. For instance, if $P = (a, b, c, d)$ is on the 3-sphere, its antipodal point is $-P = (-a, -b, -c, -d)$ and one can show (in the exercises) that these points get mapped by ϕ to points in $\mathbb{R}^3$ (pure quaternions) $q = \phi(P)$ and $u = \phi(-P)$ with the property that $q \cdot u^* = -1$. As a result, two points q and u in $\widehat{\mathbb{R}^3}$ are called antipodal points if they satisfy the equation $q \cdot u^* = -1$.

Example 8.1.4 The Poincaré dodecahedral space.

The **Poincaré dodecahedral space** has been given consideration as a model for the shape of our universe (see [25]). Start with a dodecahedron living in $\mathbb{R}^3$ (we're thinking of it as a solid now, not a surface) and identify opposite faces with a one-tenth clockwise twist (rotation by $2\pi/10$ radians). It is cumbersome to indicate all face identifications, so the figure below shows the identification of the front face with the back face. For instance, the two corners labeled with a 1 get matched.Notice: no points in the interior of the dodecahedron get identified.

With this face identification the twenty corners of the dodecahedron come together in five groups of four (one group of 4 is marked with vertices in the figure), and the angles are too small for the corners to create a full open ball of three-dimensional space when they come together. Placing the dodecahedron in elliptic space inflates the corner angles, and we may make these angles fat enough to determine a perfect three-dimensional patch of space.

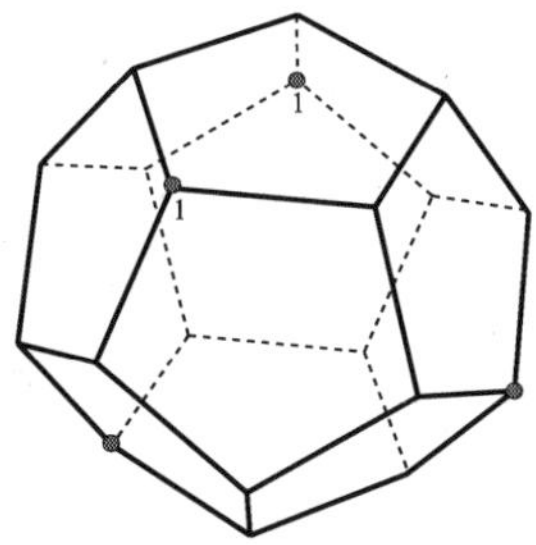

Extending the ideas of Section 7.7 to this case, one can show that the Poincaré dodecahedral space space is a quotient of the 3-sphere $\mathbb{S}^3$ by a group of isometries. The dodecahedron pictured here is a fundamental domain of the space. Just as the polygons in Section 7.7 tiled the space in which they lived, and the cubical fundamental domain of the 3-torus tiles $\mathbb{R}^3$, the dodecahedron tiles $\mathbb{S}^3$. Although far from obvious, it turns out that $\mathbb{S}^3$ is tiled by 120 copies of this dodecahedron!

Hyperbolic 3-manifolds have not been completely classified, but a remarkable relationship exists between geometry and shape in this case: a connected orientable 3-manifold supports at most one hyperbolic structure. This marks an important difference from the two-dimensional case. If a two-dimensional being knows that she lives in a two-holed torus, say, then the area of her universe is determined by its curvature, thanks to the Gauss-Bonnet formula, but other geometric properties may vary, such as the length of minimal-length closed geodesic paths in the universe, as we saw in Example 7.6.6, p. 181. No such freedom exists in the three-dimensional case.

Here is one hyperbolic 3-manifold, also built as a quotient of the dodecahedron.

Example 8.1.5 The Seifert-Weber space.

Identify opposite faces of the dodecahedron with a three-tenths clockwise turn. With this identification, all twenty corners of the dodecahedron come together to a single point, and no such identification is possible unless we drastically shrink the corner angles. We may do this by placing the dodecahedron in hyperbolic space. The resulting hyperbolic 3-manifold is called the **Seifert-Weber space**.

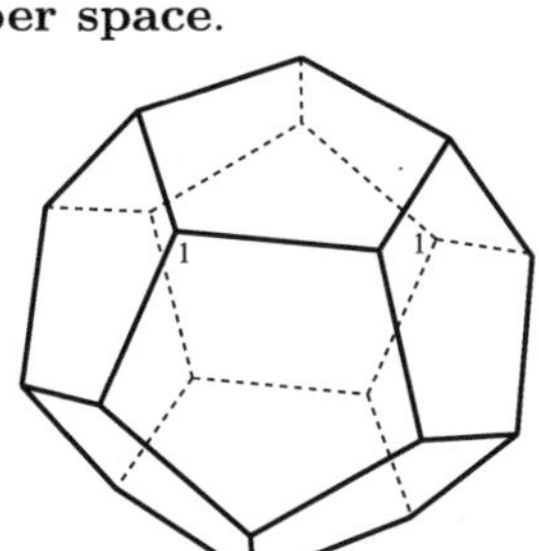

Example 8.1.6 Lens spaces.

The lens spaces $L(p,q)$ form an infinite family of elliptic 3-manifolds. Assume $p > q$ are positive integers whose largest common factor is 1. The lens spaces may be defined as follows. Consider the unit solid ball living in $\mathbb{R}^3$ whose boundary is the unit 2-sphere. The ball consists of all points (x, y, z) such that $x^2 + y^2 + z^2 \leq 1$. Any point on the boundary 2-sphere can be expressed in coordinates (z, t) where z is a complex number, t is real, and $|z|^2 + t^2 = 1$. The **lens space** $L(p,q)$ is obtained from the solid ball by identifying each point (z, t) on the boundary 2-sphere with the point $(e^{(2\pi q/p)i}z, -t)$. Note that the north pole of the boundary 2-sphere is $(0, 1)$ and it is identified with the south pole $(0, -1)$. Any other point u in the northern hemisphere is identified with a single point in the southern hemisphere. This point is found by reflecting u across the xy-plane, then rotating around the z-axis by $2\pi q/p$ radians. Each point on the equator is identified with $p - 1$ other points.

The lens space $L(p,q)$ can be obtained from a cell division of the unit solid ball. The cell division has $p + 2$ vertices: the north pole n, the south pole s, and p equally spaced vertices along the equator, label them $v_0, v_1, \cdots, v_{p-1}$. The following figure depicts this scene for $p = 5$. There is an edge connecting v_i to each of its neighbors on the equator, creating p edges around the equator. There is an edge connecting each v_i with n and an edge connecting each v_i with s, as pictured, for a total of $3p$ edges. The vertices and edges create $2p$ triangular faces on the boundary sphere, half of them in the northern hemisphere. The 3-complex has a single 3-cell, corresponding to the interior of the solid ball.

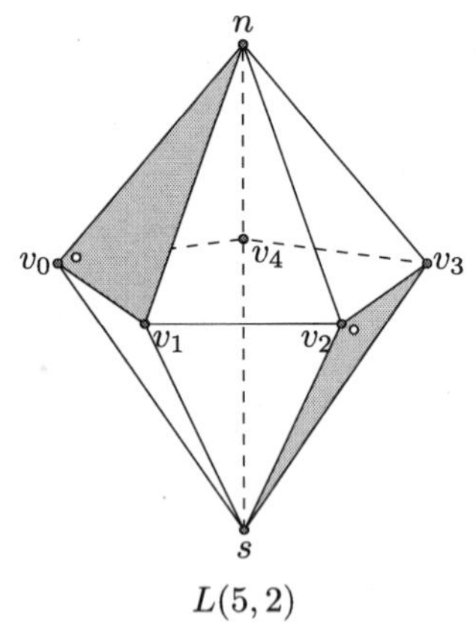

$L(5, 2)$

Let N_i denote the face in the northern hemisphere whose vertices are v_i, v_{i+1}, n. Let S_i be the face in the southern hemisphere whose vertices are v_i, v_{i+1}, and s. The lens space $L(p,q)$ is created by identifying face N_i with face S_{i+q} where the sum $i+q$ is taken modulo p. For instance, in $L(5, 2)$, the shaded face N_0 in the figure is identified with the shaded face S_2 (and the circle of points pictured in N_0 gets sent to the circle of points in S_2). The faces N_1 and S_3 are identified, as are N_2 with S_4, N_3 with S_0 and N_4 with S_1.

Example 8.1.7 The Hantschze-Wendt manifold.

This interesting manifold can be constructed from two identically sized cubes that share a face, as in the following figure. The resulting box has 10 faces to be identified in pairs. A three-dimensional bug with a jet pack living in the manifold would experience the following face identifications. The top and bottom faces are identified just as they were in the 3-torus. Each point on the top back face (see the circle in the figure) is identified with a single point on the bottom back face. This point is the reflection of the given point across the vertical segment bisecting the face. The top front face and the bottom front face are identified the same way. The figure shows two square points on these faces that are identified. The top left face and bottom right face are identified with a 180° rotation (see the elliptical point and its image point), as are the bottom left face and the top right face (the two triangular points are identified). This 3-manifold also inherits Euclidean geometry.

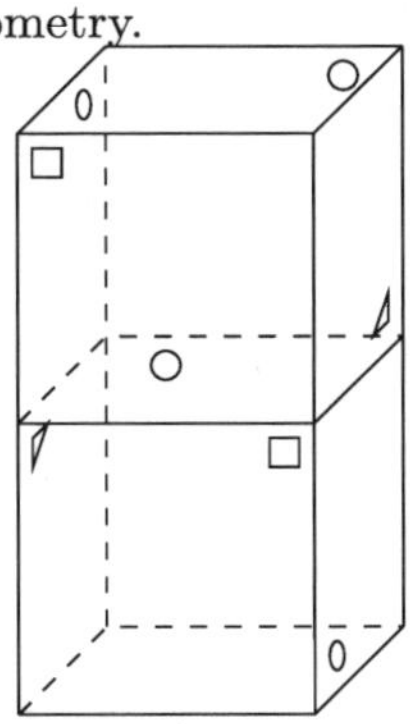

A more elegant description of this manifold makes use of the orbit space construction of Section 7.7. Consider a unit cube sitting in $\mathbb{R}^3$. Let T_1 be the following Euclidean transformation: Rotate by 180° about segment 1 in Figure 8.1.8, p. 204(a) and then translate along the length of that segment. The original cube and its image are pictured in Figure 8.1.8, p. 204(b). Let T_2 be defined similarly using segment 2 of Figure 8.1.8, p. 204(a). The original cube and its image under T_2 are pictured in Figure 8.1.8, p. 204(c). The transformation T_3 is defined the same way using segment 3, and Figure 8.1.8, p. 204(d) depicts its effect on the original cube. Each of these transformations is a screw motion. In particular, each screw motion consists of rotation by 180° and translation by unit length. The Hantzsche-Wendt manifold is then the quotient of $\mathbb{R}^3$ by the group of Euclidean isometries generated by the three screw motions, and it inherits Euclidean geometry.

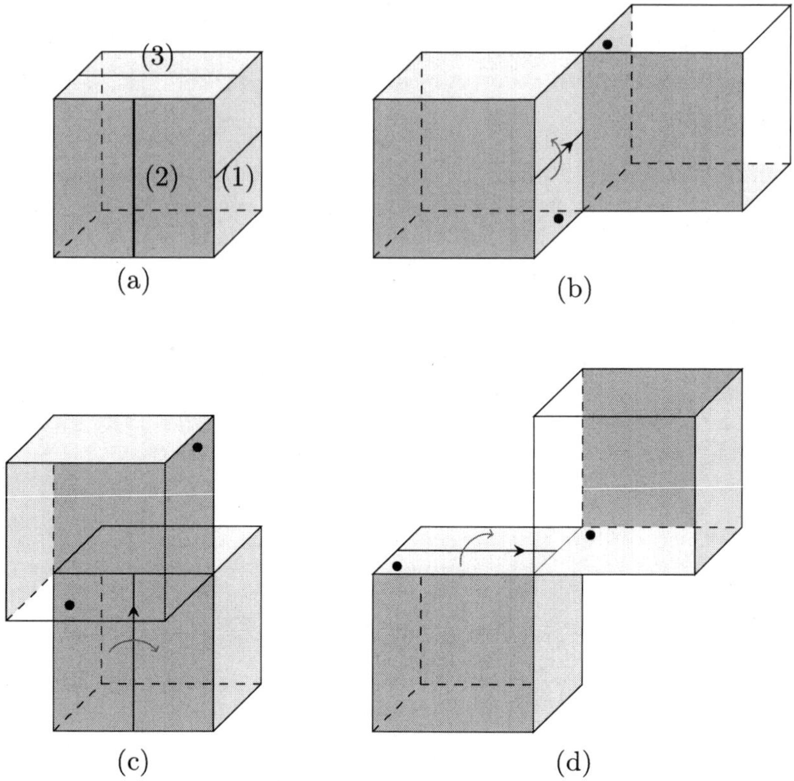

Figure 8.1.8 Describing the Hantzsche-Wendt Manifold via a group of transformations.

By repeated applications of the three transformations and their inverses one may produce image cubes covering half of $\mathbb{R}^3$ in a checkerboard pattern. The other points in $\mathbb{R}^3$ are themselves grouped into cubes and form the other half of the checkerboard pattern. It follows that the ten-faced solid in Example 8.1.7, p. 203 is a fundamental domain of the manifold, and the face identifications are determined by the transformation group.

Example 8.1.9 Four more Euclidean 3-manifolds.

Two orientable 3-manifolds arise from slight changes to the 3-torus construction of Example 8.1.2, p. 197. The **quarter turn manifold** results when the front and back faces of a cube are identified with a 90° rotation, while the remaining 2 pairs of opposite faces are identified directly, as they were for the 3-torus. Figure 8.1.10, p. 205(a) depicts this identification. The F on the front face is identified with an F on the back face by a one-quarter turn.

The **half turn manifold** results when the front and back faces of a cube are identified with a 180° rotation, while the remaining 2 pairs of opposite faces are identified directly, as they were for the 3-torus. See Figure Figure 8.1.10, p. 205(b).

The remaining two connected, compact, orientable Euclidean 3-manifolds have a hexagonal prism as the fundamental domain. A hexagon can be used to tile the plane, and copies of a hexagonal prism as in Figure 8.1.10, p. 205(c) can tile $\mathbb{R}^3$. Note that the prism has two hexagonal faces and the other six faces are parallelograms. The **one-third turn manifold** is obtained as follows: directly identify parallelograms that are opposite one another, and identify the two hexagonal faces with a rotation of 120°, as in Figure 8.1.10, p. 205(c). The **one-sixth turn manifold** is obtained by identifying the parallelograms as before, but the two hexagonal faces by a rotation of just 60°, as in Figure 8.1.10, p. 205(d). More detailed discussions of these and the non-orientable Euclidean 3-manifolds can be found in [12] and [16].

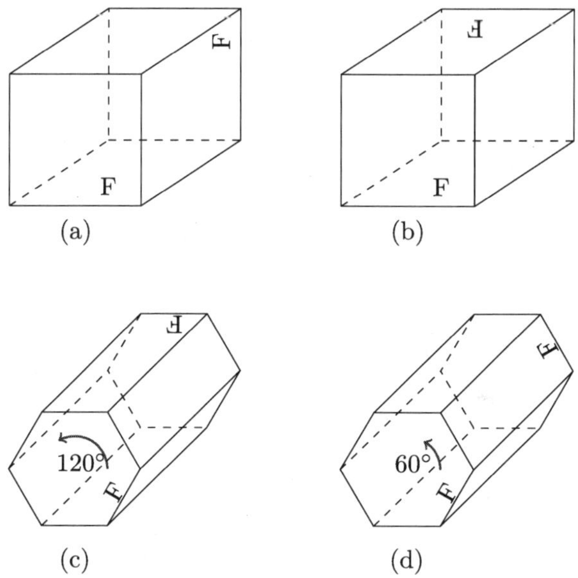

Figure 8.1.10 Four Euclidean 3-manifolds: (a) the quarter turn manifold; (b) the half turn manifold; (c) the one-third turn manifold; and (d) the one-sixth turn manifold.

Exercises

1. *Investigating quaternions.*

a. Show that $\mathbf{ij} = \mathbf{k}$, $\mathbf{jk} = \mathbf{i}$, and $\mathbf{ki} = \mathbf{j}$.

b. Show that $\mathbf{ji} = -\mathbf{k}$, $\mathbf{kj} = -\mathbf{i}$, and $\mathbf{ik} = -\mathbf{j}$.

c. The conjugate of a quaternion $q = a + b\mathbf{i} + c\mathbf{j} + d\mathbf{k}$ is $q^* = a - b\mathbf{i} - c\mathbf{j} - d\mathbf{k}$. The modulus of q is $|q| = \sqrt{a^2 + b^2 + c^2 + d^2}$. Prove that $q \cdot q^* = |q|^2$ for any quaternion.

d. Prove that $|uv| = |u| \cdot |v|$ for any quaternions. Thus, the transformations in three-dimensional elliptic geometry, which have the form $T(q) = uqv$

where u, q, v are unit quaternions, do send a point of $\mathbb{S}^3$ to a point on $\mathbb{S}^3$.

2. Suppose $P = (a, b, c, d)$ and $-P = (-a, -b, -c, -d)$ are diametrically opposed points on $\mathbb{S}^3$. Prove that

$$\phi(P) \cdot \phi(-P)^* = -1,$$

where $\phi : \mathbb{S}^3 \to \widehat{\mathbb{R}^3}$ is stereographic projection.

3. Verify that in the 3-torus of Example 8.1.2, p. 197, all eight corners come together at a single point.

4. Verify that in the Poincaré dodecahedral space of Example 8.1.4, p. 200, the corners come together in five groups of four. Specify the five groups.

5. Verify that in the Seifert-Weber space of Example 8.1.5, p. 201, all 20 corners come together in a single point.

6. What happens if you identify each pair of opposite faces in a cube with a one-quarter twist? Convince yourself that not all 8 corners come together at a single point, so that the result is not a Euclidean 3-manifold.

8.2 Cosmic Crystallography

Imagine once again that we are two-dimensional beings living in a two-dimensional universe. In fact, suppose we are living in the torus in Figure 8.2.1, p. 206 at point E (for Earth). Our world is homogeneous and isotropic, and adheres to Euclidean geometry. Our lines of sight follow Euclidean lines. If we can see far enough, we ought to be able to see an object, say G (for galaxy), in different directions. Three different lines of sight are given in the figure.

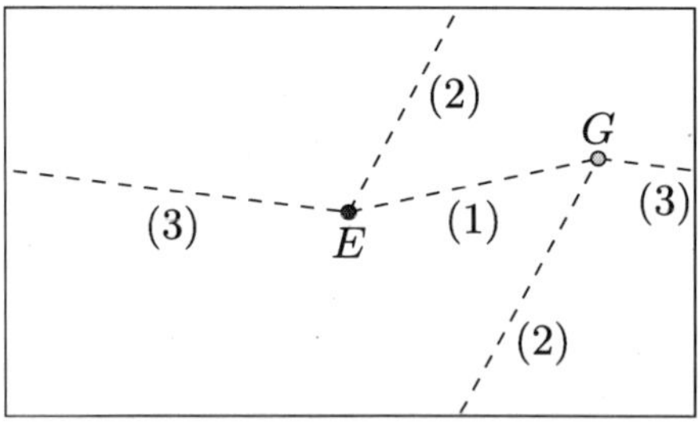

Figure 8.2.1 Seeing multiple images of the same object in the torus.

In fact, if we suppose for a minute that we can see as far as we wish, then we would be able to see G by looking in any direction that produces a line of sight with rational slope. In reality, we can't see forever, and this limitation produces a visual boundary. We will let r_{obs} denote the distance to which we can see, which is the radius of our observable universe. To have any hope of seeing multiple images of the same object, the diameter of our observable universe, $2r_{obs}$, must exceed some length dimension of the universe.

Getting back to the torus, the easiest way to find the directions in which one can view G is to tile the plane with identical copies of the torus. Place the Earth at the same point of each copy of the rectangle, and the same goes for other objects such as G. Figure 8.2.2, p. 207 displays a portion of the tiling, and our visual boundary. According to Figure 8.2.2, p. 207, in addition to the instance of G in the fundamental domain, 5 of its images would be visible.

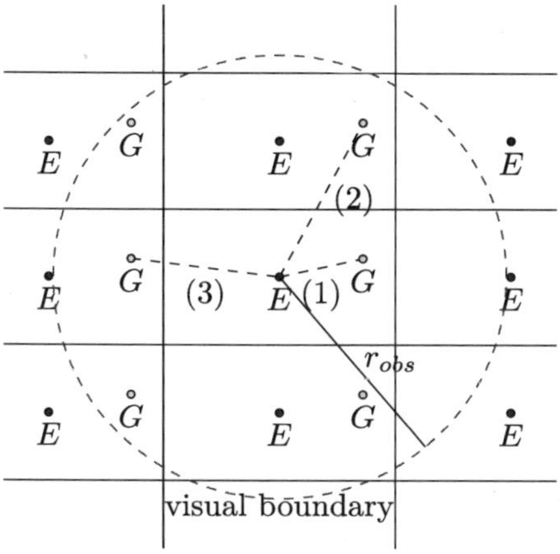

Figure 8.2.2 Detecting multiple images with a tiling of the universal covering.

Practically speaking, detecting multiple images of the same object is complicated by the finite speed of light. Since the lines of sight in Figure 8.2.2, p. 207 have different lengths, we see the object G at different times in its evolution. In reality, galaxies evolve dramatically over time. So even if we found an image of G looking in some "longer" direction, it might look so different we wouldn't recognize it.

Still, humanity has pondered the tantalizing possibility that one of the many distant galaxies we've detected with our telescopes is actually the Milky Way galaxy. Based on recent lower-bound estimates of the size of our universe, however, it is now clear that we will not be treated to such a sight.

Rather than spotting different images of a particular object, perhaps we can detect multiple images of the same object indirectly. Consider a catalog of similar objects that don't evolve too rapidly (such as galaxy superclusters). Assume we have observed N such objects and they appear to be sprinkled randomly about the universe (the universe is homogeneous and isotropic after all). In Figure 8.2.3, p. 207 we have generated a two-dimensional random distribution of point sources.

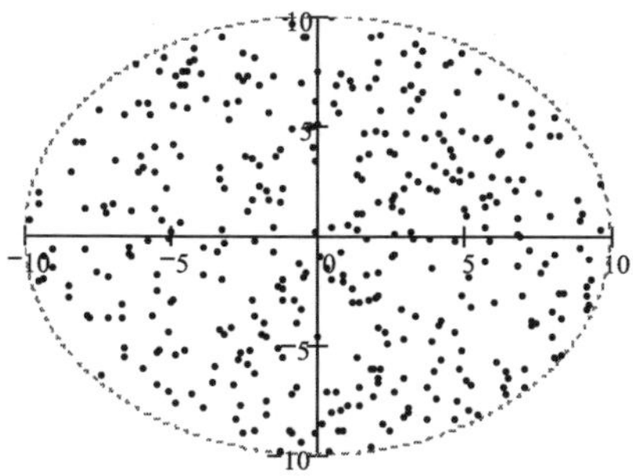

Figure 8.2.3 The positions of N objects in a catalog.

Rather than hunt for two copies of the same source, we compute the distance between each pair of sources in the catalog (we must make an assumption about the geometry of space to compute these distances), giving us $N(N-1)/2$ distances. If the catalog contains no repeat images, then the distances ought to follow a Poisson probability distribution. The histogram of the $N(N-1)/2$ distances is called a **pair separation histogram** (PSH) and is given in Figure 8.2.4, p. 208.

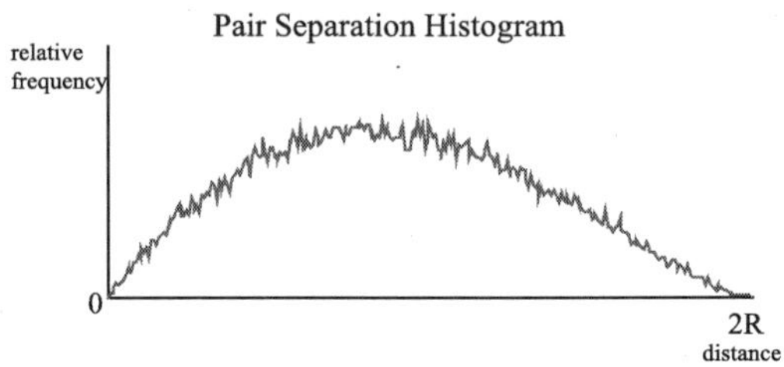

Figure 8.2.4 A pair separation histogram in a simply connected universe.

Now consider the catalog in Figure 8.2.5, p. 208(a). As in Figure 8.2.3, p. 207, the observable radius has been scaled to 10 units. The objects we can observe may look evenly distributed, but in fact there are multiple images of the same object. In this simulation the universe is a torus and the observable radius exceeds the dimensions of our universe. Placing ourselves at the origin in this catalog, our Dirichlet domain in this torus universe has been superimposed on the catalog in Figure 8.2.5, p. 208(b).

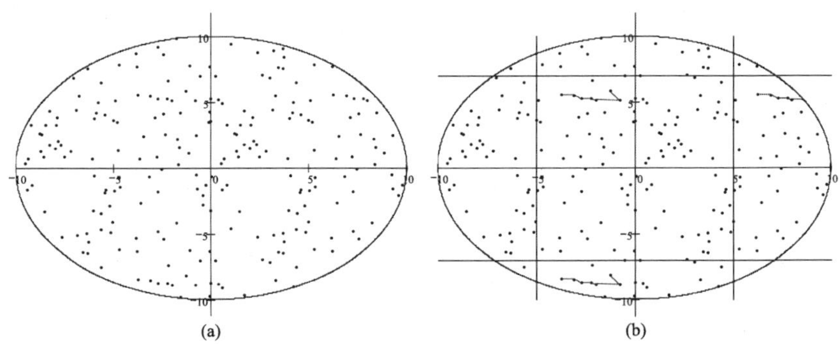

Figure 8.2.5 The positions of N objects in a catalog.

The pair separation histogram for this simulated catalog appears in Figure 8.2.6, p. 209. Notice the spikes in the histogram. Some distances are occurring with higher frequency than one would expect by chance alone. At first glance, it looks like the spikes occur at distances of about 10, 14, and 17 units.

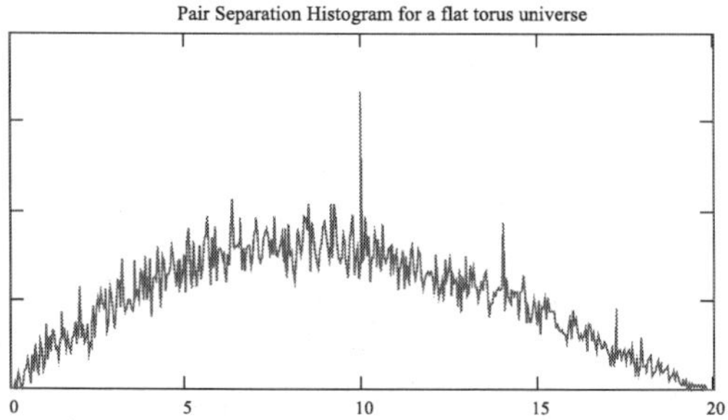

Figure 8.2.6 A pair separation histogram in a torus universe.

What causes these spikes? Look at the catalog plot again in Figure 8.2.5, p. 208(b), and find an object near the top edge of the fundamental domain. We've highlighted a group of objects that look a bit like a sled. There is a copy of this object just below the bottom edge of the fundamental domain. The distance between a point in this sled and its image below equals the length of the width dimension of our torus, which is 14 in this simulation. Indeed, there are lots of points for which we see an image displaced vertically in this manner, so this distance will occur lots of time in the pair separation histogram.

Another copy of our big sled appears just to the right of the right edge of the fundamental domain. So, the distance between a point and its horizontally displaced image will be equal to the length dimension of the torus, which is 10 in this simulation. There are also lots of these pairs in the catalog - in fact more than before since this dimension of the fundamental rectangle is smaller. This accounts for the larger spike in the histogram above the distance 10.

Finally, there are some objects in the fundamental domain for which a diagonally displaced copy is visible. The length of this diagonal is $\sqrt{10^2 + 14^2} \approx 17.2$, and this accounts for the third, smallest spike in the histogram.

Spikes appear in the PSH precisely because the torus universe $\mathbb{C}/\Gamma$ is constructed from isometries that move each point in the space by the same distance. A transformation T of a metric space with the property that

$$d(p, T(p)) = d(q, T(q))$$

for all points p and q in the space is called a **Clifford translation**. Any translation in $\mathbb{C}$ is a Clifford translation; every point gets moved the same distance. However, a rotation about the origin is not: the further a point is from the origin, the further it moves. In the exercises you prove that non-trivial isometries in the hyperbolic plane are not Clifford translations.

Recall that to create the PSH of a catalog in the cosmic crystallography method we must first make an assumption about the geometry of the universe. The PSH in Figure 8.2.6, p. 209 was generated by computing the *Euclidean* distances between points in the catalog. If we assumed a hyperbolic universe and used the hyperbolic metric to produce the PSH, the spikes would vanish.

In essence, the method of cosmic crystallography pours over catalogs of astronomical objects, computing distances between all pairs of objects in the catalog, and then looking for spikes in the pair separation histogram. The detection of a spike in the histogram that cannot be reasonably explained by chance in the distribution of objects indicates a finite universe.

The method of cosmic crystallography has limitations beyond the obvious challenge of accurately measuring astronomical distances. As you will see in the exercises, different shapes might produce identical spikes, so finding a spike in a PSH doesn't precisely determine the shape of our universe (though it would certainly narrow down the list of candidates). All ten Euclidean 3-manifolds will reveal a spike (or spikes) in the PSH if we can see far enough to detect the finite dimensions. Some of the elliptic 3-manifolds will produce spikes in the PSH, but no hyperbolic 3-manifold would reveal itself by this method, since hyperbolic isometries are not Clifford translations.

To date, no statistically significant spikes have been found in the pair separation histograms computed from real catalogs. Two good surveys of this method, including information about generating simulated catalogs, can be found in [26] and [24].

More sensitive methods have been proposed that might detect any 3-manifold, regardless of geometry, and we look at one such method below.

Example 8.2.7 Collecting correlated pairs.

In a catalog of images, there are two types of pairs that might generate recurring distances. The cosmic crystallography method outlined previously detects what have been called Type II pairs in the literature: A Type II pair is a pair of points of the form $\{p, T(p)\}$, where T is a transformation from the group of isometries used to generate the manifold. If T transforms each point the same distance (i.e., if T is a Clifford translation), then this common distance will appear in the PSH as a spike.

The other type of recurring distance can arise from what's been called a Type I pair of points in the catalog. A Type I pair consists of any pair $\{p, q\}$ of points. If we can see images of these points in a copy of the fundamental domain, say $T(p), T(q)$, then since transformations preserve distance, $d(p, q) = d(T(p), T(q))$, and this common distance will have occurred at least twice in the PSH. The figure below shows a portion of the torus tiling of the plane depicted in Figure 8.2.2, p. 207. The two types of pairs of points are visible: Type I pairs are joined by dashed segments, and Type II pairs are joined by solid segments.

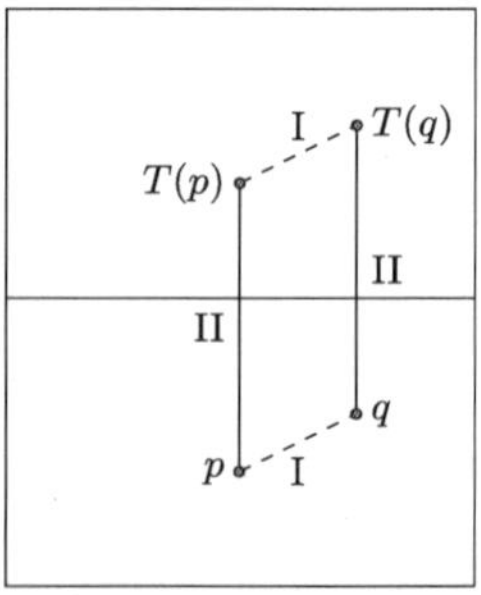

Type I pairs will not produce discernible spikes in the PSH. Even in simulations for which several images of a pair of points are present, the spike generated by this set of pairs having the same distance is not statistically significant.

The **collecting correlated pairs** (CCP) method, outlined below, attempts to detect the Type I pairs in a catalog.

Suppose a catalog has N objects, and let $P = N(N-1)/2$ denote the number of pairs generated from this set. Compute all P distances between pairs of objects, and order them from smallest to largest. Let Δ_i denote the difference between the $(i+1)$st distance and the ith distance. Notice $\Delta_i \geq 0$ for all i, and i runs from 1 up to $P-1$.

Now, $\Delta_i = 0$ for some i if two different pairs of objects in the catalog have the same separation. It could be that unrelated pairs happen to have the same distance, or that the two pairs responsible for $\Delta_i = 0$ are of the form $\{p, q\}$ and $\{T(p), T(q)\}$ (Type I pairs). (We're assuming there are no type II pairs in the catalog.)

Let Z equal the number of the Δ_i's that equal zero. Then

$$R = \frac{Z}{P-1}$$

denotes the proportion of the differentials that equal zero. This single number is a measure, in some sense, of the likelihood of living in a multi-connected universe.

In a real catalog involving estimations of distances, one wouldn't expect Type I pairs to produce identical distances, so instead of using Z as defined above, one might let Z_ϵ equal the number of the Δ_i's that are less than ϵ, where ϵ is some small positive number. For more details on this method, see [28].

Exercises

1. *The Klein Bottle.* We may view the Klein bottle as a quotient of $\mathbb{C}$ by the group of isometries generated by $T_1(z) = z + i$ and $T_2(z) = \overline{z} + 1 + i$. A fundamental domain for the quotient is the unit square in $\mathbb{C}$. The edges of the square are identified as pictured. The a edges are identified as they would be for a torus, but the b edges get identified with a twist.

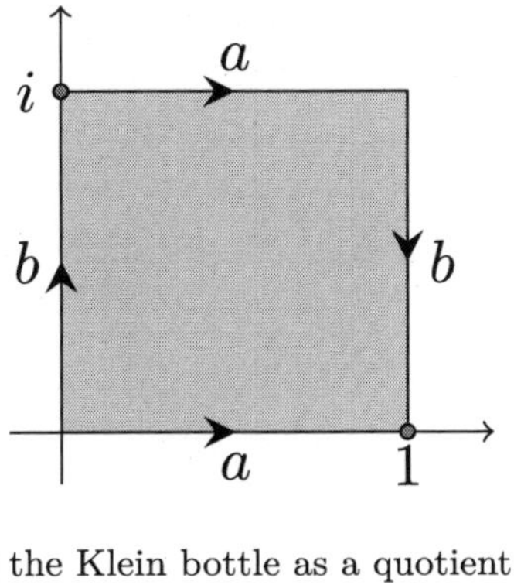

Figure 8.2.8 Building the Klein bottle as a quotient of $\mathbb{C}$.

a. Verify that T_1 maps the bottom edge of the unit square to the top edge of the unit square, and that T_2 maps the left edge of the unit square to the right edge with a twist.

b. Determine the inverse transformations T_1^{-1} and T_2^{-1}.

c. We may compose any number of these four transformations T_1, T_2, T_1^{-1}, and T_2^{-1} to tile all of $\mathbb{C}$ with copies of the unit square. In the following figure we have indicated in certain squares the transformation (built from the four above) that moves the unit square into the indicated square. Complete the figure below by indicating a composition of the four transformations that maps the unit square to the indicated square in $\mathbb{C}$.

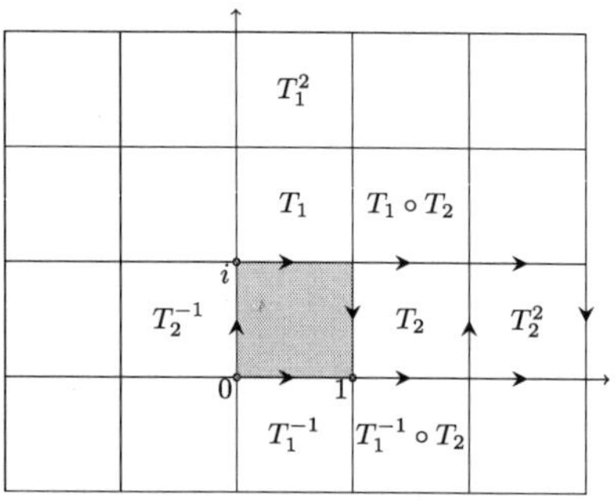

d. Verify that $T_2 \circ T_1 = T_1^{-1} \circ T_2$.

e. Show that T_1 is a Clifford translation of $\mathbb{C}$ but T_2 isn't. It follows that in a Klein bottle universe, cosmic crystallography would only be able to detect one dimension of the Klein bottle.

2. Figure 8.2.9, p. 212 shows a simulated catalog from a two-dimensional Euclidean universe with the corresponding pair separation histogram. There are two Euclidean surfaces: the Klein bottle and the torus. Based on the cosmic crystallography analysis, what do you think is the shape of the universe? Explain your answer. Also, make an estimate at the total area of the universe.

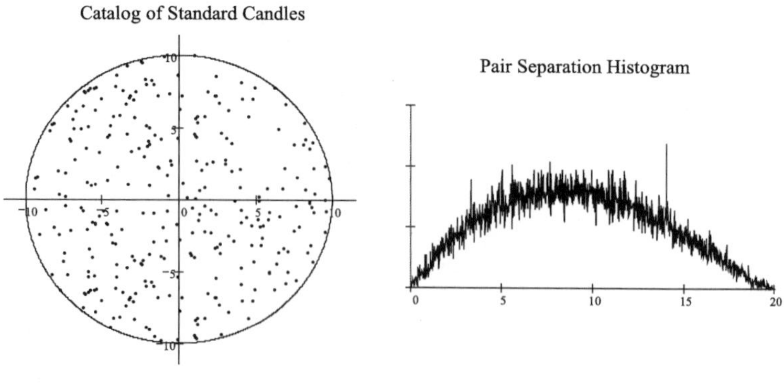

Figure 8.2.9 A catalog of images for a two-dimensional Euclidean universe, with corresponding PSH.

3. Prove that the transformation T_a in Example 7.7.11, p. 190 used to generate the two-holed torus as a quotient of $\mathbb{D}$ is not a Clifford translation. Can you generalize the argument to show that any isometry in $\mathbb{D}$ that takes one edge of a regular n-gon to another edge is not a Clifford translation?

4. A rough estimate for the number of images of an object one might see in a catalog can be made by dividing the volume of space occupied by the catalog by the volume of the Dirichlet domain at our position in the universe. Suppose we live in an orientable two-dimensional universe. In fact, suppose we live in H_g for some $g \geq 2$, and our Dirichlet domain is the standard $4g$-gon as in Figure 7.5.24, p. 176. Set the curvature of the universe to $k = -1$.

a. According to Gauss-Bonnet, what is the area of the Dirichlet domain?

b. What is the area of the observable universe, as a function of r_{obs}? That is, what is the area of a circle in $(\mathbb{D}, \mathcal{H})$ with radius r_{obs}?

c. Determine the ratio of the area of the observable universe (A(O.U.)) to the area of the fundamental domain (A(F.D.)). Your ratio $A(O.U.)/A(F.D.)$ will depend on r_{obs} and g.

d. Complete the following table in the case $g = 2$. Assume r_{obs} has units in light-years.

Table 8.2.10 Estimating the number of images of an object one might see in a catalog

r_{obs}	A(O.U.)	A(F.D.)	Ratio
2			
4			
6			
8			

e. Repeat part (d) in two other cases: $g = 4$ and $g = 6$.

5. Repeat the previous exercise in the case of the non-orientable two-dimensional universe, C_g.

8.3 Circles in the Sky

Immediately after the big bang, the universe was so hot that the usual constituents of matter could not form. Photons could not move freely in space, as they were constantly bumping into free electrons. Eventually, about 350,000 years after the big bang, the universe had expanded and cooled to the point that light could travel unimpeded. This free radiation is called the cosmic microwave background (CMB) radiation, and much of it is still travelling today. The universe has cooled and expanded to the point that this radiation has stretched to the microwave end of the electromagnetic spectrum, having a wavelength of about 1 or 2 millimeters.

The CMB radiation is coming to us from every direction, and it has all been travelling for the same amount of time - and at the same speed. This means that it has all traveled the same distance to reach us at this moment. Thus, we may think of the CMB radiation that we can detect at this instant as having come from the surface of a giant 2-sphere with us at the sphere's center. This giant 2-sphere is called the **last scattering surface** (LSS).

It is perhaps comforting to think that everyone in the universe has their own last scattering surface, that everyone's LSS has the same radius, and that this radius is growing in time.

The CMB radiation coming to us has a temperature that is remarkably uniform: it is constant to a few parts in 100,000, which makes the temperature of the radiation in the LSS very nearly perfectly uniform. As Craig Hogan points out in [14], this is much smoother than a billiard ball. Nonetheless, there are slight variations in the temperature. These variations, due to slight imbalances in the distribution of matter in the early universe, were predicted well before they were finally found (when our instruments became sensitive enough to detect them). These very slight temperature differences might reveal the shape of the universe.

Imagine our universe is a giant 3-torus. Assume a fundamental domain for the universe is a rectangular box as shown in Example 8.1.2, p. 197, and that this box is our Dirichlet domain (we're at the center of this box). We may tile $\mathbb{R}^3$ with copies of this fundamental domain, placing ourselves in the same position of each copy of the fundamental domain. Now, imagine our last scattering surface in the fundamental domain. In fact, there will be a copy of our last scattering surface surrounding each copy of us in each copy of the fundamental domain.

If our last scattering surface is small relative to the size of the fundamental domain, as in Figure 8.3.1, p. 214(a), then it will not intersect any of its copies. However, if the last scattering surface is large relative to the size of the fundamental domain, as in Figure 8.3.1, p. 214(b), then it will intersect one or more of its copies. Moreover, adjacent copies of the LSS will intersect in a circle. In this happy case, our last scattering surface will contain circles with matching temperature distributions. Look again at Figure 8.3.1, p. 214(b). We have three copies of our fundamental domain pictured as well as three copies of the LSS (only one of which is shaded to make the situation less cluttered). Two vertical circles of intersection appear in the figure. From our point of view at the center of the LSS, the two images of the circle will be directly opposite one another in the sky. Since these circles are one and the same, the temperature distribution around the two circles will agree. Therein lies the hope. Scan the temperature distribution in the last scattering surface for matching circles.

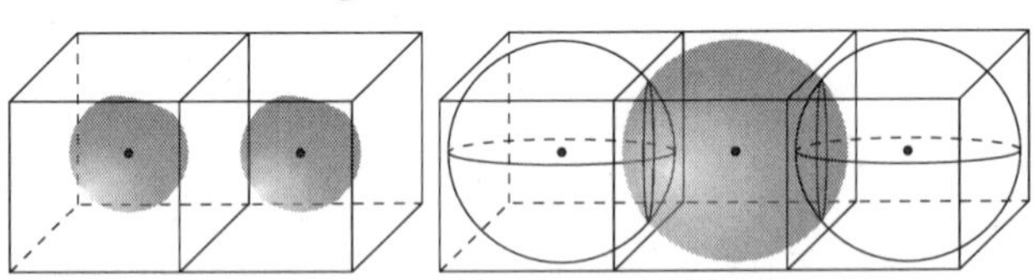

(a) (b)

Figure 8.3.1 The LSS compared to the size of a 3-torus universe. In (a) the LSS is small, so it won't reveal the shape of the universe; in (b) the LSS intersects itself and will have circles of matching temperature distributions.

This strategy for detecting a finite universe is called the **circles-in-the-sky** method, which, in cosmic topology, has advantages over the cosmic crystallography method. In theory, the circles-in-the-sky method can be used to detect any compact manifold, regardless of the geometry it admits. Also, the search for matching circles is independent of a metric. One doesn't need to make a claim about the geometry of the universe to detect a finite universe.

This method is computationally very intensive. The search for matching circles on this giant 2-sphere involves the analysis of a six parameter space: the center (θ_1, ϕ_1) of one circle on the LSS, the center of the second circle (θ_2, ϕ_2), the common angular radius α of the two circles (since these circles are copies of the same circle they will have the same radius), and the relative phase of the two circles, say β. (See the diagram that follows.) In general, $\beta \neq 0$ if the face identifications in the 3-manifold involve rotations. It remains for us to analyze whether a statistically significant correlation exists between the temperatures as we proceed around the circles.

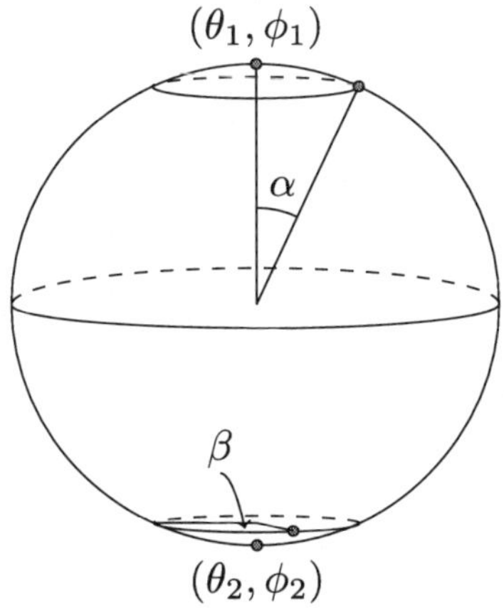

When comparing the size of the LSS relative to the size of space, it is convenient to define the following length dimension. The **injectivity radius** at a point in a manifold, denoted r_{inj}, is half the distance of the shortest closed geodesic path that starts and ends at that point. A necessary condition, then, for detecting matching circles in the LSS at our location is that our observable radius r_{obs} exceeds our injectivity radius r_{inj}.

Example 8.3.2 Detecting the 3-torus from the LSS.

If the universe is a 3-torus, and our LSS has diameter larger than some dimension of the 3-torus, then the LSS will intersect copies of itself, and the matching circles would be diametrically opposed to one another on the LSS. Suppose our Dirichlet domain in a 3-torus universe is an a by b by c box in $\mathbb{R}^3$, where $a < b < c$. Our LSS is then centered at the center of the box. The injectivity radius of the universe is $a/2$. In the following figure, we assume that r_{obs}, the radius of the LSS, is greater than $a/2$ but less than $b/2$. In this case, the circles-in-the-sky method would detect one pair of matching circles in the temperature distribution of the LSS. From the Earth E, we would observe that circle C_1, when traced in the counterclockwise direction, matches circle C_2 when traced in the clockwise direction, with no relative phase shift.

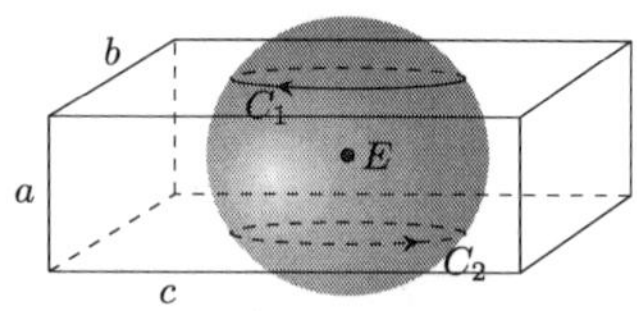

If the size is right, all six compact orientable Euclidean 3-manifolds would have matching circles that are diametrically opposed to one another on the LSS. The phase shift on these matching circles will be non-zero if the faces are identified with a rotation.

Example 8.3.3 LSS in a Poincaré dodecahedral space.

If we live in a Poincaré dodecahedral space and our LSS is large enough, we might see six pairs of matching circles, each pair consisting of diametrically opposed circles in the sky with matching temperature distributions after a relative phase shift of 36°. The following figure indicates the matching circles that would arise from the identification of the front face and rear face of the dodecahedron. From the Earth E, we would observe that circle C_1 when traced in the counterclockwise direction matches circle C_2 when traced in the clockwise direction, with a phase shift of 36°.

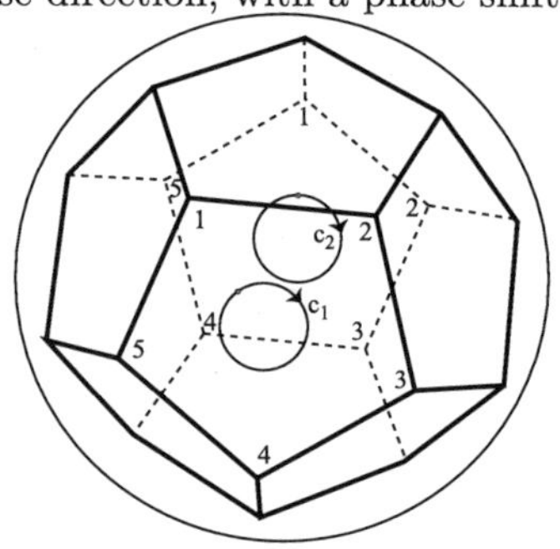

In general, the matching circles we (might) see can depend not only on the shape of the universe, but also on where we happen to be in the universe. This follows because the Dirichlet domain can vary from point to point (see Example 7.7.14, p. 192 for the two-dimensional case). Of the 10 Euclidean 3-manifolds, only the 3-torus has the feature that the Dirichlet domain is location independent. Some (but not all) elliptic 3-manifolds have this feature, and in any hyperbolic 3-manifold, the Dirichlet domain depends on your location. Thus, if we do observe matching circles, it can not only reveal topology but also the Earth's location in the universe.

Searches to date have focused on circles that are diametrically opposed to one another on the LSS (or nearly so). This restriction reduces the search space from six parameters to four. Happily, most detectable universe shapes would have matching circles diametrically opposite one another, or nearly so. At the time of this writing, no matching circles have been found, and this negative result places bounds on the size of our universe. For instance, an article written by the people who first realized a small finite universe would imprint itself on the LSS [19], concludes from the absence of matching circles that the universe has topology scale (i.e., injectivity radius r_{inj}) bigger than 24 gigaparsecs, which works out to $24 \times 3.26 \times 10^9 \approx 78$ billion light-years. So, a geodesic closed path trip in the universe would be at least 156 billion light-years long.

This stupendous distance is hard to fathom, but it appears safe to say that we might abandon the possibility of gazing into the heavens and seeing a distant image of our beloved Milky Way Galaxy.

In addition to [19], other accessible papers have been written on the circles-in-the-sky method, as well as the cosmic crystallography method. (See [23], [26], and [24].) Jeff Weeks also discusses both programs of research in *The Shape of Space*, [12].

8.4 Our Universe

Our universe appears to be homogeneous and isotropic. The presence of cosmic microwave background radiation is evidence of this: it is coming to us from every direction with more or less constant temperature. This uniformity can be explained by the inflationary universe theory. The theory, pioneered in the 1980s by Alan Guth and others, states that during the first 10^{-30} seconds (or so) after the big bang, the universe expanded at a stupendous rate, causing the universe to appear homogeneous, isotropic, and also flat.

The assumptions of isotropy and homogeneity are remarkably fruitful when one approaches the geometry and topology of the universe from a mathematical point of view. Under these assumptions, three possibilities exist for the geometry of the universe - the three geometries that have been the focus of this text. Each geometry type has possible universe shapes attached to it, and Section 8.1 showcases some of the leading compact candidates.

The mathematical point of view gives us our candidate geometries, but attempts at detecting the geometry from the mathematical theory have proved unsuccessful. For instance, no enormous, cosmic triangle involving parallax has produced an angle sum sufficiently different from π radians to rule out Euclidean geometry.

Adopting a physical point of view, we have another way to approach the geometry of the universe. Einstein's theory of general relativity ties the geometry of the universe to its mass-energy content. If the universe has a high mass-energy content, then the universe will have elliptic geometry. If the universe has a low mass-energy content, then it will be hyperbolic. If it has just a precise amount, called the critical mass density, the universe will be Euclidean. From a naive point of view, this makes it seem highly unlikely that our universe is Euclidean. If our mass-energy content deviates by the mass of just one hydrogen atom from this critical amount, our universe fails to be Euclidean.

A little notation might be helpful. It turns out that from Einstein's field equations, the mass-energy density of the universe, ρ, is related to its curvature k by the following equation, called the Friedmann Equation:

$$H^2 = \frac{8\pi G}{3}\rho - \frac{k}{a^2}.$$

Here G is Newton's gravitational constant; H is the Hubble constant measuring the expansion rate of the universe; $k = -1, 0$, or 1 is the curvature constant; and a is a scale factor. In fact, a and H are both changing in time, but may be viewed as constant during the present period. Current estimates of H (see [17] or [22]) are in the range of 68 to 70 kilometers per second per megaparsec, where 1 megaparsec is 3,260,000 light-years.

In a Euclidean universe, $k = 0$ and solving the Friedmann equation for ρ gives us the critical density

$$\rho_c = \frac{3H^2}{8\pi G}.$$

This critical density is about 1.7×10^{-29} grams per cubic centimeter, and is the precise density required in a Euclidean universe.

We let Ω equal the ratio of the actual mass-energy density ρ of the universe to the critical one ρ_c. That is,

$$\Omega = \frac{\rho}{\rho_c}.$$

Then, if $\Omega < 1$ the universe is hyperbolic; if $\Omega > 1$ the universe is elliptic; and if $\Omega = 1$ on the nose then it is Euclidean.

Until the late 1990s all estimates of the mass-energy content of the universe put the value of Ω much less than 1, suggesting a hyperbolic universe. In fact, different observational techniques for estimating the total mass-energy content of the universe put the value of Ω at about 1/3, contrary to the value of 1 predicted by the inflationary universe model.

But at the dawn of the 21st century, this all changed with detailed measurements of the cosmic microwave background radiation, and the remarkable discovery that the universe is expanding at an accelerated rate.

Careful analysis of the WMAP data on the cosmic background radiation[1] suggests that the universe is flat, or nearly so, in agreement with the theory of inflation. (This analysis is different than the circles in the sky method, which searches for shape.) The five-year estimate from the WMAP data (see [21]) put the value of Ω at

$$\Omega = 1.0045 \pm .013.$$

So if the mass-energy density is about 1/3 of what is required to get us to a Euclidean universe, but it appears from the CMB that the universe is Euclidean, or nearly so, some other form of energy must exist. Evidence for this was presented in 1999 (see, for instance, [18]) in the form of observations of distant exploding stars called Type Ia supernovae. These distant supernovae are fainter than expected for a universe whose expansion rate is slowing down, suggesting that the universe is accelerating its expansion. In 2011, Saul Perlmutter, Brian Schmidt, and Adam Riess won the Nobel Prize in Physics for their work on this discovery.

When Einstein first proposed the 3-sphere as the shape of the universe, his theory predicted that the 3-sphere should be expanding or collapsing. The idea of a static universe appealed to him, and he added a constant into his field equations, called the cosmological constant, whose role was to counteract gravity and prevent the universe from collapsing in on itself. But at roughly the same time, Edwin Hubble, Vesto Slipher and others discovered that galaxies in every direction were

[1]The Wilkinson Microwave Anisotropy Probe was launched in 2001 to carefully plot the temperature of the cosmic microwave background radiation.

receding from us. Moreover, galaxies farther away were receding at a faster rate, implying that the universe is expanding. Einstein withdrew his constant.

But now the constant has new life, as it can represent the repulsive dark energy that seems to be counteracting gravity and driving the accelerated expansion of the universe. So the density parameter in the Friedmann equation can have two components: ρ_M, which is the mass-energy density associated with ordinary and dark matter (the mass-energy density that cosmologists have been estimating by observation); and ρ_Λ, which is the dark energy, due to the cosmological constant. In this case, Friedmann's equation becomes

$$H^2 = \frac{8\pi G}{3}(\rho_M + \rho_\Lambda) - \frac{k}{a^2}$$

and dividing by H^2 we have

$$1 = \frac{8\pi G}{3H^2}\rho_M + \frac{8\pi G}{3H^2}\rho_\Lambda - \frac{k}{(aH)^2}.$$

We let

$$\Omega_M = \frac{\rho_M}{\rho_c}, \qquad \Omega_\Lambda = \frac{\rho_\Lambda}{\rho_c}, \qquad \Omega_k = \frac{-k}{(aH)^2}.$$

So the simple equation

$$1 = \Omega_M + \Omega_\Lambda + \Omega_k$$

fundamentally describes the state of the universe. The inflationary universe model suggests that $\Omega_k \approx 0$, which is supported by recent reports. Nine-year analysis of the WMAP data combined with measurements of the Type Ia Supernaovae (see [22]) suggest

$$-0.0066 < \Omega_k < 0.0011,$$

with $\Omega_\Lambda \approx .72$ and $\Omega_M \approx 0.28$. As the universe evolves, the values of the density parameters may change, though the sum will always equal one.

Now is probably as good a time as any to tell you that the fate of the universe is tied to its mass-energy content and the nature of the dark energy, which is tied to the the geometry of the universe, which is tied to the topology of the universe.

If the cosmological constant is zero then the relationship is simple: if $\Omega > 1$ so that we live in an elliptic 3-manifolds, the universe will eventually begin to fall back on itself, ultimately experiencing a "big crunch". If $\Omega = 1$, a finite Euclidean universe will have one of 10 possible shapes (6 if we insist on an orientable universe) and its expansion rate will asymptotically approach 0, but it will never begin collapsing. If $\Omega < 1$, the universe will continue to expand until everything is so spread out we will experience a "big chill."

With a nontrivial vacuum energy the situation changes. While the gravitational force due to the usual mass-energy content of the universe tends to slow the expansion of the universe, it seems the dark energy causes it to accelerate. Whether the universe is hyperbolic, elliptic, or Euclidean, if the dark energy wins the tug of war with gravity, the curvature of the universe would approach 0 as it continued to accelerate its expansion, and the density of matter in the universe would approach 0.

The European Space Agency launched the Planck satellite in 2009. In its orbit at a distance of 1.5 million kilometers from the Earth, the Planck satellite has given us improved measurements of the CMB temperature, enabling sharper estimates of cosmological parameters, as well as more refined data on which to run circles-in-the-sky tests. Alas, no circles have been detected. Regarding the curvature of the universe, the Planck team concludes in [17], in agreement with the WMAP team, that our universe appears to be flat to a one standard deviation accuracy of 0.25%.

In short, the universe appears to be homogeneous, isotropic, nearly flat, and dominated by dark energy. The current estimates for Ω_k leave the question of the geometry of the universe open, though just barely. It is still possible that our universe is a hyperbolic or an elliptic manifold, but the curvature would have to be very close to 0. If the universe is a compact, orientable Euclidean manifold, we have six different possibilities for its shape. Since Euclidean manifold volumes aren't fixed by curvature, there is no reason to expect the dimensions of a Euclidean manifold to be close to the radius of the observable universe. But if the size is right, the circles-in-the-sky method would reveal the shape of the universe through matching circles.

Perhaps we will be treated to matching circles some day. Perhaps not. Perhaps the universe is just too big. In any event, pursuing the question of the shape of the universe is a remarkable feat of the human intellect. It is inspiring to think, especially looking up at a clear, star filled night sky, that we might be able to determine the shape of our universe, all without leaving our tiny planet.

A

List of Symbols

Symbol	Description	Page
$\mathbb{C}$	the complex plane	15
$\mathbb{S}^1$	the unit circle	38
$i_C(z)$	inversion in the circle C	39
∞	the point at ∞	49
$\mathbb{C}^+$	the etended complex plane	49
$(\mathbb{C}, \mathcal{T})$	translational geometry	73
$(\mathbb{C}, \mathcal{E})$	Euclidean geometry	75
$(\mathbb{C}^+, \mathcal{M})$	Möbius geometry	78
$(\mathbb{D}, \mathcal{H})$	the Poincaré disk model for hyperbolic geometry	81
$\mathbb{D}$	the hyperbolic plane	81
$\mathbb{S}^1_\infty$	the circle at ∞ in $(\mathbb{D}, \mathcal{H})$	81
$\mathbb{P}^2$	the projective plane	130
$(\mathbb{P}^2, \mathcal{S})$	the disk model for elliptic geometry	130
$(\mathbb{P}^2_k, \mathcal{S}_k)$	the disk model for elliptic geometry with curvature k	150
$(\mathbb{D}_k, \mathcal{H}_k)$	the disk model for hyperbolic geometry with curvature k	152
(X_k, G_k)	2-dimensional geometry with constant curvature k	158
$\mathbb{R}^n$	real n-dimensional space	166
$X_1 \# X_2$	the connected sum of two surfaces	168
$\mathbb{T}^2$	the torus	168
H_g	the handlebody surface of genus g	169
C_g	the cross-cap surface of genus g	169
$\mathbb{K}^2$	the Klein bottle	172
$\chi(S)$	the Euler characteristic of a surface	175
X/G	the quotient set built from geometry (X, G)	187
$\mathbb{H}^3$	hyperbolic 3-space	196

(Continued on next page)

Symbol	**Description**	**Page**
$\mathbb{S}^3$	the 3-sphere	197
$\mathbb{T}^3$	the 3-torus	197

References

Textbooks

[1] Anderson, J.W. *Hyperbolic Geometry, 2nd Ed.* Springer, London, 2005.

[2] Boas, R.P. *Invitation to Complex Analysis.* Random House, New York, 1987.

[3] Coxeter, H.S.M. *Introduction to Geometry, 2nd Ed.* Wiley, New York, 1961.

[4] Heath, T.L. *The Thirteen Books of Euclid's Elements, 2nd Ed.* Dover, New York, 1956.

[5] Henle, M. *Modern Geometries: The Analytic Approach.* Prentice Hall, New Jersey, 1997.

[6] Hilbert, D., and H. Cohn-Vossen, *Geometry and the Imagination.* AMS Chelsea Publishing, Rhode Island, 1952.

[7] Jennings, G.A. *Modern Geometry with Applications.* Springer, 1998.

[8] Schwerdtfeger, H. *Geometry of Complex Numbers.* Dover, New York, 1979.

[9] Sieradski, A.J. *An Introduction to Topology and Homotopy.* PWS-KENT Publishing Company, Boston, 1992.

[10] Stillwell, J. *Geometry on Surfaces.* Springer, New York, 1992.

[11] Thurston, W.P. *Three-Dimensional Geometry and Topology, Vol. I.* Princeton, New Jersey, 1997.

[12] Weeks, J.R.*The Shape of Space, 2nd Ed.*. Dekker, New York, 2002.

Other Books

[13] Gray J., ed. *The Symbolic Universe: Geometry and Physics 1890-1930.* Ofxord University Press, New York, 1999.

[14] Hogan, C.J. *The Little Book of the Big Bang.* Copernicus Springer-Verlag, New York, 1998.

[15] Rucker, R. *Geometry, Relativity and the 4th Dimension.* Dover, New York, 1977.

Articles

[16] Adams, C. and J. Shapiro. *The Shape of the Universe: Ten Possibilities.* American Scientist, Sept - Oct 2001, **89**, 443–453.

[17] Ade, P. A. R. and others. *Planck 2015 results. XIII. Cosmological parameters.* e-Print: arXiv:1502.01589v3 [astro-ph.CO], 2016.

[18] Bahcall, N., J. Ostriker, S. Perlmutter, and P. Steinhardt. *The Cosmic Triangle: Revealing the State of the Universe.* Science, 1999, **284** no. 5419, 1481–1488.

[19] Cornish, N.J., D.N. Spergel, G.D. Starkman, and E. Komatsu. *Constraining the Topology of the Universe.* Physical Review Letters, (2004), **92** no. 20, 1302.

[20] Foote, R. L. *A Unified Pythagorean Theorem in Euclidean, Spherical, and Hyperbolic Geometries.* Math. Magazine, February 2017 **90** no. 1, 59–69.

[21] Hinshaw, G. and others. *Five-Year Wilkinson Microwave Anisotropy Probe (WMAP) Observations: Data Processing, Sky Maps, and Basic Results.* e-Print: arXiv:0803.0732, 2008.

[22] Hinshaw, G. and others. *Nine-Year Wilkinson Microwave Anisotropy Probe (WMAP) Observations: Cosmological Parameter Results.* eThe Astrophysical Journal: Supplement Series, 2013.

[23] Levin, J. *Topology and the Cosmic Microwave Background.* Phys. Rep., 2002, **365**, 251–333.

[24] Luminet, J.-P. and M. Lachieze-Rey. *Cosmic Topology.* Phys. Rep., (1995), **254**, 135–214.

[25] Luminet, J.-P., J.R. Weeks, A. Riazuelo, R. Lehoucq, R., and J.-P. Uzan. *Dodecahedral space topology as an explanation for weak wide-angle temperature correlations in the cosmic microwave background.* Nature, (2003), **425**, 593–95.

[26] Rebouças, M.J., and G.I. Gomero. *Cosmic Topology: A Brief Overview.* Phys. Rep., December, 2004, **34** no. 4A, 1358–1366.

[27] Schwarzschild, K. *On the Permissible Curvature of Space.* Vierteljahrschrift d. Astronom. Gesellschaft, (1900), **35**, 337–47.

[28] Uzan, J.-P., R. Lehoucq, and J.-P. Luminet. *New developments in the search for the topology of the Universe.* Nuclear Physics B Proceedings Supplements, January 2000, **80**, C425+.

Web Resources

[29] Joyce, D.E. *Euclid's Elements*, http://aleph0.clarku.edu/~djoyce/java/elements/elements.html 1994.

Index

(X_k, G_k), 158
$(\mathbb{D}_k, \mathcal{H}_k)$ with $k < 0$, 152
$(\mathbb{P}^2_k, \mathcal{S}_k)$ with $k > 0$, 150
H_g, 169
∞, 49
$\mathbb{P}^2$, 130
$\mathbb{S}^1$, 38
i, 15
2-sphere, 51
3-manifold
    3-sphere, 199
    3-torus, 197
    half turn manifold, 204
    Hantschze-Wendt, 203
    one-sixth turn manifold, 205
    one-third turn manifold, 205
    Poincaré dodecahedral space, 200
    quarter turn manifold, 204
    Seifert-Weber space, 201
3-sphere, 199
3-torus, 197
8, the greatness of, 18

all-star equation, 18
angle
    between curves, 34
    between rays, 20
    determined by three points, 21
    transformation preserves, 34
    transformation preserves magnitudes, 34
angle of parallelism, 154
antipodal points of $\mathbb{C}^+$, 121
Apollonian Circles Theorem, 45

Beltrami, Enrico, 6
Bessel, Friedrich, 156
block, 107
Bolya, János, 4
Bolyai, Farkas, 4
bounded set in $\mathbb{R}^n$, 167

cell complex, 173
    n-dimensional, 173
    edge, 173
    face, 173
    vertex, 173
cell division, 174
circles of Apollonius, 46, 60
Clifford translation, 209
cline, 40
closed geodesic path, 181
closed set in $\mathbb{R}^n$, 167
compact space, 168
complex number, 15
    addition of, 15
    argument, 18
    Cartesian form, 15
    conjugate, 16
    division of, 19
    imaginary part, 15
    modulus, 16
    multiplication, 16
    polar form, 18
    real part, 15
    scalar multiplication, 15

cone point, 11, 179
Coneland, 9
connected sum, 168
construction
  antipodal point, 125
  cline through three distinct points, 41
  elliptic line through two points, 131
  hyperbolic circle centered at p through q, 90
  hyperbolic line through two points, 90
  hyperbolic reflection sending a point to the origin, 82
  octagon in $(\mathbb{D}, \mathcal{H})$ with 45° interior angles, 111
  right-angled hexagon in $(\mathbb{D}, \mathcal{H})$, 107
  symmetric point $i_C(z)$
    when z is inside C, 47
    when z is outside C, 48
cosmic background radiation (CMB), 213
cosmic crystallography, 209
  collecting correlated pairs, 211
  pair separation histogram, 208
cosmic topology, 195
  circles-in-the-sky method, 214
  cosmic crystallography method, 209
cross ratio, 57
  invariance of, 58
cross-cap, 169
curvature of a space at a point, 147
curve, 34
  smooth, 34, 95

De Sitter, Willem, 199
Dirichlet domain, 192
Dostoevsky, Fyodor, 6

Einstein, Albert, 7, 198, 218
  general theory of relativity, 217
  special theory of relativity, 7
elliptic geometry, 130
  arc-length, 132
  area, 133
  circle, 134
  distance formula, 133
  line, 131
  lune, 135
elliptic geometry with curvature k, 150
equivalence relation, 185
Erlangen Program, 6, 71
Euclidean distance between points, 75
Euler characteristic, 175
extended plane, 49

fractional linear transformation, 52
Friedmann Equation, 217
fundamental domain, 186

Gauss, Carl Friedrich, 4, 146
Gauss-Bonnet Formula, 183
general linear transformation, 32
general theory of relativity, 217
geodesic, 8
geometry, 72
  (X_k, G_k), 158
  congruent figures in, 72
  Euclidean, 75
  figure in, 72
  homogeneous, 75
  hyperbolic geometry, Poincaré disk model, 81
  invariant function, 74
  invariant set, 74
  isotropic, 75
  metric, 76
  minimal invariant set, 74
  point, 72
  rotational, 77
  translational, 73
geometry with curvature $k = 0$, 159
geometry with curvature $k > 0$, 150
geometry with curvature $k < 0$, 153
golden ratio, 109
great circle, 8
great circle in $\mathbb{C}^+$, 122
group of homeomorphisms, 187
group of isometries, 187
group of transformations, 71
Guth, Alan, 217

half turn manifold, 204
handlebody surface of genus g, 169
Hantschze-Wendt manifold, 203

Hogan, Craig, 214
homeomorphic spaces, 165
homeomorphism, 165
homogeneous geometry, 75
horocycle, 84
Hubble constant, 218
Hubble, Edwin, 218
hyperbolic cosine function, 101
hyperbolic geometry
    $\mathcal{H}$, the transformation group in hyperbolic geometry, 81
    $\frac{2}{3}$-ideal triangle, 102
    $\mathbb{D}$, the hyperbolic plane, 81
    arc-length, 96
    area, 100
    circle, 89
    circle at infinity, 81
    circle centered at p through q, construction of, 90
    distance between points, 93
    ideal point, 87
    ideal triangle, 102
    line, 87
    line through p and q, construction of, 90
    parallel lines, 87
    Poincaré disk model, 81
    upper half-plane model, 114
hyperbolic geometry with curvature k, 152
hyperbolic plane, 81
    reflection of, 82
    rotation of, 84
    translation of, 85
hyperbolic refelction, 82
hyperbolic sine function, 101
hyperbolic transformation group, 81
    parallel displacement, 84
    rotation, 84
    translation, 85

image of a set, 33
inflationary universe theory, 217
inverse pole of a Möbius transformation, 64
inversion in a circle, 38
involution transformation, 68
isometry
    Euclidean, 35
    fixed-point free, 189
    hyperbolic, 97
    properly discontinuous, 189
isotropic geometry, 75

Klein Bottle, 211
Klein bottle, 172
Klein, Felix, 6, 81

last scattering surface (LSS), 214
lens space, $L(p, q)$, 202
Lobachevsky, Nikolai, 4
Lobatchevsky's formula, 154

Möbius geometry, 78
Möbius strip, 171
Möbius transformation, 52
    determinant of, 52
    elliptic, 63
    fundamental theorem of, 55
    hyperbolic, 63
    inverse pole of a, 64
    loxodromic, 64
    normal form
        one fixed point, 67
    parabolic, 67
    pole of a, 64
manifold, 166
metric, 76
    Euclidean, 76
    hyperbolic, 97
multiconnected space, 165

one-sixth turn manifold, 205
one-third turn manifold, 205
one-to-one, 29
onto, 29
open n-ball, 166
orbit of a point, 187
orbit space, 187
orthogonal clines, 42

parallax, 155
    of star 61 Cygni, 156
Parallel Postulate, 4
partition, 186
Perlmutter, Saul, 218
planar curve, 34
Planck Satellite, 219
Platonic solids, 173

Playfair's Axiom, 4
Playfair, John, 4
Poincaré, Henri, 81
point at ∞, 49
pole of a Möbius transformation, 64
polygonal surface
    boundary label, 170
power of a point, 43
projective plane, 130

quarter turn manifold, 204
quaternion, 197
    conjugate, 197
    modulus, 197
    pure, 199
    scalar term, 197
    unit, 197
quotient set, 186
    X/G built from geometry (X, G), 187

radius of curvature, 151
real n-dimensional space, 166
reflection, 35
relation on a set, 185
Riess, Adam, 218
rotation, 31

saddle point, 179
Schmidt, Brian, 218
screw motion, 196
Seifert-Weber space, 201
simply connected space, 165
Slipher, Vesto, 218
smooth curve, 34
sphere
    diametrically opposed points, 121
spherical geometry, 129
square root, 23
stereographic projection, 51

surface, 167
    cross-cap surface of genus g (C_g), 169
    handlebody surface a genus g (H_g), 169
    non-orientable, 172
    orientable, 172
    polygonal, 170
symmetric points
    with respect to a circle, 38
    with respect to a sphere, 196

Theorem Egregium, 146
three-dimensional geometry
    elliptic, 197
    Euclidean, 195
    hyperbolic, 196
Thurston, William, 147
transformation, 29
    dilation, 32
    fixed point, 35
    fractional linear, 52
    general linear, 32
    inverse, 29
    involution, 68
    Möbius, 52
    preserves angle magnitudes, 34
    preserves angles, 34
    reflection, 35
    rotation, 31
    screw motion, 196
type I cline of p and q, 60
type II cline of p and q, 60

unit 2-sphere, 51
unit circle, 38
universal covering space, 188

Weeks, Jeff, 217
Wilkinson Microwave Anisotropy Probe (WMAP), 218